KAFKA'S LAST LOVE

For Lenore
who, like Dora, feels
everything deeply~
with love,
Kathi

La Jolla, July 27, '03

KAFKA'S LAST LOVE

The Mystery of Dora Diamant

KATHI DIAMANT

BASIC
BOOKS

A Member of the Perseus Books Group

The following publishers have generously given permission to use extended quotations from the following copyrighted works. From *There Goes Kafka* by Johannes Urzidil, translated by Harold A. Basilius. Copyright © 1968 Wayne State University Press, Detroit, MI. Used with permission of Wayne State University Press. From *Letters to Friends, Family and Editors* by Franz Kafka, translated by Richard & Clara Winston, English translation copyright © 1977 by Schocken Books, a division of Random House, Inc. Used by permission of Schocken Books, a division of Random House. From *Franz Kafka, a Biography* by Max Brod, translated by G. Humphreys Roberts & Richard Winston, © 1947, 1960 and renewed 1975, 1988 by Schocken Books. Used by permission of Schocken Books, a division of Random House. From *Letters to Ottla and the Family* by Franz Kafka, edited by Nahum Glatzer, translated by Richard & Clara Winston, copyright © 1974, 1982 by Schocken Books. Used by permission of Schocken Books, a division of Random House. From *The Trial, Definitive Edition* by Franz Kafka, translated by Willa and Edwin Muir, copyright © 1925, 1935, 1946, renewed 1952, 1963, 1974 by Schocken Books. Copyright © 1937, 1956, renewed 1964, 1984 by Alfred A. Knopf. Used by permission of Schocken Books, a division of Random House. From *Franz Kafka: The Complete Stories* by Franz Kafka, edited by Nahum Glatzer, translated by Willa and Edwin Muir, copyright © 1946, 1947, 1948, 1949, 1954, 1958, 1971 by Schocken Books. Used by permission of Schocken Books, a division of Random House. From *Franz Kafka: The Diaries 1910–1923* by Franz Kafka, edited by Max Brod, translated by Joseph Kresh and Martin Greenberg with the cooperation of Hannah Arendt, copyright © 1948 and renewed 1976 by Schocken Books. Used by permission of Schocken Books, a division of Random House. From *Conversations with Kafka* by Gustav Janouch, copyright © 1968, 1971 by S. Fischer Verlag GMBH Frankfurt-am-Main. Reprinted by permission of New Directions Publishing Corp. From *The Nightmare of Reason: A Life of Franz Kafka* by Ernst Pawel, copyright © 1984 by Ernst Pawel. Used by permission of Ruth Pawel. From *A Hesitation Before Birth* by Peter Mailloux, copyright © 1989 Associated University Presses, Inc. Used by permission of Associated University Presses. From *The Blue Octavo Notebooks* by Franz Kafka, edited by Max Brod, translated by Ernst Kaiser and Eithney Wilkins. Copyright © 1991 Exact Change, published by arrangement with Schocken Books. Used by permission of Exact Change, Cambridge. From *Leseerfahrungen, Liebeserklärungen, Aufsätze Zur Literatur, Volume 12*, by Martin Walser, edited by Helmut Kiesel and Frank Borsch, 1997 Suhrkamp Verlag Frankfurt. Used by permission of Suhrkamp Verlag.

Cover Photo credits:
Photo of Dora Diamant © Lask Collection used by permission.
Photo of Franz Kafka. Used by permission of Archiv Klaus Wagenbach, Berlin.

Published by Basic Books,
A Member of the Perseus Books Group

Library of Congress Cataloging-in-Publication Data
Diamant, Kathi.
    Kafka's last love : the mystery of Dora Diamant / Kathi Diamant.
        p.   cm.
Includes bibliographical references and index.
    ISBN 0-465-01550-6 (alk. paper)
    1. Diamant, Dora, 1902-1952. 2. Kafka, Franz, 1883–1924—Relations with women. I. Title.
PT2621.A26Z6758 2002
833'.912—dc21   2002153099

03 04 / 10 9 8 7 6 5 4 3 2 1

For Bill and Peggy Diamant
and Byron La Due

CONTENTS

	Acknowledgments	*ix*
	Author's Preface	*xiii*
1	The Threshold of Happiness	1
2	A Dark Creature from the East	15
3	A Free Life in Berlin	32
4	The Idyll in Berlin	48
5	The Burrow	63
6	The Killing Winter	75
7	The Most Fearful Day of Disaster	90
8	The Best of Beginnings	101
9	Funeral in Prague	121
10	In Memoriam	128
11	Life After Kafka	135
12	Between Two Worlds	143
13	The Nature Theater of Oklahoma	150
14	Description of a Struggle	165
15	Exodus from Berlin	180
16	The Workers Paradise	193
17	The Great Escape	211
18	The Isle of Man	222
19	Friends of Yiddish	234
20	Something Indestructible Within	250
21	The Promised Land	265

22   A Memory Come Alive   282

23   "Mach Was Du Kannst"   303

24   Kafka's Daughter   317

25   A Redwood Grows in Hampstead   332

     Epilogue   *341*
     Notes   *345*
     Sources   *387*
     Index   *395*

ACKNOWLEDGMENTS

You will do not anything without others.
—Franz Kafka, *Diaries*

This book would not have been possible without the love, encouragement and material assistance of a legion of people, beginning with my wonderful parents, Bill and Peggy Diamant, who taught me that I can do anything; and my husband, Byron La Due, the love of my life. For their generous contributions of advice, talent, knowledge, expertise, inspiration and all manner of help, I want to thank the following: Ruth Alon-Diamant, Inbal Aviram, Breffni Barrett, Kim and Nancy Bennett, Doreen Berry, Raina and Theodora Betow, Mira Binford, Wyatt Blassingame, Erica Boddie, David Brin, Jerome Chanes, Joyce Chapman, Anna Cohn, Paul and Kathy Corey, Annamaria Diamant, Lori Diamant, Trudi Diamant, Tershia d'Elgin, Marti Emerald, Ulrike Eisenberg, Susan Emrich, Fotine Fahouris, Noel Riley Fitch, Arielle Ford, Harley Gaber, Murray Galinson, Joan Gannij, Kit Goldman, Lucy Goldman, Kathy Dugle Goodman, Terry Barlin Gorton, Dita Guery, John Guth, Harvey Hagman, Nora Harlow, Ron Harrison, Christine Harrison, David Hendin, Johanna Hoornweg, Divina Infusino, Luba Johnston, Bonnie Klein, Yehuda Koren and Eilat Negev, Betsy Lane, Rachel Lasserson-Rossiter, Rachel Leisorek, Glorie Levinson, David Lichtenstern, Sara Loeb, Barbara London, Mitra Makbuleh, Michael Nyman, Betsy Nolan, Felix Pahl, Ruth Pawel, Michelle Polk, Arnon and Yoram Porat, Leonard Prager, Barbara Press, Rosina Reynolds, Morris and Sophie Rubinstein, Jack Salb, Sue Schaffner, Hillel Schenker, Brenda Schulman, Pauline Siegel, Paulette Singer, Sofia Sunseri, Deborah Tabart, Tanya Taskila, Judith Teitelman, Mr. and Mrs. Joop van Dormolen, Sara Vickers, Susan Vreeland, Andrea Walker, Bree Walker-Lampley, Donna Walker, Robert Walker, Geoffrey Weill, Laurence Weinbaum; Writing Women: Georgeanne Irvine, Sharon Whitley Larsen, Dee Anne Traitel, Judi Strada, Lynn Macey, Jackie Shannon, Kitty Morse, Linda

Susan Dudley, Julie Castiglia, Jacque Foltyn and Mary Duncan, who helped find Dora's diary in Paris; Beverly Cassell, Cherril Doty, Catherine Cooper, Marta Chaussee-Kelly, Virgina Mason, Sue Knuth, Richard McMillan and the members of the Artists Conference Network of Laguna Beach; my editors, Nanette Wiser, Alison Ashton and Glenda Winders of Copley News Service, whose travel assignments allowed me to research Dora in England, Germany and Israel.

Dora's first biography has been shaped by my interviews with individuals who knew Dora, her family and friends, and experts in historical and political aspects of her life, who have provided the first-person accounts in this book. I am deeply grateful to Angele Argy, Leon Askin, Sara Baumer-Dimant, David Aurbach, Bernd Rainer Barth, Zelig Besserglick, Majer Bogdanski, Branka Diamant, Etty Diamant, Zvi Diamant, Dorothy Emmett, John Erpenbeck, Colette Faus, Ora Fein, Miron Grindea, Michael Hamburger, Betty Kuttner, Dina Lask, Noga Maletz, Ottilie McCrea, Michel de M'UZAN, Ilse Muenz, Ruth Pawel, Bracha Plotkin, Leonard Prager, Luise Rainer, Uziel Raviv, Dasha Rittenberg-Werdygier, Carol Shaw, Marianna Steiner, Tova Perlmutter and Anthony Wilson. For sharing the Lask Collection photographs and opening family records, I am indebted to Ruth Kessentini and the Lask family.

Hanny Lichtenstern's contributions to this book are enormous. In addition to sharing her personal collection of letters and papers, she translated Dora's Yiddish articles, Dora's collected letters and diaries from German, and the letters of Robert Klopstock and Ester Hoffe in this book. I am also personally indebted to Anthony Rudolf, who, since 1990, has helped and encouraged me in ways too numerous to mention. My friend and mentor Nikki Symington read and edited each page before I submitted it and provided gainful employment over the long years of research. Stefanie Groenke joined the Kafka Project as research assistant in 1998 and has devoted hundreds of hours to translating Dora's papers and published German texts, as well as conducting research in Berlin. My gratitude to them is as deep as the friendship that has grown between us.

For help with Kafka matters, I am appreciative of the work of biographers Peter Mailloux, Ernst Pawel, Ronald Hayman and Nahum Glatzer (whose great-grandfather was also a Diamant), whose books allowed me to understand Dora's fascination with Kafka. I am grateful to Klaus Wagenbach for sharing the results of his search (conducted with Max Brod in the 1950s) for Kafka's lost letters to Dora and for his collection of Dora's papers from his archive. I am indebted to Kafka Project Advisory Committee members Niels Bokhove of the Kafka Circle of the Netherlands, Rolf Goebel, president of the Kafka Society of America, and Maja and Detlev Rehbein in Berlin. I owe a special debt of appreciation to Hans-Gerd Koch, of the Critical Edition of Kafka's letters at Wuppertal, who carefully read the manuscript for errors and added critical and rich new details.

For archival and research help, I thank Yoram Mayorek, who produced remarkable results in Russia, Israel and Poland, Rochelle Rubinstein for her diligent efforts in Switzerland, Robert Adamek and Aneta Zaspa of the Muzeum Miasta Pabianic, Tim Rogers, deputy keeper of Western Manuscripts at the Bodleian Library at Oxford University, Norbert Winkler of the Franz Kafka Gesellschaft, Wien-Klosterneuburg, Gisela Erler at the Landesarchiv-Berlin, Roger Sims of Manx National Heritage, Irene Runge of the Jüdische Gemeinde Berlin, Michael Matzigkeit and the staff of the Theater Museum, Düsseldorf. I am also grateful for information provided by Seymour Barofsky, Barry Davis, Bernhard Echte and Remigiusz Grzela and to Heather Valencia of the University of Stirling, Scotland, for her research on Stencl. For research guidance in Poland, I thank Carol Baird, Zdzisław Les, Jaroslaw Krajniewski, Wiktor Wotjas, Albert Stankowski and Jeffrey Cymbler, who shared his vast knowledge and archive of Bedzin.

I am grateful to Michael Steiner and the Kafka estate for ongoing support of the Kafka Project and permission to reprint letters to the Kafka family from the Bodleian Library; Yosl Bergner of Israel and Clive Sinclair of the London *Jewish Chronicle* for permission to reprint Melech Ravitch's story about meeting Dora; Carol Shaw for sharing her mother's writings about Yealand Manor School and for the connection to the wonderful late Dorothy Emmet, with help from Cressida Miles and Susan Hartshorne; and David Mazower for collecting Dora's Yiddish articles.

I will always praise the heaven on earth provided by Nancy Nordhoff and Cottages at Hedgebrook Writer's Colony, where this book was born, and for the financial support provided by grants from Hadassah International Research Institute on Jewish Women at Brandeis University, Ludwig Vogelstein Foundation, Weingart Foundation, and the sponsorship of the North Coast Repertory Theatre in Solana Beach and the Spiro Institute, London. I am indebted to Kathleen Jones and San Diego State University College of Arts and Letters for my academic home.

And finally I bow before my agent, Betsy Lerner, and the team at Basic Books: my editor, Liz Maguire, Will Morrison, Felicity Tucker, Chrisona Schmidt, Rachel Rokicki and all those who made this book real.

AUTHOR'S PREFACE

I was nineteen the first time I heard her name. It was spring 1971 in a German Language Literature class at the University of Georgia. We were translating "The Metamorphosis," a short story by Franz Kafka, when the instructor interrupted class. "Are you related to Dora Diamant?" he asked me. I had never heard of her. "She was Kafka's last mistress," my teacher said. "They were very much in love. He died in her arms and she burned his work." I promised to find out and let him know.

After class, I ran to the library. From Max Brod's biography, I learned that Dora was nineteen when she met Kafka—my age, or so I thought. It was the first of several facts that later turned out to be incorrect, but at the time, I was thrilled by what I read: Dora was a passionate, vibrant and intelligent young Eastern European Jewish woman who gave one of the most important writers of the twentieth century the happiest year of his life. I wanted to know more, but I could find nothing written about her after Kafka's death in 1924. I had reached, it seemed, a dead end.

In 1984, a new biography of Franz Kafka appeared with intriguing news of Dora. *The Nightmare of Reason: A Life of Franz Kafka* by Ernst Pawel revealed amazing aspects of Dora's life after Kafka, a history that encompassed evading the Gestapo in Berlin, escaping Stalin's purges in Russia and surviving the bombing of London. After Kafka's death, Dora married an idealistic German communist and gave birth to a daughter, whom Pawel mistakenly reported to be alive and living in England. The question that haunted me for years—*was Dora still alive?*—was finally answered. Dora died on August 15, 1952, three months to the day after I was born.

Inspired by Dora's sense of adventure and motivated by strange coincidences that connected us, I began the search for the missing pieces of Dora's life. On my first "mission to find Dora" in 1985, I traveled to Prague, Vienna and Jerusalem. On that trip, I learned more about myself than I did about Dora, but since then, my search has taken me on many more fruitful research trips retracing Dora's steps to Poland, Germany, France, England and the Isle of Man, as well as back to the Czech Republic and Israel several times. In 1996, I initiated the Kafka Project at San Diego State University with an international advisory committee of Kafka scholars and researchers to search for Kafka's lost papers, confiscated from Dora by the Gestapo in Berlin 1933. This biography finally became possible with documents and photographs found during a four-month Kafka Project research trip to German archives in Berlin in 1998, as well as Dora's diary, uncovered in Paris in 2000.

Dora's perspective provided me a light to understanding and appreciating Franz Kafka, one of the most misunderstood writers of the past century. In turn, Kafka's words and aphorisms have guided my search for Dora, providing the courage, humor, insight and strength necessary to persist in the long unraveling and writing of her story. At first I relied solely on intuition, an unrelenting sense that Dora wanted this story to be told. When I found her letters, published Yiddish writings and unpublished notebooks on Kafka, and the revealing documents from her Gestapo and Comintern files, Dora's own words took over. My most significant collaborator in this book has been Dora herself, through her words and actions and the legacy she left: the generous outpouring of love and support of her friends, family and those who, like myself, continue to be moved by her indestructible spirit.

Ironically, while I have solved the most intriguing mysteries surrounding Dora's life, I have not been able to find the answer to the original question. While her family in Israel has warmly welcomed me and my family into the "mishpoche," I still don't know if I am related to her. I do not doubt, however, that we are connected. Dora has changed the way I see the world. In learning about her life, I have been inspired to improve my own. Before Dora gave her first public interview about Kafka in 1948, she began with a disclaimer, part of which I would like to repeat on my own behalf: "I am not objective and can never be. Therefore, it is not the facts which are so important; it is a rather a matter of pure atmosphere. The story I have to tell you has an inner truth, and subjectivity is a part of that."

Kathi Diamant
San Diego, California
December 2002

1

THE THRESHOLD OF HAPPINESS

I am a memory come alive. Hence the inability to sleep . . .

—Franz Kafka, *Diaries*

KIERLING, AUSTRIA, JUNE 3, 1924

Franz had fallen asleep at midnight. As the minutes of his last day ticked away, Dora sat at his bedside, watching his frail body, alert for any change in his breathing. A lamp on the table cast elongated shadows on the high walls of the room. The balcony door was open to give his lungs the fresh air he desperately needed. Dora watched the slow rise and fall of his chest and studied his profile, the sharp outline of his long, bony nose, high cheek bones, deep-set eyes. Now more than ever, Franz looked like an American Indian, as she had imagined him to be that first time she saw him.

He was no longer handsome. His face was skeletal, and his brilliant gray eyes had sunk into his skull. In the past months, he had aged quickly. Until this year, his face had been boyish. Dora had thought him a young man when she first met him. He was still only forty. His forty-first birthday was exactly one month away.

Dora believed she could will him into wellness. Miracles happened. The tuberculosis had spread to his larynx, making eating or drinking a sip of water nearly impossible. Despite the agony each time he swallowed, Franz wanted to live. When the specialist from Vienna came for a visit and told him his throat seemed improved, Franz cried and hugged and kissed Dora. Joyfully he told her over and over that he had "never wished for life and health so much as now." Never mind what Dr. Beck and the other doctors said. Dora felt positive Franz would recover, if only she could get him to eat a little more.

For Franz, sleep was a blessing. Nights racked by insomnia often left him drained and exhausted for the struggle of the day ahead. Lately Dora had been tempting him with sips of beer and wine during his evening meals. Without his knowledge, she was slipping in a sleeping powder, So-matose. The drug was working and Kafka had slept peacefully through the past few nights. In the mornings, he had felt much better. In fact, earlier this afternoon he had worked on correcting the galleys of his latest collection of short stories, *A Hunger Artist*, which had recently arrived from the publisher.

"They waited so long to send me the material. With what strength I have am I to write it?" he complained before resolutely getting down to work. The irony of Franz's story—about a sideshow artist who starves as an art form—and his current emaciated state and inability to eat was not lost on anyone.

Dora gently stroked his forehead. In a weak moment, she had per-suaded him to agree to a death pact. If Franz died, she swore to die with him. She took comfort in that emotional blackmail. Dora was desperate, and she would use all tools at her disposal, including his wish to protect her. As the early hours of June 3 slowly passed, Dora dwelled on the posi-tive, keeping alive their shared dream for a life together in Palestine, a dream that had begun only eleven months earlier.

MÜRITZ, BALTIC SEA, NORTHERN GERMANY, JULY 13, 1923

Dora Diamant stood in the kitchen of a summer holiday camp at Haus Huten in Müritz, a seaside resort on the Baltic Sea, cleaning fish. Light fil-tered into the room from an open doorway and a small window near the sink. The clouds cleared and the afternoon sun cast a golden glow in the small kitchen. As she worked, she thought about the tall, dark man, the man she had seen on the beach playing with two children. The man she couldn't forget.

Dora was twenty-five years old. Back home in Bedzin, Poland, she would be called an old maid, unmarriageable, long past her prime. In Germany, es-pecially in Berlin, where she had lived for the past three years, the attitude toward women was different. The modern ideal in Germany was no longer "the childlike, well-behaved virgin" of past years but the "independent, knowing, self-reliant woman . . . with her own career (and income)." Dora didn't have to worry; she looked younger than her age. Most people assumed she was only nineteen or twenty. She didn't tell them otherwise. Why should she? It was one of the advantages of starting a new life in the West: She could recreate herself and be whatever she wanted to be.

She wasn't beautiful, although people often said she was. She was short, about five feet, two inches, and tended to put on weight, but her legs and ankles were slender. Her features were attractive, but her face was too round, lips too full and mouth too wide for classic beauty. When she smiled broadly or laughed, the gums under her upper lip were visible. She compensated by smiling, especially in photographs, with her lips closed or only slightly parted. It gave her a mysterious, Mona Lisa sort of look that she favored. Her eyes were dark and her light brown hair was cut short—an attempt at the revolutionary bob currently popular in Berlin. Her hair was too wavy to fit the sleek look, and as she worked at her task, unruly strands tumbled into her eyes, which she pushed away with her forearm.

With well-aimed whacks, Dora severed the heads from the fish. Tonight's *Oneg Shabbat* dinner was special. Earlier in the afternoon, it had been announced that a guest, a Dr. Kafka from Prague, would be attending the holiday camp's customary Sabbath dinner that evening. One of the other volunteers, sixteen-year-old Tile Rössler, had invited him. Tile talked incessantly about Dr. Kafka after meeting him two days earlier and seemed to have quite a crush on him. Like Dora, Tile was working as a volunteer at the Berlin Jewish People's holiday camp for refugee children.

Dora was in charge of the kitchen. The camp was organized and run by the Berlin Jewish People's Home, a center for Jewish relief work founded during the Great War. Designed to develop Jewish national traditions among Eastern European refugees, the Berlin Jewish People's Home catered to orphans and children forced from towns, villages and shtetls across Galicia and Silesia in Poland and Russia. Displaced by war, famine and pogroms, these children struggled to build a life in the slums of Berlin's overcrowded Scheunenviertel, the old Jewish Quarter. Since her arrival in Berlin, the Jewish People's Home had provided Dora with a sense of community and family. Modeled on the settlement house system developed in England and the United States for use in Palestine, it sponsored a variety of activities, including organized comradeship meetings, self-governed youth groups, Hebrew and rhythmic dance classes, hiking trips, political and intellectual discussions, Jewish legends and Chassidic storytelling, at which Dora excelled. The holiday camp, housed in a rambling two-story hostel

known as Haus Huten, nestled in a forest of birch trees at the eastern edge
of the village of Müritz. For these children—and Dora, too—it was a
breath of fresh air, a healthy respite from a hard life as stateless foreigners.

Shortly after arriving in Berlin as a Polish Jewish émigré, Dora learned
about the programs offered by the Home and volunteered her training and
skills as a *Fröblerin,* or kindergarten teacher, to help prepare the younger
children for eventual resettlement in Eretz Yisroel. She, too, had come
from the East and knew the overwhelming obstacles and hatred faced by
the Jews. She believed fervently in the necessity of a national Jewish home
in Palestine, in Eretz Yisroel, the Promised Land. In her daydreams, she often saw herself, as she said, "in the fields of Galilee," living on a kibbutz,
working side by side with other free Jews, men and women from all lands,
reclaiming the swamps and barren land, planting gardens and building a
safe and just world for her future children and grandchildren.

Theodore Herzl, the founder of modern political Zionism, first called
for a Jewish state in Palestine in 1897, the year before Dora's birth. Like
Herzl (whose mother was also named Diamant), Dora had grand dreams.
That's all she had. But as Herzl said, "If you will it, it will not be a dream."
Her dreams kept her warm at night. She owned nothing, had no money or
savings. She left everything behind when she turned her back on her father's beliefs and traditions. If Dora would not consider marriage, then
there were only two choices available to her as the eldest daughter of a respectable and pious father: kindergarten teacher or accountant. Accounting she wouldn't even discuss. Although Dora loved children—she helped
raise her younger brothers and sisters after her mother died—she didn't
want to be a kindergarten teacher. She wanted more for her life, more than
what her mother had endured. Dora took hope from the myriad opportunities that had opened up for young women, even for Jewish women, more
than at any other time in recorded history. Dora wanted to take advantage
of all of them. Women were advancing in the arts, sciences and politics in
Germany. Dora wanted to make something of herself, to make her world—
and people's lives—better. One of her role models in Berlin was Clara
Zetkin, a passionate socialist and feminist, a founder of the women's international suffrage movement, a leading political figure and member of the
German Reichstag.

After her mother died, added responsibilities fell on Dora as the oldest
daughter. Consequently, Dora grew up more independent than most girls.
Her responsibilities were heavy—taking care of her siblings, filling her
mother's role in lighting the candles on Friday night and reciting the "God

of Abraham" prayer at the end of the Sabbath. But she also had more free-dom to read, learn and dream of other possibilities for her life. When she entered womanhood, she began to reject the role in which she had been cast from birth.

As Dora followed the desires of her heart and mind, friction with her father erupted in arguments and terrible words. Her desire to learn more about her religion was considered unnatural and destructive. She pre-tended, for a while, to follow the rules imposed by her father and society. Without her father's knowledge, Dora joined a Bedzin theater group and acted in some plays. When her father finally remarried a decade after his first wife's death, Dora was almost twenty. Something had to be done with her, and she was packed away to a girl's school, the Sarah Schirmer Beis Ya'acov in Krakow.

It was in Krakow that Dora's eyes were opened and she learned that she did have another choice for her life. With a new age of secularism and hu-manism dawning in Europe, waves of young people were leaving homes and tradition behind to seek opportunities, a new way of life in the scien-tifically and socially advanced Western countries. Dora wanted to be a part of it, as she said, "to make the pilgrimage to Western Europe, to study in their tabernacles the laws of humanity, light and beauty."

Twice Dora ran away from the Beis Ya'acov in Krakow. She went to Germany with "an eager soul," seeking the light of the West she had heard so much about, with "its knowledge, clarity and lifestyle." When she left Poland, Dora envisioned herself "as a character springing from a Dos-toyevsky novel, a dark creature filled with dreams and premonitions." The first time, her father tracked her down and found her in Breslau, on the German border, and returned her to the school. The second time, her fa-ther gave up—what else could he do?—and let her go. Dora's choice shamed her family and deeply disappointed her father, Herschel Dymant, a beloved and devout Orthodox Jew—a respected follower of the Chas-sidic Gerer Rebbe. But how could she have done otherwise? The quick-ness of her mind, the depth of her thoughts, the strength of her will were all worthless in the face of her sex. The God of her father denied her, re-fused her the chance to continue to study and learn the Jewish laws and condemned her to a life she could not live.

For the past four years, Dora had managed to earn her own way. Her first job in Berlin was as "the governess in the home of Dr. Hermann Badt, a leader in Berlin's orthodox community and a senior official at the Prussian Interior Ministry—the first Jew ever admitted to the Prussian civil service."

Later she found lodging in the orphanage where she worked as the house seamstress.

Although Dora was no longer religious, as defined by her father's brand of Orthodoxy, and no longer practiced the rituals, she was consumed with her Judaism. She was studying the laws of the Torah, curious about its deeper and humanistic questions, and seeking her place in the world as a modern woman. Had Dora chosen to stay in Bedzin, her books would have been put away forever. Had she given in and married one of the penniless religious scholars of whom her father approved, she would wake every morning, as her mother and grandmother had done before her, to a day of hard labor, only to hear her husband's daily prayer of gratitude that he was not born a woman.

As Dora sliced open bellies and gutted the fish, her thoughts wandered down to the beach, with white-capped waves and the Müritz pier stretching into the distance. It was a five-minute walk down the path through the understory of pine, birch and linden trees to the shore. Would the dark, mysterious man be there now, where she had first seen him two days ago, in his covered beach chair? When she saw him standing on the beach, she noticed how tall, slim and dark he was. Two children, a little girl and her older brother, were playing around. A woman stood nearby, probably his wife. She watched him laughing with the boy, who looked about eleven. A happy family, Dora thought.

She couldn't tear her eyes away from the man. There was something about him. What was it? He was tall and dark and handsome. His jet black hair was a leonine mane framing his angular face. His laughter was youthful, his voice a melodious baritone. When the man, along with the woman and children, left the beach and started walking on the road into town, Dora, despite the absurdity of her actions, followed them.

It was midsummer, but the weather was cool and the north wind from the Baltic Sea was cold and damp. There were two roads into town, both ending at the pier. The beach promenade followed the dunes along the coastline in a westerly direction to the town center. The Hauptstrasse began at the end of Strandstrasse, the street in front of Haus Huten, and continued past windmills and thatched roof farmhouses through pastures with tidy haystacks dotting the harvested fields.

During the walk into town, Dora kept a polite distance behind the foursome, her eyes never leaving the man. He took long strides and swayed a little as he walked. He was obviously a foreigner like her, not German, but from where, she couldn't tell. He stood straight and tall, except for his head, which he held a little to one side, especially when he was listening. It was his loping walk that finally made Dora realize that he wasn't European at all. "He had to be a half-breed Red Indian from America," she decided.

Long, deep ruts made the road muddy as it curved north into the cluster of hotels, villas and pensions interspersed with restaurants and shops at the entrance to the Müritz pier. The stones that once covered the Hauptstrasse were missing and scattered, and the road was in a sad state of disrepair. Although the war had ended four years ago, the staggering cost of the reparations that the Versailles Treaty forced Germany to pay following its defeat precluded fixing the only paved road in this quiet town on its northern coastline.

Once in the town center, Dora regained her common sense to a certain degree and left the man and his family to their own diversions. With a history dating back six centuries, Müritz offered hotels, grand and small, restaurants, outdoor cafés and shops. The pier, originally built in 1882 and reconstructed many times after brutal winter storms, stretched from the beach pavilion due north out into the choppy sea. Couples walked arm in arm, strolling along the promenade and pier, where steamships and ferries docked, loading and unloading passengers and supplies.

The sun, when it finally appeared late in the afternoon, lit up spectacular skies with rosy golden rays filtering through pastel clouds. Only a few of the hardy souls decked out in the new knee-length bathing suits braved the bracing water. An enclosed bathing area, set up at the left side of the pier, was empty. Most beach goers sat protected from the wind in covered wicker beach chairs that dotted the long stretch of coarse sand.

Dora finally remembered her neglected duties in the kitchen and rushed back to the camp. On the road ahead of her, Dora saw the man with the woman and children. Hurrying, she passed them by with only a nod and a quick glance. She turned back once but could only make out his tall, thin silhouette against the setting sun.

Dora slapped the fish down on the counter. No matter what she was doing, she could not forget him. He wouldn't leave her mind, her thoughts. Who was he? Why did he attract her so strongly? He was obviously married. Awful as it was, it didn't matter! Common sense and decency abandoned her. She knew she must see him again.

Suddenly the room turned dark. Someone stood outside the kitchen window, blocking the light. Dora looked up as the shadow moved and the light streamed into the room. A man's silhouette filled the doorway. His head tilted to one side. It was the man from the beach! He was taller than

Dora originally thought: at least six feet. When he stepped inside the kitchen, Dora was paralyzed by his eyes, which were large and brown—or were they gray?—and wide, wide open. His mesmerizing gaze took in the room, the pile of fish in front of her and finally, at last, her eyes. She couldn't move or speak. He spoke to her, his voice low and gentle: "Such tender hands, and such bloody work that they must do!" he said softly.

Dora stared down at her fingers, stained red and encrusted with entrails, and felt her face flush. She looked up and found herself smiling back at him. He tipped his hat and was gone.

At dinner that evening, Dora saw the man again. As everyone sat down on the benches at the long tables, she learned that her mysterious man from the beach was the evening's guest of honor, Dr. Kafka from Prague. He was staying at the neighboring hotel, Haus Gluckauf, and had stumbled into her kitchen, trying to find the front door of the holiday camp. He had come alone. Hope fluttered in Dora's breast. It could only mean one thing. Her new optimism was soon confirmed: Dr. Kafka was not married! He was staying at the nearby family hotel in the company of his sister and her two children. Dora was "overrun with joy," she said. Her prayers had been answered.

Dora had fallen in love before. Living on her own in one of the most sexually permissive cities in the world, she had learned a thing or two about the ways of the world. Men had been in love with her, too; in fact, there was someone in her life now, someone she knew from home who was a student at the Gardening School in Dahlem. They had talked and planned of going to Eretz Yisroel to work in a vineyard. But all thoughts of him—and everyone else—flew out the window when Kafka stepped in the door.

Besides his lifelong single marital status, Dora gleaned a few other facts about the evening's dinner guest. When he passed on the fish, she learned that he was a vegetarian. He was a highly placed lawyer until his recent retirement, the senior secretary of the Workers Accident Insurance Institute in Prague, where he lived. What was more, according to Tile Rössler, he was also a published writer. Tile boasted that she had placed with her very own hands Kafka's book in the display window of Jurovics Bookshop in Berlin, where she worked.

During dinner an incident occurred, something small, but something Dora thought spoke volumes about Kafka, about the kind of person he was. The children were being especially good and were eager to be noticed. They sat up straight on the benches at the tables, doing their best to impress the distinguished dinner guest. A little boy around five or six years old, in Dora's estimation, "perhaps the most anxious of all," responded too eagerly to a request to fetch something. As the child stood up, his feet tangled underneath him and he fell down. Embarrassed, he quickly scrambled to his feet. "Laughter and jeers were about to be unleashed, all the more because the other children were just as paralyzed by embarrassment," Dora said. "But before the laughter began, before the child was publicly humiliated, Kafka exclaimed in a voice full of admiration: 'How nimbly you fell and how well you got up again!' Not only was the self-respect of the child safe, but he could also feel an additional glory which would not be the envy of anyone." As long as she lived, Dora never forgot the incident or its significance. Twenty-five years later, she still pondered Kafka's thoughtful attention to the little boy: "When I thought of these words again, their core meaning seemed to be that everything could be saved—except Kafka. Kafka could not be saved."

After dinner, Kafka and Dora continued to talk. When Kafka, a struggling Hebrew student himself, learned that Dora's Hebrew was excellent, he asked her to read aloud. Dora was delighted to show off her language skills. She'd learned to read the "aleph-bayz," the Hebrew letters, as a child, eavesdropping on her brothers' cheder lessons. As an adult, the study of Hebrew had become Dora's first open rebellion against her father. To Dora's father, Hebrew was the sacred language of the Torah, not the language spoken in the streets or for secular matters. He abhorred the Zionist plan to revive Hebrew as the national language of Palestine and forbade her participation in special Hebrew classes for girls and women taught by a Zionist group in Bedzin. Dora defied her father and enrolled in the classes, making no attempt to keep her action secret. Not only did Dora become a student, but she posed with her class for an official school photograph.

In a corner of the Haus Huten communal living room, with Franz Kafka sitting in rapt attention, an audience of one (and the only one she wanted), Dora opened the book of the prophet Isaiah. Kafka smiled warmly, nodding his head, encouraging her. How alive he was, she thought, how alert to every detail! Dora knew these passages by heart and recited them from memory, transforming the reading into a dramatic declaration of scriptural text. When she finished, Dora luxuriated in Kafka's glowing admiration and effusive praise.

Franz Kafka had been intrigued by the Berlin Jewish People's Home holiday camp, located only fifty steps from his balcony at Haus Gluckauf, since arriving three days earlier, on June 10. In letters to friends in

Jerusalem written the morning he met Dora, Kafka had written, "Through the trees I can see the children playing. Cheerful, healthy, spirited children. East European Jews whom West European Jews are rescuing from the dangers of Berlin. Half the days and nights the house, the woods, and the beach are filled with singing. I am not happy when I'm among them, but on the threshold of happiness." He ended his letter saying, "Today I shall celebrate Friday evening with them, for the first time in my life, I think." A few hours later, Kafka crossed that threshold.

From its beginnings in 1916, the Berlin Jewish People's Home had filled Kafka with hope. Through his good friend Max Brod and others he knew who served on its board, such as the philosopher Martin Buber, Kafka was well aware of its practical and forward-looking approach to solving problems and was an enthusiastic supporter and advocate of its Zionist goals. While he was engaged to his former fiancée Felice Bauer, who lived in Berlin, Kafka had frequently urged her to get involved with the Home as a volunteer helper for the children, just as Dora was now doing. He wrote dozens of letters encouraging Felice to take advantage of the opportunities presented by the Home, which he thought offered her "the only path, or threshold to it, that could lead to spiritual liberation." Moreover, he wrote, "the helpers will attain that goal earlier than those who are being helped." Now Kafka was delighted to meet Dora, a young, intelligent woman who embraced the principles of the Berlin Jewish People's Home with heart, body and soul.

Dora's fluency in Hebrew, the lingua franca of Palestine, impressed him deeply. For several years, Kafka had been struggling to learn Hebrew. He had studied with several tutors but had not made any satisfying progress. Dora's personality was steeped in the Chassidic lore and tales of miracles, the eastern mysticism to which he had been deeply attracted for years. Her speech and expressions were infused with the sage sayings and wise old Yiddish parables of her grandmothers. Perhaps most significantly to Kafka, Dora was independent and free. Fifteen years his junior, she had done what he had yet to do: break the psychological and emotional chains imposed by her father and community and defy the authority of the religion in which she had been raised. On her own, Dora was making of herself a person, living a free life in Berlin, a life Kafka had long dreamed of.

Except for short excursions and vacations, and various stays in sanatoriums, Franz Kafka had never left Prague, had never fully cut his ties with his father's authority. Although seemingly calm on the surface, the relationship between father and son was a war zone. Herrmann Kafka had always been brutally critical of his son, whom he loved but experienced as a constant source of disappointment and irritation. Franz had been an early casualty of this war, deeply wounded and scarred as a young boy. Franz resented his victimized state, which he felt tied him to his parents forever. In his diary in 1922, the year before he met Dora, Kafka wrote, "As a little child I had been defeated by my father, and because of ambition have never been able to quit the battlefield after all these years despite the perpetual defeat I suffer."

Not a single day passed after Kafka and Dora's first *Oneg Shabbat* meeting on Friday, July 13, that they did not spend some time together. Kafka returned to the Home every day, he wrote in a letter, as well as each Friday evening for the Sabbath celebration for the remainder of his three-week stay in Müritz, until the last week. He was drawn there, fascinated by the mechanics of the camp, the children's classes and his conversations and growing friendship with Dora, who was equally fascinated by him. In a diary that Dora wrote in the last year of her life, she recalled certain sparkling moments from these days: "Franz helping peel potatoes in the kitchen. The night on the pier. On the bench in the Müritz woods."

In a letter to Tile, who had returned to Berlin at the end of July, Kafka wrote that he had received the latest letter from her—the second one that day from her—with the evening mail, while he was at the beach. "Dora was with me," he wrote. "We had just read a little Hebrew. It was the first sunny afternoon for a long time, and probably for a long time to come." Kafka admitted that he was once again experiencing "fatigue, sleeplessness and headaches" and wondered why those things bothered him so much less at the beginning of his stay. "Perhaps I'm not allowed to remain too long in one place; there are people who can acquire a sense of home only when they are traveling. Outwardly, everything is just as it was; all the people in the Home are very dear to me, much dearer than I am able to indicate. Dora, especially, with whom I spend most of my time, is a wonderful person."

Almost every day, Kafka and Dora walked through the woods to the beach and sat in the covered beach chair looking out at the sea. It had been ten years since Kafka had been to the seashore, and he said he found it "truly more lovely, more varied, livelier and younger" than ever before. They spent hours talking, mostly about her life but also about the many subjects that interested them both. Kafka knew how to ask questions, Dora said, and how to listen "with both ears." He never tired of her stories of family life in Bedzin, the stories her mother and grandmother had told her and the magical legends from the Baal Shem Tov, the founder of Chas-sidism. Like Scheherazade, every night she wove a magical spell around Kafka, slowly revealing her hidden treasure of remembered *bubeh meises*, fairy tales and Jewish folk legends, which came alive with her telling.

There were many things Kafka admired about Dora. She was natural, healthy, pretty and uncomplicated, and she was living what he considered an authentic life, leading to no less than "spiritual liberation." Dora had never met anyone like Franz Kafka. He was a unique and extraordinary man, someone special. Others sensed it too and "walked on tip-toe or as if on soft carpets" in his presence. He was elegant and refined, yet playful and full of fun. His eyes were warm, but his manner reserved. He didn't talk about himself, but had an insatiable curiosity about everyone else.

Until Kafka, none of the Western Jewish men Dora met had lived up to her expectations. She had come to Germany with "an eager soul" but soon realized that the people there were restless and lacked something essential in their understanding of their humanity. Kafka had no rest, either. But it seemed to Dora that Kafka was in constant connection with something outside himself. His search for what he called "the indestructible" was at the core of his being. "It was not exactly a listening," she said. "There was also something very affectionate about it." It was as if he were saying, "On my own I am nothing. I am only something when connected with the outer world."

Despite what one Kafka biographer called their "manifest disparities," Franz Kafka found, in the young East European Jewess, the fulfillment of his expressed longings and the first woman with whom he could share his life. Another biographer observed, "It is easy to see why they were so comfortable together since if Kafka had created Dora himself, she could not have suited him better." According to Max Brod, Kafka's closest friend and first biographer, "the two suited one another quite marvelously. The rich treasure of Polish Jewish religious tradition that Dora was mistress of was a constant source of delight to Franz; at the same time the young girl, who knew nothing about the many great achievements of Western culture, loved and honored the great teacher no less than his dreamlike, curious fantasies, which she entered into easily and like a game."

They represented opposite ends of European Jewry. Dora, born into the ultra-Orthodox Chassidic Jews of Poland (and therefore anywhere), had broken free of religious taboos and societal bonds with her Jewish soul intact. Kafka, descended from rabbis on his maternal side, had lived almost all his life within the narrow radius of Prague's Jewish Quarter but was so assimilated that at the age of forty he had never once attended a Friday night Sabbath celebration. Kafka's bar mitzvah, his ritual passage into manhood, had been for show only. Franz had dreaded the event but hoped that the religious ceremony might reveal some aspect of the mysterious significance of Judaism to him. Required to memorize a Torah portion in Hebrew, Franz had little concept of the meanings of the strange sounds and letters. The party following the ceremony was an ordeal for the sensitive thirteen-year-old, a torturous exercise in meaninglessness. As an adult, Kafka longed for a mystical connection to his Jewish roots but bore the burden of being a Jew in an anti-Semitic society without any of the restorative benefits of Judaism's sustaining spirituality.

To Dora, it was paradoxical that Western Jews were condescending toward *Ostjuden* like herself. At the same time they looked down on her, they also saw her as a font of Jewish insight and wisdom. "After the catastrophe of the war, everyone expected salvation through the intermediary of the East," Dora said. "But I had run away from the East because I believed the light was in the West. . . . Over and over again I had the feeling that the people there needed something which I could give them. Europe was not what I had expected it to be, its people had no rest in their innermost being. They lacked something. In the East, one understood what a human being was: perhaps one could not move so freely in society or express oneself so easily, but one did know the consciousness of the unity of man and creation. When I saw Kafka for the first time, I realized that his image corresponded to my idea of man. But even Kafka turned to me attentively, as if he expected something from me."

Kafka had come to the Baltic Sea to recuperate from a serious illness. After barely surviving pneumonia on top of tuberculosis, from which he had suffered for five years, he had been bedridden for the past year. This trip to Müritz, he explained, was "a short test run for the greater journey" and to "test my transportability." He wanted to go to Palestine, Kafka told Dora, hopefully, in the autumn. He knew that he must do something drastic if he wanted to continue living. What could be more drastic than to finally break free of his parental home in Prague and move to Palestine?

The wife of Kafka's friend, Hugo Bergmann, a professor at the Hebrew University, had thrown Kafka a lifeline a few months earlier. Else Bergmann had invited Franz to come and live in their apartment in Jerusalem. Kafka's health would quickly improve in the hot, dry climate of Palestine, she promised. Kafka would recover his health, rediscover his roots in Judaism and, at the same time, participate in building the future

Jewish national home in Palestine. Amazingly, Kafka said yes and told his friends he hoped to come in October.

This was the great dream Dora Diamant and Franz Kafka shared: to immigrate to Palestine. Within days of their first meeting, Dora and Kafka were talking excitedly of making the journey together. The days flew by quickly and the summer season was nearly over.

Kafka dreaded the thought of returning to Prague. He and Dora had begun to discuss Berlin as a stepping-stone to Palestine, but, with Kafka's health in its fragile state, it was still too far away to be a serious consideration. Now that he had met Dora, Kafka wanted, more than ever, to live in Berlin. For the past decade, Kafka had dreamed of moving to the German capital. Ten years earlier, when he was thirty, he had written in his diary, "If only it were possible to go to Berlin, to become independent, to live from one day to the next, even to go hungry, but to let all one's strength pour forth!" He had not been able to convince friends to join him, though he had tried. He couldn't go alone. His illness now prevented it and, besides, he was used to having someone, usually one of his sisters, take care of him.

Dora provided the perfect solution. She had lived in Berlin for three years and knew her way around, and she could help him. Dora embraced the idea: She could find him a nice inexpensive flat and get him settled. She would take care of everything. She was already enrolled in classes at the Academy of Hebrew Studies, which he wanted to attend. They could go together. He wouldn't be alone! Faced with this new opportunity, this long cherished dream, along with the awareness that he must change his life if he wished to continue living, how could Kafka refuse?

2

A DARK CREATURE FROM THE EAST

There is no one here who wholly understands me. To have someone possessed of such understanding, a wife perhaps, would mean to have a foothold on every side, to have God.

—Franz Kafka, *Diaries*

MÜRITZ, EARLY AUGUST 1923

Dora Diamant and Franz Kafka had known each other less than three weeks and already they were discussing living together in Berlin, a radical concept for both of them. Dora had never lived with a man. In Berlin's modern, postwar society, unmarried couples lived together without raising an eyebrow, but in the eyes of most people outside the city it was still disgraceful, scandalous behavior. In Bedzin, her name and reputation would be sullied forever. Kafka had never lived with a woman, other than one of his sisters, usually Ottla. Although he had been in love many times (seeing the best in people, he fell in love fairly easily) and had been engaged three times, twice to the same woman, he had never married. The diagnosis of tuberculosis, six years before he met Dora, had effectively ended his fitness for marriage. In those days, tuberculosis was a death sentence. In Kafka's opinion, no respectable or loving father would give his permission to such a match, only to see his daughter become a young widow.

Kafka wanted to marry, longed to be a father. "A man without a wife is not a man," he once quoted from the Talmud. But the "all-consuming demands of his writing" and his refusal to live a normal, middle-class existence led to an "unshakable conviction" that he would never marry. When his niece Gerti was born, Kafka wrote in his diary that he felt "envy, nothing but furious envy at my sister, or rather of my brother-in-law, because I will never have a child."

But with Dora, the possibility of marriage, even fatherhood, was born anew. Dora's independence, her youth, vitality, fearlessness, her immediate understanding and loving reaction to him, gave him courage and a new optimism. In one of his last letters to Milena Jesenska, the woman Kafka had loved—and lost—before Dora, he wrote, "In July, something momentous had happened to me—what momentous things exist!—I had gone to Müritz on the Baltic with the help of my eldest sister. Away from Prague in any case, away from the closed room. At first I didn't feel too well. Then in Müritz the Berlin possibility unexpectedly developed. I had actually meant to go to Palestine in October, I think we talked about it, of course it would never have come off, it was a fantasy, the kind of fantasy someone has who is convinced he will never again leave his bed. If I'm never going to leave my bed again, why shouldn't I travel as far as Palestine?"

Kafka talked of his attraction to the summer colony at the Jewish People's Home from Berlin, where "I began considering the possibility of moving to Berlin. At the time this possibility was not much more real than the Palestine plan, but then it grew stronger. To live alone in Berlin was of course impossible, in every respect, not only in Berlin but for that matter anywhere. For this, too, a solution—surprising in its special way—offered itself in Müritz."

Their meeting in Müritz had also changed the course of Dora's life. Going to Palestine had not been a fantasy for her. But she would put her dream on hold until Kafka's health improved enough for him to survive the journey. It was a fair trade. With Kafka, Dora had discovered a magical new world and had found a new version of herself, a new appreciation for who she was.

PABIANICE, POLAND, 1898

On a late winter day in central Poland, in the waning years of the nineteenth century, "Dworja Diament" was born to Horn Aron Diament, age twenty-four, and Frajda Frid Diament, twenty-five, in Pabianice, near Lodz, according to her official Polish birth certificate. Her birthdate is listed as March 4, 1898. Dora's father's name, according to Sara Baumer-Dimant, his youngest child, was "Herschel (Zvi) Aron Lizer Dymant."

The last name is also spelled, in other documents, as Dimant, Dimont and Dymand. The various spellings come from different translations of the original Hebrew writing, with "Dymant" being the Yiddish version, and "Diamant," "Dimant" or "Diament" the Germanized spellings. When Dora arrived in Germany, she registered her name as Diamant, and that's how she spelled it when Kafka knew her.

The earliest civil records of the Dymant family in central Poland begin with the family of Szlama Efroim Dymant, probably Dora's grandfather, a weaver born in Brzeziny, near Lodz, in 1827. He married Fajga Bryl, and their first daughter, Malka, was born in 1847. About that time, the family moved to Pabianice, a large textile manufacturing town on the opposite side of Lodz, and six more children were born.

The first mention of Dora's father, Hersz Aron Dymant, and his wife, Frajda, in the Pabianice official records is the death of their six-month-old daughter, Mirel, in 1892. Frajda was known by her Yiddish name, Friedel. Her first two babies, both daughters, died. Herschel, who was eighteen when his first child was born, and Friedel were never listed in the permanent dweller books for Pabianice. According to the archival historian in Pabianice, Herschel and Friedel probably lived with their relatives. In 1897, when Friedel was twenty-five, she gave birth to her first son, David, a strong and healthy boy. The next year, Dworja, or Dora, was born. The year after came Jakub. Dora's first sister, Nacha, was born at the beginning of 1903 and Abram came at the end of that same year. Before her death, Friedel gave Herschel one more son, Arje, who was born in 1905.

There is no record of Friedel's death. She was probably buried in the old Jewish cemetery in Pabianice. The cemetery now stands in ruins, locked behind a stone wall covered in graffiti, the headstones cracked and toppled, the records destroyed in the flames of anti-Semitic hatred. Friedel may have died in childbirth, but when or exactly how old Dora was at the time is unknown. What is certain is that with her mother's death, Dora's childhood was effectively over. As the eldest daughter of five children, her small shoulders bore responsibility for running the household.

After Friedel died, Herschel moved his family to Bedzin, a predominately Jewish city under Russian control in Silesia, a coal mining region near the German border. It was an old town, with a ruined medieval castle at the top of the hill and a river flowing through the wide valley below. The family moved to a four-story building at the top of the hill on Modzejowska Street across the road from the old castle and the town's largest synagogue.

Herschel Dymant was a learned man, and in time he became one of the town's most respected citizens. Many people came to ask his opinion and get his advice. His house was full of books. He spoke Polish, German, Yiddish and Hebrew. Every morning at four he got up to recite his prayers, to study and learn before breaking bread and going to work. The name on his tombstone reads "Herschel der Paviancer," after the town from which he had come. He prospered in Bedzin and, after a couple of years, owned a factory that manufactured suspenders and garters, located on the upper floor of the same building that served as the family home. Then he became known as Herschel *der Shleikesmacher,* or shoulder strap maker.

In Bedzin, Jews judged one another "not by their tastes, literary preferences, or style of dress, but by the character of their observance." Dora's father was the very model of the pious Chassidic scholar, with a great beard and earlocks, black caftan, and his fur *shtreimel* covering his head on the holidays. As the *Gabbai,* or leader, of the Gerer Rebbe's *shtiebel* in Bedzin, he was in charge of the prayer house and collected the money. Every Sabbath, after the prayers in the large synagogue, and more in the small prayer house, the members came to Dora's home to drink tea and study and engage in Talmudic discussions.

The character of Reb Herschel's observance was beyond reproach; his kindness, generosity and hospitality were legend. A Friday evening never passed that Dora's father didn't come home from the prayer house with a poor man to share the rich blessings of the Sabbath table. When she was alive, Dora's mother would cook and bake all day on Fridays and send the children out to deliver baskets to poor families, so that "God forbid" they wouldn't go without food on the Sabbath.

Dora's father did nothing without permission from the Gerer Rebbe, whom Herschel worshiped as a miracle-working holy man. The Gerer Rebbe called Herschel "his diamond," his youngest daughter later reported. "Ein diamant hob ich," the Wonder Rabbi said, "Herschel der Paviancer."

When Herschel became a man at thirteen, the Gerer Rebbe was Avraham Mordechai, who had inherited the Chassidic dynastic throne from R. Issac Meir, known by the initials RIM. RIM became the first Rebbe of Ger when he moved his rabbinical court from Warsaw to the small town of Ger (Gora Kalwaria) in 1859. A disciple of the famous Rabbi of Kock, RIM established one of the most powerful Chassidic dynasties in Poland, which continues to this day in Israel, where it constitutes the largest

Chassidic group. It was only after his death in 1866 that a rival court arose to challenge the predominance of the Gerer Rebbe, who "put his stamp on Polish Chassidism . . . [and] charted its course for the future."

The Ger Chassidim devoted themselves to the study of the Talmud as a fundamental way of life, above all the other commandments, and were identified by their "inflexible and extreme conservatism." A popular saying with the Chassidim of Ger was, "Anything new is forbidden by the Torah." This was based on the verse from Leviticus 26:10: "And ye shall bring forth the old from before the new."

And so much was new. The Haskalah movement, known as the Jewish Enlightenment in Europe, had begun in the eighteenth century. With the rise of the modern revolutionary movements, liberal political parties popped up and championed equal rights for Jews, which were finally accorded in the 1870s. With emancipation, European Jews jumped with both feet into worlds previously forbidden them, entering politics, philosophy, finance, industry, the arts, science and technology. With the growth of the bourgeoisie, the new middle class, Jewish culture in Berlin, Vienna, Prague, Budapest, Vilna and Warsaw swirled with new streams of cultural, religious and political activism.

But the Haskalah movement never really took hold in Poland, where the population was mostly rural. The Chassidim in Poland and Galicia did not warm to any of these new movements but in fact fought them all the way. As early as the mid-1840s, the Gerer Rebbe opposed any modernization in the lives of his followers. He wrote poems warning against the "plague of the Haskalah" and denounced popular romance novels and political journals of the "freethinkers." He opposed building new schools and campaigned against a royal decree forbidding the traditional Jewish mode of dress and requiring all Jews to adopt the style of Western Europe. Because of the Gerer Rebbe's influence, pious Polish Jews adopted the Russian style of dressing, which allowed for a full beard and longer coats, rather than the German style, which barely covered their bottoms when they sat. As the nineteenth century drew to a close and the twentieth century dawned, the Chasidim of Ger grew even more isolated and conservative.

Dora's life was strictly organized according to her father's rigorous religious observances. It was a "highly structured symbolic universe," according to author Eva Hoffman in *Shtetl: The Life and Death of a Small Town and the World of Polish Jews:* "The day, the week, the year were shaped and parsed by ritual signposts: the day by morning and evening prayers, the week by the climax of the Sabbath, the year by the sequence of holidays.

Each part of life, from food to sex to marriage and personal hygiene, was governed by a highly elaborate and precise body of religious principles and rules."

As a child, Dora learned the legends of the Baal Shem Tov, who taught through simple parables that every human being "was capable of direct contact with God" and that "layers of doctrine and years of study were unnecessary to achieve a holy state." Amid these communal rituals, Dora reached adolescence secure in a joyous communion with God's presence. Throughout her life, even after she lost her belief in the Absolute, Dora maintained an otherworldly awareness, the recognition of the holy act of living a simple life every day, in the joy of eating, dancing, laughing and loving.

Mandatory secular education for both boys and girls was instituted in Poland only after the Great War, but even before that, Dora attended Polish schools, where she encountered secular literature, such as the writings of Goethe and Dostoyevsky. Dora's studies were permitted because girls, unlike boys, were allowed to "waste" their time learning something other than Talmud. Dora's worldly education was seen as a form of adornment, to help her make a good match in marriage. But Dora yearned for more knowledge, more understanding of the outside world; she wanted to take part in the advances in modern society. In some western countries, women had already won the right to vote. Women now attended institutions of higher learning and universities and studied to become doctors, lawyers, scientists, even artists and actresses.

Dora managed to escape an early marriage, her prescribed future. Most likely, Dora was so necessary to the smooth running of his household that Herschel neglected to arrange a timely match for her. On the other hand, Herschel may have tried to find a suitable husband, but his headstrong daughter wouldn't discuss it. Marriage for women in Dora's world meant the end of hours spent reading and studying and dreaming, the end to her life as a individual, in charge of her own mind. She would have to cut off her luxuriously thick, wavy hair and cover her head with a scarf whenever she left the house or, worse, wear a stiff wig made of horsehair. She would exist only to serve her husband's will. She would work only to support him and the children she bore him. Her future seemed to be already inscribed in the Book of Life.

But then the war came and changed everything. When Dora was sixteen, the world exploded with the assassination of Archduke Franz Ferdinand, the heir to the throne of the Austro-Hungarian Empire. Cataclysm followed

as Austria-Hungary declared war on Serbia, forcing the Russians to come to
the aid of the Serbs. Germany declared war on Russia and France and invaded Belgium. Three days later, Great Britain declared war on Germany
while Austria-Hungary declared war on Russia. The madness mounted as
country after country joined in. World War I, then called the Great War, the
war to end all wars, had begun. Poland became the major battlefield between Germany and Russia. Young men, even the religious, rushed to join
the fight. Jews and Christians volunteered or were conscripted to fight on
both sides. The ensuing slaughter was unbelievable. By the end of the first
month, each side had suffered about half a million casualties.

A major influence on Dora's life during the four long years of world war
was Theodor Herzl. A journalist and an assimilated Jew from Vienna,
Herzl had published a pamphlet, *Der Judenstaat* (The Jewish State) (1896),
advocating the establishment of a Jewish state in Palestine. The idea of a
return to Israel as a solution to the problem of anti-Semitism was not new,
but Herzl took unprecedented political action and created an internationally recognized plan. He called for a Zionist congress, and the first one
convened in Basel, Switzerland, in 1897, the year before Dora's birth. That
same year, the World Zionist Organization was established to help lay the
economic foundation for the proposed state. Although other locations in
Europe, South America and Africa were proposed, Palestine was chosen as
the site of the future Jewish homeland because of its religious and historical significance to the Jews. They had remembered it in their psalms and
daily prayers ever since the Romans destroyed the temple in Jerusalem
and banished them from their land: "If I forget thee, O Jerusalem, let my
right hand forget its cunning!" Each year they had repeated the resounding congregational chorus at the close of Yom Kippur, the holiest day of
the year: "Next year in Jerusalem!"

At the beginning of the Great War, Zionist factions in Bedzin began an
organized effort, called the Hebraica Association, to reach young people
who were searching for their place in the world. One of the founders,
Moshe Rozenkar, reported on the formation of this group and the chal-
lenges facing them in the *Pinkas Bedzin*, a memory book compiled after
the destruction of the entire Jewish population of Bedzin during World
War II. Building on the work of the Hovevei Zion (Lovers of Zion) Hebraica reached out to spread the "national language to the masses."

Dora, along with a large number of Jewish teenagers from a variety of
families—assimilated, Zionists, Socialists, Bundists, even the most extreme
Communists and those from the most religious Orthodox quarters—

signed up for classes. They "served as the foundation for the Zionist movement in our city, with all its various political parties and modalities,"
Rozenkar said, and provided "a source of encouragement and filled our
hearts with joy."

But tuition fees didn't cover the costs of running the classes, and consequently lectures, parties, plays and movie days were instituted to raise
funds. A theater group was founded under the direction of one of the
teachers and presented plays that "were received with great love by the audiences." The ultra-Orthodox religious groups, however, saw their work
"as a desecration of the holy language." At one point, the followers of the
Rabbi of Ger, led by Dora's father, "threatened to excommunicate the parents of the students who visited the Hebraica and were being led astray."
It is not known how Herschel handled the situation, which must have
been personally embarrassing once he realized his own daughter was a
"student-trainee."

Dora joined a special class for older girls and young women, who would
instruct their children in Hebrew. Her teacher was a former yeshiva student, David Maletz, who, many years later, again played an influential role
in her life. Like most Jewish boys, David Maletz had learned to read and
speak Hebrew at an early age. Beginning as early as age three, boys studied
in the cheder for up to ten hours a day, six days a week. Most Jewish boys
could read Hebrew by the time they were six. Gifted students, such as
David Maletz, were sent away to a yeshiva, a tuition-free school or college,
usually supported by a synagogue. Education was an integral part of Judaism—for boys. Girls were not encouraged to learn more Hebrew than
the prayers every pious Jewish woman recited on the Sabbath.

In the earliest known picture of her, Dora posed with ten other class-
mates of Hebraica's Zionist Hebrew class for women and girls, and the official school photograph was later published in the *Pinkas Bedzin*. Her
teacher, the solitary male, stands in the center of the back row. Dora sits at
the far right, at the end of the front row. Dora's expression is wistful. Her
large eyes and full lips define her round face, a widow's peak framing her
features in the shape of a heart.

By the time Dora was a teenager, Herzl's dream had become her own.
When she was nineteen years old, the document that became known as the
Balfour Declaration finally promised a Jewish National Home in Palestine.
On November 2, the British Foreign Secretary, Arthur James (later Lord)
Balfour declared that His Majesty's Government, which, since the end of
World War I had held the mandate for Palestine, viewed "with favour the

establishment in Palestine of a national home for the Jewish People." With this declaration, the fulfillment of work begun by Theodor Herzl seemed imminent and Dora's hopes became *takke*, really possible.

Dora turned her sights toward what had truly become for her the Promised Land. She studied Hebrew with a passion. The more knowledge she gained, the greater the help she could give to building the Jewish State. But her destiny in Palestine seemed far in the future. The departure of the Jews from Europe was not designed to be sudden. Herzl had predicted the emigration would be gradual and take many decades: "The poorest will leave first and these will make the land workable. According to a pre-conceived plan, they will build roads, and bridges, railways and a telephone system; they will redirect the rivers and build homes. Their work will bring trade, and trade will bring markets, which in turn will attract new settlers, who will come by their own means. The work then done on the land will raise the value of the country. The Jews will soon see that their hitherto hated and despised determination has opened up a new and prosperous age."

Before the war ended in November 1918, two marriages took place in Dora's family in Bedzin. Dora's older brother David married Gittel Auerbach, whose family owned a cocoa importing company. It was a good match and made David a wealthy man. The other marriage affected Dora's life to a much greater degree: Herschel finally remarried. His new wife, also named Gittel, was a young widow with a daughter whom Herschel adopted. By the end of the war, the Dymant family had grown considerably. Dora's stepmother had given Herschel two more sons, Nathan and Avner, and David had made Dora an aunt for the first time with his daughter, Helusha. Over the next few years, Gittel gave birth to three more children, Pinche, Sara and Matitiahu.

With a new wife, Herschel had someone to run his household. Dora, almost twenty years old, refused to discuss marriage, and her involvement with the Hebraica Association was a growing embarrassment. She had even begun acting with a theater group.

In 1917, the first Beis Ya'acov schools for girls were established in Eastern Europe. Until that time, there was no formal higher education for religious Jewish girls. Beis Ya'acov schools were created in part as a response to the economic necessity for Orthodox Jewish women to support their pious, scholarly, but often poor husbands. The schools were also designed "to protect Jewish girls from the subversive influence of the Polish feminist movement." According to Dora's youngest half sister, Sara, Herschel took Dora to Krakow, where the first Beis Ya'acov seminary had just opened. "She was supposed to study there to become a teacher in a religious Orthodox school."

It took two days, traveling by horse and wagon, for Dora and her father to reach the famed city of Krakow, the royal and cultural capital of Poland. The ancient road from Bedzin passed through a lush green valley along a rushing creek, with medieval castles perched on high white limestone cliffs. At first Dora was excited about the possibility of training as a *Fröblerin,* named after German educator Friedrich Fröbel, who in the 1830s invented kindergarten to teach young children about art, design, mathematics and natural history. It was a solid career choice. By 1872, kindergarten had become compulsory throughout the Austro-Hungarian empire for all children under six, and instruction in the Fröbel method was made obligatory for all students of normal schools and teacher training classes.

In Krakow Dora learned about the "bloody persecutions of Jews in the newly liberated Poland." The Jews who had fought for Polish independence had been slaughtered like sheep. It shocked Dora to her core, and "for the first time as a thinking and conscious person," Dora said. She began to question her political beliefs about a free Poland.

Dora stayed at the Beis Ya'acov long enough to realize "that it was not for her." She didn't like the other girls "who got up in the morning and didn't take the feathers [from the pillows] out of their hair." She packed her small suitcase and took off without saying anything to anyone in her family about it. She got as far as Breslau, Germany; now Wroclaw, Poland, before her father tracked her down and brought her home. He ignored her pleas and returned her to the school in Krakow. He threatened to mourn her as dead if she disobeyed him again. When she ran away the second time, Herschel gave up on her.

Dora returned to Breslau, which lay in a direct line halfway to Berlin and was home to people she knew. Dora lived there for a year, working in a children's home and learning to speak German. She joined student and literary circles and met interesting young men, including Manfred Georg, who later immigrated to New York and became a well-known journalist, and Ludwig Nelken, a medical student who went on to practice medicine in Berlin and Jerusalem. In a newspaper interview many years later, Dr. Nelken recalled hearing Dora speak at a left-wing Socialist rally in the former Preussisches Herrenhaus, sharing the stage with a leading Russian revolutionary author, Angelica Balabanoff. He remembered Dora as a "pretty and intelligent woman whose strong Jewish commitment influenced a number of Jewish youngsters who might otherwise have gone into the assimilationist or left-wing camp."

By 1920, Dora moved to the vortex of action, the German capital, Berlin, and found a home in the largest Jewish community in Germany. Berlin's growing reputation as the modern cultural, artistic and intellectual center of the Western world attracted thousands of young—and Jewish—foreigners, like herself, seeking freedom and the latest modern ideas. At first, Dora "was intoxicated with Germany."

There had never been a better time to be a Jew in Berlin. The earliest known reference to Jews in Berlin is a 1297 discriminatory decree, forbidding weavers to buy yarn from Jews. Despite periods of cooperation and peace, anti-Semitism prevailed throughout the centuries as the Jews became scapegoats for every disaster. During the Black Death in the mid-fourteenth century, Jews were blamed for the plague and expelled from the city, a pattern that continued until 1671, when fifty Jewish families were given permission to resettle in the area. From 1800 the Jewish community numbered a little more than thirty-three hundred.

By the time Dora moved to Berlin, about 170,000 Jews lived in the city and suburbs. At their peak, Jews represented no more than 5 percent of the population, yet they played a prominent cultural role in the city. Many Jews held leadership positions in the new German democracy, the Weimar Republic. Since emancipation fifty years earlier, Jews had become enormously influential in commerce, dominating the banks and giant department stores. The two biggest newspaper groups, Ullstein and Mosse, were owned by Jews. "To a very considerable extent," one historian noted, "the spectacular culture of Berlin in the 1920s . . . was a Jewish culture."

On August 6, Kafka left Müritz. Dora stayed behind to complete her responsibilities at the Berlin Jewish People's Home holiday camp before returning to Berlin later in the month. Kafka went first to Berlin and formulated his next steps. He had planned to visit his parents, Herrmann and Julie Kafka, who were vacationing in Marienbad, but changed his mind due to bad weather. For a while he thought he might continue on to Karlsbad, where Brod was attending the Thirteenth World Zionist Conference in the second week of August, before returning to Prague to prepare for the move to Berlin. That didn't happen, either.

On August 8, Kafka wrote a postcard from the garden of a Berlin tavern. Away from Dora's enthusiastic influence, Kafka's resolve was weakening. His health had not improved at all in the past three weeks on the Baltic Sea, and he now felt drained and weak. He didn't have the strength to stay in Berlin and was returning directly to Prague. Berlin was "continually menacing," Kafka admitted to Max. "As for myself, I don't know exactly how I am. With each passing hour, I feel more intensely the evil effect of being alone."

Ensconced in his parent's home in Prague, Kafka watched his temperature climb steadily. The headaches, coughing and insomnia were driving him to "the verge of complete physical collapse." He was overcome with "my own great fatigue." On August 16, Max Brod went to visit Franz Kafka in his old room at his parents' home on the Old Town Square. In his biography of Kafka published fourteen years later, Brod said that "Franz came back from his summer holiday full of high courage. His decision to cut all ties, get to Berlin, and with Dora stood firm." Max thought his friend was dealing with his usual "anxiety—ghosts, nothing specific." Despite the disturbing tone of his earlier postcard, Kafka seemed optimistic and was continuing his Hebrew lessons. Max noticed that Kafka had become intrigued with Jewish prayer rituals. During their visit, Franz recited the curses from Leviticus in Hebrew and told him that he "wanted tefillim—the phylacteries used by Orthodox Jews for the daily morning prayers." On top of that, according to his mother's unpublished memoirs, Franz Kafka "borrowed the family's Hebrew prayer book."

But Kafka's body continued to sabotage his dreams. It was clear that he couldn't leave Prague in his current weakened condition. His weight continued to decline until he was "a six-foot skeleton weighing 118 pounds." When Franz's sister Ottla returned to Prague in the third week in August for a quick visit from her rented summer cottage in the Bohemian countryside, she was shocked by her brother's appearance, and "she quickly whisked him back with her to Schelesen, along with her two children."

Ottla was Kafka's youngest sister and perhaps his best friend. Nine years his junior, Ottla looked the most like him and, like him, was a vegetarian. She wasn't generally considered pretty, but she was "bright, sensitive, independent, funny, and remarkably kind and generous." Kafka admired Ottla's "humility and pride, sympathetic understanding and distance, devotion and independence, vision and courage in unerring balance." He envied the personality traits she shared with their father, such as "vigor, resolve, and self-confidence." Ottla had rebelled against their father's heavy-handed authoritarian behavior. Ottla's refusal "to be bullied in any way" was especially wonderful in Kafka's eyes.

Ottla's older sisters, Ellie and Valli, had submitted to marriages arranged by their father, but not Ottla. After a secret six-year courtship, Ottla married the man she loved, a boisterous Czech Christian, over the vehement objections of her family. Except Franz. Despite misgivings, he always encouraged Ottla to follow her heart. When she was younger, before she married Josef David, she had wanted to study agriculture and work on a farm to prepare for immigration to Palestine. Franz even offered to pay for her schooling, so that she wouldn't have to ask their father for the money. They often saw themselves as coconspirators against the rest of the family.

Once she even gave up her house for him. She had rented the magical little house on Alchemist's Lane in the winter of 1916 as a meeting place for her and her Christian lover. When Franz, who had been suffering from writer's block for a couple of years, asked if he could borrow it for a few days, Ottla quickly agreed. The few days turned into several months as the miniature house became "the monastic cell of a real writer." Over the next six months, throughout the winter of 1916–1917, Kafka conducted his own alchemy in the fairy-tale dwelling perched at the ramparts of Prague's Castle district, where he wrote the majority of parables and short stories published during his lifetime.

Franz was Herrmann and Julie Kafka's only living son. When he was five years old, his two younger brothers, George, born when Franz was three, and Heinrich, born the following year, died suddenly of childhood illnesses. His grief-stricken parents turned to each other for comfort and left Franz in the care of his governess and the household servants. They never discussed or explained the deaths of his brothers to him. As a result, Franz carried a horrible secret childhood guilt, certain that his jealousy for his siblings had somehow caused their early death.

Elli Kafka Hermann, who had been in Müritz with Kafka (whom Dora had mistaken for Franz's wife), was the oldest of his three younger sisters. She was born in 1889, when Franz was six years old. Valli was born the next year, and two years later, Ottla followed. Elli wasn't as beautiful as Valli or as courageous as Ottla, but had, like her brother, often been the butt of her father's irritation. Herrmann thought Elli was fat and criticized her in front of the entire family "at almost every meal," with such statements as, "She has to sit six feet away from the table, the great fat lump."

With conflicted feelings (because when Franz was younger, he too found Elli irritating), he watched in silence as their father, "without the slightest trace of pleasantness or good humor would exaggeratedly imitate the way she sat," which he "found utterly *loathsome.*"

Before their parting in Müritz, Dora promised to find an apartment for Kafka in Berlin. Immediately on returning to the city in mid-August, Dora set about her task. She had always managed to find places to stay, a bed or a room where she worked, or with friends in Mitte, the center of Berlin, or in the orphanage in Charlottenburg, near the royal palace just east of the city, where she was the house seamstress. It was easier to obtain residential permits in the suburbs, and there Dora began to search for a home for Kafka. In the quiet, leafy district of Steglitz south of Berlin, Dora found it.

From the moment she saw the furnished room for rent on the tree-lined Miquelstrasse, not far from the Steglitz Rathaus, Dora knew Kafka would love it. A peaceful, green neighborhood populated by civil servants and pensioners, Steglitz was a half hour by trolley from the center of Berlin. The room was a large and light-filled, with bay windows and a verandah. It was comfortably furnished and had a private bathroom and kitchen. The rent was well within his budget. It was close to the Dahlem School of Gardening, where Franz had said he wished to study someday. The room was warmed by a stove and a fireplace. A grand piano had been left behind by a recent tenant. The former lodger promised to move it, but Dora liked it. It gave the room elegance and warmth. Even silent, it filled the room with music.

Dora wrote to Kafka and waited in breathless anticipation for his response.

August passed into September. Dora carried on as best she could, praying for his arrival. Kafka stayed on in the Schelesen countryside with Ottla and her two daughters. Ottla's new baby, Helene, was only three months old. The weather was pleasant, Kafka reported, the air clean and fresh, but despite Ottla's and his best efforts, it wasn't enough. "Too many counterforces," he explained in a letter to Max Brod. "I must be a very precious possession of those counterforces; they fight like the devil, or are it." In a postcard to Max on September 14, Franz reported that his weight was "up a little, scarcely noticeable outwardly; but that is offset by some greater defect every day. There's a trickling in the walls."

This was Kafka's fourth retreat to Schelesen, a small town on the Elbe River in the hilly countryside northwest of Prague. Kafka first went there in 1918 to recuperate from the Spanish influenza, the pandemic that claimed almost 20 million lives. The year before, 1917, Kafka had been diagnosed with tuberculosis. On top of the weakened condition of his lungs, the deadly influenza had been complicated by double pneumonia, and for several days "his life hung in the balance."

On his second visit to Schelesen, in January 1919, Kafka had met and fallen in love with Julie Wohryzek, a young Jewish woman from Prague, also there for a rest cure. The two spent two months talking, laughing and holding hands. In Prague, the romance continued and Kafka proposed to Julie, although he had warned her in the beginning of their relationship that he could not possibly marry her, given the state of his health and his all-consuming need to write. His second engagement to Felice Bauer had ended because of the tuberculosis, which still presented a serious problem.

Julie Wohryzek, the pretty daughter of a shoemaker and *shammes* (synagogue custodian), had lost her fiancé in the war. She was, in Kafka's words, "brave of heart, honest, unassuming," although not well educated. When he first mentioned her to Brod, Kafka described her rather unkindly—although only to his closest friend and in confidence—as "in general very ignorant," belonging to the "race of shop girls." Nevertheless, he fell in love with her, and when he proposed, she accepted. They planned to marry that November. When Franz announced his marriage plans to his family, Herrmann Kafka exploded. He accused Franz of mixing sexual attraction with marriage and ignoring his requirement that his children marry at least within (preferably above but not significantly below) their social station. "She probably put on a fancy blouse, something these Prague Jewesses are good at, and right away, of course, you decided to marry her. And that as fast as possible, in a week, tomorrow, today," Herrmann said. "I can't understand you; after all, you're a grown man, you live in the city, and you don't know what to do but marry the next-best girl."

Instead of marrying Julie that November, Franz returned to Schelesen for his third stay, this time in the company of Max Brod. There Kafka penned a seventy-six page letter to his father, pouring out his anger and frustration. Franz said he had never felt more humiliated, or felt his father's contempt so keenly, than at the rejection of his latest marriage plans. Franz gave the letter to his mother to deliver, but Julie read it and returned it to her son. Edited by Max Brod and published in 1953, long after the death of everyone mentioned, *A Letter to His Father* is a searing psychological portrait of the relationship between a father and son. Although

Kafka continued to see Julie Wohryzek for several more months, the engagement was called off in July 1920.

Kafka couldn't bear to think what his father would say about Dora Diamant. Herrmann despised *Ostjuden* and had nothing but contempt for the old-fashioned Orthodox Jews, who he thought gave all Jews a bad name. When the Emperor Franz Joseph granted equal rights of citizenship to the Jews of Bohemia, Herrmann was a boy living in wretched poverty. As a young man, Herrmann moved to Prague, where he worked hard to take advantage of the new freedom by opening a business, marrying, providing for his family, prospering and fitting into Czech society. When his first son was born on July 3, 1883, Herrmann named him after the reigning emperor in a salute of gratitude.

To succeed in business, it was smart, if not essential, to assimilate—to appear less Jewish. Herrmann abandoned the ancient Pinkas Synagogue, where the old rituals were still practiced, for the liberalized Altneu Synagogue, which he attended four times a year and on High Holy Days. Later Herrmann sat on the board of the Heinrich Synagogue, the first Reformed synagogue that held services in Czech, instead of Hebrew. After she knew him longer, Dora realized that Kafka had "missed so much, never having learned devout praying, never having been taken to experience the profound devotion of a congregation."

At home again with his parents in Prague, Kafka said nothing about Dora or his intended move to Berlin. He didn't even mention her by name to Brod. He did confide everything to Ottla, who was very encouraging and supported his plan to go to Berlin and live there with Dora's help, as soon as his health allowed it.

As the late summer days slipped away, Kafka struggled in vain to get better. Dora continued to write letters, enthusiastically encouraging him toward Berlin. The leaves on the trees lining Miquel Street were changing and falling, but summer lingered in the warm afternoons. In the evenings, the air was sweet from the gardens surrounding every house and villa in the neighborhood. At the end of the street, the verdant countryside began. Fifteen minutes away were the tropical greenhouses of the famous botanical gardens, and within a half-hour walk was the Gruenewald, a 745-acre birch forest.

Ottla's husband had leased the country cottage in Schelesen until mid-October, so Kafka could stay with them until then, he wrote to inform her.

What Kafka needed, Dora countered, was to come to Berlin. Kafka agreed with her, perhaps now more than ever.

"Berlin is a medicine against Prague" Kafka had written in September 1922, one year earlier, encouraging Robert Klopstock, a young medical student, to move to Berlin. "Since the West European Jew is a sick man and lives on medicines, it is essential for him . . . not to pass up Berlin. However, Berlin today is a good deal more; one also has, I think, a stronger view of Palestine from there." But now Kafka found himself unable to "stretch out my hand from my bed and reach for the medicine." On September 13, Kafka wrote to Klopstock that "Berlin, too, is almost beyond me. (My temperature has gone up, and there are other problems.) And the danger remains that the voyage to Palestine will shrink to a trip to Schelesen. May it at least remain that, rather than end up as the elevator trip from the Old Town Square to my room."

As summer faded into fall, Kafka's health did not improve. His hope for a free, peaceful life in Berlin began to fade into the fantasy world to which it had been relegated for more than a decade.

3

A FREE LIFE IN BERLIN

There is a point of no return. This point has to be reached.

—Franz Kafka, *Blue Octavo Notebooks*

BERLIN, SEPTEMBER 1923

Yom Kippur, the holiest day on the Jewish calendar, fell on September 20, the autumn equinox. Ten days earlier, on Rosh Hashanah (the anniversary of the day of creation, which marked the beginning of the High Holy Days), Dora still hoped Kafka would be in Berlin to celebrate the Jewish New Year. Seven weeks had passed since she had seen him, more than twice the time they had actually spent together. With her nudging, Kafka had rented the apartment on Miquelstrasse and paid the rent for August and September in advance. The rental, along with his frequent letters to her, sustained Dora's hope. Still, he did not come. Time was running out. The brilliance of the leaves and the nip in the night air warned of a cold winter, and the chances of Kafka moving to Berlin grew dimmer as the days grew shorter.

Even if God had already decided against Kafka and Dora finding happiness together, according to Jewish belief, Dora's actions during the ten days between Rosh Hashanah and Yom Kippur could change everything, through the three t's: "*teshuvah, tefilah and tzedakah,*" or repentance, prayer and charitable good deeds. On Rosh Hashanah, God wrote in his book for the upcoming year, decreeing who would live and who would die, who would have a good life and who a bad one. On Yom Kippur, Dora's father, his head and shoulders covered in a white prayer shawl, would daven in the prayer house and fast for the entire day, plus one hour, as was the custom.

During the Days of Awe, the ten days between Rosh Hashanah and Yom Kippur, Dora had done all she could. Now it was truly in God's hands. Tonight, on Yom Kippur, the book would be sealed after nightfall when the long final blast of the ram's horn sounded. She prayed for her name to be inscribed beside that of Franz Kafka in the Book of Life.

The contrast between Dora's Orthodox childhood and her current life in Berlin was stark on this day. In Bedzin, the High Holy Days were observed by the whole town. Only a few goyim moved quietly on the empty streets, lighting the ovens and providing the necessary labor religious Jews could not perform on this day. Inside the synagogue and prayer houses, filled to over-flowing, the men cried and rejoiced, praying that their names would be writ-ten in the Book of Life for the coming year. Behind the grating in the back and in the balconies, the women, mothers, daughters, wives and sisters mur-mured along in their prayer books. Others remained at home with the chil-dren, solemnly awaiting the return of the men, the blowing of the shofar that signaled the end of the fasting and prayers and the closing of the holiday.

In Berlin, life went on as if it were any other day, not the Day of Atone-ment, the day set aside for contemplation of one's sins and the opportunity to ask for forgiveness. Dora knew the blessings and wisdom of these ritu-als. It was, perhaps, the loss of this introspection, the deep examination of one's personal responsibility for causing pain and suffering in others, that lay at the root of the restlessness she felt around her. The ritual act of rec-onciliation—of seeking forgiveness and healing, with God and with one's loved ones, family, friends, neighbors and business associates—provided joy and peace of mind that sustained those who observed the practice dur-ing the coming year.

The next day, on Friday, September 21, a miracle occurred. Kafka sent a telegraph from Prague: He had left Schelesen in the morning and would be arriving in Berlin on Monday, September 24. Would Dora be able to meet him at the station?

How could she possibly wait three more days?

PRAGUE, SEPTEMBER 21, 1923

On the first day of the Jewish year 5684, Kafka left Schelesen and returned to Prague. The violent coughing and headaches had subsided and he had even gained a few pounds. Protected with this "fatness from Schelesen," as he called it, Kafka returned to his parents' home to begin packing for Berlin. On Saturday, he wrote a postcard to his friend Robert Klopstock: "I'm leaving tomorrow, unless in the next twelve hours some great obstacle is thrown at me from a dark ambush." Kafka played down the move, saying he was going to Berlin "only for a few days."

Given the precarious state of his health on top of the current political and economic situation in Germany, his trip, even if only for a few days, was viewed by almost everyone as a very bad move. On Sunday Kafka spent the day engaged in the "frightfully complicated packing" of his trunks. On Monday morning, as he got ready to leave for the train station, Herrmann made one last effort to discourage his son from leaving. Ottla's husband, Josef David, nicknamed Pepa, reminded him of the latest news of inflationary disaster, food shortages, escalating unemployment and nightly fights in the streets of the German capital.

On the other side of the exciting artistic and creative glitter, Berlin was indeed a violent city, and much of the killing was official. "People were capable of a greater degree of physical violence than one was accustomed to living with elsewhere," reported an Englishman, one of many who moved to Germany in 1923 to take advantage of the higher standard of living enjoyed by foreigners during an inflationary period. "You felt that you could be easily arrested; and that if you were, there was no knowing what might become of you. It was a town in which it seemed remarkably easy to get shot, beaten up or generally maltreated."

In 1919, in its struggle for control in the chaotic aftermath of Germany's defeat in the Great War, the Weimar Republic had sanctioned the political murders of radical socialists and communists. The victims included Rosa Luxemberg and Karl Liebknecht, leaders of the revolutionary Spartacist movement, who had proclaimed their government at the same time the Weimar Republic was created. In the four following years, the leadership of the democratic republic had also been riddled by the assassination of mostly Jewish leaders by right-wing fanatics and nationalists.

The large newspapers backed the government's position and reported sympathetically in favor of the army and police, who were forced to shoot strikers, usually communists, when strikes turned violent. Fights broke out nightly following rallies and marches in working-class neighborhoods, such as "Red" Wedding, between leftists and the growing ranks of the fascists, the NSDAP—the National Socialists, or Nazis—who had begun infiltrating poorer districts. The government, controlled by the moderate

Social Democratic Party, favored the Nazis, who seemed manageable when compared with the highly organized communists, who were backed by the powerful and dreaded Soviet Union. Only when the leftists appeared to be winning did the police step in. A typical newspaper headline read, "Police obliged to open fire on a demonstration—ten dead."

"Within the limits of my condition," Kafka admitted to a friend, Oskar Baum, the move to Berlin was "a foolhardiness whose parallel you can only find by leafing back through the pages of history, say to Napoleon's march to Russia." Despite the inner and outer forces that threatened to defeat him, Kafka was taking a stand for his own personal happiness. As Max Brod later reported in his biography, "His decision to cut all ties, get to Berlin, and live with Dora stood firm—and this time he carried it out inflexibly."

The night before Kafka left his parents' home in Prague was "one of the very worst" of his life. The indecision that always haunted him now tortured him, and he spent the night unable to sleep. First, he told Ottla, he faced "an assault by all my many anxieties, and no army in the history of the world is as large as these." After eating and dozing off for a quarter of an hour, "I occupied myself for the remainder of the night with drafting the cancellation telegram to the landlord in Berlin, and with my despair over that. But in the morning (thanks to you and Schelesen) I did not collapse when I got up and went away, comforted by the Fräulein, alarmed by Pepa, lovingly quarreled with by Father, looked at sadly by Mother."

BERLIN, OCTOBER 1923

Max Brod still didn't know anything about Dora Diamant or her increasingly important role in Franz Kafka's life. Brod was already in Berlin when Kafka arrived, having left the day before him, and was spending several days in the city. They arranged to meet one afternoon at Josty's, a popular Berlin café. Kafka successfully deflected questions about himself and centered the conversation on the issues and events happening in Brod's life and career, which was flourishing. Brod was in Berlin to arrange for the performance of a Czech opera by Janacek, *Jenufa*, which he had translated, at an opera house next spring. But his personal life was a mess. Brod had another reason for visiting Berlin so often: His mistress lived here. For almost two years, Brod had been having a tumultuous affair with Emmy Salveter, an aspiring young actress who was currently employed as a chamber maid in a Berlin hotel. Although married, Brod was in love with Emmy, whom he had idolized in a recent book, *Life with a Goddess.*

"She is charming. And so entirely centered on you. Whatever came up, she made it a pretext to refer to you," Kafka reported to Max in July, after meeting Emmy for the first time in Berlin on his way to Müritz. At that first meeting, Kafka thought Max's lover had "a truly vital originality, straightness, seriousness, a dear and childlike seriousness." After detailing the time he spent with Brod's mistress in Berlin, Kafka signed the post-card: "Warm regards to you and your wife, Franz."

The affair had reached a crisis point. Emmy's family was causing diffi-culties and wanted it to end. At first, her parents approved of their daugh-ter's relationship with the married but well-regarded Czech writer and critic but changed their minds when Brod did not divorce his wife.

Ironically, Kafka, who had not been able to sustain a happy romantic relationship with any woman in his own life, was asked for advice in deal-ing with Emmy and her family. Brod thought his "wonderfully helpful friend" had the ability to identify the essential element of any problem and had come to rely on Kafka's "knowledge of the world, his tact, his advice, which never failed to be right." But not always. As a solution to Max's concern over the cost of maintaining two households, one in Prague and another in Berlin, Kafka blithely posed the idea of moving Emmy to Prague, so that Max, his wife and his mistress could all live under one roof in a sort of ménage à trois.

The friendship between Max Brod and Franz Kafka has been labeled as "unique in the history of literature." The relationship, which became for Brod "the mainstay of my whole existence," began while they were teenage students at Prague's Charles-Ferdinand University. Their first meeting took place in the fall of 1902, following a talk Brod gave on the philosophers Schopenhauer and Nietzsche at Prague's Reading and Lec-ture Hall for German Students. A passionate believer in the ideas of Schopenhauer, Brod disliked Nietzsche's nihilistic principles to such a de-gree that he referred to the philosopher, who had died two years earlier, "quite simply and baldly as a swindler."

Kafka was nineteen, a year older than Brod, and in many ways his social opposite. Normally quiet and reserved, Kafka kept to himself at these meetings, but not this time. Kafka approached Brod and introduced him-self. They walked home together, engaged in an "endless conversation."

As Brod remembered it, Kafka "began with a strong protest against the extreme uncouthness of my way of putting things. From that we went on to talking about our favorite authors, and defended them against one another."

In his biography of Kafka, published thirty-five years after that first meeting, Max Brod described their first conversation. It was Kafka's "simplicity and naturalness of feeling," Brod said, stemming from that first conversation, that led him away from what he called "my confused and corrupt state of mind, puffed up with childish pride and the completely false assumption of a blase air."

"At school I modeled myself on the classics, and rejected everything 'modern,' but in one of the upper classes I swung round, and at this time in a proper 'storm and stress' mood, I welcomed everything that was out-of-the-way, unbridled, shameless, cynical, extreme, overcaustic," Brod said. "Kafka opposed me with calm and wisdom. I quoted him 'purple passages' by heart. One from Meyrink's *Purple Death* compared butterflies to great opened-up books of magic. Kafka turned up his nose. That sort of thing he considered too farfetched . . . everything planned for effect, intellectual, or artificially thought up, he rejected—although he himself never used labels of this kind. In him there was something of the 'softly murmuring voice of Nature' of which Goethe spoke, and it was that he liked to hear in other writers. As a contrasting example, Kafka quoted a passage from Hofmannsthal, 'the smell of damp flags in a hall.' And he kept silent for a long while, said no more, as if this hidden, improbable thing must speak for itself. This made so deep an impression on me that I remember to this day the street and the house in front of which this conversation took place."

Until then, Max had taken little notice of Franz Kafka. His "outward appearance was above all deeply unobtrusive—even his elegant suits, which were mostly dark blue, were as unobtrusive and reserved as himself." His first impression of Franz Kafka was that of a healthy nineteen-year-old, who though "remarkably quiet, observant, reserved" was also "brave, a good horseman, swimmer, and oarsman."

The friendship developed slowly. From the very beginning, Brod had been deeply impressed with Kafka's "absolute truthfulness, one of the most important and distinctive features of his character." Kafka's "*Conscientia scrupulosa*—his unimaginably precise conscientiousness," in Brod's words, "revealed itself in all questions of a moral nature, where he could never overlook the slightest shadow of any injustice that occurred."

Kafka and Brod were young Jewish law students interested in art and literature, but there were significant differences. Where Kafka was unsure, introspective and thoughtful, Brod was social and ambitious. He was a *Wunderkind*, already a musician, composer, poet and budding novelist while still in his teens. "While Kafka floated through college," said one biographer, "Brod swept through, making use of every opportunity to develop his ubiquitous interests." Brod spoke fluent German and Czech and worked with "energy and initiative" to achieve positions of cultural prominence. He entered politics and ran as a candidate for a Zionist party. At the age of twenty-six, "Brod had published four books. By thirty, he had published nineteen. And by the time he died, he had published eighty-three books, including novels, books on philosophy and religion, biographies, literary essays, plays, poems, and journalistic articles of various kinds."

While still in high school, Kafka announced his intention to become a writer, but his standards for his art were very high. He destroyed the evidence of his earliest attempts, burning everything he wrote before his twentieth birthday. As a boy, Kafka lived to read. Fairy tales enchanted him. He devoured adventure stories, true accounts of polar expeditions, voyages to distant lands and the mysteries of Sherlock Holmes. When he was still a teenager, withdrawn and self-conscious (he referred to himself as "shamefaced lanky"), his reading tastes expanded to scientists and philosophers, including writers such as Goethe, Darwin, Nietzsche, Spinoza, and the thirteenth-century German mystic Meister Eckhart. In literature he discovered a way to use books, he said, as a key "to unfamiliar rooms in one's own castle."

In 1901 Kafka enrolled at the German-language university within walking distance of his parents' home, where he developed a circle of intellectual friends and writers who remained close to him for the rest of his life. At first he studied chemistry but switched to law, which he soon discovered he also didn't like. His true passion was German literature. He wanted to go to Munich to study literature but decided to stay the course in Prague and become a lawyer, as his father wished. He graduated with a doctor of law degree in 1906. Brod was behind him, earning his law degree the following year.

The physical differences between the two friends were striking. To Kafka's thin, tall frame, Brod was short and hunchbacked. When he was four years old, Max was diagnosed with "a life-threatening curvature of the spine." According to Kafka biographer Ernst Pawel: "Abandoned by the luminaries of the local medical establishment, who considered the case beyond help or hope, his frenzied mother whisked the child off to a miracle healer in Germany's Black Forest. For one entire year, the five-year-old lived with this sullen sorcerer, a shoemaker by trade, who built him a monstrous harness into which he was strapped day and night." While the cure was "effective to a degree," it "left Brod with a permanently deformed physique, whose apparent frailty seemed accentuated by the strikingly massive head."

In one of his published photos, Brod's languid brown eyes gaze halflidded through round wire-rim glasses. His wide forehead, patrician nose, delicately formed lips under a short mustache and a dashing cleft chin disclose part of his appeal to women. As Pawel noted, "If his subsequent promiscuous generosity as a lover was inspired by the need to reaffirm his wholeness, he should have been reassured well into old age by an impressive roster of attractive women who succumbed to his charms, presumably including his wife."

Although Max Brod was the far more successful as a writer and better known within the literary circles of Prague, Vienna, and Berlin, he always acknowledged that Kafka was the senior partner in their friendship, "although an equality of rights was cheerfully acknowledged" on both sides. Brod also thought Kafka the superior writer. Before anyone else, Max Brod believed that someday his friend would be recognized as "the most important writer of his time."

Neither Kafka nor Dora discussed his first days in Berlin or the terms of their cohabitation. Exactly when Dora moved into the apartment on Miquelstrasse was never documented, but clearly she was a presence there from the very beginning. She may have kept her bed at the orphanage in Charlottenburg, where she still helped out, but as Kafka came to need her more, she spent less time there and more with him. Living together outside marriage was still frowned on. Not mentioning Dora or their living arrangement was a way to protect her. Kafka's parents would have been deeply disapproving had they known, and Dora, as the woman, would be the one whose character was faulted. It wasn't that unmarried couples didn't live or sleep together; they just didn't talk about it. Neither did Dora or Kafka.

Kafka loved the apartment and the neighborhood. One week after moving in, he described it in a postcard to Ottla: "In the evenings, on these warm evenings, when I step out of the house, a fragrance comes to me from the lush old gardens, a perfume of such delicacy and strength as I think I have never sensed anywhere. And so far, everything else is in keeping with that. It is hard to describe anything in greater detail." He wanted Ottla to experience it herself and invited her for a visit, underlining his request: "By the way, wouldn't you feel like seeing it for yourself?"

The immediate problem he faced was the wildly escalating prices. "The landlady is allegedly satisfied with me," he wrote Ottla, "but unfortunately, the room no longer costs 20 crowns, but for September some 70 crowns and for October at least 180 crowns; prices are climbing like the squirrels where you are. Yesterday I became almost a little dizzy from it." In a postcard written to Max the same day, Kafka admitted, "I had a severe fit of numerical obsessions."

Economically speaking, Kafka could not have come to Berlin at a worse time. As its headlines screamed the latest economic disaster, the price of the newspaper itself told the story. In January 1923, a single copy of the *Berliner Morgenpost* cost a whopping forty marks, or ten dollars, due to the inflation that had started in 1914 and was now spiraling out of control. In August, eight months later, the newspaper sold for 100,000 marks, or 250 dollars. By September, it had risen to a 150 million marks for a single copy. According to the *Morgenpost*, a loaf of bread, which already cost 69,000 marks in August, rose to almost 4 million marks in September, the same month Kafka arrived in Berlin.

Descriptions of Germany's Great Inflation of 1923 defy belief, or at least rational comprehension. The cost of living rose 20 percent *every day*. A new currency index, or exchange rate, was announced daily at noon. The bulk and weight of the nearly worthless money was too heavy to carry; wheelbarrows were necessary to cart home a day's wages.

Before the war, the German mark was valued against a gold standard, with one paper mark equal to one gold mark; one dollar was valued at a little over four marks. Before the Great Inflation reached its crescendo on November 20, 1923, the value of the mark continued to fall until one billion paper marks equaled one gold mark, and almost a *trillion* paper marks equaled one U.S. dollar. Marks were no longer individually counted but measured in stacks with rulers. Life savings disappeared overnight. Small and medium-sized family businesses, after generations of profitability, suddenly collapsed. Unemployment rose exponentially. Those who still had jobs were not much better off. Eyewitness accounts describe how the moment people were paid, they grabbed the armfuls of cash and "rushed off to the shops and bought absolutely anything in exchange for paper about to become worthless." For wives whose husbands worked away from home and sent money through the mail, it was "virtually without value by the time it arrived. Workers were paid once, then twice, then five times a week. One luckless author received a sizable advance on a work only to find that within a week, it was just enough to pay the postage on the manuscript."

Patriotic nationalists blamed the inflation on the enormous war debt, the massive reparations imposed by the Treaty of Versailles. In *The Rise and Fall of the Third Reich*, William Shirer points the finger of blame squarely on the big industrialists and rich landlords, who forced the government to "deliberately let the mark tumble in order to free the state of its public debts, to escape from paying reparations." If it is true, it worked: "destruction of the currency enabled Germany's heavy industry to wipe out its indebtedness by refunding its obligations in worthless marks." Although the final death knell for the Weimar Republic did not sound for another decade, the inflation of 1923 was the beginning of the end for Germany's first attempt at democracy.

Kafka kept his relationship with Dora private. In the postcards he wrote during the first days and weeks after arriving in Berlin, Kafka didn't mention her name, except once in a postcard to Max. The postcard contained a report of Emmy Salveter's first visit to Kafka's apartment on September 27, three days after he arrived in Berlin: "Yesterday—Thursday—she came to see me. It was my first social occasion, the 'housewarming.' . . . Dora was there; she was indispensable for the occasion." He said nothing more about Dora until Max complained and demanded an explanation. To Robert Klopstock he only wrote, "When conditions here, my personal ones, I mean, have clarified, I'll write in more detail." But he never did.

Tile Rössler was the first to learn the truth about Kafka's relationship with Dora, and it devastated her. Tile's family lived in Steglitz, and as soon as she found out Kafka was in Berlin, she went to visit him. She brought a friend with her, a painter. Although Kafka had written in a letter to Tile that he was spending most of his time with Dora, it never occurred to Tile that there was anything romantic between the two of them. The teenager, who eventually became a well-known dancer and Israeli choreographer, harbored her own daydreams about Kafka. He had given her a parting gift before she left Müritz, which, along with her memories of him, she cherished as her most prized possession.

The day she met Kafka in Müritz, Tile had found herself pouring out her troubles to him. He was "infinitely patient" with her, and she marveled at "how youthful and cheerful" he was, "this tall, overly thin man with the dark, rather long hair and deep blue eyes." Kafka's eyes were gray, not blue, but Dora had made a similar mistake in regard to the color of his eyes, although she thought they were brown, when she first met him. Kafka's kindness to Tile "filled her with a stunned gratitude and love for the understanding goodness of this great man."

Not only Dora and Tile had fallen for Kafka; nearly everyone at the holiday camp had been taken with him. "All of these young people, most of whom had surely not read a single line of his, fell completely under his spell, sensing that his increasingly frequent visits to their circle were events of unique significance, honoring them all." Another sixteen-year-old volunteer from Berlin, Sabine (nicknamed Bine), was with Tile when they encountered Kafka while window shopping at Müritz's only department store. Tile had been admiring a candy dish made of bright ruby red glass.

"I'd give God knows what to own this bowl," Tile had sighed.

"What could you give?" Bine retorted. "You don't own anything."

Suddenly the two girls noticed Dr. Kafka and realized he must have overheard them. Embarrassed, the two girls "got themselves out of there."

When Tile left Müritz at the end of July, she was miserable at the thought of having to leave her new friend, who always listened to her with the "tenderest empathy." With her last penny, she purchased a vase to give him as a parting gift and went to the Haus Gluckhauf to deliver it. Outside, the pouring rain was "the very symbol of her own desperation." As Tile waited in the lobby, the player piano appropriately played the funeral march by Grieg. When Kafka entered, she presented a pitiable sight. Damp from the rain, her "slender arms pressed close to her thin body, her face bowed to the ground," sadness dripped "from her in long falling raindrops."

"Wait here a moment," Kafka had said. "I'll be right back!" He bounded up the stairs and returned a moment later with a big package, which he carried with an exaggerated caution. With elaborate ceremony he presented the box to her. To her delight, buried in the tissue paper was the ruby red glass candy bowl. It was, she thought, "unequaled in beauty." Kafka told her that she should, according to the old custom, "smash this glass at her wedding."

In October, Tile was stunned to arrive at Kafka's new address in Berlin to find the door opened by "the kitchen supervisor" from Müritz! Seeing

Dora Diamant there with Kafka, acting the part of a *"Hausmütterchen,"* a little housewife, "cost her deep pain, much anguish and effort of will before the whole truth sank in." Tile's secret romantic fantasies about Kafka, lovingly embellished in daydreams over the past two months, were as crushed as her sensitive soul.

On October 8, after two weeks in Berlin, Kafka wrote to his sister Ottla, repeating the invitation to visit Berlin. But, he stipulated, he didn't want anyone else to come: "We do not have to discuss whether you would disturb me. If everything in the world were to disturb me—and it has almost reached that point—not you. But anyone in addition to you, I must say I am very much afraid of that. It is much too soon for that; I am not yet firmly enough established here; the nights still pitch too badly. This whole Berlin business is such a tender thing, has been snatched with my last strength, and for that reason has probably remained very delicate. You know the tone in which others, obviously under Father's influence, often speak about my affairs. To hear such judgments, no matter how good-natured, no matter how well-meaning, would seem to me like Prague's reaching all the way out here to Berlin for me."

Kafka began to settle into a new—but not unfamiliar—routine. His issue of *Selbstwehr* (Self-Defense), a Zionist weekly, had arrived, which he read from cover to cover, as he did faithfully since 1913. His friend Felix Weltsch, whom he'd known since their university days, was the editor of the Zionist publication and had sent him the latest issue. A writer and philosopher, Felix Weltsch had been good friends with Franz Kafka for a long time. Weltsch resembled Kafka so much that from a distance they were often mistaken for each other. Felix was also shy, with a "wry and sometimes bitter sense of humor, not unlike Kafka's own."

Kafka thanked Felix for sending the latest issue of *Selbstwehr*. "I have after all stayed longer than I thought and would not like to have missed it." He apologized for not yet visiting Felix's sister, Lise, who lived in Berlin: "The days are so short, pass for me even faster than in Prague, and happily, much less noticeably. Of course it is a pity that they pass so swiftly, but that is the way time is; once you've taken your hand off its wheel it starts to spin and you no longer see a place for your hand to check it."

Kafka described his life in Berlin much as he had to others: "I scarcely go beyond the immediate vicinity of the apartment, but this neighborhood is wonderful; my street is about the last half-urban one. Beyond it the countryside breaks up into gardens and villas, old, lush gardens. Then in addition there are the great botanical gardens, a fifteen-minute walk from where I am, and the woods, where I have not yet been, are less than half an hour. So the setting for this little emigrant is beautiful." Kafka had another request: "If you can, do something for poor Klopstock (like finding a job for him)." Klopstock, a young medical student from Budapest, who also suffered from tuberculosis, was struggling to live on a pittance in Prague, and Kafka was always trying to get his friends to help him.

After two weeks in Berlin, Kafka was confident enough to declare to Ottla, Max and Robert Klopstock that he intended to stay. Despite "the real agony of the prices" and the anxiety he admitted experiencing on the rare occasions he left the autumnal avenues of Steglitz and went into the city center ("I have trouble with my breathing, start to cough, become more anxious than I ordinarily am, see all the dangers of this city uniting against me"), Kafka didn't want to leave.

In mid-October, Kafka wrote to Klopstock: "If it proves at all possible, I shall be very glad to spend the winter here. If my case were altogether new in history, the anxiety would be justified, but there are precedents. Columbus, too, for instance, did not turn his ships around after a few days." Despite the bad news pouring from the city, he reported, "Life here in Steglitz is peaceful, the children look well, the begging is not frightening. . . . I do keep out of the inner city, though, have been there only three times; my Potsdamer Platz is the square outside the Steglitz town hall. Even that is too noisy for me; happily I then duck into the wonderfully quiet tree-lined avenues."

Kafka wrote another postcard that same day, responding to Brod's earlier queries: "I don't want to return to Prague, not now, perhaps in two months. Your fears are unfounded; I am not reading the newspapers, have so far not personally suffered from the evil consequences of the times; as far as meals go I am living exactly, but exactly, the way I did I Prague; in bad weather I stay in my room; the cough that I casually mentioned has not come back. What is worse is that in the last few days the phantoms of the night have tracked me down, but that too is no reason for returning. If I'm to fall prey to them, I'd rather it were here than there; but we haven't reached that point. Besides, I'll be seeing you soon. Would you be so kind as to bring me a suitcase with winter clothes. It would go along with your own baggage. Would you do that?"

After Kafka had been in Berlin one month, Brod wrote another letter to Kafka, in stronger language this time, asking for an explanation of precisely how Kafka was living. After a twenty-year friendship, Brod knew Kafka was concealing something, and he demanded answers: What was

Franz doing with his time? What was he eating? And who exactly was Dora?

"It is true that I am not writing to you, but not because I have anything to conceal (except to the extent that concealment has been my life's vocation)," Kafka answered in a lengthy letter that took three days to complete. "If I do not write, that is due chiefly to 'strategic' reasons," Franz said. "I do not trust words and letters, my words and letters. I want to share my heart with people but not with phantoms that play with the words and read the letters with slavering tongue. Especially I do not trust letters, and it is a strange belief that all one has to do is seal the envelope in order to have the letter reach the addressee safely. It seems to me, that the nature of art, the existence of art, is explicable solely in terms of such 'strategic considerations' of making possible the exchange of truthful words from person to person."

Kafka's past relationships with women, especially Felice and Milena, had been carried out largely through letters. Now, living with Dora in Berlin, Kafka was able to express his feelings in person to the woman who inspired them, but not to Max.

He told Brod he was reading a Hebrew novel, one page a day. "In spite of all the difficulty, the thirty pages read so far is no achievement I can offer in justification if I am asked to give an accounting for four weeks." He wrote at length about Emmy, who was his most frequent visitor. Although her troubled love affair with Brod brought her suffering, she was happier, more vigorous, more courageous, Kafka said. She'd been cast in a play at the Actor's Theater and was going to sing in an upcoming church concert. Kafka had seen her on several occasions, and they had met one day in the Botanical Gardens. She telephoned often, canceling one appointment and rescheduling another. As he was writing the letter to Max, the telephone rang again. "Emmy," Kafka reported to Max after the interruption. "She was excited. Berlin excitements. (Fear of a general strike, difficulties in changing money . . .)."

It wasn't until the third day that Kafka answered Brod's most pressing question. "Diamant is her name," Kafka wrote, and said no more. The next day, in another letter, he tantalizingly mentioned her again, but only by her first initial, "D." He said Brod was worrying needlessly about the quality or quantity of the food he was getting and cited a lunch he and Dora had eaten recently at a vegetarian restaurant on Friedrichstrasse. "D. and I. We had spinach with fried egg and potatoes (excellent, made with good butter, in quality enough to be filling by itself), then vegetable cutlets, then noodles garnished with applesauce and plum compote (the same could be said of this dish as of the spinach), then an extra plum compote, then tomato salad and a roll. The whole thing, with excessive tip, cost about eight crowns. That isn't bad."

The meal Franz described to Max marked only the second time Kafka had eaten in a restaurant since arriving in Berlin. Although Kafka hadn't admitted it yet, Dora cooked most of his food. During the day, he ate fresh fruit, yogurt and kefir, and bread from the small neighborhood bakery, with excellent Czech butter that his family had been sending in great quantities from Prague.

In mid-October, Kafka began a correspondence with his parents that exceeded the total output of the previous forty years. Between October 1923 until his death nine months later, Kafka wrote more than thirty letters to his parents, reassuring them that despite reports to the contrary, food was plentiful for those who could afford to by it. As a vegetarian, Kafka needed butter medicinally; it was absolutely necessary to keep his weight up. But it was prohibitively expensive now for most Germans. In October a pound of butter cost *six million marks*. For those who could afford it or were paying in foreign currency, butter was available, "as much as anyone could want, only it isn't edible," Kafka had written on his second day in Berlin. He had asked Ottla to send him, "now and then, a small package of the good Czech butter."

As a foreigner in Berlin, Kafka had a tremendous advantage over the average German citizen. Kafka's monthly pension of a thousand crowns from the Workers Accident Institute was paid in Czech kronen, or crowns, which held its value against the U.S. dollar, the international standard. As if the rapidly spiraling cost of everything—rent, food, the streetcar fares—weren't enough trouble, Kafka's parents, who received the pension at their home, were withholding his money and forcing him to write letter after letter asking them for it.

Kafka still had not mentioned Dora's existence to Klopstock, who had written a letter enthusiastically commending Kafka on achieving his goal. "Please, do not exaggerate in regard to Berlin," Kafka wrote on October 31. "It was monstrous that I came here, but for the time being other monstrosities have not occurred, so there is no point in jinxing it by congratulations. It is not even out of the question that the fantastic inflation will drive me out—not yet, but if prices go on climbing with the same indefatigability," Kafka cautioned. Obliquely referring to Dora, he added, "So far things are going well for me; I could not be better cared for than I am."

In fact, Kafka's move to Berlin was worthy of heartfelt congratulations. At the age of forty, despite seemingly insurmountable obstacles, he had finally realized a long-cherished dream. As he told Dora, "Tearing himself away from Prague, was, even though very late, the great achievement in life without which one has no right to die."

4

THE IDYLL IN BERLIN

*This is a place where I never was before: here
breathing is different, and more dazzling than the
sun is the radiance of a star beside it.*
　　　　　　　　—Franz Kafka, *Blue Octavo Notebooks*

BERLIN, NOVEMBER 1923

"To have lived one single day with Franz means more than all his work, all his writings," Dora confided to the philosopher Felix Weltsch after Kafka's fame as a literary genius was established. Dora had not fallen in love with a writer, but with a man who embodied her conception of what a human being should be, who constantly amazed and delighted her: "Everything was done with laughter." Being with Kafka, she said, "was as if one lived in Paradise."

To Dora, Kafka's writings, or his "scribblings" as he called them, were the least of what he was as a human being. No matter how great his literary work, he himself was even greater, although he never saw it that way at all. He was truly an "exceptional being." Dora had known it the first time she saw him. Almost everyone sensed it. Friends and acquaintances spoke of Kafka's influence on them. Dora thought there was glow around him that attached itself to other people. After meeting Dora and hearing her talk about Kafka, one writer felt that she was "taller, ennobled, definitively marked by the contact with an exceptional being."

Dora and Franz spent hours alone together, a party of two, talking, reading aloud and amusing each other. "Kafka was always cheerful," Dora said. "He liked to play; he was a born playmate, always ready for some fun." He made a game of everything, from putting the plates on the table to opening letters to resolving a dilemma. Dora threw herself into the game with him, not sure if he was half playing or truly serious. It didn't matter to her.

"The content of my consciousness is entirely nebulous," Kafka had once written. "I remain undisturbed by this, so far as it concerns only myself, and am even occasionally self-satisfied." However, as he pointed out, relationships with others usually required "pointedness, solidity, and sustained coherence, qualities not to be found in me. No one will want to lie in clouds of mist with me." He was wrong. To his delight, Dora did want to lie in clouds of mist—or wherever—with him and entered his dreamlike games with a dramatic flair and an exuberant sense of adventure.

They constantly played with the idea of leaving Berlin and immigrating to Palestine to begin a new life. They imagined different scenarios, centered on the plan to live in Tel Aviv, where they would open a restaurant. Dora was to be the cook, and Kafka would make himself useful as the waiter. "That way he could stand in the midst of everyday life, seeing everything without being seen," she later explained. "He loved to play with great seriousness and care the role of waiter for me," Dora remembered. "He had an entire room to serve, and the game lasted sometimes fifteen minutes while the meal got cold."

Dora realized that going to Palestine was only a dream, a fantasy, for him: "With the state of his health he could never do such a thing. But if it was only a game, it was a serious game, like everything he undertook." Many years later, when Kafka was proclaimed a nihilist, a progenitor of existentialism, Dora thought the idea absurd: "A person who ate and drank with such joy as he did, how he took such pleasure in eating a banana! Whoever saw Franz drink a sip of wine would become a wine drinker. How could a human being who lived so intensely, who gave such an intensity to acts of daily life, how could he have hated life?"

Kafka was curious about everything from her life in Poland, about her father, how she had grown up as a young girl in a Chassidic family. "There aren't enough words to explain the intensity of his interest," Dora said. "He listened so intently that he trembled." Kafka's experience of Eastern European Judaism, Dora believed, "brought up something in him, which had been buried, archaic. It touched on the mystical." She recognized in Kafka many of the traits of Hasidism: "His love of daily life, the little things of daily life. He found the presence of God within the smallest gestures of daily living, his joy in helping and service to others."

Kafka loved to talk. "When he spoke, his eyes lit up," Dora remembered, many years later. "There was humor in them; but it was not so much irony as mischievousness—but as if he knew something that other people didn't. He was totally without solemnity. He had a very lively way of talking. His conversational style was full of imagery, like his writing. His wrists were very slender, and he had long, ethereal fingers, speaking fingers which took on shape while he was telling a story." It was another form of speech for him, as if he were musically painting his words with his fingers. When Kafka was particularly successful in expressing himself, Dora noticed a sense of "craftsman-like satisfaction."

"His voice was a hesitating, muted baritone, wonderfully melodious, although it never left the middle range in strength and pitch," wrote Gustav Janouch, a young writer, the son of a respected colleague, whom Kafka had befriended a few years earlier. Following every conversation with the older man, Janouch recorded not only Kafka's words but also the impression they made on him. Twenty-five years later, with the help of Max Brod, Janouch published his notes as *Conversations with Kafka*, filled with detailed descriptions of Kafka's mannerisms. Although many of Kafka's friends talked about laughing long and hard with him, no one but Janouch ever described *how* Kafka laughed: "Depending on how much he was amused, he threw his head back quickly or slowly, opened his mouth a little and closed his eyes into narrow slits, as if his face were turned up to the sun. Or he laid his hand on the desk, raised his shoulders, drew in his bottom lip and shut his eyes as if someone were going to shower him with water."

Where Dora thought Kafka spoke with his fingers, "Kafka speaks with his face," Janouch said. "Whenever he can substitute for words a movement of his facial muscles, he does so." Kafka's facial expressions—his mercurial smile, a slight contraction of his dark eyebrows, a wrinkling of his forehead or the pursing of his lips—replaced whole spoken sentences. Kafka also used gestures to the same effect, Janouch said, but he used them sparingly. His gestures were not only an accompaniment to his speech but "an independent language of movement, a means of communication, a deliberate expression of intention."

But it was what Kafka said rather than how he said it that Janouch considered significant. Almost fifty years later, shortly before his death, Janouch wrote a postscript to the second edition of his book, a summary of Kafka's impact on his life that echoed Dora's experiences:

The smiling Franz Kafka, who in the years when I knew him already lived in the shadow of death, awakened me to feeling and to thought. He was spiritually the greatest figure, and also the most powerfully formative character, of my youthful years, a real man who fought for truth and to preserve life, of whose bitter struggle, waged in silence, for human existence I was a witness. The look of his face, his soft voice and loud fits of coughing; the image of his tall, slim figure; the elegant gestures of his gentle hands; the shadows and the brilliance of his large changeable eyes, whose light gave emphasis to his words; something that was imperishable and unique, and that was therefore unrepeatable and eternal, in his personality, in his outer and his inner self; all this vibrates in me like an echo, which reverberates, in an endless series of images, through the corridors and abysses of my days and years, and with time does not die but only stands out in greater and clearer relief.

While the weather was good, Kafka and Dora took walks together. Two or three streetcars passed through the square, and there was a small amount of traffic, but nothing like that on the Kurfürstendamm or Friedrichstrasse in central Berlin. The publishing houses of Ullstein, Mosse, and Scherl had branch offices on the Steglitz town square, and in the windows passersby could read the news of the day without paying the exorbitant cost of a newspaper: "From the front pages of the newspapers on display," Kafka reported to Max, "I absorb the poison that I can just manage to bear, sometimes momentarily cannot bear (just now there is talk in the anteroom about street battles)."

One day, as they wandered through a small neighborhood park, they met a little girl, weeping. "She appeared to be in complete despair. We spoke to her," Dora said. "Franz questioned her, and we learned that she had lost her doll. At once he invented a sufficiently plausible story to explain the disappearance of the doll: 'Your doll has simply gone on a journey,' he said. 'I know because she's written me a letter.' The little girl was a bit suspicious: 'Have you got it on you?' 'No, I left it at home by mistake, but I'll bring it with me tomorrow.' Intrigued, the child had already almost forgotten what had so upset her. Franz went home immediately to write the letter. He set to work with the same seriousness he displayed when composing one of his own works, and in the same state of tension he always inhabited at his table, even when writing a postcard. It was a real labor, as essential as any of his other writings, because the child must at all costs not be cheated, but truly appeased, and since the lie must be transformed into the truth of reality by means of the truth of fiction.

"The next day, he ran with the letter to the little girl who was waiting for him in the park. As she did not know how to read, he read the letter out to her. The doll declared that she was tired of living in the same family all the time, expressed her longing for a change of air, in a word, to go a little way away from her—a little girl whom, indeed, she loved, but from whom she had no choice but to separate. The doll promised that she would write every day and, in fact, Kafka wrote a daily letter telling of new adventures, which evolved very rapidly, according to the special rhythm of the life of dolls. After a few days, the child had forgotten the loss of her real toy and had no thought for anything but the fiction she had been offered in exchange.

"Franz wrote every sentence with an attention to detail, with a precision full of humor, which made the situation perfectly acceptable. The doll grew up, went to school, got to know other people. She continued to assure the child of her love, but made allusions to the complexity of her life, to other obligations, to other interests, which made it impossible, for the time being, to live with her. The little girl was invited to reflect upon this and was made ready for the inevitable renunciation. The game lasted at least three weeks. Franz was in terrible distress at the thought of having to bring it to an end, because the ending had to be exactly right. It had to substitute order for the disorder brought about by the loss of the doll. He cast about for a long time and finally decided to marry off the doll. He described the young man, the engagement, the wedding preparations in the country, then, in great detail, the house of the young couple: 'You yourself will understand,' said the doll, 'we must give up seeing each other.' Franz had resolved a child's conflict through art, the best method he possessed for bringing order into the world."

Dora's story of Kafka and the doll, which she repeated many years later to friends and Kafka biographers, was, in the words of its English translator, "a simple, perfect and true Kafka story. In it Kafka the man and Kafka the writer seem to merge joyously, in harmony." The story, first published in French in 1952, was not translated into English until 1984. In recent years prominent Kafka scholars from the Netherlands and the United States, interested in finding the little girl from the Steglitz park, conducted two separate searches in Berlin. If still alive, the little girl would now be a very old lady who might have kept letters from her childhood, written from her doll. Despite articles in several Berlin newspapers—one with the headline "Who Met Kafka in the Park?"—nothing has yet come of either search.

Dora knew Kafka was a writer but had no idea until she lived with him exactly what it meant to him. "Kafka had to write, he had to," she soon realized. "It was his life-breath. The days in which he wrote were the rhythm of this breath," she once tried to explain. It was hard to describe in words. It was a deeply personal act, as Kafka once observed, it was "a form of prayer" to him.

"His day was strictly planned to accommodate his writing," Dora said. "In the mornings he often went for a walk alone. On his walks he always took a notebook with him, or if he forgot it, he would buy one on the way." He clearly loved Nature, the whole of the natural world, although Dora never actually heard him say the word.

Kafka insisted on doing the shopping and soon became a familiar sight in the neighborhood, carrying the milk can and shopping basket. Each morning he rose early, around seven, and spent quite a while dressing before going out into what he called "the elation that comes in the early morning." He liked being among simple, everyday people. "He wanted to feel like an average person, with only a few uncomplicated wishes and needs."

All that changed when he began to write. "He would pace, heavily, uneasily. He spoke little, ate without appetite, took no interest in things, and was very sad. He wanted to be alone. In the beginning I didn't understand; later on I always felt when he was going to begin writing." When she later thought about those early days together, she saw them "in their various tensions, by comparing them to colors: purple, dark green or blue days."

Dora was sensitive to Kafka's craving for isolation and silence and left him alone. Kafka's ideal writing situation, he once said, was "an innermost room of a spacious locked cellar." He had described it in detail in a letter to his former fiancée Felice. Locked away with only his "writing things and a lamp," Kafka had fantasized that "food would be brought and always put down far way from my room, outside the cellar's outermost door. The walk to my food, in my dressing gown, through the vaulted cellars, would be my only exercise. I would then return to my table, eat slowly and with deliberation, then start writing again at once. And how I would write! From what depths I would drag it up! Without effort! For extreme concentration knows no effort. The trouble is that I might not be able to keep it up for long, and at the first failure . . . [was] . . . bound to end in a grandiose fit of madness." Felice had found her future husband's description of his ideal mode of life disturbing.

When Dora asked, Kafka told her about Felice and explained why he couldn't marry her. "She was an excellent girl," Dora explained later, "but utterly bourgeois. Kafka felt that marrying her would mean marrying the whole lie that was Europe." Felice had wanted, Kafka said, "the average: a comfortable home, an interest on my part in the factory, good food, bed at eleven, central heating." Felice's desire for normalcy and the Germanic ideal of *Alles ist in Ordnung* was demonstrated in his description of how she once took Franz's pocket watch, which he kept an hour and twenty minutes fast, and set it back, right to the minute. Felice was, Kafka conceded, "right in the end and would continue to be right in the end."

Dora understood that "his engagement was an attempt to acclimatize himself to middle-class life, and at the same time a sort of curiosity. He wanted to know everything, to experience everything." Soon after the engagement ended, Felice married someone else and was now, five years later, a wife and mother. Deemed medically unfit for marriage or fatherhood, and unable to work any longer, Kafka seemed to have come to a dead end. On the other hand, living on a pension from the Institute, relieved from the draining responsibility of his job, Kafka was free for the first time in his life to pursue the life of a writer.

When he read to her from one of his favorite stories by one of his favorite writers—*Hermann and Dorothea* by Goethe—"he, too, was moved by the love of everyday life described there," Dora said. "The chance Kafka now had to live exactly the way he wanted, made him enter into a concrete relationship towards home, money and family. In a non-bourgeois sense. In Berlin, he believed for a time in the possibility of saving his life, in a personal solution for the inner and outer confusion." For once, a family life and his "life's breath" as Dora called it, were not mutually exclusive. With Dora, it was unnecessary to choose between writing and a woman with whom he could share his life. He could live with Dora and "yield not a particle of my demand for a fantastic life arranged solely in the interest of my work."

On the days that Kafka wrote, Dora kept busy, reading for her classes at the Academy for Jewish Studies and doing her volunteer work with the Berlin Jewish People's Home, where she took a rhythmic dancing class offered for free and helped out occasionally with the children at the orphanage. These were Dora's long-standing occupations in Berlin, and nothing she did with her time could have interested or pleased Kafka more. When she returned to the apartment, Franz would want to know everything and then would often read to her what he had written with "verve and passion. Afterward, he would say, "Well, I wonder if I've escaped the ghosts."

Ghosts, Dora learned, "was the name with which he summarized everything that had tormented him before he came to Berlin. He was as though possessed by this idea; it was a kind of sullen obstinacy," she said. "He spoke of ghosts, however, with the conniving smile of a kid who knows better, and which evoked ancient bogey-men."

Dora quickly discovered what made Kafka happy, his peculiar likes and dislikes. He loved exotic fruits, such as pineapple and bananas. He was particularly fond of his pocket watch and especially of Dora's daily calendar, which revealed a new aphorism each day. She and Kafka laughed at the coincidental insights and perverse perspective that the proverbs provided. He often insisted that he must "consult the calendar."

Once, when Dora was washing grapes, the glass bowl slipped from her hands and shattered. Kafka immediately appeared in the kitchen, holding the calendar in his hand. Wide-eyed, in great seriousness, he read the aphorism to her: "One moment can ruin everything." He maintained his grave expression as long as he could, and then handed her the page, and they laughed. "The truth sounded so trivial," she remembered.

Appearance was important to Kafka, but not because of any conceit or self-admiration. "He attached great importance to being carefully dressed," Dora said. "He would have regarded it as a lack of courtesy to go somewhere without having his tie perfectly knotted. His suits were made by a first-class tailor, and he always took a long time about dressing. It was not vanity," Dora insisted. "He looked into the mirror without complacency, quite critically and judiciously. It was done in order not to offend the world."

He was extremely sensitive to sound. He hated noise. He disliked the telephone, never wanted to answer it or even speak on it and always begged Dora to pick it up. "What would I do if Prague rang and D. were not at home?" he wondered. In fact, Kafka was uncomfortable and mystified with anything mechanical. He marveled at the skills required to use a typewriter and was truly impressed by anyone who could type quickly. Kafka never used a typewriter, if he could help it. All of his writing was by hand, in his unmistakable elegant black scrawl.

They stayed home together nearly every evening. It was too expensive to go out, so they spent the long evenings and nights together, entertaining each other, Dora curled up on the sofa, Franz reading aloud from his favorite stories and books, something he never tired of doing.

"He loved Kleist," Dora remembered. "He was capable of reading his *Marquise von O—* to me five or six times in succession." One of Kafka's best-loved authors, Heinrich von Kleist (b. 1776) had broken new ground in German literature one hundred years before Kafka began writing his own groundbreaking literary work. *The Marquise von O—*, which Kafka read over and over to Dora until she knew certain passages by heart, was so shocking, according to one reviewer of the time, that "no woman could read it without blushing."

In his diary, Kafka noted many parallels with Kleist's life. Like Kafka, Kleist was a civil servant in the Austrian empire, a bachelor who despaired of ever marrying, a shy and sensitive child in a society that revered strong or even brutal men, whose parents felt only contempt for their son's foolish literary ambitions. Kleist died prematurely, committing suicide at thirty-five, and his work remained largely unknown outside of Germany. Martin Greenberg, who translated Kafka's diaries into English, found Kleist's work through Kafka's interest in it. Greenberg translated the stories into English and got them published in 1960.

Kleist had long been famous in Germany. According to Thomas Mann, one of Germany's foremost novelists, the first sentence of *The Earthquake in Chile* is "a masterpiece of succinct exposition: everything the reader needs to know has been compressed into a very few words, and the narrative, as sober as it is beautifully articulated, betrays at once the hand of a master." The opening sentence of Kafka's favorite, *The Marquise of O—*, was equally intriguing: "In M—, a large town in northern Italy, the widowed Marquise of O—, a lady of unblemished reputation and the mother of several well-bred children, published the following notice in the newspapers; that, without her knowing how, she was in the family way; that she would like the father of the child she was going to bear to report himself; and that her mind was made up, out of consideration for her people, to marry him."

The story, written in 1804 when Kleist was twenty-eight years old, mixes sweet innocence with perverse eroticism. The incestuous scene between the Marquise and her estranged father, the Commandant, secretly witnessed by the mother, is still strange and disturbing after two hundred years:

> Finally she opened the door and peered in—and her heart leaped for joy; her daughter lay motionless in her father's arms, her head thrown back and her eyes closed, while he sat in the armchair, with tear-choked, glistening eyes, and pressed long, warm and avid kisses on her mouth; just as if he were her lover! Her daughter did not speak, her husband did not speak; he hung over her as if she were his first love and held her mouth and kissed it. The mother's delight was indescribable; standing unobserved behind the chair, she hesitated to disturb the joy of reconciliation that had come to her home.

Kafka cherished Kleist's creative ability to tamper with sacred conceptions and understood that Kleist's motive was not merely to shock the reader. *The Marquise of O—* and Kleist's other strange stories questioned the established equilibrium of the world, discarded artificial language and attempted to set down extraordinary things in plain, bare, matter-of-fact words. It was a search for a new truth, a style Kafka adopted in his own literary work. Kafka concurred with Kleist that one needed "to risk the ludicrous to achieve the sublime," a technique Kafka employed in his life and his work.

Kafka had brought his favorite books with him to Berlin, which he read over and over again to Dora. *The Life and Opinions of Kater Murr* by E.T.A. Hoffman quickly became one of her favorites. Kafka's dramatic flair, with his deep melodic voice and dancing fingers, enchanted her for hours. She never tired of it. The memoirs of an adventurous adult tomcat, Kater Murr, inspired laughter from the opening paragraphs of the cat/author's introduction. Kafka held the book in one hand, as he illustrated the words with the elegantly expressive fingers of his right hand: "Modestly—with trembling heart—I offer the world a few pages of the life, the sorrow, the hopes, and the longings, which, during sweet hours of leisure and poetic inspiration, flowed from my innermost being."

Kafka's tone and bearing changed as he turned the page to reveal the true nature of the tomcat's attitude: "Should anyone be so bold as to wish to raise doubts about the genuine value of this extraordinary book, let him consider that he will have to deal with a tomcat who possesses spirit, intelligence and sharp claws."

Kafka had a real gift as an actor, Dora said, as he interpreted Murr's passion for his world: "O Nature! Sublime and holy Nature! How your raptures, your ecstasies fill my sympathetic breast!" When Kater Murr, prowling a rooftop, spies a cooing dove near the church steeple, he purrs: "Something is stirring marvelously in me; a certain rapturous appetite is possessing me with irresistible power! Oh, if she would only come to my lovesick heart, that sweet goddess, I would embrace her, never let her go."

Hours passed this way, magical hours.

Although they were alone most of the time, they had occasional visitors. Dora invited someone she knew, a Palestinian student at the State Gardening Institute and Nursery in Dahlem, to come and talk with Kafka about the school Kafka had dreamed of attending. Now that he lived only fifteen minutes away, Kafka was interested in taking a class there. But after Dora's friend spoke enthusiastically about the school and its programs, Kafka was completely discouraged. He realized, as he wrote to Max, "I am too weak for the practical classes, too distracted for the theoretical instruction. Moreover the days are so short, and I cannot go out in bad weather."

Tile and her friend, a young painter, came for a visit one day. Another visitor was Pua Bentovim, a beautiful young nineteen-year-old Palestinian Jewess who had been Kafka's Hebrew teacher in Prague. Pua, who was now studying in Berlin, came to the flat twice to resume the Hebrew lessons she had begun with Kafka in Prague. Dora was always there when the lessons were conducted, and as Pua later said, "it soon became quite clear to me that Dora, who had a good basic command of the language, could assist him in his Hebrew study as well as I could." After two visits, Pua never returned.

There were problems with the landlady, who thought at first she had stuck gold with her Czech tenant. "I believe she had found out in the first half hour of our first meeting that I have the 1000 K pension (back then, a lot, today a small fortune) and afterwards she began to raise the rent," Kafka wrote to his mother at the beginning of November. "For example, in the end of August the room was rented to me for 4 million marks per month and today it costs about one half trillion, and this is not really too much, but the uncertainty, caused by the fact that it can be increased monthly and also other things of this kind, is unpleasant."

The trouble began with Kafka's overuse of electricity, since the gaslight was not bright enough for him to write at night. When the landlady complained bitterly about the electric bill, Dora found a solution. Because of fuel shortages, kerosene lamps were scarce and impossible to buy. So Dora made do, borrowing and buying the separate pieces and assembling it herself. Kafka was absolutely delighted by it. "He loved its soft, living light, and always wanted to fill it up himself," Dora said. "He would play about with the wick, and continually found new virtues in it."

In a letter to Valli, written by the light of this example of Dora's self-sufficiency and practical ingenuity, Kafka continued to praise it: "My kerosene lamp burns marvelously, a masterpiece both of lamp-making and of purchasing. It's a lamp with a burner as large as a teacup and a construction that makes it possible to light it without removing the chimney and shade." It had only one flaw, he noted, that it wouldn't burn without the fuel, "but then we, too, are the same."

The landlady had raised the rent from 28 Czech crowns in August, to over 70 in September, to 180 in October. In November, she informed them she was doubling it again, to 360 crowns, more than a third of Kafka's entire pension for the month. Dora had been looking for a new apartment, but with foreigners pouring into Berlin and taking advantage of the highly advantageous foreign exchange rates, reasonably priced furnished flats were now difficult to find. Once she thought she might have found something in the city and took Franz to see it, but it wasn't right for him. He was spoiled, he admitted later, "by the Steglitz air." Dora renewed the search within their current neighborhood, and at the beginning of November, with her characteristic good luck, she found it.

It was an even nicer place only two streets away on Grunewald Strasse, the road running from the Steglitz town hall to Dahlem. Dora was thrilled with it, and Kafka, once he saw it, agreed wholeheartedly. They would move on November 15. Until then, Dora warned Franz, they must maintain utmost secrecy. They were not obliged to announce they were leaving until the fifteenth. Then they would leave immediately. Between themselves, in whispers, they talked about the move to their new home. If Frau Hermann knew they had another place, she might well kick them out early or make life even more unpleasant for them.

"A highly advantageous move, so it seems to me" Kafka wrote to Max. "I am almost afraid to commit this news to paper, my landlady is not to know until November 15th, and here I go writing it down among her furniture which reads it over my shoulders; but then the furniture, at least some pieces of it, is partially on my side."

Kafka also wrote to his parents, letting them know about his change of address, and described the place: "Not far, two lanes further away, to a small villa with nice garden on the second floor, two (two!) nicely furnished rooms, of which one, the living room, is as sunny as my present one." The smaller one, the bedroom, got only the morning sun. Further advantages of the new apartment, included "central heating and electric light." The price was the same as his current rent, but, as he pointed out, "it is more stable against increases and other cheatings."

Kafka dealt with landlady the way he knew best: He wrote a story. He never said who the woman was in "A Little Woman," but Dora clearly recognized her as their landlady when he read it to her: "This little woman, then, is very ill-pleased with me, she always finds something objectionable in me, I am always doing the wrong thing to her, I annoy her at every step; if a life could be cut into the smallest of small pieces and every scrap of it could be separately assessed, every scrap of my life would certainly be an offense to her." Even his death, he said, would not assuage the little woman's distress at his existence. "Her objection to me, as I am now aware, is a fundamental one; nothing can remove it, not even the removal of myself; if she heard that I had committed suicide she would fall into transports of rage." Despite this, Kafka remained untouched by her malice and ended his story on an optimistic note: "I shall quietly continue to live my own life for a long time to come, untroubled by the world, despite all the outbursts of the woman."

Knowing he was leaving soon, the furnishings in the room had begun to turn away from him. Even Dora's calendar seemed changed, had become "utterly taciturn," Kafka said, even sarcastic. Once he had needed its advice and rushed to it. All it said was "Feast of the Reformation," a Protestant holiday observed in northern Germany. It "probably has its deeper meaning," Kafka admitted in a long, cheerful letter to his sister Valli, "but who can fathom it?" Another time, he had "an idea that seemed to me very good, or rather significant, so much so that I wanted to ask the calendar about it (it answers only on such odd moments in the course of the day, not when you pedantically tear off the calendar leaf at a particular hour)." The aphorism he read seemed designed to humble him: "Sometimes even a blind chicken finds a grain." Another time he had been horrified by the coal bill, which cost as much as the rent that month. "Happiness and contentment are life's blessings," the proverb declared. "Perhaps," he ruminated, "after the calendar leaf for the day I move, there will be a leaf I'll no longer see that will say something like: 'It is determined by divine decree,' etc. No, it isn't right for me to set down everything I think about my calendar," Kafka admonished himself to Valli, "after all, 'it's only human.'"

On November 9, Max Brod returned to Berlin. He needed to see Emmy and to determine for himself how Kafka was doing. He also wanted to meet Kafka's mysterious new friend, Dora. From Prague he brought a heavy suitcase filled with Kafka's winter things, which provided him entrée to the house, instead of having to meet him, as in September, at a Berlin café.

Fresh flowers adorned the table as Dora and Kafka made final preparations for their first guest from Prague. Dora felt that she already knew Max Brod. Hearing about him from both Franz and Emmy, she was acquainted with intimate details of his personal life. Franz had described Max in vivid detail, with love and admiration shining in his eyes. Nearly everyone Kafka spoke of reflected the light he cast on them. He always found something to admire—in everyone. For example, when the moving men came to take away the grand piano, Dora marveled at Kafka's awed appreciation as he "followed the two furniture movers to the stairs, open-mouthed with astonishment," as they maneuvered the gigantic piano through the narrow spaces. Many years later, Dora described the scene, as "he, in the middle of breakfast, with the eggcup in his hand, quickly ran back from the staircase, to the window, to watch them until they vanished." "If there is a moving men's school where everybody can be turned into a mover," Kafka wrote to Ottla the next day, "I would enter it with passionate eagerness. So far I haven't yet found the school."

Max Brod's visit to Kafka and Dora, the first of three during the next six months, went brilliantly. "I found an idyll," Brod reported in his biography. "At last I saw my friend in good spirits; his bodily health had gotten worse, it is true. Yet for the time it was not even dangerous. Franz spoke about the demons which had at last let go of him. 'I have slipped away from them. This moving to Berlin was magnificent, now they are looking for me and can't find me, at least for the moment.' He had finally achieved the ideal of an independent life, a home of his own. He was no longer a son living with his parents, but to a certain extent, himself a paterfamilias." It was obvious, Max said in answer to intellectuals who had decided that Kafka was a loner who sought a solitary life, that "Kafka was not at all striving after a paradox," an unachievable ideal, but "wanted an intelligently fulfilled, good and proper life."

Brod said that Kafka was "sleeping well—an unheard of novelty in these last years." He noted that Kafka was working with pleasure and had read aloud to him from "A Little Woman." Kafka was clearly and significantly happier. "It was not only to me that Franz seemed to have found salvation in his whole existence, to have become a new man," Brod said. "From his letters you can see his good spirits and the firmness he had finally won."

Outside the paradise that Dora and Kafka had created for themselves in the warmth and safety of their room in Steglitz, a few miles north to the backrooms and cellars in the center of the city, and beyond to beer halls and meeting rooms in cities throughout Germany, evil forces were gathering. On the same day that Max Brod arrived in Berlin to visit Kafka and

Dora, four hundred miles south, in Munich, a violent political drama was unfolding. The night before, at a meeting of some three thousand citizens in the cavernous Burgerbrau beer cellar attended by Bavarian government officials, industrial leaders and the directors of municipal and patriotic organizations, "a small troop of armed men with submachine guns" forced their way in "led by a short fellow excitedly brandishing a Browning."

It was Adolf Hitler, a former Austrian corporal, now the leader of the right-wing National Socialist Workers Party, surrounded by his Brownshirts, the thugs who served as his paramilitary protection. The former corporal mounted a chair and fired at the ceiling. "The national revolution has started," he announced, and then told a boldfaced lie. The hall was surrounded, he said, "by six hundred heavily armed men." No one was allowed to leave. Hitler proclaimed a new German government with himself as the new leader. At gunpoint he secured loyalty oaths from the current leaders. His big mistake was letting them leave the crowded hall, as he continued to proclaim his new policies and programs. But by the next morning, the Bavarians had rallied their forces and mobilized the militia against him. At noon, Hitler and his commander in chief, General Ludendorff, marched several thousand armed Brownshirts and members of the "Fighting League" to one of Munich's main squares. They were greeted by policemen, and shots rang out. Several people lay dead and wounded in the street. The Nazis and their sympathizers fled.

Kafka and Dora may have seen the newspaper accounts of the latest power grab in the provincial southern capital. The stories in the windows at the Steglitz town square gave the "Beer Hall Putsch" a great deal of attention, laced with ridicule. Two days later the ex-corporal Hitler was arrested in a Munich suburb and sentenced to five years in prison for high treason. It seemed the Nazi Party was dead.

5

THE BURROW

*There I can curl myself up in comfort and lie
warm. There I sleep the sweet sleep of tranquillity, of satisfied desire, of achieved ambition; for I
possess a house.*

—Franz Kafka, "The Burrow"

BERLIN, NOVEMBER 15, 1923

The move to the apartment at 13 Grunewaldstrasse went smoothly and
effortlessly, especially for Kafka. At half past ten in the morning, he left
the old flat and went into Berlin to attend a lecture, while Dora stayed
home to pack and prepare for the move. Dora was missing her class, but
there was no point in both of them doing so, and she encouraged Kafka
to go alone.

Two to three days a week since the beginning of November, Kafka and
Dora took the tram together to the heart of the Scheunenviertel, "the dirty
Jewish streets of Berlin," as Kafka had once referred to the district, to attend lectures and classes at the Academy for Hebrew Studies. While
Kafka was learning about the Hagadah, the legends and stories, Dora was
studying Halacha, the laws, forbidden to women in Orthodox Judaism.
The academy was one of the reasons Dora loved Germany: the opportunity to learn about her own religion. For over fifty years, the Academy for
Hebrew Studies had trained reform and liberal Jewish scholars and rabbis,
within strict scholarly guidelines, and allowed women to attend classes
and study as well. While Dora educated herself in the laws, the foundation
on which Judaism was built, Kafka was, Dora said, "literally 'drinking in'

the words of Professor Torcziner, whose stories he valued as he would Grimm's."

Kafka described it to a friend: "A whole building of handsome lecture rooms, large library, peace, well heated, few students, and everything free of charge. Of course I am not a proper student, am only in the preparatory school, and have only one teacher there, moreover, go seldom, so that in the long run almost all the glory evaporates again; but even though I am not a student, the school exists and is a fine place." Unfortunately the school did not exist much longer. Less than twenty years later, with Leo Baeck as its last director, the heavy wooden doors of the school on Artillerystrasse were closed forever by the Nazis.

After the lecture, Kafka headed down Friedrichstrasse, toward one of two restaurants where he and Dora usually ate. "I wanted to go to eat and afterward ride right back to Steglitz and after all take some small part in the moving," he said. There were two restaurants he and Dora liked. One was the vegetarian restaurant on Friedrichstrasse he had described to Max and the other near the corner of Dorotheenstrasse. From this second restaurant, a sign was visible above a shopkeeper's door: "H. Unger." Kafka never failed to point it out to Dora: "Hunger," he'd say quietly, his lips set in a bitter smile.

"He did not need such accidental puns to see everywhere the presence of madness, of decay," Dora said. Kafka walked the streets of Berlin observing the frightening beggars and cripples, the starving children and desperate old people, wretched victims of inflation, begging outside giant department store windows filled with the latest luxury goods. He did not try to protect himself from it. "He felt that the only way to react was to dive into it and to identify with the suffering and the deprivation of others. He wanted to face the lamentable spectacle of humans in quest of a piece of bread, which everyday, became smaller."

Before he reached the vegetarian restaurant on Friedrichstrasse, someone called out his name. It was Dr. Lowy, an acquaintance from Müritz. As Kafka related the story to Ottla, Dr. Lowy "was very kind and friendly, and promptly invited me to dine with him at his parents' home, where he was going. I hesitated at this gift worth billions [Kafka meant that literally] after all, I did want to go out to Steglitz, but finally I went anyhow, entered the peace and warmth of a well-to-do family. Before I rang the bell at the garden door in Steglitz it was already six o'clock and the moving completed without one item left behind. I cannot say that it proved especially strenuous for me."

BERLIN, NOVEMBER 20, 1923

On the day that the new German mark, the rentenmark, was introduced, effectively ending the Great Inflation of 1923 (although the damage the inflation caused would be felt for many years to come), Kafka wrote two cards. The first was to Milena, his former lover, who, knowing nothing of Dora, had been writing to him again. "Things in Berlin are not so bad as you seem to think," he wrote. "I've never yet had such a beautiful apartment. I'm also sure I'll soon lose it—it's too beautiful for me. . . . So far the food here isn't essentially different from Prague—though only my food. The same holds true for my health. This is all. I don't dare say much more, what I've said is already too much, the ghosts are already drinking it greedily down their insatiable throats. And you say even less in your letter. Is the general condition a good, a bearable one? I cannot unriddle it. Of course one can't even do it in one's own case; that's what fear is, nothing else."

To his parents, he repeated how beautiful his new flat was and his fear that he would lose it. "It is expensive, of course," he admitted. He began by acknowledging the letters he'd just received from them. "This time it was a special joy, both your letters and above all father's nice information about his health. A pity that I don't have sufficient stamps to reply to you in more detail, maybe next time." A letter he had sent the week before with an 18 billion mark postage stamp, had been returned due to insufficient postage, and Kafka was not taking any chances. His father, ever practical, had asked how Franz intended to support himself in Berlin. "Your question, dear father, whether I will have 'a future for later' here is very delicate. Up to now, I don't have the smallest hint of a possibility of earning money. Of course, I treat myself here like an ill person in a sanatorium. I can not easily live in the city, especially now that I am spoiled by the Steglitz air."

Kafka always began his letters to his parents, "Dearest parents," and his tone was always solicitous, if not completely open or honest. Dora believed Kafka no longer loved or respected his father. He saw him as "the man who dominated through possessions and 'possesses' even his family," Dora said. "Kafka was very bitter about him, and time and again, with biting humor, he would tell the story of how he had dedicated a book to him, and when he wanted to present it to him, his father only said coldly: 'Put it on the table beside my bed.'"

Nevertheless, Kafka's correspondence to his "dearest parents" was respectful and affectionate, if sometimes exasperated. He was grateful for the packages of butter they sent and masked his resentment that his pension was being doled out in such small installments, haphazardly, which caused him constant worry. The German post office, with the wildly fluctuating costs of postage, was in disorder: packages didn't arrive in the order they were sent, and some went missing. Kafka was never sure whether his money was lost in the mail.

In a letter to Ottla, urgently asking her to have money sent to him, he complained that his mother had promised to send small amounts in every letter but had not done so. "Now I have repeatedly asked for them, but nothing comes; today is the 16th and I have received only 70 crowns all told for this month. Is it that the money from the Institute hasn't come, or has a letter with money possibly gone astray? Or do they aim to teach me in this way about earning money."

He could not ask the Institute to send it directly to him for two reasons. Technically, he wasn't supposed to be living in Berlin. According to the legal conditions of his pension, a letter from the director of the Institute was necessary to approve the change of address and a letter from Kafka authorizing his parents to receive the remittances. The second reason Kafka wanted the money to go to his parents' address in Prague was that any other form of transmittal would result in loss of funds due to exchange fees and other deductions.

On November 23, Kafka wrote again to his parents, letting them know that "the parcel arrived in excellent condition, nothing is missing, nothing was forgotten, the slippers are incomparably warmer than the previous ones. How much the sending must have cost you and how much trouble it must have given you! There was no urgency, but to have all this is very pleasant . . . it is autumn now, so beautiful, as I believe it has never before been in my life, we might have a hard winter, I am in every respect well prepared for it."

With Franz's constant assurances that he was being well taken care of in Berlin, Julie was feeling jealous that someone else was taking her place in her son's life: "Dear mother," he wrote, "you need not worry because of the competition in care, you'll retain your position. Anyhow, what didn't I get in the last days? A bottle of excellent red wine which I sniff with delight, a gigantic bottle of homemade raspberry juice and four plates. Not bad, don't you think?"

BERLIN-STEGLITZ, NOVEMBER 25, 1923

"Today Ottla is here, approving of everything she sees," Kafka wrote in a quick note to Max. Despite her husband Pepa's wish that she not go, Ottla had left her two little girls in Prague for a quick trip to see her brother. She brought linens and more of his winter things, including shirts, socks and underclothes, all of which he had requested in a long and detailed list. He had also asked for "the heavy overcoat, a suit (perhaps the black one, whose lighter brother I have with me), and any trousers I can wear at home." He wanted his old blue raglan robe, which could be made into a housecoat, gloves for daytime, his foot muff, and three hangers for the suit and coats.

In addition to the several heavy suitcases, Ottla also brought money, the balance from his pension payment. The rentenmark had stabilized the daily index, which now reflected the prewar exchange rate, 4.2 rentenmarks to US\$1. For the time being, Kafka's money worries were resolved.

Kafka had been looking forward to Ottla's trip since he first proposed it two months earlier. In a card written in October, he had imagined possibilities for their visit: "When I sit just looking out the window: the blue sky, all the greenery, then back into the room: fruit, flowers, butter, kefir, then go on thinking: the lovely parks, the botanical garden, the woods of Grunewald, then let myself be carried further: an inordinately expensive theatre performance (I haven't gone to any), window-shopping (our funds would enable us to do no more)."

Even before meeting her, Dora loved Ottla, based on Franz's radiant descriptions of her, and Ottla felt the same way about Dora. Mutual admiration and affection were present from the first moment. The two women had much in common and held similar political and social views. Ottla shared the dream of Palestine, or had before she married and had children. Both were independent Jewish daughters of successful businessmen and leaders in their communities. Both were sensitive, intelligent, generous women who consciously worked to improve the world around them. At thirty-one, Ottla was six years older than Dora, the older sister Dora never had, a confidante, a knowing adviser, and, as she had been with her brother, a coconspirator. As the first member of Kafka's family to meet Dora, Ottla bore witness to Dora's good character and obvious love for Franz. Seeing her brother's newfound joy, his sense of play unleashed, how could Ottla not love Dora, too?

As soon as Ottla returned to Prague, according to one Kafka biographer, "she moved heaven and earth on the couple's behalf. She saw to it that they received several food packages a week, arranged for regular money remittances, and sent them whatever linen and household necessities she and her sisters could spare."

"I have not been sick," Kafka wrote to Max on the day of Ottla's visit, "it's just that the lamp flickers a little; otherwise, it's not been bad so far. It

did prevent me from going to E.'s performance, though; D., too, was unfortunately not altogether well that day. But perhaps the play will be repeated at Christmas-time." He signed off with an uncharacteristically intimate greeting to their mutual friends: "Give Felix and Oskar a caress or
two for me."

It wasn't until Kafka wrote his short story "The Burrow" that Dora
glimpsed the shadows of what she later called the "unfathomable depth"
of Kafka's inner life. "In Berlin," Dora said, "Kafka believed that he had
liberated himself from the tyranny of his past. But the earlier problems
were too tightly bound up with his life. As soon as one touched even a single string of it, all the others vibrated, too."

He dealt rigorously with himself, Dora said. He allowed himself no
quarter, no relief. He voluntarily restricted himself from things he needed
because "he wanted to accustom himself to a Spartan life." Where he
could have kept himself apart from the sufferings of others, he refused.
"Whatever might happen around him, he felt he had no right to shut himself off from it," Dora observed.

While Dora could pass unscathed through the poverty and misery,
Kafka could not. "Every time Franz goes from our quiet suburb to Berlin,
he comes home as if he were coming back from the field of battle," Dora
told Max. "The sufferings of the poor touch him to the heart; he comes
back ashen and grey. He lives with such intensity, that he has died a thousand deaths in his life."

"We too must suffer all the suffering around us," Kafka once explained
in one of his blue octavo notebooks. "We all have not one body, but we
have one way of growing, and this leads us through all anguish, whether in
this or in that form. Just as the child develops through all the stages of life
right into old age and to death, so also do we develop (no less deeply
bound up with mankind than with ourselves) through all the sufferings of
this world. There is no room for justice in this context, but neither is there
any room either for fear of suffering or for the interpretation of suffering
as a merit. You can hold yourself back from the sufferings of the world.
This is something you are free to do, and is in accord with human nature.
But perhaps, it is precisely this holding back that is the only suffering that
you might be able to avoid."

For hours, Kafka stood in line with other shoppers, the price of potatoes and bread rising as the queue slowly advanced. It wasn't just that he
wanted to buy something: "blood was flowing, and so his must flow, too."
In this way, Dora said, he achieved "communion with an unhappy people

in an unhappy time." But it affected him physically. When Kafka returned home to Steglitz after a day in the city, he would almost collapse. "He was often more than depressed; it was a revolt." Kafka's journey to the city, she said, was often a "kind of Golgotha for him." Comparing Kafka's empathy for the suffering of others to the hill up which Jesus carried his cross and on which he was crucified was no exaggeration, Dora insisted: "With Kafka, no exaggeration is possible."

While living with Kafka, Dora developed a new understanding and appreciation of literature. Growing up, she loved the stories of Mendele Mocher Sforim, Sholem Aleichem and Isaac Leib Peretz, who were creating their finest works, already considered classics when she was still a little girl. These three, the fathers of modern Yiddish Literature, died when Dora was a teenager and many of her ideas were born in the flowering of modern Yiddish literature, which continued in Russia, Poland, Lithuania, Germany and the United States. Later she eagerly read Dostoyevsky and Tolstoy and saw reflections of herself.

But for Kafka, literature was something else entirely. "Literature for him was something sacred, absolute, incorruptible, something great and pure," Dora said. By literature, he did not mean the journalism or modern books of the day, which he regarded as "merely wavering reflections of the present." Literature held an almost religious significance in his life. "Kafka felt unsure about most things in life and expressed himself very cautiously," Dora said. "But when it was a matter of literature, he was unapproachable and knew no compromise. There he was concerned with the whole. He not only wanted to penetrate to the bottom of things. He was at the bottom. Where the solution of human confusion was in question, he would not have any half measures. He experienced life as a labyrinth; he could not see the solution. He never got further than despair."

Literature was Kafka's way of understanding, interpreting and putting order in the world, but he never believed he achieved what he wanted with his own writings. As a young man of twenty, Kafka wrote: "I think we ought to read only the kind of books that wound and stab us. If the book we're reading doesn't wake us up with a blow on the head, what are we reading it for? So that it will make us happy? Good Lord, we would be happy precisely if we had no books, and the kind of books that make us happy are the kind we could write ourselves, if we had to. But we need the books that affect us like a disaster, that grieve us deeply, like the death of someone we loved more than ourselves, like being banished into forests far from everyone, like a suicide. A book must be the ax for the frozen sea inside us. That is my belief."

The year before, in 1903, Kafka had one of his first bouts of writer's block: "God doesn't want me to write, but I—I must. So there's an ever-lasting up and down; after all, God is the stronger, and there's more an-guish in it than you can imagine. So many powers within me are tied to a stake, which might possibly grow into a green tree."

When Kafka completed law school in 1906, Brod reported, he "insisted that the job have nothing to do with literature; that would have seemed to him a debasement of literary creativity. The bread-and-butter job had to be kept strictly separate from his writings," Brod said. "What we were both desperately looking for was a job with a single shift . . . till two or three in the afternoon . . . with afternoons free." Kafka was lucky to find what he was looking for at the Workers Accident Insurance Institute, but it didn't work out the way he had hoped. Because he couldn't do anything halfway and devoted his complete attention to every task, no matter how trivial, Kafka's work for the insurance company sapped his energy, drained his emotions and left no time for his writing.

Dora described in her diary the way he prepared a cup of tea for one of their guests: "The final thoroughness, the all-consuming demands to prop-erly prepare the cup of tea claimed his all attention, kept him so busy, that he didn't manage to put the tea on the table. He used his strength up in the preparation. The countless preparations delayed his readiness to re-ceive the guest. 'I am not ready! He can't come yet!'"

In these remarks, written in the last year of her life, Dora was still trying to explain the "apparent pedantry of Franz," even to herself: "The count-less preparations—the number was legion—that he had to make, held him back from receiving a guest, from marrying, from bringing what he had written to an end. That's why the guest could not come yet, why one could not start a family, why one would not publish a book, or finish the writing, complete it."

At other times, "in blessed moments, he was the glowing, shining, rac-ing messenger, fully aware of his strength and filled with belief and hope, removing the closest obstacles in his way. But behind these obstacles, and again behind the others, and the next ones, new obstacles were rearing up which he could not see. So never, never could he succeed."

As he had written every night during the winter of 1917–1918 in Ottla's miniature house on Alchemist Street in Prague, Kafka now wrote in Berlin. He would begin to write in the late afternoons or in the evenings, after dinner, and well after midnight for days, even weeks, in a row. For the first time in his life, he no longer wanted to be alone when he was writing and asked Dora to stay in the room with him. Happy to oblige, she got her sewing things and worked or she read. One night, after he had written for a very long time, Dora fell asleep on the sofa. She woke suddenly to find the electric light still blazing and Kafka sitting by her side. She looked at him in surprise. "A palpable change was visible in his face," she said. "The traces of spiritual tension were so obvious that they had changed his face utterly."

One evening after dinner Kafka began a new story called "The Burrow." As Dora remembered it, he wrote all through the night and by morning he had finished it, although he worked on it again. When he read the story to her, Dora began to understand her role in his life. Kafka's move to Berlin represented his hope for survival, his last chance to salvage what was left of his life. Despite his accomplishments, he considered himself a failure up to this point, amounting to nothing. "It must have been the foreboding of the return to his parents' house, the end of freedom, which aroused this panic feeling of fear in him," she later realized.

Although Kafka never analyzed, never explained what he had written, in regard to this latest story, he "told me about it, jokingly and seriously. The story was autobiographical. He pointed out that I was the 'citadel' in the burrow," his "Castle Keep," the "refuge in case of extreme danger."

The story began on a satisfied note: "I have completed the construction of my burrow and it seems to be successful." But within the first paragraph, the fears and anxieties creep in: "Even now, at the zenith of my life, I can scarcely pass an hour in complete tranquillity; at that one point in the dark moss I am vulnerable, and in my dreams I often see a greedy muzzle sniffing around it persistently."

Dora might well have blushed when Kafka read his story to her. The mole—or whatever the small burrowing creature was, Kafka never explained—moves through labyrinthine passageways to the remotest rooms throughout the burrow, in a never-ending struggle to create, maintain and protect his shelter from the terrifying forces just outside his burrow that constantly threaten to annihilate him. Building the burrow, in particular its center, the castle keep (the place that Dora occupied in Kafka's life), required "the most arduous labor of my whole body," the creature explained: "Just at the place where, according to my calculations, the Castle Keep should be, the soil was very loose and sandy and had literally to be hammered and pounded into a firm state to serve as a wall for the beautifully vaulted chamber. But for such tasks the only tool I possess is my forehead. So I had to run with my forehead thousands and thousands of times, for whole days and nights, against the ground, and I was glad when the blood came, for that was a proof that the walls were beginning to harden."

As time passes, the creature moves ever closer to the center of his burrow, where he enjoys "periods of particular tranquillity in which I change my sleeping place by stages, always working in toward the center of the burrow, always steeping myself more profoundly in the mingled smells, until at last I can no longer restrain myself and one night rush into the Castle Keep, mightily fling myself upon my stores, and glut myself with the best that I can seize until I am completely gorged. Happy but dangerous hours; anyone who knew how to exploit them could destroy me with ease and without any risk."

The creature now realizes that the burrow has become too important to him. "It is his castle, the thing he loves best, which he does not want to share with anyone." Thus it has become a new source of anxiety. And so the endless time passes "with new anxieties, new threats, new disturbances every day, in a constant rhythm of panic and despair until finally, one day, there is a disturbance of different sort."

The final deadly assault on the creature's life begins as "an almost inaudible whistling noise." The sound grows louder and more threatening, increasingly impossible to ignore, while the creature comforts himself with positive thoughts and assurances that he has nothing to worry about. Finally, he must accept that a great beast "dangerous beyond all one's powers of conception" is encircling him. As both Dora and Max remembered it, Kafka's story ended with the fearsome beast killing the terrified creature, but the ending was lost and never published. As it stands, the story closes with the terrible beast quieted for the moment, with the final line, "But all remained unchanged."

In late November, Max Brod returned to Berlin see Emmy and to pay a second visit to Kafka and Dora, this time at the new apartment. His earlier impressions of Kafka's newfound happiness were confirmed. "He was working with pleasure," Brod observed. In the past, Kafka had "frequently experienced great happiness in writing, although he never dignified it with any other name than 'scribbling.'" During his visit, Kafka read aloud passages from his latest work, to Brod's delight: "Anyone who was ever privileged to hear him read his own prose out loud to a small circle of intimates with an intoxicating fervor and a rhythmic verve beyond any actor's power, was made directly aware of the genuine irrepressible joy in creation and the passion behind his work."

One of the most startling changes in Kafka was his new, positive attitude toward publication. Recalling the "embittered struggles preceding every single publication," Brod was now astounded by Kafka's willingness to actively assist in publishing his own work. "I wrested from Kafka nearly everything he published either by persuasion or guile," Brod said in the preface to the posthumous edition of Kafka's first novel, admitting that many of Kafka's manuscripts had been "extorted from him by force and often by begging." Because of Kafka's extremely high standards for judging his work, "there were many obstacles to be overcome before a volume of his saw the light of day."

In October, less than a month after joining Dora in Berlin, Kafka received a letter from his publishers, Kurt Wolff Verlag, with the royalty statement for the fiscal year 1922–1923, saying they had closed his account, since no sales of his books had occurred since the beginning of July. "We use this opportunity to express again that the insignificance of the sale of your books does in no way reduce our joy about them belonging to our company," the letter informed him. Despite the lack of sales, they assured him, they would continue to promote Kafka's books, because they were "convinced that at a later time the extraordinary quality of these prose pieces would be recognized." As a gesture of their good will, the publishers offered to send him several copies each of the six volumes of his book published by their firm, including "The Metamorphosis," *The Penal Colony,* "The Judgment," "The Stoker," "The Country Doctor" and "Reflections," along with a selection of his choosing of other books from their catalogue.

Kafka wanted to continue to live in Berlin, to maintain his independence (albeit with Dora's help). Because of this, he was now willing to do what was necessary to further the publication of his work. To Brod's amazement, Kafka negotiated a new contract himself with Die Schmiede publishing house and handled all the details for a new collection of his stories, which would be published the following fall under the title of one of them, "A Hunger Artist."

BERLIN, DECEMBER 18, 1923

Dora interrupted the card Kafka was writing to ask how he was feeling. His fever had returned every evening lately. After reassuring Dora, Kafka went back to his note to Klopstock: "I am just being asked about my condition and can say of my head only that it is 'coiffeured like a lion.'" Klopstock's last letter was peppered with questions as to how Kafka was living and why he wasn't writing. "You must not imagine, Robert, that my life is such that I have the freedom and energy to report, even to write, at any given moment. There are abysses into which I sink without even noticing, only at best to creep up again after a long time."

Kafka described the Academy of Hebrew Studies to Robert as "a refuge of peace in wild and woolly Berlin and the wild and woolly regions of the mind." Before ending the card, Kafka asked about Pua Bentovim, his young Hebrew teacher, whom Robert had mentioned: "It's very good that you will be seeing Pua; perhaps then I'll have some news of her. I have not been able to reach her for months. How have I offended her?" After signing off, he added: "Another student wishes to enclose a greeting."

For the first time in one of Kafka's letters, Dora wrote a brief hello to Robert, whom she had not yet met, and signed her name. Now that Max and Ottla knew and liked Dora, Kafka mentioned her more frequently in his letters to them and began to leave space at the bottom of the letter or card, so that Dora could add a greeting and a note of her own.

6

THE KILLING WINTER

*You belong to me, I to you, we are united. What
can harm us?*

— Franz Kafka, "The Burrow"

BERLIN-STEGLITZ, JANUARY 1924

Dora and Franz celebrated the last day of 1923 alone but not quietly. "I
also took part in the New Year," he wrote to his parents, "although only
from my bed. The noise which came for hours through the open window
was enormous, without regard for the frost, the sky full of fireworks, with
music and shouting throughout the whole district."

Kafka had fallen ill before Christmas, but he downplayed it in his letter:
"Concerning the fever, this is now an old business and was quickly gone,
already by the second day. It was not a cold, judging by its occurrence.
Well, now it is gone. The apartment is not as cold as you seem to believe, I
am sitting next to the central heating where it is quite good."

Their food, prepared by Dora, was "excellent," Kafka said. According
to Brod, their meals were "conjured up out of two methylated spirit stoves
and an improvised Dutch oven." Due to the fuel shortage, there was no
methyl alcohol for the cooking stove, and Dora was forced to improvise
again. "My nourishment, about which you ask, continues to be splendid
and varied," Kafka wrote to Ottla. "Cooking is so easy. Around the New
Year, there was no alcohol for the stove; nevertheless, I almost scalded myself while eating; the food was warmed on candle stubs."

It was probably Ottla, on returning to Prague after her visit in late November, who broke the news about Dora to their parents. When Herrmann and Julie learned the truth about how their son was managing to live

in Berlin, and why he was so insistent on remaining, they were no doubt very unhappy. Ottla must have been very persuasive in her defense of Dora's character and intentions because they continued to support him with packages from home. The Christmas package "was so splendid, so many good and sweet and juicy and banknotey things, and so well chosen and put together," that if any more packages were to arrive, especially if they contained more butter, "it would simply be too much, too expensive, too lush, too humiliating. Of course I will 'pay back' everything but you make this too hard for me with such a quantity. By the way," Kafka added, mentioning Dora for the first time in a letter to his parents, "of all the packages D. was most happy about 'the good fairy.'"

A magnificent package of "household items," according to the labeling notice, arrived the week before Christmas. "Fifteen kilograms," Kafka exclaimed in his thank-you letter to Ottla. "What all can the package possibly contain?" Kafka searched his memory for Ottla's possessions. "You don't really have all that much." He was right. The package's generous contents had come from the combined households of all his sisters. "Oddly enough," Kafka wrote, "the dishcloths and tablecloths made the greatest impression upon D.; she said she really wanted most of all to cry, and actually she nearly did do something of the sort."

Nevertheless, his parents continued to harbor suspicions and doubts about the young Polish immigrant, the runaway from the shtetl, with whom their son was living. One of Kafka's nieces, Ottla's daughter Vera, a small child at the time, remembered as an adult that her grandparents "looked down on Eastern Jewesses and on unmarried love." When Kafka became ill again after the first of the year, according to Vera, "his parents felt sure that Dora was giving him the wrong food."

Dora wanted to call a doctor. For the first two weeks in January, Kafka's high fever returned every evening. He suffered chills and intestinal troubles, and the racking cough continued until morning. He worried constantly that he might infect her. Finally, at Dora's urging, they called a well-known university professor and physician who had been recommended to him. "Luckily he didn't come himself," Kafka reported to Max, "but only sent an assistant, a young man not yet thirty; he couldn't find anything more than a temperature, and ordered nothing for the time being except to stay in bed and wait. For this visit he asked twenty marks, that is, 160 Czech crowns."

Dora took one look at the bill and had a long, obviously fruitful talk with the doctor. "Later, D. negotiated it down to half that," Kafka told

Max. "Since then I have tenfold fear of getting sick; a second-class bed in the Jewish Hospital costs 64 crowns a day, but that only pays for bed and board, apparently not for service or the doctor."

The real worry was money. The stabilization of the German mark had ended the one advantage Kafka had enjoyed, the favorable exchange rate from crowns to marks, and prices were rising inexorably. "You must earn gold marks, if you want to live here," he complained to Max. "But the rise in prices nevertheless also has its good sides, it is educational, one becomes more modest (not regarding food, which is not in my control, I only get the best and most expensive, but I am learning more and more to appreciate it) and there are other good effects apart from this, against which, however, the unruly body sometimes opposes."

It had become a private ritual between them, every Saturday night. After four months, "Franz knew the 'Got fun Avrum' by heart, as a child knows the fairy tales which have been told to him countless times," Dora said. The prayer, which Jewish women had recited for centuries at the closing of the Sabbath, was a reminder to bring the sacred into the secular for the coming week: "God of Abraham, of Jacob and of Isaac, protect your dear people of Israel in their need, that the seven days may bring us good luck and good fortune to all the good and faithful ones."

Every Saturday night he never failed to ask her, and she recited it for him: "Our dear, holy, blessed Sabbath is passing, may the dear, beloved week come with health and life, and with wealth and honor and good deeds and good gains for all. A good healthy week, a happy making week, a being alive, may come to all of us: to me, to my father, my mother, to my sister and brother, and to all of us, all of Israel."

He not only listened to the prayer but participated in it too, Dora said. "At the point in the prayer, 'May the gates of Jerusalem soon stand open. Open shall they stand,' he moved his head in rhythm, but very slowly, so that I, conducted by his nodding, slowed down the tempo progressively to the end":

Into the gates we shall go, into Jerusalem we will go. To you, the only God above the world. We shall call out and hope and pray: A good week, a healthy week, a happy week, a lucky week, a good healthy week, alive. Oh, may we be redeemed from our hard and bitter dispersion, this week, and this month, and this year.

His reaction to this prayer made Dora realize how devout Kafka was. "He missed so much never having learned devout praying," she said. His path in life was made more difficult, she believed, because he never participated in the rituals of communal prayer, nor had he experienced the "profound devotion of a congregation."

Kafka wrote his last letter to Ottla from Berlin during the first week of January. Kafka asked if Ottla had news about his friend, the Hungarian medical student who was taking time from his studies to publish literary translations in Max's newspaper, the *Prager Tagblatt*. "What is Klopstock up to?" Kafka asked. "I suppose he is badly, badly off. In this cold, to be running around after uncertain earnings—what heroes they are who can do that. Besides, in his need he always has the understandable craving for some fantastic luxury, say to buy Vera a toy or—this time—to take the train to Berlin. Ought I to encourage him? It would not be hard to find him a free place to sleep somewhere for two days, says D. Food would also be easy to obtain, for two days. But ought I to urge him to the enormous expenditure for the trip . . . No, I probably won't do it." At the end of the letter, Dora added her own postscript: "Just very, very warm regards. So tired! I'm already asleep. Goodnight."

Kafka's fears of losing the "extraordinarily beautiful" apartment were justified. The rising costs had forced their landlady to let out her own bedroom, the only other room on the floor. In mid-January, Franz wrote to Max, "We poor foreigners who cannot pay such high rents will be expelled from our wonderful apartment on February 1." Remarkably, Kafka did not seem at all fazed by this latest uprooting. "I already have the prospect of another flat," Kafka breezily informed his parents. "This is how I will get acquainted with the surrounding of Berlin, which is not bad at all. In Prague I would have felt terrible if I had to move, here I don't mind very much."

What Kafka called "the miracle of getting by on 1000 crowns" in December was not likely to be repeated in January. He did not want to leave Berlin but was beginning to think that he "must give up the struggle against Berlin prices." Leaving would also mean giving up his Hebrew and

Talmud classes, although, he admitted, he was not "really pursuing these studies, but only doing them for pleasure without the necessary ground-work."

The last thing Kafka wanted to do was return to Prague. He saw it as the final defeat. He roundly rejected Max's proposal that he return to "warm, well-fed Bohemia. . . . I had warmth and good feeding for forty years, and the result does not tempt me to go on trying them." Kafka described himself to Max: "If the creature were not so decrepit, you could almost make a drawing of his appearance: On the left D. supporting him; on the right that man [a Hebrew teacher]; some sort of 'scribbling' might stiffen his neck; now if only the ground beneath him were consolidated, the abyss in front of him filled in, the vultures around his head driven away, the storm in the skies above him quieted down—if all that were to happen, then it might be just barely possible to go on for a while."

In his letters to Franz, Brod had continued to ask for Kafka's assistance in dealing with Emmy. "Of course, I'll try to all I can with E., to the limits of my strength and cleverness," Kafka promised. But his limitations were becoming greater. A telephone call with Emmy had been arranged that day, but he couldn't take the call when it came; he had a temperature of 100 degrees and had to stay in bed. "It's nothing special, I frequently have such a temperature without any further repercussions," Franz said, and blamed the change in the weather as a cause. He would be better by tomorrow. "Still," he conceded, "it is a serious obstacle to freedom of movement, and the figures of the doctor's fee float in fiery letters over my bed."

Kafka added eight separate postscripts before the letter was finally mailed, several days after he began writing it. Max had sent a food parcel, for which Kafka thanked him while admitting that he had not kept the contents: "D. had a big cake baked and took it to the Jewish orphanage where she had been a seamstress last year. I hear that it was great event for the children, who lead a depressed, joyless life there." This was not the first gift Kafka had given to the orphanage. In early October, soon after arriving in Berlin, he had given twenty crowns, a small fortune, to the children's shelter.

He asked what Max thought of well-known journalist Manfred Georg, who had written an essay on Brod for an anthology, *Jews in German Literature,* just published in Berlin. "Dora knows Manfred Georg of Breslau quite well (he's in Berlin now) and would be curious to hear your opinion of him," Kafka wrote. Whatever Brod (or Dora) thought of him, Georg became well-known in the United States after he emigrated to New York in 1938 and developed the Jewish-language weekly *Aufbau* into a major newspaper for Yiddish-speaking immigrants.

Kafka was understandably concerned. Five days before they were supposed to vacate their apartment on Grunewaldstrasse, they still had not found a place to live. In a postcard written to Klopstock on January 26, Kafka wrote, "At the moment we have apartment troubles, an overabundance of apartments, but the fine ones march right past us, beyond our means, and the rest are questionable. If only I could earn something! But nobody here is paying wages for lying in bed until twelve."

The young Berlin artist whom Tile had introduced to Kafka had managed to find "a fine job" for himself in the midst of the economic chaos, an occupation that Kafka admired. "I've envied him for it more than once," Kafka admitted. "He is a street book-peddler; around ten o'clock in the morning he goes to his stand and stays there until dusk. Around Christmas, he made ten marks a day, now three or four."

The next day, their problem was solved: Dora located a new place for them. On January 28, Kafka wrote to Felix Weltsch. "It's true that I write to you only when I move (out of fear that an issue of *Selbstwehr* might fail to arrive.) On February 1 (that is, for the next issue) my address will be: c/o Frau Dr. Busse, Heidestrasse, 25–26, Berlin-Zehlendorf. I am possibly making a mistake (and am being punished in advance by the exorbitant rent, which as rents go is really not at all excessive for this apartment, but is in reality beyond my means) by moving into the home of a deceased writer, Dr. Carl Busse (he died in 1918), who at least during his lifetime would certainly have detested me."

The new lodgings consisted of one room, and the building itself was much less charming. The rambling two-story house was owned by the middle-aged widow of Dr. Busse, a neo-romantic author and literary critic who died at the age of forty-eight. Dr. Busse might well have "rolled over in his grave" knowing that the modernist writer and his girlfriend were living unmarried under his roof. "But I'm moving nevertheless," Kafka told Felix. "The world is everywhere full of perils, so let this special one emerge if it will from the darkness of all the unknown dangers."

Zehlendorf was a wealthy district, only two stops further southeast of Berlin on the local S-Bahn line. Yet it seemed far more cut off from Berlin than Steglitz had. It was a long walk from the elevated station above the Teltowdamm, across the broad straight boulevard that led to Potsdamm, through a forested park and down the long Heidestrasse, today known as Busse Allee, with stately villas and mansions scattered along the wide street. In the summer it would be lovely. There were forests and clear lakes nearby, perfect for walks. The house had a pleasant verandah, where he could sit outside when it got warmer. But now it was bitingly cold, and Kafka rarely left the house.

BERLIN-ZEHLENDORF, FEBRUARY 1, 1924

On Thursday, February 1, the same day that Kafka and Dora splurged on a taxicab to cart them and their belongings to their new apartment, a telegram arrived from Ludwig Hardt, who was giving a performance that Saturday evening in Berlin's Master Hall. Kafka wanted very much to go. In his opinion, Hardt, a well-known orator, was "a magician," an enchanting performer of poetry and literature, and "a servant of the word. He revives and brings to life poems that are buried under the dust of convention. He is a great man."

Kafka was excited by Hardt's invitation. "But sad to say, sad to say, I cannot come," Kafka wrote in response. "Not only because I just moved this afternoon, with all the paraphernalia of the massive household I am running, but chiefly because I am sick, feverish, and haven't been out of the house in the evening throughout these four months in Berlin." Kafka offered another solution: "Couldn't I see you here in Zehlendorf—it's been such a long time. Tomorrow evening a Fräulein Dora Diamant will be coming to your reading to discuss this matter with you. Warm regards and blessings on your evening."

It was not unusual for Kafka to ask Dora, "the other student," as he sometimes referred to her, to go to events and readings in his place. With the program fresh in her mind, Dora described everything to him. Kafka seemed to get as much enjoyment, maybe even more, than had he attended the performance himself. Afterward, Kafka always praised Dora on her natural acting gift. It was her responsibility to her God-given talent that she get professional training, he said. A career in the professional theater, once a romantic impossibility, was a dream that now took root in Dora's imagination.

A few days earlier, a friend of Kafka's, the actress Midia Pines, also encouraged Dora to get training. Pines had performed at a Berlin gallery, and
Dora attended alone because Kafka wasn't feeling well. Midia, who
worked as a language teacher in Prague to earn her keep, was performing
the life story of the hermit from *The Brothers Karamazov* by Dostoyevsky,
"reciting the whole thing by heart." Dora had been thoroughly delighted
by Midia's performance and longed to be on stage herself.

On Saturday night, Dora went alone to Ludwig Hardt's performance at
the Master Hall. In her pocket, Dora carried a second letter to Hardt from
Franz, which she hoped would explain her mistake of the day before.
"Dear Ludwig Hardt," Kafka had written, "I have just received the report
of a very unhappy young lady." Even the qualifier "very" didn't begin to
describe Dora's misery. "The doorman misunderstood her when she asked
whether Hardt had arrived yet and called him personally to the telephone," Kafka explained. "I have made her even more unhappy by recol-
lecting that H. usually takes a nap before a reading (which is surely still
true), but then offered the consolation that nothing can disturb H. (which
is surely even truer)."

Kafka reissued the invitation to visit him in his Berlin suburb. "Fräulein
Dora Diamant, the bearer of this message, has plenipotentiary authority
and more to discuss the possibility of a journey to Zehlendorf. Will it be
possible?" Kafka wondered. Hardt wasn't able to take the time to go to
the outskirts of frigid Berlin, but other visitors did come.

Some of the well-known literary personages who found their way from
their busy Berlin city offices to the somber streets of Zehlendorf included
Willy Haas, editor of *Die literarische Welt* (The Literary World), and
Rudolf Kayser, editor of the *Die neue Rundschau* (New Worldview).
Kayser had published Kafka's novella "A Hunger Artist" in his October
1922 issue. Like Brod, Kayser recognized Kafka's literary genius:

> His nature and his books show the same basic characteristic: honesty. He
> spoke and wrote what he was, without ambition regarding form and suc-
> cess. His language is clear, objective and pure. It avoids all ornament. . . .
> Nevertheless, it is rich, gives visions and dreams and is always personal.
> Kafka's prose belongs to the best in today's German literature. Despite its
> simplicity and matter-of-factness, it knows about the magic of words.

After Kafka's death, Kayser wrote about his first and only meeting with
Kafka in the winter of 1924. The meeting, he said, took place "in a Berlin

suburb, where he led a lonely existence, living with his fateful illness, which he bore with a smile. He was living in a snow-covered street dotted by villas, close to a forest where the city, having reached here its absolute limit, is silent. From me he wanted to hear things: about life, about books, theaters and people. The existence of the world—he saw it removed from himself and observed it—as children observe the lives of adults—with longing and smiles at the same time."

Kafka's illness was, Kayser said, "something more than physical suffering, for it had passed over into his very nature. It belonged to him as much as he belonged to it. It gave this forty-year-old man a lean boy's face, a young laugh, a tender voice. He had so much youth in him." Kayser thought it must have been Kafka's impending death that "seemed to bring him closer to his childhood." Meeting Kafka for the first time, knowing him only through his literary work, Kayser couldn't have known that Kafka's youthful quality was an essential aspect of his personality. Despite his suffering, Kafka always saw the beauty surrounding him, in the simplest and smallest of things. As he once said, "Anyone who keeps the ability to see beauty never grows old."

Franz Werfel also came for a visit, but it was a disaster, as Dora recalled it. One of Kafka's circle of Prague literary friends, Werfel was already famous outside of Prague as a poet, author and playwright.

The circle had unofficially begun in 1909. Since then, Kafka and Werfel had shared their writing, reading it to each other, though recently the experience had become become painful for both of them. In the past two years, Kafka and Werfel, while respecting each other personally, saw the world very differently and were no longer able to "understand or appreciate each other's work."

Franz Werfel was short and plump, with a full round face, blond hair and blue eyes. He believed firmly in his own genius, even as a teenager, when he was considered a prodigy by the Prague literati. His future was indeed bright. After escaping from Hitler to Hollywood, California, in 1938, Werfel wrote a best-selling novel, *The Song of Bernadette,* and won an Academy Award for the screenplay.

In November 1922, Kafka and Werfel had spent a miserable evening after a reading of Werfel's latest play. According to Mailloux's biography, "the visit had been extremely difficult because Kafka had spent the evening criticizing Werfel's new play, *Schweiger.* It hadn't been that Kafka had disliked the play; rather he had felt for some not wholly explicable reason horrified by it, and he had not be able, despite his usual delicacy, to prevent himself from telling Werfel that. Afterwards, Kafka had felt terrible, but almost the same thing happened in Berlin."

Actually, the opposite occurred. When Werfel arrived, his new book in hand, Dora greeted him and ushered him into Kafka's room. The two men were alone for what seemed to Dora a very long time. Suddenly the door burst open and Werfel rushed out, weeping. "When I entered the room, Kafka was sitting there completely shattered," Dora said. "He murmured to himself several times, 'To think that something so terrible has to be at all!' He was weeping, too." Dora soon discovered what had happened: "He had let Werfel go away without having been able to utter a single word about his book."

When it came to literature, as with life, Kafka could be nothing but scrupulously honest. Just as Franz Werfel had left Kafka's room in tears following this latest meeting, "anyone who put himself into Kafka's hands either had the most encouraging experience or despaired," Dora said. "There was nothing in between. He had the same inexorable severity towards his own work." It seemed to Dora that "he never really believed that he had achieved what he wanted." That, she reasoned, was the reason he wanted to destroy it.

Dora burned Kafka's work while they lived in Zehlendorf. It was an act of love that elicited reproach and criticism for the remainder of her life. "I was so young then," she later explained, "and young people live in the present and perhaps in the future too. After all, for him all that had been nothing but self-liberation! He was possessed by this idea; it was a kind of sullen obstinacy. He wanted to burn everything that he had written in order to free his soul from these 'ghosts.' I respected his wish, and when he lay ill, I burnt things of his before his eyes."

As Kafka lay watching from the bed, Dora lit the match and touched it to the pages, dropping them into the basin as they caught fire. "What he really wanted to write was to come afterwards, after he had gained his 'liberty,'" Kafka told her. They watched as the small flames rose in a temporary warmth. He only relaxed when the ashes lay quietly at the bottom.

According to Kafka biographer Ronald Hayman, Dora may have burned the final missing pages of "The Burrow." He reported that Dora, "at his instructions and in his presence, had to burn many of his manuscripts, including a play and the story about an Odessa trial for ritual murder." But Dora didn't burn everything. She saved many of the notebooks containing his last diaries, written during his walks in Berlin. Those she tucked away, but not out of a sense of any future literary importance. That didn't concern her at all. What she saw and appreciated was how Kafka seemed to feel a balance had been achieved in their burning. "After all," he once said, "what one writes is only the ashes of one's experience."

On Max Brod's third and last visit to Kafka in Berlin, he left deeply concerned. Kafka's spirits were still high, and "he mentioned his troubles only in a jocular way." But his health had deteriorated rapidly, and neither he nor Dora was facing the situation realistically. Nearly bedridden and living in abject poverty, as soon as "he earned a few pence through his contract" with Die Schmiede, he wanted to begin repaying his "family debts." From his family in Prague, "worrying desperately about him," Brod reported, Kafka hid "the true state of his affairs."

"It was impossible to shut one's eyes to the fact that Franz's bodily health—despite his spiritual equilibrium, which continued—was getting worse," Brod said. He hated to break up the Berlin idyll, but when he returned to Prague from Berlin, Max contacted Kafka's physician uncle, Dr. Siegfried Lowy, and warned him about the seriousness of Franz's condition.

BERLIN-ZEHLENDORF, FEBRUARY 29, 1924

It was the last day of the month in a leap year, and Dr. Lowy was visiting for a couple of days. Kafka had insisted that his uncle and Dora attend a literary reading in Berlin that he, in better days, would most certainly have attended himself. Kafka stayed home and indulged in an "enervated evening orgy" of reading. Before Dora and his uncle returned, Kafka wrote the only letter that he completed that month to Robert Klopstock. Two letters and "a postcard long have been drifting around the apartment somewhere. You will never receive them," he said and thanked Robert for "all the good things you shower upon me (the wonderful chocolates that I received only a few days ago, or rather, not to hide the truth, that we received.)"

Dr. Lowy was shocked at his nephew's condition and insisted that he leave Berlin at once and go directly to a sanatorium for specialized care if he wanted to go on living. The uncle was adamant, but Franz, with Dora's support, refused to agree with his prognosis. He was not ready to give up his hard-fought struggle for independence. Dora would not accept the verdict either. They both knew that returning to Prague would mean the end for him. Their best hope lay in a second opinion from another doctor refuting his uncle. But they couldn't afford the expense. What else could they do?

BERLIN-ZEHLENDORF, MARCH 4, 1924

It was early March, but spring was already in the air. Buds were showing on the elm trees as Dr. Ludwig Nelken walked to 25–26 Heidestrasse to pay a house call as a favor to a friend. When Dora telephoned him, her voice conjured up images of the left-wing rally at the *Preussisches Herren-haus* in Berlin, where he had seen her give a speech, sharing the podium with Angelica Balabanoff. Dora had been commanding and persuasive, Nelken thought, in moving the audience with her "strong Jewish commit-ment" and sense of responsibility for humanity.

Dora first met Nelken in his hometown, Breslau, in 1919, when he was a medical student. She still spoke Yiddish then and was just learning to speak German. He thought her pretty and was attracted to "her simplic-ity, originality and intelligence." In Berlin they saw each other again, when he working at the Jewish Hospital and she was governess in the home of Dr. Badt, a leader in Berlin's Orthodox Jewish community. Nelken had not seen her in many months and was surprised and pleased to hear from her when she rang him up, asking him to come to Zehlendorf to examine her friend Franz Kafka, with whom she was living. They had no money to pay, she admitted. Could he come immediately, as soon as possible? There was no denying Dora, or the desperation in her voice.

When Dr. Nelken entered the room, Kafka was not in bed, "but he was in a wretched state," Nelken later reported. "He was leaning against the window sill with a friendly smile, almost as if he pitied me and wanted to say: 'Why are you wasting your time and your talents on me, young man? It is hopeless, I can't be helped anymore.'" In a newspaper article pub-lished in Israel in 1974, Dr. Nelken, described as "a well-known Jerusalem physician," mourned the fact that he couldn't help Kafka. "If only strepto-mycin had been available then, or any of the other medicines which have done so much for the cure of tuberculosis. All I could do at the time was to prescribe something to alleviate the cough and other symptoms."

In deference to Dora, Dr. Nelken refused to submit a bill. In gratitude, Kafka sent him a book with a personal dedication. It was not one of his own slim volumes—that wouldn't have been good enough—but rather a lovely large book on the artist Rembrandt, one of the new books he had received from Kurt Wolff Verlag as a parting gift when they closed his account.

March 4 was Dora's twenty-sixth birthday. Dora stayed home, as she usually did now. She had dropped her classes at the Academy and now devoted herself to Kafka. He hadn't been out of the house for weeks. It had been more than a month since he had been able to attend classes at the Academy. He felt well when he was lying down. But when he stood up for any length of time or attempted to take walks, "after the first step they assume the quality of a grandiose enterprise, so that sometimes the thought of peacefully burying myself alive in the sanatorium is not at all so unpleasant. And then again it horrifies me when I consider that I shall be losing freedom even for those few warm months that are predestined for freedom."

Dora was earning a little money by taking in sewing. "He loved this situation, as it meant that I would stay in the house," she later told Ottla. "He always used to follow me a little anxiously with his eyes, and then, when I took my sewing things out, his eyes lit up and looked so reassured and grateful, and he called it a present I had given him."

When Kafka could no longer leave his bed, he and Dora continued to read aloud to each other and found new ways to entertain themselves. "We very often amused ourselves making shadows on the wall with our hands," she said. The play of light and dark shadows, without the fripperies of actual bodies, danced and leapt across the wall, while they improvised stories and scenes from fairy tales and legends. They often played the game until the last candle burned out.

In his last letter to Robert Klopstock from Berlin, written in the first week of March, Kafka was still refusing to leave Berlin. "I am resisting a sanatorium, also resisting a boardinghouse, but what's the use since I cannot resist the fever. And 100.4 has become my daily bread, all evening long and half the night. Otherwise," Kafka continued, "it is very lovely here to lie on the verandah and watch the sun working on two tasks, each difficult in its own way: to awaken me and birch alongside me to natural life (the birch seems to be somewhat ahead). I am very reluctant to leave here, but I cannot entirely reject the idea of going to the sanatorium." Kafka could not ignore the "morning and evening coughing lasting for hours, and the flask almost full every day that again argues for the sanatorium." Beside his bed, there was a jar for the mucus he coughed up. Arguing against the sanatorium was the "fear, for example, of the horrible compulsory eating there." In Klopstock's last letter, he announced he was coming to Berlin to help take care of Kafka. "No, no traveling, no such wild adventure," Kafka wrote back. "Perhaps—we really are thinking seriously of it—we'll soon be coming to Prague; if a sanatorium in the Vienna woods proves feasible, then certainly."

Dr. Lowy telephoned Franz repeatedly. He was not accustomed to his medical orders being disobeyed. He refused to give up on his favorite nephew. He used his connections to get Franz admitted without the customary waiting period into a sanatorium in Austria, and a bed was waiting for him there. "Uncle proposed that I go direct from here to Innsbruck," Kafka wrote, "but I explained to him today why I would prefer to go by way of Prague. Perhaps he will consent."

By March 15, the fight to stay in Berlin was lost. In the last letter to his parents written from Berlin, he was still trying to delay the inevitable by a day or two: "I might not finish with the travel preparations until Monday, and then I'll come several days later. Definitely, Robert should not come. I know he would like to do it, and I know from experience that you are as safe with him as in the arms of a guardian angel, but for this short familiar distance it is definitely not necessary. Please be sure to talk him out of it." Once more, he said, he might be staying longer. "The uncle's servant does not need to wait at the train station on Monday, since it is quite unsure whether I'll come."

BERLIN-ZEHLENDORF, MARCH 17, 1924

On Monday morning, Kafka leaned heavily on Dora as they left his room for the last time and walked to the waiting taxi. Supporting him on the other side was Robert Klopstock, who had come to Berlin despite Kafka's request for him not to do so. Max Brod was waiting for them at the train station. Max was in Berlin for the premiere opening of his translation of *Jenufa* at the Staatsoper. Max, not Dora, would accompany Kafka to Prague.

Dora wasn't going to Prague. Franz didn't want to subject her "to the house from which all his disasters had come." He was afraid of the disdain and disrespect his parents would certainly show her. He couldn't bear to think how his father might treat Dora, what abysmal things he might say. In many matters, Kafka was completely helpless, but in this one case he could do something, even if it meant a personal sacrifice: he would protect Dora from his parents.

Wait, Kafka alternatively commanded and begged her. Wait. Later, when he went to a sanatorium, she could join him there. In the meanwhile, he promised to write her every day from Prague. Dora stood on the platform until the train pulled away from the station, until it disappeared and she could no longer see it.

7

THE MOST FEARFUL DAY OF DISASTER

A man is only fully aware of himself when he's
either in love or in danger of death.
—Franz Kafka, in *Conversations with Kafka*

BERLIN, SPRING 1924

Berlin was beginning to thaw and drip. The birds were noisy and the trees in full bud. Dora noticed little of it. She missed Kafka. She longed to hear his hypnotic voice, to sit in his lap with his robe wrapped around both of them for warmth. She still believed their separation was temporary. When he left, he said he would stay in Prague no more than two or three days. As the days extended into weeks, Dora sometimes despaired but refused to allow such thoughts for long. Instead, she concentrated on a positive, happy outcome.

Kafka wrote to her every day from Prague, sometimes twice and three times a day. His letters warmed her like a blessing, as if he were there. Afterward, his presence lingered in the atmosphere around her. A particular moment of a day, a certain look in his eyes, the touch of his hand, became the present moment. "I have to be careful," she wrote in her diary almost thirty years later, about her tendency to vividly imagine him. "Sometimes when I think of an incident, an experience with Franz, I glide into fantasizing, which is equally real and intense as the original experience."

Dora treasured her letters from Kafka and reread them over and over again. It gave her the greatest joy to find a new letter waiting for her in the morning or afternoon mail—or both—with her name written in his distinctive bold handwriting: *Fräulein Dora Diamant*. She counted the days he had been gone by the growing stack of letters and cards.

He had begun working on a new story about a mouse singer named Josephine. He was reading Tolstoy's diaries and was concerned with a problem he encountered in the writings, "technical errors" in the way man acts toward himself. He probed the problem at length, from many angles. Dora had never known anyone who approached the search for solutions as thoroughly as Franz did. At times like this, Kafka reminded Dora of a great Talmudic sage or rabbi, who could never come to a decision without intricately, with infinite patience and great precision, dissecting every question until an answer could be produced. But who knew if that was the final solution to the argument? With Kafka, it was a question of fairness, of divine justice: there was always the possibility of another perspective, yet another "but on the other hand" for every solution.

In another letter, Franz told her about a dream he had the night before. "Highwaymen had taken him from his room in Berlin, shut him up in a shed in some backyard and gagged him. 'I know that I am lost, because you can't find me,'" Franz told her. Then, in his dream, he suddenly hears that Dora is still in sight, close by. He tries to tear himself free, he thinks he is already free—he has pulled the gag out of his mouth—all he has to do is cry out for her to hear him "but at this very moment is discovered by the highwaymen and they gag him again."

The dream served its purpose. Dora heard Kafka's cry for help and would never abandon him. If Kafka stayed in Prague in his parents' care without her, Dora believed, he would die. Franz had to live. His frightening dream strengthened her resolve, renewed her purpose, and refocused her vision of the future for the two of them together. This decision was not based on reason; it was purely emotional and therefore irrefutable.

As soon as Kafka returned at the end of March, Klopstock visited Kafka at his parents' home. Franz was in bed, propped up with pillows. A tray stocked with fresh fruit, juices and water stood nearby, untouched. He spoke in ragged whispers. "I think I began to investigate that animal squeaking at the right time," he said. "I have just finished a story about it."

Klopstock wanted very much to read it but lacked the temerity to ask. Instead, he talked about other things, mostly the problems in his own life.

A Hungarian Jew and medical student from Budapest, Robert Klopstock was twenty-five. He also suffered from tuberculosis but showed "no outward signs of his illness." As Kafka described him, he was a "tall, strong, broad, red-cheeked, blond fellow; when dressed he is almost too heavy." His boyish appearance and tousled hair reminded Kafka of illustrations in classic German children's stories: "earnest and tense, yet also dreamy."

Kafka first mentioned Robert Klopstock in a letter to Brod after meeting him in a sanatorium in the High Tatra Mountains in winter of 1921. Kafka thought the young man was "very ambitious, intelligent, also highly literary. He has a hunger for people, the way a born doctor does." Klopstock was also an "anti-Zionist" whose "guides are Jesus and Dostoyevski." Two months later, still recovering at Matliary, Kafka wrote to Brod again about the young man, asking for help on his behalf. Klopstock's father was dead, and Kafka wanted them both to sponsor Klopstock into the university, their alma mater.

When Kafka left Matliary after a six-month stay and returned to Prague, he and Klopstock stayed in touch with frequent long letters. Once Kafka wrote of a new cure prescribed by his latest doctor, whom Kafka described as "sublimely, childishly ridiculous, like most of them." Kafka was not uniformly cynical about doctors and their cures. "I end up being very fond of them," Kafka said. "After all, what matters is that they do the best they can, and the less that is, the more touching it is." Besides, Kafka said, "sometimes they spring a surprise."

During the visit at his parents' house Kafka said something that shocked Klopstock to his very core: On the third day back home, he had begun to notice an odd burning sensation at the back of his throat. Franz felt it "whenever he drank certain beverages, especially fruit juices, and was worried that his larynx might also be affected." As a medical student specializing in lung and thoracic disorders, Klopstock was well aware of what would happen if Kafka's larynx became infected by the tuberculosis. The bleak look in his eyes suggested that Kafka knew what it meant, too.

For three weeks, Kafka remained at his parents' apartment on the Old Town Square. Max Brod came to see him every day. "Come tomorrow again at this time," Kafka commanded at the end of each visit. "Now he wanted me to go to see him every day," Brod later reported. "Other times he had never spoken so energetically, had always been extremely considerate towards the piles of work that overwhelmed me. This time he spoke as if he knew we should not have one another much longer." In spite of the "tender care that surrounded him" at this parents' home, Kafka felt defeated and "he grew worse and worse."

SANATORIUM WIENERWALD, ORTMANN, AUSTRIA, APRIL 5, 1924

Dora did not go to Prague while Kafka was alive, although most of his biographers, beginning with Brod, claimed she did. She wanted desperately

THE MOST FEARFUL DAY OF DISASTER

to go and told people she was going; nevertheless, she respected Kafka's wishes. With news of the ominous burning in Kafka's throat, everything was up in the air, and then, at the last minute, it was decided. Kafka's uncle prevailed and Franz was sent to an Austrian sanatorium without further interference or delay. Arrangements were being made for an available bed at the prestigious and expensive Sanatorium Wienerwald in Ortmann, near the town of Pernitz, in the Vienna Woods. As others discussed his fate, Kafka helplessly fretted about the costs. Dora immediately left Berlin for Vienna, where she found a room, to await news of Kafka's arrival and exact destination.

On April 7, Kafka wrote a card to his parents describing the Sanatorium Wienerwald. After signing his name, he added, "If anyone of us should speak to Dora, she should write to me with her Vienna address and not come to Pernitz (endless journey) before I've written to her about it."

Dora arrived at the sanatorium the next day. Kafka lay on a hospital bed in an entirely white, sterile room, where he received his treatments. It had been over three weeks since she had seen him, and his appearance shocked her. She vowed never to let him go again. On the postcard Kafka sent to Brod when he arrived at the clinic, Dora added her own frightened postscript before mailing it: "The patient's condition is very grave."

Kafka sent a postcard on April 9 to his parents, worrying about the exorbitant costs of his care and wondering if his uncle, who knew the attending physician, might not be able to arrange for a 10 percent cut in the billing that had been promised. "D. is with me, that is very good," Kafka wrote. "She is staying at a farmhouse next to the sanatorium, but only for a couple of days, then she'll go back home." At the bottom of the card, Dora added her own note: "It is not sure yet whether I'll go home. If possible, I'll postpone the journey. For your lovely sweet letter, a thousand thanks, D."

With Klopstock, Kafka discussed "only medical matters—everything else is too involved." The treatment was "delightfully simple," he wrote, although he thought its simplicity "its only merit." He outlined the treatments: "Against fever, liquid Pyramidon three times a day. Against coughing, Demopon (unfortunately it doesn't help) and Anastesin lozenges. Along with the Demopon, atropine. Probably the larynx is the chief problem."

At first, the doctors at the Sanatorium Wienerwald were unwilling to make a diagnosis. In discussing his case, Kafka noted, "everybody drops into a shy, evasive, glassy-eyed manner of speech," using phrases like "swelling at the rear," "infiltration," "not malignant," and finally, "but we cannot yet say anything definite." Kafka knew what those terms meant. Combined "with a very malignant pain," it seemed to him that the diagnosis was self-evident. During the admission process, he was asked to step on a scale: Fully dressed in his winter clothes, Kafka stood six feet tall and weighed 108 pounds.

KIERLING, APRIL 10, 1924

"I am being transferred to the University Clinic of Prof. Dr. M. Hajek, Lazarettgasse 14, Vienna IX. It seems my larynx is so swollen I cannot eat; they must (they say) undertake alcohol injections into the nerve, probably also surgery," Kafka wrote in a quick postcard to Klopstock. While Dora packed, Franz also wrote informing his parents of the sudden decision. "Obviously, I could not manage this whole undertaking without D.," he said. Dora, too, felt that she needed some help. Before she mailed Kafka's card to his parents, she added a line: "It would be good, if it is at all possible, that the uncle or somebody else comes here."

Brod was devastated by Kafka's diagnosis. "The most fearful day of disaster," he wrote in his diary. "All my terrors surpassed on April 10th by the news that Kafka has been sent back from the Wienerwald Sanatorium to the Vienna Clinic—tuberculosis of the larynx discovered."

The tubercular lesions forming at the back of Kafka's throat made talking extremely painful. The air passing over his vocal cords stabbed like sharp knives. "A little water," he wrote on a note, "these bits of pills stick in the mucus like splinters of glass." Swallowing food was an ordeal, becoming at times an impossibility. There was no known prevention or treatment yet for this "most exquisitely painful of afflictions, a protracted martyrdom only relieved by such palliative measures as anesthetizing lozenges and alcohol injections into the laryngeal nerves."

Surgery was a last-ditch effort to keep Kafka alive by opening a passageway through his throat to allow him to eat. Klopstock had recommended a stronger prescription, but Kafka didn't want to take it. "I am afraid of your codeine," Kafka admitted, saying he was already taking a small dosage of the drug, but the symptoms were worse than ever. The sanatorium staff was not hopeful or encouraging: "I wonder what it looks like inside?" Kafka had asked the nurse after she examined his throat that morning. "Like the witch's kitchen," the nurse replied honestly.

Kafka took the news of his death sentence calmly. He seemed to worry mostly about the huge expenses he was now incurring. "It is expensive, might well be frightfully expensive," Kafka wrote in a note to Max before he left the sanatorium. To help defray the medical bills, he asked Brod to offer his last story, "Josephine the Singer, or the Mouse-Folk," to their mutual friend Otto Pick, the literary editor at the *Prager Presse*. "'Josephine' must help out a little, there's no other way," Kafka said. "If he takes it, please send it to Die Schmiede *later*; if he doesn't, then ship it over *right away*. As for me, it's evidently the larynx. Dora is with me. Regards to your wife and Felix and Oskar."

This request marked the first time Kafka urgently asked Brod to arrange for publication of his work, and Max leaped at the opportunity to help his friend—as did Otto Pick. "Josephine the Mouse-Singer, or the Mouse-Folk" was published in the Easter Sunday edition of the literary supplement of the *Prager Presse*.

Thursday morning, the day of Kafka's emergency transfer to Vienna, was cold and rainy. Low dark clouds rumbled, the wind blustered and a chilling fog muted all colors. As the open car drove up the circular driveway to the entrance to the enormous sanatorium, Dora stared in disbelief. How could Kafka travel in an open car in such weather? The trip from Pernitz to Vienna took almost four hours. Kafka had called it an "endless journey." Despite all Dora's arguments, nothing could be done; no other transportation was available. Dora bundled Kafka into the back seat of the large Benz and tucked two warm blankets around him. As the open Benz pulled away, the wind blew harder. Dora stood up in front of Kafka, protecting him from the wind and rain with her own body for the entire journey to Vienna.

VIENNA, APRIL 11, 1924

High on a hill with a panoramic view of the city, the University Clinic in Vienna was billed as the best and "most beautiful Laryngological Clinic in the World." As soon as they arrived, Kafka was whisked away by white-coated orderlies. Dora was not allowed to follow and had to stay away until official visiting hours. Dora left the clinic and wandered down the hill. With money from Franz, she checked into the Hotel Bellevue and waited until the next afternoon.

The University Clinic, under the leadership of the highly respected Prof. Dr. Marcus Hajek, was run more like a military camp than a hospital, with Dr. Hajek acting as commander in chief over a veritable army of doctors and their assistants. Kafka was assigned to a large ward that was lined with beds filled with dying men. Visiting hours were restricted to two hours a day. Dora was at Kafka's bedside every minute she was allowed to see him, and more.

The first day at the clinic, Kafka wrote a short note to his parents: "I am very well taken care of here, under the best medical supervision that one can have in Vienna." He interrupted his note to assure his parents that he was receiving specialized attention: "I cannot write, Dora disturbs me all the time with questions about what she should bring me." The next day, April 12, Kafka wrote again to his parents: "From two to four Dora is always with me, in fact, she already comes by one, which I fear will destroy the whole hospital organization." Kafka had resisted the drugs and painful injections as long as he could, but now reported he would be receiving one that day. "Then we'll see what happens," he said.

That afternoon, just before the end of visiting hours, Karl Hermann, Elli's husband, arrived at the clinic from Prague. He stayed two days to make sure Kafka was being taken care of properly and that the necessary financial arrangements were made. Before mailing the postcard, Dora added her own postscript: "Herr Hermann has just arrived. Now everything will be all right." After warmly returning their sweet greetings to her in Franz's letters, Dora squeezed in three more words: "Franz cheerful and merry."

The following day, Dora added another postcript to Kafka's postcard, his third since arriving in Vienna three days earlier. She asked his parents to send, if possible, "a down-filled quilt, or just a simple one, and a pillow. He only gets the most basic in the clinic, and he is a bit spoilt, you know."

"I am quite well, as Karl will confirm. I have already received three injections, none today, which is of course especially pleasant," Kafka wrote to his parents on April 15. He described his abundant meals, which he admitted that only he—not the rest of the hospital—enjoyed. "This lunch, for instance, chicken soup with egg, chicken with vegetable, sponge cake with whipped cream, and banana, in order not to exaggerate, although the whole hospital does not generally live this way, but only he for whom D. cooks."

Once Kafka pointed across the ward to a happy, cheerful man with a big mustache and shining eyes. The man had a tube in his throat but otherwise seemed robust and healthy. He walked around and chatted with other patients and obviously enjoyed himself. Kafka was especially taken with the man's enormous appetite. Since Kafka couldn't eat without pain, it gave him great pleasure to watch someone else eat with gusto.

The next day, as soon as she arrived, Dora immediately noticed Kafka's darkened aura. Before she could even ask a question, he pointed across the ward to the empty bed of the jovial man, who had died during the night. "Kafka was not shaken, but positively angry," Dora reported, "as if he could not grasp that the man who had been so gay had to die." It frightened her. For the rest of her life, Dora would never forget Kafka's "malicious, ironical smile."

That night, alone in her room at the Hotel Bellevue, Dora wrote her first letter to Kafka's parents: "Dear Parents of Franz! Forgive me, that I allow myself on this one occasion to represent Franz by writing. I know that it cannot in the least way be a substitute, but it is in any case better than nothing." She apologized that Kafka hadn't written more that day. Kafka was asleep when she arrived, and she didn't want to wake him. Kafka usually wrote his correspondence while she was there, so she could take it with her to the post office. The visiting hour "passed away quite imperceptibly," Dora wrote, "the first half with sound sleep, the other half with chatting, without leaving time for chatting [with you]. So, my fault!" She promised that "Tomorrow he'll write at once." "Franz is well," she reported. "The pains in his throat have lessened considerably through the treatment. Eating is much easier and he is in good spirits. We hope shortly to be able to go outside again, where he can start the full recovery." Dora concluded her card with a note of gratitude: "I hope to thank you personally for the greetings and all the love you send to me. The written word is too bland. I hope you understand how happy it makes me. Many best wishes to all from Franz and me." She signed the letter, "D."

Every night somebody died on the ward. In the early hours of Kafka's seventh day at the clinic, the man in the bed next to Kafka passed away. His name was Josef Schrammel. Only one year older than Kafka, he was a shoemaker, a poor husband and father of three. When Dora arrived that day, Kafka mutely pointed to the empty bed across from him. With gestures and expressions and notes, Kafka told her about the shoemaker's death and the "extraordinary patience of the priest who waited on at the dying man's side with words of comfort, until the last moment, when all the doctors had run away long ago."

"I've cried without reason several times today," Kafka admitted in a postcard to Brod. It was clear that Kafka's physical health was improving under Dr. Hajek's care, but his emotional well-being was diminished with each corpse carried out of the ward.

In Prague, Brod was doing all he could to help. Alarmed by Dora's reports, Max wrote letters to important doctors and other influential people in Vienna, including Franz Werfel, trying to arrange a private room for Kafka. Werfel did everything he could to help Kafka and sent a dozen roses, along with a copy of his latest book, about the Italian composer Verdi. Before Werfel left for Italy, where his novel was causing a sensation, he enlisted a friend, a woman doctor, to examine Kafka and wrote a letter to Dr. Hajek requesting a private room for Kafka.

Professor Hajek was unimpressed by the appeals on Kafka's behalf and refused to provide any preferential treatment for his patient. He dismissed Werfel's request coldly: "A certain Werfel has written to me that I should do something for a certain Kafka," he said. "I know who Kafka is. He is the patient in number 12. But who is Werfel?"

Dora had written Klopstock, informing him of the harsh restrictions on Kafka at the clinic and asking advice for finding an alternative to the clinic, where Dora was afraid for Kafka's emotional stability. Her thoughts about the possibility of a nature cure sent Klopstock into a panic, inspiring a long letter to Ottla in which he insisted Ottla must write to Dora and instruct her that under no circumstances was she to remove Kafka from Hajek's care.

In her reports to his parents, Dora wrote with as much cheer and delicacy as she could, refraining from telling them the worst. Kafka's weight dropped under one hundred pounds, but after he spent one week at the clinic, Dora was able to write truly good news. The regular spraying of Kafka's larynx with a solution of 20 percent menthol oil was working, and his symptoms were fading, making surgery unnecessary. Kafka could now swallow solid food again and was even eating meat for the protein he needed.

Dora wrote to Franz's mother, who was concerned, as always, about how her son was eating. "The food in the clinic is not as bad as one might imagine," Dora said. "For breakfast, always rich milk or cocoa, as one prefers. For the second breakfast, egg dishes. I cook lunch for him. It mostly consists of chicken or calves cutlet, fried, mashed potatoes, mixed with butter and egg, cauliflower or young peas. For dessert, a sweet tart with whipped cream, sometimes also bananas or an apple. At teatime he gets cocoa or milk with buttered rolls. For supper always something similar with eggs."

On April 16, Kafka and Dora wrote another postcard to his parents. "The weather has become very beautiful, with the window open all day long," he said. "I suspended the injections today for the second time, which contributes also to the brightening of the days." He was already beginning to suffer from the thirst that would become the greatest agony before he died. "If you would like some good advice, then drink a lot of water," he wrote. "I neglected this while I had the opportunity, and now I am not allowed to make up for it. Life pleases me here apart from this, although it is a very small and pale retrospective compensation for the military life that I missed."

Felix Weltsch had come to Vienna and was helping to get the best care for Kafka. He had learned from a famous specialist of the small private sanatorium in Kierling, near Klosterneuburg, on the rural outskirts of Vienna. The first thing that morning, Dora went to Kierling and spent half a day there convincing herself that it was just the right place for Franz, "where he can have exactly the same treatment and be at the same time in absolutely the right surroundings," she reported in a postcard to Julie.

The decision was made: "Franz goes Saturday into the sanatorium," Dora wrote. "It is 25 minutes from Vienna. The physician will come for treatment. I was there today. I was able to get a splendid balcony room, facing south. It is in a forested area, and is situated marvelously. Starting from Saturday the new address will be: Sanatorium Dr Hoffmann, Klosterneuburg Kierling."

Their plan to leave caused a furor. Professor Dr. Hajek wouldn't let Kafka go without a fight. He correctly maintained that the treatment at the sanatorium in no way rivaled that of the clinic. According to what Werfel told Brod, "Professor Hajek maintained the only chance for Kafka was to stay in the hospital, because there all the medicines and treatments were ready to hand. He put up a direct struggle against letting him go."

Nevertheless, Dora and Kafka held firm: "Tomorrow he will move to the sanatorium," she restated to his parents on April 18. "This happens with the agreement of the doctors and friends," she wrote, somewhat incorrectly. "Next time I will send you the prospectus of the sanatorium so you can convince yourself how beautiful it is there. If the food should not agree with him, I have arranged to cook for him. It is a small establishment and the wishes of everyone are considered." Dora ended her letter on a strongly positive note: "I am of the firm conviction that the summer in the open, in fresh good air, with careful treatment, will repair all the harm Berlin and 'the coming and goings' did. All the best, many affectionate greetings, D."

Into the midst of this maelstrom came Klopstock's letter. He was abandoning his medical studies at once and coming to Vienna to help Dora take care of Kafka. "Robert, dear Robert," Kafka quickly wrote back. "No acts of violence, no sudden trip to Vienna. . . . Since I left that luxurious, depressing, and yet ineffectual (though wonderfully situated) sanatorium I have been feeling better; the procedures in the hospital (except for details) have done me good; the pain in swallowing and the burning have decreased. On Saturday, if no special misfortune intervenes, I intend to go to Dr. Hoffman's sanatorium, Kierling bei Klosterneuberg, Lower Austria."

In the stony face of Kafka and Dora's determination, Professor Hajek was forced to release Kafka. Reluctantly, he signed his name, releasing the patient into "home care" and washing his hands of the patient in number 12.

KIERLING, LOWER AUSTRIA, APRIL 19, 1924

Saturday, April 19, was a glorious day in every sense. It was warm and sunny, the sunniest day of the month so far, with soft clouds drifting on a gentle northwesterly wind. The journey to the small private sanatorium of Dr. Hoffman in the countryside near Klosterneuberg was the opposite of the difficult journey to Vienna nine days earlier.

This trip had the exhilaration of a successful getaway. Kafka radiated happiness. He inhaled the fresh air of the countryside as they drove out of Vienna, heading north to the new sanatorium. Early wildflowers brightened the fields and meadows with bursts of color. Behind them was the past. Ahead, the future looked brighter than it had in months.

8

THE BEST OF BEGINNINGS

*My life was much sweeter than other people's,
and my death will be more terrible to the same
degree.*

                    —Franz Kafka, letter to Max Brod

SANATORIUM HOFFMANN, KIERLING, SATURDAY, APRIL 19, 1924

The private clinic and sanatorium of Dr. Hugo Hoffmann was situated in the village of Kierling near the town of Klosterneuberg, in the countryside less than thirty minutes from Vienna. The sanatorium was housed in a unprepossessing three-story building at 187 Hauptstrasse on Kierling's main street, near a little post office.

Dora and Kafka entered through a tall, narrow entrance, located oddly on the far right corner of the building. An elevator near a staircase took them up to Kafka's room on the second floor. When pressed into operation, the old elevator made an appalling racket, with earthshaking bumps and metallic scraping and screeching. The electricity required to operate the mechanical beast drained a good part of the village's reserves, and each time it was used the lights flickered in surrounding houses. In this way news of an arrival at Dr. Hoffmann's sanatorium was immediately broadcast to the village.

Since 1913 a private clinic specializing in treatments for diseases of the lungs, Sanatorium Hoffmann was not well regarded, medically speaking. It did, however, have a reputation for fine dining and privacy and was, with the exception of the dying patients, very much like the hotel it would soon become. Twelve large, sun-filled bedrooms offered private balconies with expansive views of the surrounding area. Geraniums brightened the window boxes along the wooden railing. Upstairs were smaller rooms for guests and family members, where Dora was able to stay. Beyond its beautiful bucolic setting, the sanatorium's greatest charm to Kafka was its low cost, only "between eleven and fifteen crowns per day."

Kafka's bedroom opened onto a south-facing balcony. From early morning until about two in the afternoon, the balcony was bathed in light. On the balcony, Kafka could lie outside, which was part of the prescribed treatment for tuberculosis, without going down to the communal sun-bathing room on the ground floor. From here he could view the garden below, with its neat rose beds cut into the green lawn. Beyond the rose garden stood a wall of pine and fir trees and the flower-bedecked valley, the Maydale, and the Kierlingsbach, the stream that runs through it. In the late afternoon, the sun's lengthened rays focused golden spotlights through the trees onto the hilly vineyards and beyond to the Wienerwald, the Vienna Woods.

The bedroom was simple and clean. The high ceiling and walls were white. In fact, everything (including all the furnishings) was white, except the floor, a terrazzo floor painted an ugly shade of yellow. They would simply have to focus their eyes upward.

KIERLING, EASTER SUNDAY, APRIL 20, 1924

Kafka wanted to be outside as much as possible. Having been bedridden or housebound since January, he wanted to feel the wind and breathe the fresh air, to experience the world coming to life in the spring. He even felt well enough to take a short walk into the village and enjoyed the excursion so much that he wanted to explore more of the surrounding areas. Dora located a horse and buggy for rent, and Kafka went for an afternoon ride, engrossed in the sights and smells of the countryside, the neighboring farms and forests. The next day, the weather turned cold again and Kafka's fever rose. He never left his room again.

On April 23, Dora wrote a card to Kafka's sister Elli, apologizing for not immediately answering the letter from her husband, Karl. "Felix Weltsch returned to Prague yesterday, so I know that he will tell you everything," Dora explained. "His throat is not troublesome and outwardly at least gives no cause for alarm. More disturbing is the stubborn fever, 101.5 F–102 F in the evening. Until noon almost free of fever. The main thing is that since yesterday the fever has made Franz very depressed."

Armed with letters of recommendation from Brod and Weltsch, Dora was planning to go to Vienna the next day to arrange for two doctors, top specialists in their fields, to urge them to come to Kierling to examine Kafka. "I am building my hopes very much on the two doctors," Dora reported. One specialized in the larynx and the other, the lungs. They were "dreadfully expensive," she said, but came highly recommended. The lung specialist, Dr. Oskar Beck, "is said to be almost a genius."

Dora and Kafka were desperately looking for a miracle and were running out of options. As she told Elli, "Unfortunately we had to discontinue with the nature-cure doctor, since the Sanatorium does not allow any unorthodox treatment from outside." Before closing, she asked a favor: "Is it possible to arrange at once that Franz gets the featherbed. Otherwise it's too cold to leave the windows open, which is absolutely necessary. In addition, that he gets all the newspapers. He has nothing to read and that makes him very grumpy." She signed the letter, "Yours, D. who loves you very much."

At the end of April, Kafka's parents asked Dora to keep them apprised of their son's condition. In a postcard she and Kafka wrote together, Dora began, "It is good that you have given me the task of writing to you. I'm very proud of that. Though it is a pity that it deprives you of your real joy. But that won't last long. Gradually Franz will take up all his duties. For the time being he is still weak, has a temperature sometimes during the day. The throat is unchanged. It impedes his speaking, but eating or otherwise, not too bad. Not a lot of coughing, either. If only the sun would come out at last! Then it would be so much faster and easier to get well. The sun will come out! Today the weather looks more peaceful than yesterday." She filled the card before she knew it. "Franz will grumble because I've left him so little room," she wrote, before handing the card to him.

Kafka wrote his note on the address side of the card: "Dearest Parents, the postal route to here seems to be very long, so the route from here must be too; don't let that disturb you. The treatment for the present—the fever prevents anything else—consists in lovely compresses and in inhalations. I am fending off arsenic injections. You should not imagine the fever as too bad; now, early in the morning, for instance, I have 98."

That weekend, Kafka wrote to Brod, thanking him for all his help and generosity. "My condition is bearable; for the present I can swallow again," he wrote. "Your two packages, especially the second, have given me the greatest pleasure, and the Reclam books seem virtually predestined for me." The slim Reclam volumes were nearly weightless and contained the gems of classic literature. "How good you are to me and how much I owe you these last weeks," he continued. "I am very weak, but very well taken care of here."

Kafka's medical care was limited at the clinic. Dr. Hoffmann himself was little or no help. He was, as Kafka admitted to his parents, "a sick old man who cannot devote much time to my affairs." The second doctor lived in Vienna, worked in Klosterneuberg, and only stopped by the clinic from time to time. With Franz Werfel and Felix Weltsch, as well as Max Brod, actively involved in arranging quality care for him, other, more highly regarded sanatoriums and clinics were still in discussion. Despite the worry over the inadequate medical care available at Dr. Hoffmann's, Kafka ended all arguments by telling Max: "I cannot travel now." He was reading Werfel's novel, he said, "with infinite slowness," too tired to read much: "Being closed is my eyes' natural state, but playing with books and magazines makes me happy." Kafka signed off: "Keep well, my good, dear Max."

Kafka's sisters and parents telephoned the sanatorium daily for updates, and Dora continued to send postcards as well. At the end of April she wrote, "It is really a shame that Franz's recovery is being delayed by the weather. As soon as these cold spells are completely over at last, I hope for the best from his stay here. The air is wonderful here, in spite of the boringly bad weather, you can really feel the way you are inhaling health. The food, too, leaves nothing to be desired, especially since it is permissible sometimes to prepare a meal yourself just the way you would like to have it."

Kafka's parents had begun to recognize Dora's importance to Franz and were grateful to her. Dora was equally grateful to them. "I hope to thank you personally and fully for the greetings and all the other kindness and love for me. The written word is too colorless. I hope you understand how happy it makes me."

En Route to Kierling, May 1, 1924

Dora scribbled the postcard on the train to Klosterneuberg. She wanted to send it before she saw Franz; she certainly didn't want him to know she had written it: "Not on your life must he ever know about it," Dora warned Elli. "I will start without any preamble. I need money. I'm on the way back from

Vienna, where I booked the doctor. He will be very expensive, but only once. After examining Franz, he will arrange everything necessary." She still had some money, she said, but feared an embarrassing situation if unforeseen difficulties arose. "I told Franz that we still have enough to live on for another five months. Otherwise, he would have blocked this and every undertaking." Dora was acting out of both fear and hope, she explained. "I expect a great deal from this doctor."

Two days later, Dora hung up the phone and looked up the stairs to the room where Kafka lay suffering. Now what could she do? She would never tell him what Dr. Beck had just said. She wanted another opinion. She thought of Robert Klopstock. Perhaps he could come?

In Vienna Dr. Beck, the renowned pulmonary specialist, replaced the receiver on its cradle. Dr. Beck was troubled by Dora's obstinacy, by her refusal to accept his and Prof. Dr. Neumann's expert advice. The young woman would not grasp the reality of Kafka's hopeless situation. It was Dr. Beck's professional responsibility, as he saw it, to inform Kafka's family of the situation, since the young woman was not Kafka's wife but only his companion. Her intentions were good, he realized, but she was not being logical. Dr. Beck addressed his report to Felix Weltsch:

> Yesterday I was called to Kierling by Miss Diamant. Dr. Kafka was having very sharp pains in the larynx, particularly when he coughed. When he tries to take some nourishment, the pains increase to such an extent that swallowing becomes almost impossible. I was able to confirm that there is a decaying tubercular action, which includes also a part of the epiglottis. In such a case an operation cannot even be thought of, and I have given the patient alcohol-injections in the *nervus laryngeus superior.*
>
> Today Miss Diamant rang me up again to tell me that the success of this treatment was only temporary and the pains had come back again with all their former intensity. I advised Miss Diamant to take Dr. Kafka to Prague, since Professor Neumann, too, estimated his expectation of life at about three months. Miss Diamant rejected this advice, as she thinks that through this the patient would come to realize the seriousness of his illness.

It is your duty to give his relations a full account of the seriousness of the situation. Psychologically I can quite understand that Miss Diamant, who is looking after the patient's interests in a self-sacrificing and touching fashion, feels she ought to call a number of specialists to Kierling for a consultation. I had, therefore, to make it clear to her that Dr. Kafka was in such a state, both with regard to his lungs and with regard to his larynx, that no specialist could help him any more, and the only thing one can do is to relieve pain by administering morphine or pantopon.

The next day Dora sat down to write another card to Elli. She dreaded it but had given her promise. Now what could she say? "Nothing is changed," she began. "Thanks to the injections he sleeps a bit. My only wish now is that he does not suffer. On the other hand, I am afraid that due to these remedies, nature will be deprived of its last possibilities. Medicine has no more to offer. But I am not entirely without hope. Franz must live. He carries the help within himself, and it—just like he—cannot possibly disappoint. Please, I will not write every day. I can't bear it. Have pity on me." She wanted to end on a more positive note, and so she added into the margin: "Yesterday we had a few happy hours. He wanted to have wine. I fetched it for him, and he drank it with a curious enjoyment peculiar to him, without having pain, and that was very gladdening." On front of the card, she added a final postscript: "Perhaps if Klopstock came, something could be achieved."

When Dora wrote to Kafka's mother, she did not mention Kafka's condition or the advice of the doctors. Instead, she talked about the weather, which, she said, "has changed for the better—touch wood. Franz lies outside on the balcony in sunshine and seems to sleep. If he doesn't wake up before I'm ready, he won't add a line this time." She thanked Julie for the parcels and the featherbed, which was of great use. "Every day we enjoy having it," Dora wrote. Franz still hadn't woken up by the time she finished the card. "In one way it's a pity, but really it is wonderful that he can sleep a little now and then." Dora thanked Julie for the greetings from the family and sent her "fervent regards" to them all. "Do I really deserve all this kindness and love?" she wondered.

That same day, Dora wrote to Ottla, pouring out her despair. Ottla had come for a quick visit to check on Franz at the end of April, and Dora had not written to her since. "Dear, beautiful Ottla," Dora began. "Sometimes I want Franz to get well, just to make you happy . . . but that is only sometimes. Mostly, I think of nothing. My ability to feel and think is frightfully impaired," she complained, begging Ottla not to blame her for the lapse in contact. "You are so good to me. I should think of you more, write more, call you. I can't, by God, I cannot. Not my fault. I don't know whose."

Dora rambled on about a better and happier time to come. "I am full of hope that it will come," Dora wrote. "In spite of everything. There are quite a few moments that allow hope." It was harder, she thought, for Ottla to understand, being so far away. "But when one is with him to witness all the individual moments of happiness, it is easier. You should have hope, too. Be—like I am—sure of a turn for the better, and then it'll happen more easily. How could it be otherwise? This is not prattle," Dora assured her. "It is just the unshakable conviction that the most Impossible of all Impossibles must give way to the Absolute Necessity. If only I could give you my heart, so full of hope and trust!"

To Dora's great relief, Robert Klopstock proved his love and loyalty, as Brod said, and dropped his studies (which would later lead to important medical advances in the treatment of the lungs) to devote himself entirely to Kafka's care. For the time being, he was staying in the guest room upstairs. "Klopstock's being here is favorable in every respect," Dora reported to Ottla. The family had financed Klopstock's journey from Prague, but they were saving money by having him there, Dora said. "Through him we save more, or as much as, we two (Klopstock and I) consume, in the medications which Franz needs urgently and which, until now, we had to get from the sanatorium. Since he is here, he orders the prescriptions himself and the night visits which, every time, had to be paid for separately!"

Again Dora had to ask for money. It was even "a little bit urgent," she said, but not yet an emergency. She had already paid for the coming week and had a little left over. "But it would be embarrassing to get into financial difficulties if some sudden expenditure would become necessary."

Robert took over the task of writing to Kafka's parents and sisters. His first letter was to Kafka's mother, written in his effusive style: "Dear Madam! My dear Madam! I thank you for your warm words and will report to you again." He told her about a new young doctor, Professor Tschiassny, who was coming out to the sanatorium to see Kafka. The physician was very encouraging, Klopstock said, and considered it a privilege to treat Franz. Robert agreed wholeheartedly: "It really is a privilege!" They'd managed to keep Kafka's temperature down for the past two days, which refreshed his mind and made him feel much better. In a card to Ottla, he reported that his earlier concerns about Kafka remaining in Vienna at the clinic under Hajek's care had evaporated in the healthy fresh air and countryside that "gives Franz so much joy and pleasure, which cannot be replaced."

Kafka's mother, Julie, wanted to visit her son, fearing that she would never see him again. "Nobody should come!" Dora had written to Elli at the beginning of the month. Klopstock, too, tried to dissuade anyone from coming after initially telling Julie that it would be all right. "Of course it would be terrible if his mother came here (every new person excites him so much . . .)." Instead, Kafka's uncle, Dr. Lowy, came to Kierling. The uncle disapproved of the sanatorium's medical care and wanted a more professional setting for his nephew. Dora was terrified that he might make Franz return to Prague or move to a stricter sanatorium. The three of them, Dora, Robert and Franz, were greatly relieved when the uncle departed, allowing Franz to remain at Kierling, at least for the time being.

When Robert wrote to Kafka's family, he wrote about Dora, too, of whom he was growing increasingly fond. His descriptions are grammatically odd and incorrect but capture the passionate exuberance he felt in Dora and Franz's company. After the uncle left, Robert commented on how wonderful it was to see Kafka more relaxed. On Sunday evening, after saying "Good night to the Franzs," he had retired to the guest room upstairs, where he sat at the table to write a letter to Ottla. He rhapsodized over the intense happiness he felt with them. "Dora was even more happily cheerful than usual," he said. "When he turns those lively, shining eyes on us, and both of them, Dora and he, jolly, happy, wonderful, God's Magnificence, those two, so together!"

In Klopstock's medical opinion, it was no longer a matter of deciding which treatment would lead to healing, but finding one that would alleviate the painful swallowing. After finishing his detailed report on two new specialists who would be coming from Vienna and the various possible treatment options, he added, "There should now be a chapter about Dora, of whom every day one, a new one could be written; she is a limitless source of wonder!"

No one knows for sure when Kafka actually proposed to Dora, but it was probably in the hopeful days at the end of April. In his excitement at her acceptance, Kafka decided he must write to her father in Bedzin to ask his permission. To Dora, it was unnecessary—the permission and, for that matter, the marriage. She had freed herself from such conventions, especially in regard to her father. Dora was not impressed with the necessity for a legal, bureaucratic document proving her undying love and commitment. In her heart, body and soul, she had become his wife months ago. But for Kafka, who wanted to do everything in the most impeccably correct manner, the request for permission from her father was a formality he could not ignore.

In his carefully crafted letter, Kafka declared his love for Dora and his desire to marry her. In asking Herschel's blessing for his daughter's hand in marriage, he pointed out that "although he was not a practicing Jew in her father's sense, he was nevertheless 'a repentant one, seeking to return,' and therefore might perhaps hope to be accepted into the family of such a pious man."

Franz's letter to her father was so respectful and eloquent that even Dora hoped it might succeed. Miracles happened, she knew, and perhaps her father could forgive her. It had been more than four years since she had seen or spoken to him or any member of her family. The last time she had seen her father, Herschel had threatened "to sit *shiva* for her, to tear his shirt and mourn her as dead" if she ran away again.

When Dora's father received the letter from Dr. Franz Kafka, currently living in a sanatorium near Vienna, where Dora was apparently living too, with a request for his wayward daughter's hand in marriage, Herschel the Pavianizer knew what must be done. He sent one of his sons, probably either Avram or Arje (they, like their father, were very religious), to Ger. Only the Gerer Rebbe could answer this impossible question. When the beloved Mordechai Alter read the letter from Kafka, the miracle-working rabbi uttered only one word: "No."

KIERLING, MAY 12, 1924

The letter from Dora's father arrived just moments before Max did. As Dora carried the envelope, addressed in her father's hand to Dr. Franz Kafka, up to Franz's room, the envelope assumed, with each step, the weight of an omen. When they opened the letter and read it, Franz was devastated. It didn't matter to him that her father's permission wasn't necessary. To him, it was another defeat, another failure to find acceptance from a father. Moments later, when the bell announced Max's arrival at the front door, Kafka put the letter away and tried to smile. After all, he had been eagerly looking forward to Max's visit for days.

The visit was predicated on a lie—the pretext that Max had business in Vienna. It would have upset Franz to know that he was making the journey from Prague just to see him. Brod's visit to Kierling was beset with strange omens from its outset. When he arrived at his *Prager Tagblatt* office on Saturday, someone yelled, "Telephone! Immediately! There's a woman just calling up from Vienna!" Brod dashed into the telephone booth and was surprised to hear Dora on the line from Kierling. "You rang me up," she said. "No," Max replied, "I've just arrived this moment." "Prague rang up," Dora insisted. "That's why I asked for you."

After they hung up, the mysterious connection haunted Max. "While it is true the *Prager Tagblatt* often rings up Vienna, it never rings up Kierling," he mused. "Further, none of Kafka's sisters had rung Kierling that day." Despite his best efforts, the affair of the strange telephone connection remained unexplained. It was the first of several coincidences that culminated eerily on June 11, the day of Kafka's funeral.

"In a remarkable fashion," Brod wrote in his biography, "the whole journey after that lay under the shadow of death." As Brod was leaving his home, he received sad news: "I was told that a young man in the flat below ours was lying on his death-bed." On the train, a woman dressed in black spoke to him as if she knew him. He was taken aback until he realized that she was the widow of a politician he knew. During the journey, the bereaved widow told him "all about her husband's death and her own unhappiness." Arriving in Vienna, Brod "spoke to no one, but went straight from the train station to the hotel."

Brod stayed all day at the sanatorium and returned to Vienna in the evening. When he arrived, Brod reported, "Franz had been quite fresh; despite all the doctors' testimony, his position didn't seem hopeless to me. We spoke of our next meeting; I was planning a journey to Italy which was to take in Vienna again."

Under doctors' orders, Kafka was not supposed to speak. He communicated largely through pantomime and gestures, and by means of short, hastily written messages. About one hundred of Kafka's notes were saved and later published as *Conversation Slips*. These slips testify to Kafka's sense of humor, appreciation of nature, and sensitivity toward others, which he maintained until the end, despite the agonizing pain he suffered. "Does my larynx hurt so much because for hours I have done nothing with it?" he asked at one point. "Tremendous amount of sputum easily, and still pain in the morning. In my daze it went through my head that for such quantities and the ease somehow the Nobel Prize."

The notes became a kind of game they played. Kafka often restricted his messages to a single sentence or fragment. "Dora and Klopstock would then try to guess at the rest, asking questions that Kafka would answer by shaking his head yes or no." Some notes revealed his sadness and fear: "How many years will you be able to stand it? How long will I be able to stand your standing it?" and "Of course, it causes me more pain because you all are so good to me."

Out of earshot from Kafka, Brod agreed with Dora and Klopstock that Franz should remain at Kierling. If he were sent back to Prague, Dora argued, he would lose hope, the essential ingredient for his recovery. Klopstock concurred: Even if a reason were concocted for the return to his parents' home, "no pretext would be so opaque that *his* gaze would not be able to penetrate it."

Brod was deeply touched by the love that surrounded Kafka: "These two, Dora and Dr. Klopstock, now referred to themselves playfully as Franz's 'little family'; it was an intimate living together in the face of death. Franz himself knew he was desperately ill, but was . . . full of hope and courage. He seemed to be unaware of the imminent danger."

The first thing they talked about was the letter from Dora's father, "which more or less formed the topic of the day for the 'little family,' as a bad omen." Dora told Max "the remarkable story of his wooing" about Franz's letter to her father and the refusal he had just received. "He smiled, and yet he was affected by it," Brod said. "We made efforts to put other thoughts into his head. But afterwards, Dora took me to one side and whispered to me that that night an owl had appeared at Franz's window." From early in her eastern European childhood, Dora knew the significance of the owl, which she now whispered to Max: "The bird of death."

Brod had known Kafka for over twenty years, through many different periods of their lives. As ill as he was, it seemed to Brod that Kafka was a new man. In the months since meeting Dora, Kafka's "whole existence took an unforeseen turn for the better, a new, happy, and positive turn, which did away with his self-hatred and nihilism." Now Kafka wanted to live. "Dora told me about how Franz cried for joy when Professor Tschiassny told him things looked a little better with this throat. He embraced her again and again, and said he had never wished for life and health so much as now."

Kafka's new vitality contrasted to a time four years earlier, on a journey he and Brod took together to Schelesen during his doomed engagement to

Julie Wohryzek. As the train stopped at a station along the way, Kafka intoned in "the deepest despair: 'How many stations there are on the journey to death, how slowly it passes!'" Now, at the end station of his life, Kafka not only wanted to live but, with Dora's help, "would have known how to live."

"They often joked together like children," Brod wrote. "I remember how they used to dip their hands together in the same wash-basin and call it our 'family bath.' Dora's care for the invalid was touching; touching too was the late wakening of all his vital energies. Franz wanted to live; he followed the doctor's instructions with an exactitude I had never observed in him before, and without protest. Had he gotten to know Dora sooner, his will to live would have become stronger sooner, and in time. That is my impression."

Throughout the month of May, Klopstock wrote to Kafka's sisters and parents about Franz's treatment, usually in hopeful and positive terms, only lightly mentioning the intestinal problems that cost Kafka whatever weight and strength he had gained earlier. Robert also wrote about Dora: "One must of course again and again talk of Dora, of whose extraordinariness one either does not talk at all or never-endingly. It is entirely due to Dora that Franz is now eating a great deal, and such nourishing food—she always improves the meals by adding something, eggs, etc.—and keeps at him until he has eaten everything. Now, for instance, he drinks beer with his meals (and wine, too, frequently), into which Dora smuggles Somatose without Franz's knowledge—of course he notices that the beer is not especially good, but he drinks it anyhow."

Four days later Robert wrote again to Julie, apologizing for the gap in the correspondence. Franz's condition had not changed noticeably, and there was not much to say. Yet "of Franz's eager, sparkling and cheerful intellect alone there is so much to tell that one could write the whole day about it." Kafka was drinking beer with his meals and "enjoying it so much that it is a pleasure to watch him," Robert said. He described the large amounts of food that Kafka was consuming, "everything that is put in front of him," and his intense enjoyment of the fruits and flowers Robert brought back with him from the city. "His joy makes even the way to Vienna a triumphal expedition: to fetch those cherries."

To Robert, Kafka seemed to enjoy life more than ever. "For instance the day before yesterday we had such a jolly evening, Franz made jokes, was lively, did not want to go to bed. Dora is very strict and at nine or nine-thirty, all is quiet and Franz is in bed to sleep."

A few days later, Robert admitted to Elli that he was worried about Franz's inability to consume enough nourishment. "The poor dear, he makes the utmost effort—but he cannot eat, not because of the throat, which is almost completely without pain, but because of the loss of appetite."

Dora did everything she could, but it wasn't enough. It was a constant battle to get Kafka to eat. She encouraged, she scolded, she teased, she pleaded. "You praise so arbitrarily when I've eaten enough; today I ate a great deal and you reproach me; another time you praise me just as unfairly," he complained in a note. At times it seemed she made things worse for him, forcing him to eat just a little bit more. "I'm only so sad because this insane trouble over eating is useless," he wrote. "I cannot keep up the present level of eating if this pain and coughing continue." Another time, he scribbled: "If it is true—and it seems probable—that the quantity of food I consume at present is insufficient for the body to mend of its own accord, then there's no hope, apart from miracles."

Dora firmly believed Kafka could survive this crisis. If only he could eat a little more. The great shining example was the Baroness Henriette Waldstaetten-Zipperer, a fellow patient at the sanatorium, whom all her doctors had considered terminal. But the young baroness believed in the power of food. She became famous for eating everything she could, allegedly once consuming an additional eight cucumber salads not eaten by other patients. Although she suffered from stomachaches, the baroness had reportedly gained over two pounds every day for the past month! Her prognosis was now excellent.

Franz was sleeping. Dora sat upstairs in the room with Robert, writing a letter to his parents, the first since Klopstock had joined them at the beginning of the month. "I do have a guilty conscience," Dora wrote. "That the kind-hearted Klopstock writes makes it even more guilty, but on the other hand also soothes it. Also there is not much to report. Everything would be much more reassuring and convincing if you could see for yourself how well Franz is being taken care of. From seven in the morning to seven or eight in the evening he lies on the balcony. The sun shines until two p.m., then it moves on to other patients on the other side, and in its place, slowly rising out of the depths comes a wonderfully intoxicating fragrance that acts like a balm. By the evening it has reached an incredible, almost unbearable, intensity. The view and the sounds all around provide eye and

ear with lungs and breathing organs. All the senses turn into breathing organs, and all together breathe in the healing, the blessing, which is spread
abundantly all around. It is a shame that I am not able to describe it to you
more beautifully. As it really is. Through the uncle, Ottla and Max, who is
more gifted, you will get the right impression. And since the fight against
the disease is solely dependent on this, we must believe and be certain of
its success."

She heard her name called for lunch and hoped she wouldn't have to
wake Franz. She would write more, she said, but Klopstock told her he
had already written to the family about Kafka's medical status. Dora was
deeply thankful for Robert: "What a wonderful person he is!" she added.
Before signing off, she wrote, "Your relationship with me in the letters
makes me happy. I don't know that I deserve it. I will try hard to. Many,
many heart-felt greetings. May I, in your warm and cordial manner, also
extend my arms for an embrace? How good that feels! Again most sincerely, Dora."

On May 26, Dora wrote her last card to Franz's parents. In an express
letter that had arrived one week earlier, Julie said that she wanted to come
to Kierling to see Franz, as did Kafka's father, who said he would enjoy
drinking a beer with his son. "What an exchange of joys that was! If only it
were always that way," Dora began. "The card brought no less joy than the
express letter. Franz almost learned it by heart. He is especially proud of
the possibility of drinking glass of beer with his revered and dear father,"
Dora said. "I would like to stand at a distance and look on," she added,
more truthfully. "Often I am almost drunk just from the frequent conversations about beer, wine (water) and other nice things. Franz has become a
passionate drinker. Hardly a meal without beer or wine. However not in
too great quantities. He drinks a bottle of Tokay a week or other good
gourmet wines. We have three kinds of wine available, so that we can have
plenty of variety in proper gourmet fashion."

Realizing how much she had gone on about drinking, Dora apologized:
"Please don't hold it against me that I've taken up so much space with
such nonsense: I'm infected by Franz. If you want to give him again a great
deal of pleasure, then tell him stories of outings, walks and drinking bouts.
We've had to create a special place for the flowers and plants, and often
spend many happy hours with them."

A few days later, Kafka could no longer swallow without choking. The
injections and the Pyramidon, intended to ease Kafka's endless burning in
his throat, were not helping. Nevertheless, Kafka found a way through to

pleasure: "The trouble is that I cannot drink a single glass of water, though the craving itself is some satisfaction," Kafka observed in one of his notes.

Kafka's conversation slips reveal the enjoyment he savored despite the pain during the last weeks and days of his life. More than two dozen of the slips refer to flowers and nature, and water and drinking. He often urged others to take long drinks of water and beer while he watched. He wanted Dora to offer wine to the doctors and nurses. "That is a pleasure, to give someone something that gives him pleasure certainly and honestly at the moment you give it to him," he noted. The nurse who tended Kafka during his last weeks was often offered a glass of wine, and she never forgot how happily he smiled when she accepted and drank it. "It is as if I were drinking it," he told her.

The thirst became unbearable. "To think I could once simply venture a large swallow of water," he wrote. On one piece of paper, he wrote with regret: "Why didn't I once try beer in the hospital?" and "Lemonade. It was all so boundless." Kafka reminded Robert of his last visit to his parents' home, in an attempt to slake his terrible thirst by the written word: "How easy it was, and yet I didn't even have beer, just preserves, fruits, fruit juice, water, fruit juice, fruit, preserves, water, fruit juice, fruit preserves, water, lemonade, cider, fruit, water."

More than ever before, Kafka luxuriated in the sensual delights of smell, sight and sound. "Sensual like an animal—or like a child," Dora later wrote of him. "Where on earth does the supposition of Kafka as an ascetic come from?" He noticed and appreciated everything. "A bird was in the room," he wrote on one note. "And that is why one loves dragonflies," on another.

His preoccupation with flowers permeated his notes: "See the lilacs, fresher than the morning"; "somewhere in today's newspapers there is an excellent little item on the treatment of cut flowers; they are so terribly thirsty"; "do you have a moment? Then please lightly spray the peonies"; "show me the columbine; too bright to stand with the others. Scarlet hawthorn is too hidden, too much in the dark"; "and move the lilac into the sun"; "how wonderful that is, isn't it? The lilac—dying, it drinks, goes on swilling. That cannot be, that a dying man drinks."

At the end of May the page proofs for *A Hunger Artist* finally arrived from his publisher, Die Schmiede. According to Brod, Kafka "gave orders for changing the order of the stories, showed some temper with the publisher, who had not paid sufficient care to this or that instruction." The task in front of him, considering his weakness, was overwhelming. "They have waited so long to send me the material," Kafka complained in a note. "Here now, with what strength I have am I to write it?" Nevertheless, Kafka began correcting the first of the four stories, "First Sorrow," about a temperamental trapeze artist, written two years earlier. He was exhausted, "with every limb as tired as a person," but continued to work on the galleys, a few pages each day. The effort required so much that "he sometimes cried afterwards."

At the end of her own life, it was still inconceivable to Dora how good, decent people like Dr. Hoffmann and his wife could act as they had, could do what they had done to her and Franz. The fact that Dora and Kafka were unmarried disturbed the decorum of Dr. Hoffmann's sanatorium. That a wedding was purely a private matter between Dora and Franz, or that Dora's father had refused permission for her to marry Kafka meant little or nothing to Dr. Hoffmann and his staff.

"When the doctors let it be known that Franz was dying, the people in the sanatorium started to pester me to get married," Dora recorded in her diary, recalling the painful experience. "Dr. Hoffmann and his assistant were especially busy with this. They wanted to arrange everything necessary themselves: registrars, the rabbi, etc. Every day for weeks I had to listen to this." Dora ignored them until the pestering culminated one terrible afternoon shortly before Kafka died.

"I was called to the office of Dr. Hoffmann, where I saw a man unknown to me. He was an official from the Vienna Jewish community, who wanted to perform the ceremony. Dr. Hoffmann and his wife were to be the witnesses. It was one of the most horrible moments of my life, to have the most Unimaginable hammered into my head with such cruelty: a life after Franz's death. Robert was notified. Ottla was weakly and awkwardly encouraging," but the worse of it, Dora thought, was "the cruelty towards Franz, who clung so to the hope to live. No doubt they all acted in good faith," Dora conceded, but Dr. Hoffmann and the others had failed in their "most obvious duty in humanity—not to deprive the dying man of his last happy hours, of his hope."

KIERLING, MONDAY, JUNE 2, 1924

On the last full day of his life, Kafka was feeling much better. In the morning he worked on the galley proofs for *A Hunger Artist*. When Robert returned from Vienna that evening laden with fresh cherries and strawberries, "Franz was feeling very well," Brod reported in his biography. "He was jolly, showed great pleasure in everything that Klopstock had brought back from the city with him, ate strawberries and cherries, smelled them for a very long time, enjoyed their fragrance with the double intensity with which he enjoyed everything those last days."

That day, Kafka began his last letter to his parents. The little family agreed that only Franz could persuade them not to come. "Dearest Parents," Kafka wrote, getting right to the point: "Now about the visits you refer to every so often. I have been considering the matter every day, for it is very important to me. It would be so nice; we have not been together for such a long time. I don't count my stay with you in Prague; that just introduced confusion into the household. Rather, I mean spending a few days together peacefully in a beautiful place, alone."

Franz addressed the issue of sharing a glass of good beer, "from which I see that Father doesn't think much of this year's wine, and I'll agree with him there, as far as the beer is concerned." He blamed his weakness on the "shock of the larynx business," the fever and an intestinal ailment that he had been unable to shake off. "You must not think that you could do anything to improve or amplify my treatment here," he insisted. "Only now am I beginning to work my way out of all these weakening factors, with the aid of Dora and Robert—from a distance you cannot possibly imagine what a great help they are (what would I be without them)."

With utmost tact and love, Kafka asked his parents not to come. "In spite of my wonderful helpers, in spite of good air and food, and almost daily sunbathing in fresh air, I still have not properly recovered, in fact, am not even so fit as I was recently in Prague. If you also count in the fact that I am allowed to speak only in whispers, and that not too often, you will gladly postpone the visit. Everything is at the best of beginnings," Kafka said. "But the best beginnings don't amount to much if I cannot show visitors—and what is more, such visitors as you two would be—major, undeniable progress, progress that can be recognized by the lay eye, it's better to leave it. Well, then, shall we not leave it for the moment, dear Father and Mother."

Kafka wrote a few sentences before stopping, too exhausted to continue, with the letter still unfinished. "I took the letter from his hand," Dora wrote as a postscript at the bottom of the letter. "It was already an achievement. Only a few lines, but what he is asking seems very important." At midnight, Franz fell asleep. Through the first early hours of June 3, Dora stayed beside Franz's bedside, dozing occasionally, watching the slow rise and fall of his thin chest, the noble profile, the deep set eyes, now closed.

At four o'clock in the morning, Dora left Franz alone for a moment to run upstairs and wake Robert. "Franz is breathing badly," she said, and ran back while Robert quickly dressed. Robert took one look at Kafka and immediately "recognized the danger." He woke up the resident doctor, who administered a camphor injection. It didn't help. "And so the help goes away without helping," Kafka had once written. After the doctor left, Dora stayed at Franz's side, comforting him as best she could. On one of his last conversation slips, Franz wrote: "Place your hand on my forehead to give me courage."

Dora usually left the room when Kafka received injections. They were terribly painful, and he didn't want her to see. There was something else that Franz didn't want her to witness, and he now asked Robert to fulfill the secret agreement they had made to make sure she was spared. Shortly before noon, after he had given Kafka another failed injection, Robert asked Dora to go to the post office. Kafka wanted the letter to his parents mailed in the morning post. Dora didn't want to leave with Franz in his condition. But Robert convinced her to go. The nurse was applying a new ice pack, and Robert was right there. Reluctantly, Dora left to run the errand.

According to Max Brod's account, the fight for morphine had begun. Kafka roughly dismissed the nurse, Robert said, "so brusque as he never was ordinarily," and "with all his strength he tore off his ice pack and threw it on the floor."

"Don't torture me any more," Kafka cried, begging for the drug. "Why prolong the agony. . . . You have always been promising it to me for four years," he accused Robert. "You are torturing me. I am not talking to you any more. I shall die like that." Robert gave him two injections, but it wasn't enough. "Don't cheat me, you are giving me an antidote," Kafka whispered hoarsely. "Kill me, or else you are a murderer."

Robert gave him another injection, and Kafka was happy for a moment. "That's good, but more, more, it isn't helping me." As Robert moved away from the bed to clean the syringe, Franz said, "Don't leave me." "But I am not leaving you," Robert answered. "But I am leaving you," Franz replied in a deep voice. A few moments later, as Robert held Kafka's head, Franz hallucinated and thought Robert was his sister. "Go away, Elli, not so near, not so near," Franz whispered. He was always afraid that he would infect someone. Robert moved back and Kafka sighed, "Yes, like that—it's all right like that."

According to every Kafka biography since Max Brod's, those were Franz Kafka's last words before he slipped into unconsciousness and died. The story of his life always ends there, without any mention of Dora's presence during his final moments. The full account of Kafka's death has never been published in English, although it has been printed twice in Germany: first in a Berlin newspaper article and then forty years later in 1996, when it was included in a compendium of memories of those who knew Kafka, edited and published by two of Germany's foremost Kafka scholars. The original article, "FK's Death: The Last Days," written by Willy Haas, a journalist and acquaintance of Kafka's, first appeared in *Der Tagesspiegel* on November 25, 1953.

"In the event of his death, Kafka had made several arrangements," Haas wrote. "One that is known is the one with Dr. Klopstock, who, when there was no more hope, was to hasten a quick end with an injection. It seems that Kafka in a weak moment had also given his companion Dora permission to die with him. Nothing of this was done; but apparently the loyal Klopstock did fulfill a third secret arrangement, that he would send Dora away in the last hour under a pretext so that she would not see his death throes. This Klopstock did, sending Dora out to post a letter."

Willy Haas received his information from "Sister Anna," the nurse who attended Kafka at the sanatorium in Kierling and "the person who had the sad duty of closing the dead man's eyes." According to Nurse Anna, as the morphine took effect and he drifted off to sleep, Kafka awoke suddenly and missed Dora. "I sent the chambermaid after her," said the nurse, "for the post office was nearby." The nurse was afraid that it was already too late.

Sister Anna was seventy-three years old when she told her story to Willy Haas. Almost twenty years had passed since the events she described, but they—and Kafka—were indelibly stamped in her memory: "About the writer Franz Kafka, I cannot judge," she said, "but as a human being he is the only patient who remained unforgettable for me and whose death, as simply as it happened, was so shattering that all of us who stood by his bed were moved to tears."

When Dora rushed into Kafka's room, out of breath, her arms full of fresh flowers she had just bought, "Kafka seemed to be completely unconscious. Dora held the flowers up to his face: 'Franz, look at the beautiful flowers, just smell!' whispered Dora." As the nurse watched in amazement, "the dying man raised himself up once more, though he had already seemed to be in the world beyond, and he sniffed the flowers. It was incredible. And even more incredible was that his left eye opened again and appeared alive. He had such wonderfully radiant eyes and his smile was so full of meaning, and his hands and eyes were eloquent when he could no longer speak."

Dora held him as he drifted off. She felt his heart slow and then stop its faint beating, and felt the last breath leave his emaciated body. Kafka's agony had ended, and hers had begun.

9

FUNERAL IN PRAGUE

Prague doesn't let go. This old crone has claws.
—Franz Kafka, *Letters*

KIERLING, AUSTRIA, JUNE 3, 1924

"The death of Franz was the experience of my own death," Dora wrote many years later, as she lay on her own deathbed in an East London hospital. When Kafka left his body, Dora left hers, too. She ceased to exist. Then suddenly, with an agonizing shock, she was yanked back into the impossible reality of a world without Kafka.

The nurse placed her hand on Franz's eyes, closing them forever. Dora clung to him, unable and unwilling to grasp the truth. It wasn't possible that Franz was dead. There were muted voices, then silence when the door closed. Dora was alone with him. The noble profile, devoid of life, seemed cut in stone, his thick black hair disheveled from the thrashing of his head, before the drug had released him. Franz would never want to be seen like this. He was always so careful with his appearance, unwilling to offend anyone with so much as a badly knotted tie.

Dora opened the drawer of the dressing table and took out Kafka's hairbrush. It was a men's military-style brush, a good, expensive one made by GB Kent & Sons of England. The golden bristles glistened, the light-colored wood shiny and smooth in the palm of her hand. Along the edges on both sides, the bristles had broken down from the pressure of the heel of his hand. He had the brush for years and "never went anywhere without it." He had brought it with him to Berlin, then to the first sanatorium in the Vienna Woods, and to the clinic in Vienna, and finally, here, to Kierling. Franz would have had it Müritz, too, eleven months, a lifetime ago.

Dora brushed Kafka's dark hair away from the hollow temples, away from his forehead, forever free of its fever, and smoothed it over his skull. There would be no *Hevra Kaddisha*, no holy burial society members to take custody of the body, to perform the ritual washing and cleansing, to wrap his corpse in a shroud and cover it with his prayer shawl. She didn't have the ritual silver implements used to comb his hair with egg and vinegar and to clean his fingernails, but Dora knew what needed to be done to prepare the body for burial.

It was a Judaic principle: reverence must be paid to the corpse, commensurate to the soul it once housed. It is one of the most important mitzvoth because the recipient cannot express gratitude for it. Dora filled the pitcher with water and rung out a cloth. She washed him, gently, tenderly. She had no white shroud, no *kittel* in which to wrap him. She wanted to do things correctly, precisely the way Franz would want her to. Sometime later the door opened. Someone entered, and she felt arms lift her from the bed. The men were here to take Franz down to the mortuary. It was time, Robert said. Dora had to let Franz go. Robert promised they would visit him later, if she would lie down for a while. She must rest.

Dora had not slept. She'd been channeling all her energy and resources, drawing from the depths of her being, willing Kafka to live. Now there was nothing left. Only a deep abyss of blackness, of emptiness. She had nothing to do, so she agreed to lie down.

Robert stayed with her as she drifted into a restless, fitful sleep. He had already sent the telegrams and made telephone calls to Prague. Max had called at noon, after it was too late, and had broken the news to Kafka's parents. Even as she slept, Dora continued to whimper endearments to Franz. Robert could only make out a few of the words she repeated incessantly, "My dearest, my love, my good one. . . ."

Dora awoke and demanded to see Franz again. As he promised, Robert took her down to the mortuary. It was worse to see him there. "Alone in the dark, uncovered," Dora sobbed at the sight of him. "O my God! My love, my good one. . . ." But leaving him there, alone in the dark mortuary, was even more terrible. Back in her room, she continued to whimper, whispering to her Franz, her love, "who is alone, so quite alone. We have nothing to do, and sit here and leave him there alone in the dark, uncovered—O my God! My love. . . ."

Robert did what he could, but there was nothing to do. Dora was inconsolable.

KIERLING, JUNE 4, 1924

The first of two telegrams sent from Kafka's father to Kierling announced that Elli's husband and her uncle, Dr. Lowy, would arrive the next morning to make the funeral arrangements. This was Dora's greatest fear. The uncle was taking Franz away from her. Again. It didn't matter that Franz was no longer alive, no longer hers. Dora couldn't think, she said later, she could only feel.

These were difficult hours for Robert, too. He watched unhappily as Dr. Lowy took over the arrangements with a cool, detached professionalism. There was to be no ritual hocus-pocus over the body of his nephew. The deceased would wear the black suit brought from Prague. Robert was devastated by Dr. Lowy's brusqueness toward Dora. Robert felt that Dr. Lowy offhandedly disbanded what was left of the little family, dismissing Robert and Dora to get on with their own lives.

"Poor Dora," Robert wrote in a letter that afternoon to Elli, "oh we are all so poor, who is so utterly poor in the world as we." In his flowery, awkward German (his third language), Robert sought Elli's sympathy while offering her his condolences: "What is happening here with us—I say always so 'us,' we called ourselves, you see, 'Franz's little family,' is indescribable, and should never be described. Who knows Dora, only he can know what love means. So few understand it, and that increases pain and suffering. But you, won't you, you will understand it!"

Even Robert, with his medical knowledge and experience, who had known what was coming, was utterly devastated. "We still don't know what has happened to us, but slowly, slowly it will get clearer and clearer, and more painfully dark at the same time. Particularly *we* don't know it, who have him still with us. Now we are going there again to Franz. So still, so severe, so unapproachable is his face, as his soul was pure and severe. A king's face from the oldest and noblest stock. The gentleness of his human existence has gone, only his incomparable soul still forms his still, dear face. So beautiful is it as an old marble bust."

The next morning, June 4, a second telegram from Kafka's father arrived, ending any debate about what to do with Franz's body. "Dora's wish decisive." The telegram was signed, "Kafka."

In the unbearable emptiness of Kafka's room at the Sanatorium Hoffman, the epicenter of Dora's life for seven weeks, Robert and Dora gathered together Franz's belongings. Robert collected the conversation slips that Kafka had written during the last weeks. Dora folded Kafka's long white sleeping gown and, along with his personal effects, including his hairbrush, pen and notebooks, put it in her battered suitcase. After their last visit to the mortuary, Kafka's body was placed in a coffin and taken to the depot for the train to Prague. Franz's funeral was scheduled to take place one week later, on Wednesday, June 11, at four o'clock in the afternoon.

PRAGUE, JUNE 1924

Dora dissolved into her sorrow. Someone, Robert, or perhaps Karl, helped her get on the train to Prague. In a haze, she arrived in the city of Kafka's birth, the majestic city of towers, spires and bridges, the city from which he had escaped for those few months with her. The city, Kafka's old crone with claws, was claiming him again, swallowing him within herself. At the Kafka house, she recognized the beloved faces of Elli and Ottla. When she was introduced to Kafka's mother, Dora sobbed in her arms. Julie's heart, touched by Dora's grief, went out to her. Kafka's father stayed back. The outpouring of emotion embarrassed him as undignified.

According to Kafka biographer Peter Mailloux, obituaries appeared in all the German-language newspapers in Prague, written by Kafka's closest friends. Brod published his emotional eulogy in the *Prager Presse* and an obituary by Oskar Baum. Felix Weltsch, editor of the Zionist weekly *Selbstwehr*, dedicated a whole page to him. The *Communist Review* extolled Kafka as a writer who "saw deeply into present-day social injustice . . . and in obscure but penetrating language, mercilessly condemned the rich." Three other Czech-language newspapers published obituaries in the days following Kafka's death, "although one of these misspelled his name (turning him into Franz Kavka) and another was so perfunctory as to be negligible." The following was written by Milena Jensenska, Kafka's Czech translator who lived in Vienna, the married woman Kafka loved before he met Dora. This obituary, published in the *Narody Listy* on June 5, 1924, revealed the love and admiration Milena still felt for her former lover:

Dr. Franz Kafka, a German writer who lived in Prague, died the day before yesterday in the Kierling Sanatorium at Klosterneuberg near Vienna. Few knew him, for he was a loner, a recluse wise in the ways of the world and frightened by it. For years he had been suffering from a lung disease, which he cherished and fostered even while accepting treatment. . . . It endowed him with a delicacy of feeling that bordered

on the miraculous, and with a spiritual purity uncompromising to the
point of horror. . . . He was timid, fearful, gentle and kind, but
the books he wrote were terrible and painful. He saw the world full of
invisible demons preying on defenseless humanity. . . . His knowledge
of the world was exceptional and profound, and he was a deep and
profound world in himself. He wrote the most significant works of
modern German literature; their stark truth makes them seem natura-
listic even where they speak in symbols. They reflect the irony and
prophetic vision of a man condemned to see the world with such blind-
ing clarity that he found it unbearable and went to his death.

The day before the funeral, Kafka's parents, on behalf of the bereaved
family, placed notices in the newspapers, in German and in Czech, announcing the death and funeral of their son, JUDr. Franz Kafka. At the
bottom of the announcement, bordered in black, was the request for no
visits of condolence.

The morning of kafka's funeral dawned sunny and warm, a pleasant late
spring morning in Prague. The political climate was bright as well. After
five years of independence under the leadership of Thomas Masaryk,
Czechoslovakia was established as a new democratic nation, and was the
historic capital city of Prague basked "in a summer's light and an acceler-
ating vacation mood."

But "for the German literary artists and writers of Prague, particularly
the German Jews of this city, 11 June was sad and painful," wrote Johannes
Urzidil. An acquaintance of Kafka's who worked at the Germany embassy in
Prague, Urzidil was twenty-nine years old, a poet and essayist who wrote on
culture and politics. His wife's family had been Kafka's neighbors and her
brother, Friedrich Thieberger, had been one of Kafka's Hebrew teachers.

Urzidil was one of the younger generation of Prague's circle of German
writers, who looked on Kafka and his friends Brod, Werfel, Weltsch and
Baum as literary gods. Kafka especially was revered among the young literary artists of Prague, and "his death now tore the capstone out of this congregation, broke its arch." Although he was less famous and successful
than his friends, Kafka was the most loved and respected. "His death
struck his family, his friends and acquaintances like a bolt of lighting,"
Urzidil said, "and seemed incredible though most of them had known for
a long time that his death was imminent. But all of us—including the literary artists among us, who from youth had reflected on and poetized
death—were not up to its direct actuality within our circle."

Kafka's propensity for friendship spread throughout his milieu, altering the relationships of those who knew him and causing new friendships to be formed in his name. "I am convinced that no one could have known him personally without loving him. Moreover, all those who loved Kafka also loved his friends, for his sake," Urzidil wrote more than twenty years later, a respected professor living in New York. In this way, he said, Kafka "created an invisible bond between all who felt they were in his everlasting presence, and that by virtue of his living and doing they had become associated with something higher and better and thus were personally enhanced and sanctioned."

Urzidil believed that this "strengthening and affirming power had issued from Kafka. Would it now suddenly cease to exist? . . . We knew who it was that daily walked through our day in the old lanes, who it was we greeted across the streetcar tracks—indeed, a simple return greeting had the effect of a special event—or who it was with whom we walked here or there past a few houses or sat down somewhere for an hour over a cup of coffee."

But nobody could explain Kafka, Urzidil pointed out. Of all his friends who gathered together in Prague for his funeral or for the memorial service eight days later, none could find words to adequately express who Kafka was as a man. Not Max Brod, "the clarifier and eternal stimulator," not the "philosophical" Felix Weltsch, nor "the idealistic religious scholar" Hugo Bergmann, nor Oskar Baum, blinded since boyhood but "able to peer insightfully into the rays of the soul," could account for Kafka's ability to penetrate to the truth with every sentence, every casual word, "down deeply to the very center of the earth. How it happened that Kafka said what he said; how it happened that he said it the way he said it; how it happened that one never came into conflict with what he said or with him himself, that no one could explain."

Franz Werfel had once remarked to Urzidil, "I would love Kafka so much more, if he were not so nihilistic." Urzidil was nonplused. "Seldom has a judgment as wrong as that one been expressed, though it did sound plausible coming from Werfel," he said. All of us loved the genius of Werfel's affirmation of the world and his approval of life, for after all we all wanted the world and life. Kafka also wanted them. Indeed, no one fought as hard and as despairingly as he did in their behalf. . . . Kafka was that kind of devotee," Urzidil concluded, "not a nihilist."

By four in the afternoon, the scheduled hour of Kafka's funeral, the pleasant day had grown overcast and cold. A crowd of about one hundred mourners "rode or walked, each in his own way, to the Jewish cemetery of Strasnice, a suburb on Prague's periphery." Urzidil described the day in an essay entitled "11 June 1924." Urzidil "walked in the cortege escorting Kafka's coffin from the ceremonial hall to the open grave behind the family and Kafka's pale lady-companion, beloved Dora Dymant, supported by Max Brod."

They arrived at Kafka's grave on the outer edge of the cemetery, near the last of the large wrought-iron gates. The mourners gathered around the graveside, a sea of black veils and top hats. All week, Dora had been "the saddest of the sad," Urzidil reported, obsessively repeating endearments to him who could no longer hear her.

As Kafka's casket was lowered into the earth, Urzidil reported, Dora "let out a penetrating and painful cry" and collapsed on the ground next to the grave. "Her sobbing," he said, "died away in the echo of the Hebrew prayer for the dead." After Kaddish was recited, Franz's family and friends, one by one, stepped forward to the edge of the open grave and cast earth onto the coffin. Forty years later, Urzidil could still "recall this earth, exactly. It was light colored, lumpy, claylike, permeated with little stones and pebbles, which rumbled onto the box."

Hans Demetz, a poet and playwright who arranged the memorial, was one of those who had seen Dora collapse on Kafka's grave. "She fainted," he reported, "but no one moved. On the contrary, Kafka's father turned his back, which stirred the mourners into motion. I don't remember who took care of the girl who'd broken down. I still feel ashamed that I did nothing to help the poor girl."

Urzidil and his wife walked away from the grave on the gravel path between the wall of the cemetery and the rows of graves lined with cypress trees. "Not a word was spoken," he remembered. The weather reflected the gloomy atmosphere until "finally, the darkened sky even gave forth rain."

The strange portents that preceded Kafka's death culminated that afternoon, after the funeral. "When we got back to the house of mourning in Franz's home in the Old Town Square," Brod reported in his biography, "we saw that the great clock on the Town Hall had stopped at four o'clock, and its hands were still pointing to that hour."

10

IN MEMORIAM

The real, independent life of the books begins
only after the death of the writer.
—Franz Kafka, *Letters to Milena*

PRAGUE, JUNE 19, 1924

Eight days after Kafka's funeral, Urzidil reported, at eleven in the morning, a memorial service was held at the Kleine Bühne (Little Theater), the German-language performance hall in Prague. More than five hundred people came to honor Kafka's memory with speeches, eulogies and a reading of his works by a professional actor from the Prague German Theater. The grandiose words used to describe Kafka's writings and his importance to the future of German literature left Dora with a bitter taste. Dora didn't love Kafka as a writer but as a man, as a human being. Kafka had never spoken to her about his earlier writings, and she had not asked. Why should she? Dora believed what Kafka had told her, that his writings were not finished pieces but, in most cases, merely failed experiments.

The text of Max Brod's "great eulogy" has been lost, but those present in the crowded hall heard him speak "of an approaching Kafka-era." Brod firmly believed that future generations would recognize Kafka as a great literary artist whose attitude "cheers up slaves and horrifies foreign despots." He was one of the "great prophets," Brod asserted, in whom "the splendor of the Shekina shone, the presence of God among men." Dora recognized Max's reference to the "dazzling, radiant, shining presence of the Lord himself." Moses had seen the Shekina in the burning bush, and again in the rays on Mount Sinai when the Ten Commandments were given to the children of Israel.

The final words of the memorial service were Kafka's own from his previously published stories. A well-known Prague actor, Hans Hellmuth Koch, stepped on the stage, holding two slim volumes of Kafka stories. As the first, "A Dream," was read, Dora heard echoes of Kafka's unmistakable voice. "Josef K. was dreaming," the actor began. "It was a beautiful day and K. felt like going for a walk. But hardly had he taken a couple of steps when he was already at the cemetery." The story ended as the hero, K., sank involuntarily into his grave and "was already being received into impenetrable depths," before he woke up, "enchanted by the sight" of his own name written with great flourishes on his tombstone. The second story, "An Imperial Message," written seven years earlier in the magical house on Alchemist's Street, touched Dora deeply, and she would ponder its meanings until the end of her days.

"The Emperor from his deathbed has sent a message to you alone," Kafka's parable began. The messenger, "a powerful, an indefatigable man" to whom the emperor entrusted this momentous communication, immediately set out on his journey to deliver the message. But the messenger faces an impossible task, encountering an endless number of obstacles:

> Still he is only making his way through the chambers of the innermost palace; never will he get to the end of them; and if he succeeded in that nothing would be gained; he must next fight his way down the stairs; and if he succeeded in that nothing would be gained; the courts would still have to be crossed; and after the courts the second outer palace; and once more stairs and courts; an once more another palace; and so on for thousands of years; and if at last he should burst through the outermost gate—but never, never can that happen—the imperial capital would lie before him, the center of the world, crammed to bursting with its own sediment. Nobody could fight his way though here even with a message from a dead man. But you sit at your window when evening falls and dream it to yourself.

The next day, a Prague newspaper reported on Kafka's memorial service and noted that the actor Hans Hellmuth Koch concluded his performance of Kafka's writings "in whispers as a result of overwhelming emotion."

PRAGUE, JULY 3, 1924

It was Kafka's forty-first birthday, or would have been. Instead of the happy celebration Dora had imagined for him, July 3 marked the one-month anniversary of his death. Dora's grief was not dissipating with time, as everyone promised it would. It was worse. In the days and weeks following the funeral, Dora entered an emotional torpor, "too deeply hurt to fully realize what had happened." She grew pale, her face drawn and thin.

Unable to break her connection to Franz, Dora stayed "in the home of Kafka's parents, in the most affectionate care of his mother." Kafka's fears for Dora's shabby treatment at the hands of his parents were proven groundless. Dora later said she felt welcomed into their home. Julie Kafka opened her arms to the young woman who had selflessly devoted herself to her dying son. Dora said that Kafka's mother "was a lovely woman, infinitely kind to me."

The only activity that gave Dora solace was talking about Franz. There was no other subject for her. She spent long hours in conversation with Franz's parents, which Dora believed helped "console them on the death of their beloved and ever problematic son."

At first Dora was unable to make any decisions. Going back to Berlin seemed impossible for several reasons. On a practical level, her German residence permit had expired. Urzidil, Kafka's friend from the German embassy in Prague, had promised to help her get a new one, but Dora couldn't bear the thought of returning without Kafka. Yet Prague was full of ghosts for her. The city of a hundred spires and dark, twisted alleys seemed eerie and strange. The nightmares and regrets that once haunted Kafka began to attach themselves to her.

PRAGUE, MID-JULY 1924

Days after Kafka's death, Max Brod made a discovery that led to the greatest ethical dilemma of his professional life. His decision would alter not only his own future but the course of literary history. After the funeral, at the request of the family, Brod went through Kafka's desk in his room at his parents' home on the Old Town Square. In the midst of mourning his closest and dearest friend, Brod was overjoyed to find "a mass of papers," which he described as about one hundred aphorisms on spiritual subjects, an autobiographical sketch, a sketchbook with line drawings and several stories, some finished, some almost completed. There was also "an incomplete beast-tale." This treasure was Brod's consolation.

Already Brod had decided to publish everything Kafka had written. By orchestrating the posthumous publication of Kafka's work, Max would give his friend an extended life, a literary life after death. Only a few of Kafka's writings had appeared in print while he was still alive, and those only through the force of Brod's will. The complete body of Kafka's literary writings, which Brod estimated would fill four volumes, included three unpublished novels and dozens of short stories, parables, and incomplete fragments in his notebooks. Brod believed that these novels, although unfinished, constituted "the most wonderful treasures, and measured against his own work, the best things he has written." Their publication would ensure Kafka's legacy in German literature, Brod said, for "his specialized mastery of the short story," and would grant him a place in literature as "a great epic writer."

Brod admitted that it was too soon to begin discussion of publishing Kafka's personal letters and diaries, but he believed they contained "the same truth to nature and intensity of feeling as his literary work" and provided necessary clues to "the whole magic of Kafka's personality."

In searching Kafka's desk and room at his parents' house, Brod looked for a last will or legal document concerning his estate but found nothing. He did discover something else, potentially as binding. Among the mass of papers in Kafka's desk and closet, Max found a folded note, addressed to him in Kafka's elegant scrawl:

Dearest Max, my last request: Everything I leave behind me (in my bookcase, linen-cupboard, and my desk both at home and in the office, or anywhere else where anything may have got to and meets your eye), in the way of diaries, manuscripts, letters (my own and others'), sketches, and so on, to be burned unread; also all writings and sketches which you or others may possess; and ask those others for them in my name. Letters which they do not want to hand over to you, they should at least promise faithfully to burn themselves. Yours, Franz Kafka.

Brod also uncovered a yellowed piece of paper, written earlier. In pencil, Kafka had outlined in even more specific instructions for the destruction of his work:

Dear Max, perhaps this time I shan't recover after all. Pneumonia after a whole month's pulmonary fever is all too likely; and not even writing this down can avert it, although there is a certain power in that. For this eventuality therefore, here is my last will concerning everything I have written: Of all my writings the only books that can stand are these: "The

Judgment," "The Stoker," "Metamorphosis," *Penal Colony,* "Country Doctor" and the short story "Hunger Artist." The few copies of *Meditation* can remain. I do not want to give anyone the trouble of pulping them; but nothing in that volume must be printed again.

When I say that those five books and the short story can stand, I do not mean that I wish them to be reprinted and handed down to posterity. On the contrary, should they disappear altogether that would please me best. Only, since they do exist, I do not wish to hinder anyone who may want to, from keeping them. But everything else of mine which is extant (whether in journals, in manuscript, or letters), everything without exception in so far as it is discoverable or obtainable from the addressees by request . . . —all these things, without exception and preferably unread (I won't forbid you to look at them, though I'd far rather you didn't and in any case no one else is to do so)—all these things without exception are to be burned, and I beg you to do this as soon as possible. Franz.

Kafka had asked the impossible of him. Not once in the twenty-two years of "our unclouded friendship" had Max thrown away "the smallest scrap of paper that came from him, not even a postcard." He was "far from grateful" to him for "precipitating this difficult conflict of conscience, which he must have foreseen." It was preposterous to think that Brod could ever destroy the writings that he believed could help humanity. He could never burn Kafka's work and had said so, unequivocally, three years earlier. In 1921, when Brod was talking about his own last will and testament, Kafka showed him the folded note that Brod now held in his hands and said, "My last testament will be quite simple: A request to you to burn everything." Brod clearly remembered every word of his refusal: "If you seriously think me capable of such a thing, let me tell you here and now that I shall not carry out your wishes."

Brod, a lawyer himself, approached his ethical dilemma logically, building his case for ignoring his friend's final written wishes with solid reasoning. "Convinced as he was that I meant what I said, Franz should have appointed another executor if he had been absolutely determined that his instructions should stand."

A year later, in 1925, when Kafka's first novel, *The Trial,* was published posthumously, Brod wrote a postscript in which he described finding the handwritten requests to burn the work, even publishing Kafka's requests, before pleading his case and laying out his justifications for going ahead with publication. It was true, Brod said, that Kafka demonstrated a type of nihilism in regard to his own work. "Without ever saying so, he applied the highest religious standard to his art," Brod said, "and since this was wrung from manifold doubts and difficulties, that standard was too high. It was probably immaterial to him that his work might nevertheless greatly help many others who were striving after faith, nature, and wholeness of soul."

Brod argued that Kafka's instructions had been written in an earlier, unhappy period before his life with Dora. Kafka's newfound contentment and acceptance of life during the Berlin period contributed to his change of heart regarding the publication of his work. In the end, Kafka had ignored his own instructions: Franz had given Max explicit permission to publish a reprint of parts of *Meditation* in a journal, and had himself negotiated the contract with Die Schmiede for *A Hunger Artist* collection, which was to be published posthumously in a few months.

To Max's bitter disappointment, his search of Kafka's lodgings uncovered evidence that Kafka had taken matters into his own hands and burned his own work. Brod found "ten large quarto notebooks—only the covers remained; their contents had been completely destroyed." The pain of this loss was even more acute because he had an inkling of what was missing. Kafka's notebooks contained numerous sketches for plots, stories and fragments, many of which Kafka had read aloud to him at one time or another. These were not among the papers Max found, and he mourned their loss. "What unforgettable, entirely original, and profound thoughts he communicated to me!" Brod lamented. "As far as my memory and my strength permit, nothing of all this shall be lost." He vowed that "a small circle of Kafka's friends will see to it that all the utterances of this incomparable human being which remain in their memory shall be collected forthwith."

Brod ignored Kafka's request to destroy everything, but not his request that he collect his letters, notebooks and diaries in the possession of others. Brod was well aware of "the very insidious lure of such scruples" of those who believed he should have followed Kafka's wishes. But he saw his greater ethical responsibility as Kafka's literary executor differently: to do everything in his power to preserve all of Kafka's writings and present these gifts to humanity.

Prague, August 1924

Dora would never voluntarily give up the letters that Franz had written to her. Brod plan to posthumously publish Kafka's work horrified her; his logical arguments made no difference. Her letters from Kafka were her treasure. When Dora learned of Brod's hopes for the future publication of Kafka's personal writings, she reacted badly. When Brod asked her for any notebooks or manuscripts Kafka may have given to her or that were left after his death, Dora faced her own ethical dilemma. It was a question of honesty versus trust. Dora could not tell Max the truth and honor Kafka's last wishes at the same time. Franz still needed her, she realized: She could protect him from publication. If she told Brod about Franz's notebooks in her possession, Max would try to get them published, opening his private thoughts to people who didn't know Franz and could therefore never understand him. Franz Kafka was hers and hers alone. She didn't want to share him. "The whole world doesn't have to know anything about Franz. He is none of its business," Dora later explained.

She had burned everything, she told Max when he asked about Kafka's writings in her possession. When Brod collected himself enough to ask her what, precisely, had she destroyed, Dora told him she "burned some twenty notebooks while Franz watched from his bed." Dora's lie was entirely plausible; it held grains of truth. Dora had burned pages of Kafka's work in Berlin at his insistence, when he was very ill. Sickened by the news, Brod believed her, at first. Dora's insistence that she had burned everything in her possession was a lie she would cling to for almost a decade, until a fateful night in 1933 made her regret her decision for the rest of her life.

11

LIFE AFTER KAFKA

Begin to see who you are instead of calculating what is to become of you.

—Franz Kafka, *Diaries*

BERLIN, SUMMER 1924

After staying in Prague for two months, Dora disappeared. One morning in August she packed her suitcase and boarded the train to Germany, without saying good-bye to anyone. Once she made her decision to go, she was gone. One of Kafka's friends, an official at the German embassy in Prague, had offered to help her secure a current German residence permit. She needed the permit to audition for the National Theater School in Berlin. This was her plan, her new purpose, the design to rebuild her life.

Kafka had always encouraged Dora to dream of a career on the stage. He counseled her to take advantage of the excellent professional training programs in Berlin. This small flame flickered in her, a pinpoint of hope, a direction to travel through the wasteland in which she wandered since his death. His three sisters had all encouraged her, too. Now, in her grief, she clung to this hope: a life in the theater.

As the dark landscape flew past her reflected image in the train window, Dora's fears grew. Berlin loomed before her, she later told Elli, "as the cemetery of my life, to which I came to visit the graves." She had money in her purse, Franz's family had seen to that, with the promise of more to come. Kafka had negotiated advance payments from the publication of *A Hunger Artist*, which Die Schmiede was bringing out in October, and these royalties had been promised to her.

The German capital to which Dora now returned was bursting with energy and life. Berlin housed the largest Jewish population in the country. By the end of the 1920s, more than 200,000 Jews lived in Berlin, mixing socially and culturally with Germans and the international influx of visitors who poured into Berlin in search of excitement at bargain prices. The Dawes Plan of 1924, devised by an American banker, paved the way for foreign capital investments in the devastated postwar economy, and conditions began to improve with the influx of massive loans from America and other Western countries.

The Weimar Republic's "Golden Twenties" began to roar, with Berlin at the eye of the tempest of modernization. Necklines plunged and hemlines rose. Cabarets, revues, movies and revolutionary art theaters sprouted up and began to thrive. The whole world seemed drawn to Berlin; even Einstein lived here. His theory of relativity, which won him the Nobel Prize three years earlier, in 1921, exploded old ways of thinking and perceiving the world. All facts were now in question. Objectivity and subjectivity played equal roles in the search for Absolute Truth, and morality was just an expression of individual or group choice.

Avant-garde movements proliferated: expressionism, psychoanalysis, Dada, humanistic psychology and existentialism. The Bauhaus movement, begun after the war by Berlin-born architect Walter Gropius, brought together architects, artists and sculptors to create a modern environment, a habitat with furniture designed according to its functional nature. Sexual mores had changed seemingly overnight. The teachings of Dr. Sigmund Freud had everyone talking about the subconscious, repression and libido. It was now considered "unhealthy to repress one's impulses, absurd to feel guilty about them." Modern science advocated the pleasures of lovemaking and orgasms—even for women.

What delighted and interested Dora most were advances in the theater world, where Berlin now set the standard for innovation and creativity. A new era had dawned: the old realism had been cast aside by Max Reinhardt, one of the most influential theater directors of his time. In 1894 the Jewish Austrian-born actor-director-producer moved to Berlin, where he developed his special brand of spectacle and magic, utilizing the latest techniques of stagecraft, such as the revolving stage and mysterious smoke and lighting effects. His productions of plays by the world's greatest playwrights, Shakespeare and Molière and Ibsen, the Greek comedies and tragedies, and modern classics by Schiller, Goethe and Shaw, were huge successes and created a new audience of theatergoers hungry for glittery entertainment spectacles.

In the course of his career, Reinhardt ran more than thirty theaters, including, at the height of his fame, five of Berlin's most successful theaters. His acting schools funneled professional actors into regional companies throughout Germany and Austria. In America many of the early film stars of the 1920s and 1930s, including Marlene Dietrich and Luise Rainer, had been trained on Reinhardt's stages.

"You could always tell a Reinhardt actor by all the emotion," the well-known (and Reinhardt-trained) character actor Walter Slezak once remarked. "You know, the hand to the heart. *Oh Schmerz!* Pain!" After Reinhardt immigrated to New York in 1934 and for many years after his death in 1943, his style and contributions continued to influence both film and theater.

Behind the scenes, mirroring the anguish of those who were dispossessed by postwar poverty and inflation, an exciting revolution was beginning to take shape on Berlin's stages, a raw, expressionistic approach with a highly politicized message.

In that year, 1924, Reinhardt hired a young poet and playwright named Bertolt Brecht to work at his prestigious German Theater as dramaturg. Described as "thin, ill-shaven, unkempt," Brecht was twenty-six, exactly Dora's age, and was now responsible for the company's entire repertoire. Across town, a revolutionary Bavarian actor named Erwin Piscator had taken the helm of the Volksbühne, the People's Theater, and was producing modern plays laden with working-class and communist themes. It was a brave new world, and Dora soon became caught up in it.

After she'd been in Berlin for about a week, feeling "a little drunk from strolling around," Dora sat down to write a letter to Elli. Using Kafka's fountain pen, she began: "Dear Elli, now I should be straightened out enough, that I can think back on my departure from Prague. That was really too stupid, though, truly, it wasn't my fault. Wanted to ring you, to tell you that I was leaving at noon, but couldn't get a connection, and then it was too late to go to see you. You would have left already. And so we missed each other. It was maddening. But you aren't mad at me, are you? I was just a bit excited and fidgety," she explained.

"The fear of Berlin passes gradually," she continued. "I am getting used to everything again. There is such an enormous amount of life all around me. First of all, I've landed among quite wonderful people, friends of my friend from home. Of course, Franz intervened here, too."

Dora's girlfriend had introduced her to her friends "as the wife of Franz Kafka, and for the first two days," Dora said, "I was only addressed as Frau Kafka. It was a bit strange." Dora eventually corrected them about her name. "They booked me a wonderful room in a students' residence hall until I can find a place. And I also have the prospect of getting a job. The resident permit is almost assured. For this I am entirely indebted to Mr. Urzidil. I would really very much like to thank him, but don't dare." Dora hadn't said good-bye to him either. "There is nothing to report so far about my drama stuff. I haven't spoken to anybody yet about it."

Dora wasn't going to write to Ottla yet, she said. She still felt guilty about her departure. "It was very thoughtless of me not to go to see her." She sent her warmest greetings to the parents, about whom she also felt bad: "Just as with Ottla, I regret not having waited for the mother." She also missed saying farewell to Elli's son Felix. "A pity, but where did he escape to at the time?" She promised to stay in touch before suddenly admitting her sadness: "I am so alone," she wrote. Although it comforted her to hear from Kafka's family, Dora wasn't asking her to write. "I don't want any answer to this letter," she said, "but on the whole—you understand me, Elli. Say hello to Valli and the two girls," and she signed her name. It was the last letter Dora wrote to Elli that was saved. Any other letters that may have passed between the two women before Elli's death at the hands of the Germans almost two decades later have been lost.

BERLIN, OCTOBER 1924

The room was freezing. Dora shivered as she undressed and got ready for bed. Outside, the linden trees stood bare, the leaves piled in dry drifts against the stone curbs. Dora slipped the long white night gown over her head and hugged it tightly around her. It warmed her from the inside out.

One year had passed since the day in the Steglitz park when she and Franz had come across the little girl crying for her lost doll. Dora would never forget Kafka's desire to ease the pain of the child's loss or his "deep devoted earnestness" as he concocted the doll's adventures. Had the little girl saved the letters written to her from her doll? Would the child remember the tall, dark, thin man with the shining eyes who read them aloud to her?

Wrapped in Franz's nightshirt, Dora found the courage to begin a long overdue letter to Ottla. She had written to Elli the month before, but this was the first letter to Ottla since May, six months earlier. That letter had been written from Kierling, the month before Franz died, when she had urged Ottla to keep a positive attitude. Dora stared at the empty page for a long time, Franz's pen poised in her hand. Finally she began: "How I shall manage to write this letter, I don't know. I could pull out my hair over my carelessness and thoughtlessness. Who knows when there will be another opportunity to see you, and to miss such a good one so stupidly, I can't explain it. If only I had some sense. But is it really true? We will not see each other again? My God, Ottla!"

Good things were happening around her, but none of it seemed real. "I feel as if I am only in a dream," she said. She went through the motions, she acted and reacted, but nothing seemed to touch her. "I know that the day after tomorrow is the test which will decide my admission to the National School for Drama. I also know that I will pass it and therefore will be admitted. Only I don't know that any of it applies to me. I feel so estranged from myself." A German actress, a Reinhardt teacher, was helping prepare her for the audition and told her that she had "great talent," Dora reported. "I don't know if I should be happy or sad. The last is easier."

Dora's emotions always had been her compass, guiding her though the world. Now they failed her; she couldn't trust them, she couldn't name them. It was only through luck, she said, that she lived among such wonderful people, and she didn't feel worthy of their generosity and kindness. She still did not have a job, and that was very bad. The general conditions for most Germans were still not good, and many people were hungry. Dora said she "felt like a criminal to intrude and eat their bread."

Dora turned the sheet over and stared at the blank page. Finally, she began to write again: "I am sitting wrapped in Franz's nightgown. It is so cold. When I close my eyes I believe I am sitting on his lap and that he wraps the gown around himself and me. I was in Steglitz."

Finally Dora asked the embarrassing question that had, in part, prompted the letter. Begging Ottla not to tell anyone that she had asked— Dora couldn't ask anyone else in the family—did Ottla know if the publisher sent the royalty payment in September? "I only want to know if I can count on receiving the money this month," she said. "How is Klopstock?" she asked, changing the subject abruptly. He hadn't answered several letters, and she was a little worried. But more than that, she was worried about what Ottla thought of her: "Ottla! Don't damn me!" Dora pleaded. "Be well, you dear one." Underneath her name, in small letters, Dora added a postscript: "Will you write to me?!—"

BERLIN, JANUARY 1925

The new year started off on a hopeful note. Dora made a resolution not to be so sad. She had found a job before Christmas that had already ended, and she had earned a little money. She had not been admitted to the National School of Drama but was not discouraged. She would try again. There were other good schools in Berlin, even in Hamburg and Düsseldorf. The Reinhardt teacher who had helped her prepare for the first audition still believed in her and continued to tutor her for free. She had found a lovely new place to live, a large, pleasant room, comfortably furnished, with a wonderful landlady. Once a week Dora took various lessons, which she truly enjoyed. Next week she was looking forward to starting a gymnastics class.

Through a literary group of Polish Jews, many from the neighboring towns of Bedzin, Sosnowiec, and Czeladz, Dora was meeting fascinating people. She smiled sometimes and even laughed. But she was always sad, always a widow. She dressed in black and wore her sadness like a cloak, draped over her shoulders. It became a part of who she was.

One of her new friends, a man who would remain a very dear friend until the end of her life, was a passionate young Yiddish poet named Avrom-Nokhem Stencl. He was one year older than Dora, compactly built and ruggedly handsome. Raised as a religiously observant Jew in Czeladz, the town across the river from Bedzin, Stencl had grown up within a few miles of Dora. He attended the Sosnowiec yeshiva, where his brother was the town rabbi as well as the school principal. In 1918, when he was twenty-one, Stencl received his military call-up papers. With his father's blessing, he ran away from his home in Poland that very night, never to return. He emigrated from Poland to Holland, where he worked in an iron foundry, building his muscular frame, and arrived in Berlin in 1921, the same year as Dora.

A romantic and nomadic poet, A. N. Stencl lived a "bohemian, hand-to-mouth, spontaneous existence." His need to write was like Kafka's: it was "the central impulse of his life." But any similarity between the two ended there. Stencl slept in temporary shelters, on park benches, in the rooms of other poor Jewish artists, or with his many women friends and lovers. Sometimes he stayed up all night in working-class bars. Occasionally, after selling a poem or a translation, he indulged in "the luxury of a rented room." His pockets were always stuffed with poems, which he was constantly writing or reading to anyone who would listen. When the little

money he earned from translations of his poems in German literary journals ran out, and "day began to dawn in the pocket," he took odd jobs,
working on farms, manufacturing compost, hawking fabric on the streets
and selling straw hats in the marketplace. At one low point, he worked in a
cemetery, stamping down earth on the new graves.

Stencl spent his free hours at the Romanische Café, the center of East
European Jewish literary life in Berlin. He was "simply drunk with joy"
when he first encountered many good old friends, also in exile from
Poland, who sat at the tables along the café's "eastern wall." The Romanische Café was located at the southern end of the Kurfürstendamm at the
corner of Tauenstzien and Budapester Streets, next door to the famed
Kaiser Wilhelm Memorial Church. The barnlike structure, which seated
over one thousand patrons, was one of the most popular meeting places
for artists and intellectuals in Berlin. It also served as the center of political
and literary activities for Yiddish writers and literati, displaced from
Odessa, Kiev, Warsaw and Vilna.

The legendary café was frequented by "the most curious international
mob of people, with long hair, short hair or shaven skulls, in rags or in
furs." The Berlin-born expressionist artist George Grosz was famous for
appearing in the café "dressed as an American cowboy, booted and
spurred." In the balcony, world chess champion Emmanuel Lasker, who
held that title for over a quarter century, often played at one of the little
rows of tables. Stencl once described the café's frenetic and eclectic atmosphere: "From those fleeing from the pogroms in the Jewish-Ukrainian
shtetls, from the famine in the Russian cities, and from the Revolution, a
kind of Jewish colony formed itself in the west of Berlin, and the Romanische Café was its parliament. It was buzzing with famous Jewish intellectuals and activists, well known Jewish lawyers from Moscow and Petersburg,
Yiddish writers from Kiev and Odessa, with party-leaders from the extreme left to the extreme right wing—it buzzed as in a beehive."

Dora was troubled. She hadn't heard from Ottla since her last, "failed" (as
she thought of it) letter to her in October. In the optimism of the new year,
Dora tried again to renew her relationship with Franz's beloved youngest
sister. "Dear Ottla! Are you cross with me? Apparently yes, or else you
would have written. It wouldn't surprise me, but I would be very sad." Before her lay Ottla's earlier—"and only?" Dora wondered—letter. "You
beautiful, good one! You ask me to tell you about everything. But about

what, dear one? My life, like that of all lonely people, flows so simply and clearly that every child could imagine it." Dora told Ottla about her classes, her wonderful new flat, her angel of a landlady: "She cooks for me and looks after me like a mother for her found child. I have some new acquaintances, wonderful people. One of them, a splendid character, is in love with me, and that is so sad. Sometimes also funny, but on the whole, amusing."

Since Christmas, Dora had been on holidays, she said, using the time to study and sew. "I made two blouses and a dress for myself. That was nice. I've gotten very good." Dora remembered how, when Franz was alive, each morning his eyes would follow her around the room, a little anxiously, until she took out her sewing things. Then his eyes lit up and "he looked so grateful and reassured, and called it a gift I had given him."

Dora paused to collect herself. "See, I don't even cry. Just hesitated for a moment." She had resolved not to be so sad, she said, but admitted, "I have learned to love this sadness, so that I am not ashamed anymore of being sad. I am always sad. I laugh, and I am sad, joke and am sad, am glad and then saddest. I don't even blame myself anymore when others become sad through me." Dora wrote another sentence, dismissing her feelings as prattle, and then crossed it out.

"Write to me," Dora pleaded. She wanted as much detail as possible about everything. "Also something about Franz, any news of him, as if you had spoken with him. I can't bear it, not to hear from him for so long." She begged Ottla not to be angry, but she still could not accept Franz's death. Someday perhaps acceptance would come. But until then, Dora said, she needed to hear about him, otherwise she couldn't stand it. "Please write to me," she repeated, signed her name and added a postscript, asking for news of Elli and Valli and their children. She thought about them all constantly. In fact, she said she only felt alive when she imagined herself with them. She always felt inhibited when writing to them, trying to say what was in her heart, not knowing if they wanted to hear from her. "Maybe," she said, "if they would write I would be encouraged? Don't know."

This final letter written to Ottla, probably in January 1925, is the last letter from Dora to any member of the Kafka family that is known to exist. It is now part of the collection of Kafka manuscripts and correspondence, gifted by the Kafka Family Estate to the Department of Western Manuscripts at the Bodleian Library at Oxford University.

12

BETWEEN TWO WORLDS

*The truth is always an abyss. One must—as in a
swimming pool—dare to dive from the quivering
springboard of trivial everyday experience and
sink into the depths, in order later to rise again—
laughing and fighting for breath—to the now
doubly illuminated surface of things.*
                    —Franz Kafka, in *Conversations with Kafka*

BRZEZINY, CENTRAL POLAND, 1925

Before winter ended, Dora got very sick. She lost weight and her skin grew
pale, almost bloodless. She couldn't work and her money ran out. When
the weather improved, she did not. Finally she was forced to leave Berlin,
owing her dear and loving landlady several months in unpaid rent. She returned to Poland, not to Bedzin but to the home of her mother's family in
Brzeziny, close to Lodz, near Pabianice. This was the town where Dora
was born, where she spent her early childhood years and where her
mother was buried.

Everyone worried about her. Max Brod was doing all he could for her
from Prague, but despite his best efforts, that wasn't much. Robert Klopstock was also concerned and wrote to Brod and to Kafka's sisters asking
about her. He informed Brod that he hoped Dora was entitled to receive
royalty payments from *The Trial*, which had been published recently, but he
received no answer. Now Robert was afraid that Max was angry with him.

Max was probably not angry, just frustrated. After Kafka's death, Brod
had arranged a contract with Die Schmiede for *The Trial*, granting the

publishing house future rights to Kafka's unpublished books and specifically stipulating that Dora, whom he referred to as Kafka's bride or fiancée, was to receive payments from the royalties. It was something Max knew that Franz would have wanted. Kafka's family agreed, knowing Dora desperately needed the money.

The publication of *The Trial* had been a struggle from beginning to end. The manuscript was incomplete, with no written title. The chapters were unnumbered. Brod had to sort through the "great bundle of papers . . . separating the finished from the unfinished chapters." Fortunately Kafka had read him a large portion of the book—he had always referred to it as *The Trial*—so "memory came to the aid of judgment." Brod managed to get the book edited, proofed, corrected and finally published the year after Kafka's death. Shortly afterward, Die Schmiede went out of business. For four months, Brod wrote letters to the publishing house but failed to get any royalty payments.

At the end of October 1925, Brod wrote to Die Schmiede, withdrawing from their agreement, canceling their rights to Kafka's books and announcing his intention to grant future rights to Kurt Wolff Verlag, which had been publishing Kafka since 1913. "I was forced to do this in order to secure further payments for the heirs. I couldn't have allowed Fräulein Dora Diamant, Kafka's bride, to go under. The legacy of my friend was much too dear to do this. I have repeatedly—since the signing of the contract—drawn your attention to the fact that the lady is in dire straits."

One month later, Die Schmiede finally answered, apologizing for the delay and hoping that Dr. Brod would change his mind. Brod didn't waste another piece of paper on them. At the bottom of the letter to him he replied that it was too late; he had transferred the rights "some considerable time ago." Brod was already working on final edits of Kafka's second novel, *The Castle*, for publication by Kurt Wolff the following year, in 1926. Until then, there was nothing more Max could do to help Dora.

Dora had never heard of *The Trial* before it was published. Franz had never mentioned it to her, but then he had never discussed any of his previous writings. *The Trial* introduced her to another facet of Kafka's inner life, and she began to gain insight into his reaction to the suffering and poverty that had tormented him in Berlin. As she read his newly published work, Dora felt "the most joyous and painful emotion. I could recognize each line he had written, just by remembering his accent, the rhythm of his sentences." Dora began to collect copies of each of his works. She read all his published writings and everything written about him.

After Kafka's death, Robert Klopstock continued to write to Elli and Ottla. Two weeks after returning from a several-month stay in Budapest, Robert was overjoyed to receive a letter from Elli. He was still in deep mourning, he told her. He didn't know how long he would be able to stay in his current situation; it depended on money. He had found work but didn't have an advance and was running out of funds. Dora had sent him Kc600, he said, two hundred of which he had sent to Dora's landlady, Mrs. Weil, since Dora had been unable to settle her debt before she left. He hoped that the family could reimburse him the Kc200, since the money had come from them.

Dora had written him a postcard saying life was tolerable for her. But she had written it in a poetic, dreamlike manner, without any details, as if he were already informed about everything. Please, he asked Elli, how is she? What kind of illness was it?

The nature of Dora's illness was never disclosed, but she stayed for the rest of the year in Brzeziny, most probably in the home of a female relative named Bela Dimant. Brzeziny was a predominately Jewish tailoring center two miles east of Lodz, the epicenter of the textile industry in Poland. Here Dora was literally surrounded by family. She was descended from Dimants (or Dymants) on both sides of her family: Dora's maternal grandmother was also a Dimant, and Dora was part of a large extended family of great-grandparents, aunts, uncles, cousins, nieces and nephews.

Still she was desperately lonely, lost in memories of Kafka. She and Franz had talked of making this journey together. It had been a secret plan between them, something they didn't discuss with others. When it was clear he wouldn't be able to travel to Palestine, they talked privately of "going back home" to Poland. It became another sort of aliyah, a return to Eastern Europe, as Kafka saw it, to the repository of the genuine values of Judaism.

Kafka had long felt a mystical affinity to the Eastern European communities, where people just like his ancestors continued to pray in their ancient language, persevering through all forms of adversity, reciting the same prayers for five thousand years. "One should believe in something indestructible in order to survive," Kafka had said. In the East, Jews had

freely consented, despite the lure of modernity, to the strict discipline necessary to keep the laws. This commanded his respect.

As Dora recuperated from her illness, she began to take part in the life
around her. Lodz was the second largest city in Poland, a breeding ground
of great writers and revolutionaries, buzzing with political, social and cultural movements in a population numbering more than a quarter million,
almost a third of whom were Jews. The abundance of nineteenth-century
red brick factories, the palatial residences of industry captains contrasting
starkly with the prisonlike tenements of workers, earned Lodz the title of
"Polish Manchester." Wladyslaw Stanislaw Reymont, who won the Nobel
Prize for literature in 1924, used Lodz in an earlier novel as the backdrop
for his tale about the ruthless inhumanity of capitalist greed versus the suffering of the exploited poor. A center of political unrest since the end of
the previous century, Lodz was the site of the first mass strike in Polish history. Jozef Pilsudski, who led Poland to independence in 1918, was first
arrested in Lodz years before for printing copies of an underground newspaper, *Robotnik*.

As body and soul healed, Dora had time to read. Since living with
Kafka, literature, always important to her, had taken on a heightened significance. Once again immersed in Jewish culture, surrounded by Yiddish
speakers, she rediscovered her *mameloshen*. In the six years since she'd
left Poland, new Yiddish literary magazines and cultural journals had
sprung up. Now that Dora could read German as well as Yiddish, she was
able to read translations in both languages; with this new perspective she
gained a deeper appreciation of the magical fusion of secular and sacred
peculiar to Yiddish.

There had never been a richer period in Yiddish literature. During
World War I, the "classical" period had officially ended with the deaths of
the founding fathers of modern Yiddish literature—Mendele, Sholem Aleichem and Dora's favorite, I. L. Peretz. A second generation of writers had
quickly filled the gap, experimenting in different styles with new subject
matter, exploring every aspect of human experience. By 1925 Poland was
considered the world center of Yiddish culture, with thriving theaters,
newspapers, magazines, journals and writers clubs.

In one of these new journals, Dora found an article about Kafka, which
appeared alongside a Yiddish translation of one of his short stories. It upset her. The article was inaccurate and meaningless and the translation was
terrible. The two pieces were not attributed to anyone. Dora determined

to find out who was behind these injustices to Kafka's name and work, and to tell him what she thought.

In Warsaw, less than one hundred miles from where Dora now lived in Brzeziny, a group of Yiddish writers had formed a group called *di klaliastre* (the gang) to experiment with Yiddish expressionism. One member was a thirty-two-year-old poet and essayist named Melech Ravitch. When he was an old man, after a full life lived in world capitals—Vienna, Warsaw, Melbourne, Buenos Aires, New York, Montreal and Tel Aviv—Ravitch wrote a series of essays entitled "Stories from My Life." One of them, "I Am Franz Kafka's Wife," reprinted in the *Jewish Chronicle* in London in 1992, told the story of his two unforgettable meetings with Dora Diamant, twenty-five years apart. The first encounter was surrounded by a mystery.

In 1924, shortly after Ravitch and five friends started a new literary journal, *Literarishe Bletter,* news arrived in their Warsaw offices that Franz Kafka had died. Obituaries proclaimed him one of the foremost writers of German. Ravitch and his colleagues were put in a rather embarrassing position as people asked, "Who is Kafka?"

Ravitch was familiar with Kafka's writings and had heard a strange story about Kafka's work at the Workers Accident Insurance Institute, which further intrigued him. Before World War I, Kafka was employed in the statistics department. Someone who worked at the same company said that "in his reports to the company he would enumerate the eerie coincidences of death statistics," Ravitch revealed. "Kafka's calculations, while mathematically precise, were also mysterious and vague—vague, yet razor-sharp. So sharp indeed that they horrified the management, who eventually asked him not to carry on with these reports, and gave him another job to do." Since then, Ravitch had come across the occasional Kafka story and "was very taken by Kafka's storytelling art." The name stuck: "It had a curious ring about it," Ravitch remembered, "like a drink that does not intoxicate or dull the senses, but takes you to a different world, a ghostly world: *Kafka.*"

Few had read anything by him, since so little of Kafka's work had been published. Ravitch was the German literature expert on the journal's editorial staff, so, despite his protests that he didn't know much more than they did, it fell to him to write an article about Kafka for the journal. "To help explain Kafka to myself and the readers," Ravitch said, "I translated a short story of his for the issue. But I was far from satisfied with my article, ashamed of the inadequacy of my translation and just wanted to forget the whole thing. I did not even put my name to my contribution. Since Franz Kafka was now among the dead, I was safe—as safe as someone can be who has done something he would have preferred not to have done."

TOMASHOV-LUBELSKI, POLISH-RUSSIAN BORDER, 1925

Melech Ravitch was the pen name of Zachariah Bergner, born in Galicia in 1893. He was a strong, imposing-looking man with high, wide forehead and a full red beard. In addition to being a writer and an editor, he was also a popular lecturer. Soon after his Kafka article and story translation appeared, Ravitch traveled to Tomashov-Lubelski, a small and somewhat remote Polish Jewish community near the Russian border, to give a public talk. The subject, "not unusual for those 'wild' days, was 'Nudity as a Problem in Poetry, Literature and Art.'"

Before beginning his lecture, Ravitch found himself surrounded by a small crowd. "When a writer came to a Jewish community, the young people, boys and girls, would cluster around with all kinds of abstruse questions, often about one of his poems, or a recent article which neither they, nor, often, the writer himself, understood," he said. As he stood in a dark passageway near the stage waiting for his name to be announced, Ravitch noticed a "thin, drab girl whose face had no color except the color of pallor" approach him through the crowd until she stood right in front of him.

"In a voice with no tone, except the tone of silence, she asked if she may have a word with me about my short piece on Kafka," Ravitch remembered, "then told me what I knew very well but had been ashamed to face up to: that the article was trivial and the translation bad. How did she know it was I who had written the article and translated the story? There was no smug smile on her face, nor any hint of self-righteousness in her voice. I did not jump to my own defense, still feeling as confident as a person who has done something not quite nice, but hopes it will be forgotten—if no one concerned finds out."

It was time to give the lecture, and Ravitch "could not talk to the white-faced girl any longer. I only managed to ask her, somewhat condescendingly, how she came to be such an expert on Kafka." The girl blushed and then "answered loudly and in perfect German: 'Actually, I am the wife of Franz Kafka.'"

Ravitch was called up to the stage. "Somehow I managed to give the lecture, since I knew it more or less by heart. But the whole time, I kept hearing those words: '*I am Franz Kafka's wife.*'" The girl must be a disturbed person, he thought, with a fixation on Franz Kafka. "But how did that *idée fixe* in Tomashov come to be Kafka's wife?" he wondered, looking for her face in the crowd. "She must have been sitting in the hall," he reasoned. "She had come for the lecture, yet I could not see her anywhere. We had only met in the dark corridor and all I had seen was a white face. How could I recognize her now?"

When the lecture was over, Ravitch reported, "I took no questions and there was no discussion, I just left the stage and went searching for 'Franz Kafka's wife' among the departing audience. And there she was, waiting for me." As they talked, Ravitch realized: "She really was Franz Kafka's wife!" He had heard of her: "She was Dora Diamant, a girl from a poor home in a Polish-Jewish village, well-read and a nursery-school teacher by vocation." He had heard that "she was the instrument of Kafka's Jewish re-awakening. He was always having her sing him Yiddish songs, tell him little folk tales and teach him Yiddish and Hebrew."

Ravitch knew that "they had never been officially married. It had been love at first sight and they were joined in an eternal bond from the moment they met," he wrote. "Their time together lasted only one year, the final agonized year of Kafka's life. When Kafka died, his parents had recognized Dora as the one and only woman he loved, as their son's wife." Dora told him that after Kafka's death, she had stayed in Prague with Kafka's parents for a long time to "console them on the death of their beloved and ever problematic son."

"When I mentioned that I had heard of her, that people know about her—she nodded, she knew. We did not find anything else to talk about, and she disappeared into the crowd." For months afterward, Ravitch continued to think about "Kafka's wife," the girl with the toneless voice and colorless face. Occasionally he asked his colleagues if there was any news of her. Finally somebody mentioned hearing that Dora Diamant had left Poland forever, that she had returned to Berlin and "come to no good." Until their second meeting, which proved to be even more remarkable than the first, Ravitch admitted, "I thought no more about it for a quarter of a century."

13

THE NATURE THEATER OF OKLAHOMA

As long as you keep climbing there will be stairs,
they will magically appear under your climbing
feet.

— Franz Kafka, "Advocates"

BERLIN-CHARLOTTENBURG, EARLY 1926

Dora returned to Berlin when her health improved. She moved back to
the orphanage in Charlottenburg, according to the memories of Elizabeth
"Betty" Marcus, with whom Dora became "very friendly." Betty was four
years younger than Dora and had lived in the Charlottenburg orphanage
since the age of nine. She studied music and later taught at the Luisen
Schule, one of the best schools for girls in Berlin. According to one of her
pupils, Hanny Lichternstern, who would become one of Dora's closest
and most loyal friends, Betty was "pretty, charming, a fine and much loved
teacher."

Seventy years later, Betty Marcus Kuttner remembered Dora in an interview she gave Hanny for this book, shortly before her death in London
at age ninety-three. "Dora was very lively and had a sense of humor," Betty
recalled on a hot summer day in 1995. Despite a memory that became less
reliable every day, Betty's images of Dora remained clear and constant. She
remembered Dora as always being "very political, a strong socialist."
When asked, Betty answered, "No, I don't think she was very happy."

Dora spoke constantly about Kafka, Betty told Hanny. "What beautiful
hands Franz had," she would say and begin to tell a story about him.
"When she spoke of Kafka, she stressed how close she was to him—until
the last moment, and that he had loved her." But she added: "Most people

didn't believe her." People thought, how could this be? A poor Eastern immigrant and the writer Franz Kafka? It wasn't that anyone thought Dora was lying, Hanny explained. "It was just that she possessed such an active imagination, one never knew whether her fantastic stories were truth or fantasy."

In 1926, when Kurt Wolff Verlag released *The Castle,* Dora received a complimentary copy. For Brod, preparing *The Castle* for publication had been another editorial nightmare. Like *The Trial, The Castle* was unfinished. The last chapter ended in midsentence. To bring the novel to a close and give it a sense of wholeness, Brod decided to omit almost one fifth of the text. Because he wanted "to avoid anything that emphasized its fragmentary state," Max chose an ending to the novel, "the decisive defeat of the protagonist," when K. loses his love, Frieda. It was a difficult and problematic decision, for which Brod was never forgiven by future Kafka scholars.

Years later, after Kafka's diaries were published, Dora learned more about the creation of the novel, which is about a land surveyor who never succeeds at his appointed task but never stops trying. Kafka had begun writing *The Castle* in January 1922 in Spindlermühle, a snowbound mountain village on the Polish border, after escaping from Prague following what Kafka referred to as "something very like a breakdown." Only once in his life, he said, a terrible night two years earlier, had he known anything as bad. In his diary on January 16, he wrote: "Breakdown, impossible to sleep, impossible to stay awake, impossible to endure life, or, more exactly, the course of life. The clocks are not in unison: the inner one run crazily on at a devilish or demoniac or in any case inhuman pace, the outer one limps along at its usual speed. What else can happen but that the two worlds split apart?"

Writing offered Kafka a "strange, mysterious, perhaps dangerous, perhaps redeeming consolation," he said. "It is a seeing of what is really taking place." His only hope, he believed, was to stay close to his writing and never, no matter how difficult or painful it might be, give it up. "The existence of the writer is truly dependent on his desk," he wrote in his diary that year. "If he wants to escape madness, he really should never leave his desk. He must cling to it with his teeth."

During his weeks at the resort in Spindlermühle in the winter of 1922, Kafka went hiking, tobogganing and sleigh riding; he even tried skiing. But his depression and sense of isolation refused to lift. He feared that the solitude he had forced on himself in order to write was driving him insane, while writing was his only weapon to fight it. When he returned to his parents' home in Prague at the end of February, Kafka wrote every

day. But it didn't amount to much, he complained in a letter to Klopstock: "It is like trying to dig a foxhole with one's fingernails in the midst
of battle." Despite this, he wrote four short stories, including "A Hunger
Artist."

Kurt Wolff Verlag printed fifteen hundred copies of *The Castle* and ad-
vertised it with a quotation labeling Kafka "the best writer since 1900."
Two years after his death, Kafka's name was becoming known, if not famous. "The Metamorphosis" had recently been included in a German literature course taught at the University of Marburg in Hesse, and several
laudatory articles appeared that summer of 1926 in the *Die literarishe Welt,*
written by Kafka's friends Max Brod, Felix Weltsch and Oskar Baum. Nevertheless, Kafka's books were still not widely read. Only a few copies of *The
Castle* sold when it was first published. Seventy years later, in 1996, in an
antiquarian bookshop in Amsterdam, a Dutch Kafka scholar discovered a
rare first edition of *The Castle.* On the overleaf of the book was an inscription dated 1929, which read: "To the wonderful couple, Hela and Walter
Gohlstein," and was signed "Dora Dymant-Kafka." Nothing further is
known of the couple, but the book was priced at $350.

BERLIN, SPRING 1926

Dora was twenty-eight years old. Since her birthday, she had found a lovely
place in an artist's studio on Siegmundshof in the Hansa Quarter, steps
from the Tiergarten, Berlin's version of New York's Central Park. The
sunny, charming artist's studio had a kitchen where she could cook for herself. The best part was that the studio belonged to a girlfriend, and Dora
could stay for free. In the mornings, Dora earned a little money looking after a three-year-old boy. She also took in sewing. She spent most of her free
time preparing for upcoming auditions. Dora had resumed acting lessons
with the Reinhardt teacher, who continued to coach her for free. Dora was
hoping for an engagement at the famous Volksbühne in the fall. An engagement would make her part of a theatrical company with a guaranteed income for the entire season, from the fall until the following spring. Dora
was looking forward again to the future, with excitement.

It was very early on a fresh Sunday morning in late May, when Robert
Klopstock arrived at 11 Siegmundhof. He had taken the night train from

Kiel, where he was working on his doctoral degree, and arrived at the Zoo Station in Berlin early Sunday morning on May 23. Her flat was only one stop on the S-bahn to Tiergarten. From there it was a short walk through the morning mist under the old street lamps along the fence of the famous Zoological Gardens, over the bridge across the Landwehr canal to the quiet tree-lined street that ended after a short walk on the banks of the river Spree. Klopstock loved being back in Berlin. The air was fresh and clean, and it seemed to him the healthiest of cities.

It was the Whitsun holidays. In Kiel, a seaside resort and university town north of Hamburg where Robert was now working toward his doctorate, tourists had taken over. Its famous harbor was crowded with brightly colored sails, while Berlin was quiet and peaceful. Both Christians and Jews celebrated the weeklong holiday, and many businesses and public institutions closed to commemorate Pentecost, the fiftieth day after Passover and the seventh Sunday after Easter. Robert was planning to spend the entire holiday, eight days, in Berlin.

Like Dora, Klopstock, had been deathly ill for several months. He had moved to Kiel because of its famed sea air, but the climate hadn't agreed with him, and his tuberculosis worsened to the point where the doctors wanted him to drop out of school and move away, which Robert refused to do. He felt much improved as he walked through the cool, clean morning air in Berlin. It seemed to him "the greatest injustice" for Kafka's family to blame Kafka's move to Berlin for his death, as they had written in letters to him.

It was only seven-thirty when Robert rang the bell at 11 Siegmundshof. After a few moments, the door opened a crack and Dora's sleepy head appeared. He couldn't come in, she said. She had just jumped out of bed to answer the door. She told him to come back later, and Robert returned that afternoon and several times over the next week.

"She is incredibly wonderful," Robert reported in a letter to Ottla. "She is sad, yes, but that is only her mood. Her character is so cheerful and full of life and joy for all that is beautiful and alive." He said that Dora "looks quite well, has gained ten pounds, and has become again very, very beautiful, like she was when Franz was still alive."

But Dora wasn't entirely well. She continued to run a slight temperature, which was worrying. Nevertheless, Dora cooked several meals for him over the next week, entertaining him and his cousin, with whom he was staying, as well as another friend, a painter. Dora "cooks splendidly," Robert reported to Ottla, "even as well as you!" When it was time for

Robert to return to Kiel, Dora went to the train station to see him off and brought him half a pineapple, an exotic fruit Robert had only recently discovered.

Before Robert completed the letter on June 10, Dora's circumstances had already changed. She had gone to the Baltic Sea for a rest cure. She had received 150 marks from a royalty payment and decided to use it to improve her health. She was staying at a boardinghouse owned by a woman she knew from Berlin and only had to pay five marks a day for room and meals. At that rate, she could afford to stay the whole month.

On Dora's behalf, Robert had spoken with Willy Haas, who had recently published two of Kafka's stories in the *Literary World*. Robert had asked Haas to pay Dora the royalties from the sketches so that she might stay at the Baltic for a second month. "Perhaps she will get an engagement at the Berlin People's Theater," he concluded. Therefore "it is very important that she is really well."

DÜSSELDORF, NOVEMBER 1926

On November 8, 1926, the Academy for Dramatic Art of the Düsseldorf Playhouse sent a letter to Dora outlining her courses and instructors. She had been accepted into its highly regarded and intensive professional acting program. In the records of the Dumont-Lindemann Archive at the Theater Museum in Düsseldorf, Dora Diamant is listed as one of thirty students, fifteen men and fifteen women, accepted for the school year 1926–1927. In 1927–1928, her name appears again as one of twenty-four students enrolled that year.

The letter, probably written by Berthold Viertel, who had been hired that year as lead actor and artistic director for the company, informed Dora that Salka Steurmann would be her teacher of elocution, and she would be taking performance classes with him. She would also receive one lesson per week from each of the eleven faculty members. The rigorous weekly schedule included play reading, role studies, speech technique, theater history, fencing and gymnastics. Attendance at all classes was mandatory. In the evenings, students were required to participate in rehearsals and performances in small roles in professional plays staged in the thousand-seat theater.

An enormous rococo building built on the ruins of a medieval castle on the Graf Adolf Platz near the center of the thirteenth-century Altstadt (Old

Town), the playhouse had successfully produced the classics and master-
pieces of modern theater for more than twenty years and enjoyed a stellar
reputation throughout Germany and Europe. The theater's venerated
founder and director, the actress Louise Dumont (born in Cologne in
1862), was now in her sixties and enjoying the height of her prestige and
fame. She was known throughout the Continent for her performances of
Hedda Gabler and the plays of Henrik Ibsen. Her husband, Gustav Lindemann, a Jewish actor and director, was often her leading man and also
served as manager of the Dumont Playhouse, as the theater was commonly
known.

Dora's acceptance to the highly competitive school was a tremendous
opportunity. If she could stay the course and graduate from the two-year
program, her professional future was assured, she was told. "It was one of
the great chances in my life to become a Dumont actor," Leon Askin said
when he was in his late eighties. A popular stage, film and television character actor who enjoyed busy careers in both Europe and America, Leon
Askin joined the theater's professional company as a young man about the
same time Dora was enrolled as a student. "To be a Dumont actor was
considered a great honor for any actor, yet it also had its disadvantages. A
Dumont actor was considered to be too stilted—the way we Dumont actors used to speak. Therefore, it was not easy to get any other engagement
in another theater. Directors and producers were afraid of a Dumont actor
while at the same time they admired him."

At sixty-four years of age, Louise Dumont was an impressive and formi-
dable woman, "with the bearing of a queen of antiquity." She was still active with both the playhouse and school, although her husband, Gustav
Lindemann, several years younger than she, now directed many of the productions himself. She would come to the final rehearsals "to give a final
touch to the production." According to Leon Askin, "Louise Dumont was
difficult to describe and perhaps even more difficult to know. She was neither arrogant nor distant, but rather simply unapproachable. Her face was
strong, framed with short, metal-gray hair. With her deeply set black eyes,
she penetrated her surroundings. She looked severe, but in her look was
also kindness—even if only recognizable to those who knew her well."

According to the registry of inhabitants in the Düsseldorf city archives,
"Dwora Dimant" registered her new address at 3 Remschneiderstrasse in
Düsseldorf on December 13, 1926. Her occupation is listed as "actress,

student." Her birthdate, 1899, is wrong, one year later than her actual birth year. The process of shaving years off her true age had begun. On August 1, 1927, she moved again to a neighborhood south of the city center at 34 Heresbachstrasse, where the playhouse had subsidized flats and rooms for the company's actors and students.

Founded in the thirteenth century on the banks of the Rhine River, the heavily industrialized city of Düsseldorf sat at the western edge of the great Ruhr Valley in the most densely populated area of Germany. The horrid conditions endured by the workers during the industrial boom had ignited the ideas of Marx and Engels, and now fed the growing anger of the German Communist Party factions. Düsseldorf, near the center of the "Red Ruhr," as the area was popularly called, was a hotbed of political activity, as the working classes were raging against their exploitation. At the same time, the great wealth created by the region's coal mining and steel industry supported a large middle class, as well as many museums, art galleries, the opera and several theaters.

In early 1927, Max Brod came to Düsseldorf to premiere his new comedy, *Die Opunzie,* at the City Theater's Kleines Haus, the Little Theater on Jahnstrasse. According to the daily newspaper, *Düsseldorfer Nachrichten,* Brod gave a series of lectures at the theater between February and March. *Die Opunzie* was "a three act comedy about a celebrity," according to notices put out by the theater, that dealt lightly with the class struggle between the workers movement and the left-wing intellectuals of Brod's literary circles.

Although there is no record of their meeting each other during this period, it is highly likely that they did; Brod was playing a vital role in Dora's life. The third—and last—Kafka novel was published as *Amerika* in 1927. The royalties from Kafka's estate were making it possible for Dora to devote herself to her studies.

Another person who came to Düsseldorf that year to present a play had a huge impact on Dora. Berta Lask was an extraordinary woman who in five years would become Dora's mother-in-law. The City Theater had bought the rights for a production of Berta Lask's politically explosive and highly controversial play *Leuna-21.* In the decade since losing her two brothers on the battlefields of World War I, the forty-eight-year-old wife and mother of four had become a prolific author as well as a fervent and idealistic communist.

Before he died on a Galician battlefield in May 1915, Berta's oldest brother, Emil Lask, had been a handsome thirty-eight-year-old philosopher in the prime of his life. He had earned his doctor of philosophy at Heidelberg University, and his theories were already attracting serious attention. In his last photograph, Emil is wearing his uniform, proudly clutching his rifle, as another member of his regiment stands behind him, a hand on his shoulder. Shortly after the photo was taken, he died in a battle against the czar's forces. Two years later, Berta's other brother, Hans, was killed on the Eastern front. The double tragedy left Berta grief-stricken and bitterly angry.

The horrifying loss of life in the war "deeply stirred" Berta and gave her a purpose in life outside her family. Before the war, Berta had been a happy upper-middle-class wife and mother of four. As the world dissolved into senseless ruin around her, Berta began to fight, to speak out against the madness. Despite the potentially lethal repercussions to her husband's career as a neurologist and lecturer at a Berlin University, Berta became a pacifist, a radical opponent to the war. She began to compose antimilitaristic poems, which were published in left-wing newspapers.

Leuna-21 was Berta's second play, based on her research into the inhumane working conditions that led to a revolt at the infamous Leuna Works. The events surrounding the strike—and the slaughter—of the factory workers, later known as the Central German Revolt of 1921, went largely undocumented and unreported by the news media of the day. The struggle for basic human rights at the Leuna Works chemical plant, the biggest producer of nitrogen in the world, had remained, in the words of one observer at the time, "shrouded in mystery."

To get material for her play, Berta Lask became an investigative reporter, spending months conducting intensive research. She traveled to the Mansfelder Mountains in Central Germany, took long hikes to the mines to hold secret interviews with the workers. The Leuna Works were owned by I.G. Farben, the conglomerate that later supplied gas for the death chambers in the Nazi concentration camps. Twenty-five thousand workers labored behind the thick, impenetrable brick walls, known throughout central Germany as the Leuna Prison for its poverty-level wages and high accident rates. In 1921, when I.G. Farben rescinded the eight-hour workday, a benefit "achieved through struggle just a short time before," the workers began a series of strikes. But the bosses were heavily armed with company spies, a private police force, a full arsenal, and their own legal department, which, in those days, was an unusual tactic.

Berta's dramatization examined the causes leading to the strike: "the provocations of the factory's private police force" and "the terror conducted by industrialists against the organized meetings of the workers"—

as well as the causes of the strike's collapse: "the social-political betrayal, the emergence of irresponsible communist leaders and the massive appearances of spies"—all of which she incorporated into the play's tight plot.

The first production of *Leuna-21* never opened. It was shut down just hours before its premiere by Berlin's chief of police, a member of the ruling majority Social Democratic Party who fiercely opposed the communists. Still, the play made news when a left-wing theater critic, Egon Erwin Kisch, who had seen a rehearsal, critiqued the play in his column, giving it a glowing review. Berta Lask had created a masterpiece with factual materials, he said, and displayed "a social passion which, apart from the Russian stage, is nonexistent." Beyond its effective theatricality, he said, the real importance of the play was its "strict, unadorned truthfulness, with which Berta Lask told the story of what happened in and around Leuna. The authorities have confiscated this piece of reality. But reality and truth cannot be confiscated!"

Nor did *Leuna-21* open in Düsseldorf. Repeating the censorious actions of the Berlin police, the Düsseldorf authorities, urged by powerful industrial bosses, closed the production on the day of the opening-night performance. It was not until almost thirty years later that *Leuna-21* actually opened, in an ensemble presentation performed by the Weimar National Theater in East Berlin in 1956, when Berta Lask was seventy-eight years old.

In April 1923, the year after the KPD (Communist Party of Germany) was founded, Berta Lask abandoned her "radical antimilitarism" and "bourgeois pacifism" and officially joined. By 1927 Berta Lask, an otherwise respectable, middle-class wife and mother, was under government suspicion and surveillance. Her writings, including her plays and children's books, had been pulled from libraries and bookstores, banned as "too political" by the democratic Weimar Republic.

Until discovering Berta Lask and meeting other communists who worked in the theater, Dora had considered herself a strong socialist. But the SPD (Socialist Party of Germany), the socialist party in power in Weimar, had lost her respect and trust. In a desperate bid for control of Germany after the collapse of the monarchy at the end of World War I, the SPD had sanctioned the brutal murders of fellow socialists Rosa Luxemburg and Karl Liebknecht, the leaders of the revolutionary Spartacists.

But politics were far from being Dora's primary concern. While she met other communists during her theater school years, most notably Wolfgang

Langhoff, an actor and director at the playhouse who was later arrested by
the Nazis for his communist agitprop theater activities, Dora focused on
perfecting her art. She threw herself into her classes, immersing herself in
the plays of Schiller, Goethe, Heine, Ibsen and Shakespeare. She studied
and rehearsed the great acting scenes and infused her classroom assignments with passionate intensity.

According school records, Dora left Düsseldorf on only two occasions
during 1927. In March she politely requested permission to leave between
April 1 and May 1, "since I have to travel on urgent family matters to
Poland." Dora didn't explain further, and there is no record of the
school's response to her request. Nor is there an answer to her request
sometime later that year for "two weeks' leave of absence, since I have to
go to Paris in an urgent family matter."

The nature of these urgent family matters remains a mystery, as does the
reason for the Dora's refusal to answer letters from her family. In the Theatermuseum files is a letter dated 17 November 1927, with a return address
of Brzeziny, Poland. Addressed to "Herr Direktor," the letter was written
on stationery with a sweeping capital letter D in the upper corner. "Please
forgive me if I turn to you," the writer began in halting German. "I would
like to have news about a person who is very close to me, and in whom I am
very interested, and she is at your theater, namely Miss Dora Dimant from
Bedzin, of whom I have had no news for a long time, although I write to
her constantly. I believe I will not cause you too much trouble if you,
please, are good enough to send me this information." Requesting that the
director "kindly to keep the whole matter discreet from the above-men-
tioned person," the letter was respectfully signed, "Bela Dimant."

From the beginning the teachers at the Academy acknowledged Dora's
"strong and individual" talent, as well as something else. At twenty-nine,
Dora was older and had more life experience than the other students.
Dora's talent, like Dora herself, was unusual: alternatively described as
self-willed, with a touch of extraordinary stubbornness, independence of
mind, originality and unconventionality. Although Dora exhibited strong
devotion to her studies, she tended to follow her own instincts and sometimes got into trouble. In September, Dora received a letter of reprimand
from the school's artistic director, which was placed in her school file.
"Dear Miss Diamant," Viertel wrote, "I hear complaints that you repeatedly miss the lessons of Mr. Kyser; it should be well known to you that you

are not allowed to miss any lessons without my permission. I expect your explanation."

Throughout October and November, Dora spent her evenings in rehearsals and performances of the playhouse's professional productions. In October she appeared in *The Prince of Homberg* and *The Broken Pitcher,* both plays by Heinrich von Kleist. He had also written Kafka's beloved *The Marquise of O—*, which Dora still remembered by heart. Kafka was never far from Dora's thoughts, especially now, with the ironic preponderance on Kleist in the repertoire and the publication of Kafka's third and last unpublished novel, which opened a new window onto Kafka's psyche and eerily reflected her own life.

Written in 1912, before World War I, *Amerika* was lighter and more optimistic than his other writings. According to Brod, Kafka was in "unbelievable ecstasy" and was "greatly inspired" while writing the novel, which he would work on all night long. When questioned how he could write a book set in America, where he had never been, Kafka replied, "I know the autobiography of Benjamin Franklin, and I have always admired Walt Whitman, and I like the Americans because they are healthy and optimistic." Kafka saw America as a vast, heroic landscape and "imagined that all Americans wore a perpetual smile."

Kafka had referred to the story as his "American novel," "The Man Who Disappeared," or "The Stoker," the title of the first chapter. The last chapter, and Kafka's favorite, was "The Nature Theater of Oklahoma." The young hero, Karl Rossman, joins a traveling theater company, a large public works theater "financed by invisible but extremely powerful benefactors." Kafka had confided to Max that in the end, "within this 'almost limitless' theater his young hero was going to find again a profession, his freedom, even his old home and his parents, as if by some celestial witchery." Kafka was so pleased with this unfinished chapter that, according to Brod, "he used to read it aloud with great effect."

Like Kafka's young hero, Dora was building a new life, a career with promise, a profession that demanded all the attention, love and passionate focus she had once devoted exclusively to Franz. It wasn't easy. Louise Dumont demanded perfection. As a performer in several crowd scenes, Dora received several typed notices demanding explanations for minor infractions, such as missing an entrance in the third scene. Once Dora's enthusiasm on stage went too far, and she refused to leave the stage when her scene was over, resulting in the following reprimand: "It was reported that you lingered on stage during a performance of 'The Broken Pitcher' and that you did not leave the stage in spite of the stage manager's request. I draw your attention to the fact that unoccupied students and company members are not allowed to enter the stage during performances."

On January 24, while appearing in *The Prince of Homburg,* Dora received a letter offering her the part of the Moorish girl in the playhouse's production of *Peer Gynt.* Unfortunately, no photographs remain of that production, with Dora in blackface.

DÜSSELDORF, EARLY 1928

In January, Dora notified the academy that she had changed the spelling of her last name to "Dymant." Why she took this step at this time is not known. According to her friends, Dora pronounced her last name with only two syllables, with the accent on the first syllable, and this spelling promoted a more correct pronunciation. For the rest of her life, even after she got married, Dora kept her name Dymant.

Dora was also experimenting with her first name. A fellow classmate at the academy, Luise Rainer, knew Dora only as "Doris." A seventeen-year-old beauty born in Düsseldorf, twelve years younger than Dora, Luise was already a star. She only sporadically attended classes and was immediately cast in leading roles. "Doris took a shine to me, I don't know why," Luise Rainer Knittel remembered during an interview in 2002, when she was ninety-two. Although she had no memory of any other student actors in the company, Luise never forgot Dora, even though she lost touch with her and never knew what became of her. "We were so different. I was so young in every way—I'm still not mature today. I was so very full of life and romantic. I didn't think she was particularly attractive. She was a dark kind of person, always dressed in black, as if in mourning. I had never read Kafka, but she always talked to me about Kafka. I could not tell you today any particular conversation, other than we always talked about him. It seemed to me that she was completely fulfilled by him." When asked why she remembered Dora and no one else from that period, she answered simply: "Doris was a figure. She was *somebody.*"

In February, three months before she graduated, Dora started setting up auditions for professional work. The ideal situation was to be hired as a member of a theater company for a full season, which typically ran eight months, from September to May. Dora wanted to have a job lined up before graduation; by May, all the other graduates of the academy and all other professional actor training programs throughout the country, along with every other out-of-work actor, would also be making the same rounds, trying to find work. Although the German economy was on the rebound, many theaters throughout Germany had not survived the inflation period, and the competition for jobs, always fierce in the theater, was now brutal.

In March, in an act of both boldness and desperation, Dora wrote a letter to Louise Dumont. While Dora's auditions had yielded the invaluable experience necessary for every actor, they had produced no jobs. She was thirty years old and had no time to waste. "The circumstance that I am still without engagement for the next year in spite of extreme efforts may be regarded as a part excuse for this demand," she wrote, asking for Dumont's personal help.

"Dear Mrs. Dumont!" Dora began. "In the hope that my request will reach you in this way, I permit myself, although I find it difficult, to make demands of you regarding the following—I was advised to approach Miss Madeleine Lueders, the director of the Hamburg Theater for a possible engagement. And since Miss Lueders, as I have been told, was a student of yours for many years and belongs among your most sincere admirers, I permit myself—if it would not be considered presumptuous on my part—to ask you fervently, whether you couldn't help me in a way that is worry free for you." Dora signed the letter, "With reverence and gratitude for you."

Dora kept Max Brod informed of her situation. She had written him shortly after her thirtieth birthday in early March and again on May 15, pouring out her plans for her graduation performance and upcoming recitation evening, her final project as a student of the academy. She had decided on a reading from Kafka's most recently published novel, *Amerika,* and had already gotten Ottla's blessing. Later Dora sent Brod a handwritten program from the evening.

Near the end of May, two faculty members, Hermann Greid and Franz Evereth, wrote a letter of recommendation for Dora: "From the beginning, she was recognized to have a strong, unusual talent. During these two years she completely fulfilled these expectations and—by outstanding dedication and intensive diligence—has proven her educational and developmental ability, so that we, the undersigned teachers, can say with full conviction: Miss Dymant will, with affectionate, correct direction, be able to produce strong, yes even very deeply moving, performances. We wish Miss D., with all our hearts, the success which her diligence, her devotion and her unusual gift deserve."

Dora's persistence finally paid off when she was hired by the Collective Theater of the Rhine in Neuss for a professional engagement for the season. According to microfilm records in the Düsseldorf municipal archives, that fall Dora moved to Neuss, a small city of 45,000 inhabitants located across the Rhine River just southeast of Düsseldorf. She lived at 59 Kanal Street with another actress in the theater company that season, Mia Engels, who had graduated from the academy the year before Dora.

The theater in Neuss had officially opened three years earlier, in 1925. It was an ambitious company, presenting five new plays along with a classical repertoire. Dora was one of seven women and twelve men hired for the company that season, which performed in the new six-hundred-seat Collective Theater of the Rhine in Neuss, and at regional theaters throughout the Rhineland. Over the course of the next eight months, Dora traveled with the theater troupe to thirty-six theaters dotting the Rhine River valley. They performed in the low-lying towns of Emmerich, Kleve and Bocholt on the Dutch border, in Alsdorf near the Belgian border, and in Lüdenschied and Gummersbach in the mountains east of Düsseldorf and Cologne.

Two theater programs from the Rhineland Theater found in the archives of the Theater Museum in Düsseldorf list Dora Dymant as a cast member. In *Kabale und Liebe* (Intrigue and Love), "a middle-class (bourgeois) tragedy in 5 acts" by Friedrich von Schiller, Dora played the part of Sophie, the lady's maid. Dora was double-cast with her roommate Mia Engels as the female lead, Princess Alma, the daughter of the title character, in a new play produced that season, Frank Wedekind's *King Nicolo, or Such Is Life.*

The role was Dora's great triumph and her first rave review. On opening night in Gladbach, a small town twenty miles east of Cologne, the theater was filled to capacity. The play, which lasted well over three hours, received "a storm of applause at the end of the performance," according the local daily newspaper. "Not only was the directing promising, but also the artistic quality of the largely newly-hired company. No negative criticism can be made, the ensemble acting was outstanding." The role of Princess Alma garnered the critic's highest praise. The actress, he said, "raised the creation of the princess to some truly effective heights, and managed the extraordinarily difficult role, which poses the most varied demands on the performer, so well that one can certainly welcome her entry to the ensemble, which last year was rather short of good actors."

One month later, Dora was back in Neuss in a production of *The Fool and Death,* a play about love and death written by Hugo von Hofmannsthal.

The opening night performance on November 2, 1928, was reviewed in the *Düsseldorf News.* "The play is moving," the newspaper reported, and described it in the words of a Greek philosopher who "claimed that we don't know if life is rather a state of death, and death, in reality, life." While the reviewer felt the lighting was too heavy-handed and the overall direction too shrill and exaggerated, "the performance was finely balanced. Tilla Hohmann, Dora Dymant and Albert Loeffner as well as E. Wagner adapted themselves splendidly to the play."

As 1928 drew to an end, Dora was a working professional actress, earning a living at her trade, doing what she had dreamed of, and gaining admiration and respect for her hard work and talent. For the first time since Kafka's death four years earlier, anything seemed possible. For Dora's classmate, Luise Rainer, anything was possible. After starring on stages in Berlin, Vienna, and other cities, Luise Rainer went to Hollywood, where she married the playwright and screenwriter Clifford Odets. She signed a contract with Louis B. Mayer and made eight films for MGM in less than four years. In 1936 and 1937, Luise Rainer won the Academy Award for best actress for her roles in *The Great Ziegfield* and *The Good Earth,* making her the first actor to win the award twice.

14

DESCRIPTION OF A STRUGGLE

*That which is possible will surely happen, but
only that which happens is possible.*

—Franz Kafka

BERLIN, SPRING 1929

Dora's theatrical engagement ended on April 30 and she returned to
Berlin without a job. She found an apartment to share with a young
woman, Eva Frietsche, at 17 Lohmeyerstrasse, just south of the vast Charlottenburg Palace. The neighborhood was lovely, close to the landscaped
parks and Baroque museums, but with an explosive mix of politics. Located in the midst of one of the wealthiest districts in Berlin, the area was
known as "Little Wedding," for its active communist enclave. It was
named after the northern suburb of Wedding, the largest working-class
district in Berlin and a major KPD stronghold.

As soon as Dora returned, the city exploded in violence. The traditional
May Day demonstrations, the communist workers' holiday, had a long history in Berlin, with more citizens joining in the marches and rallies each
year. However, this year, an emergency measure banned all demonstrations within the city. The Social Democratic police chief, Karl Zoegiebel—
the same man who had shut down Berta Lask's *Leuna-21* in Berlin on its
opening night—refused to lift the ban, ignoring all warnings that the communists "would feel obliged to challenge the ban in the name of socialist
tradition," which is precisely what happened.

The police went into "a senseless rage," according to the lieutenant in
charge of the Friedrichshain precinct, and began shooting bystanders as
well as demonstrators. "All over the city," one historian reported, the

police "employed their weapons with an indiscriminate ruthlessness that served only to outrage and provoke onlookers." The civil liberties of not just the targeted communist radicals, but all members of the working classes were disregarded. Normally law-abiding citizens were repeatedly attacked and their freedoms restricted. For many, and Dora included, the failure of the socialist government—a democracy—to uphold the most basic socialist ideals of human rights and freedom was a warning signal and a call to action.

Despite the bloody political street warfare, Berlin was arguably the most vibrant city in the world. The freewheeling prosperity sparked by billions of dollars in loans from American investors made the last years of the "Golden Twenties" the epitome of the cultural, artistic, social and scientific glory of Weimar Germany. "Berlin's art and artists exerted a magnetic force," noted a Berlin journalist. "People came from all over the world to take part in the town's intellectual activities. It was a great happiness to be alive in those days."

In 1928 the young poet W. H. Auden moved to Berlin after graduating from Oxford and fell in love with the city. Writing home to England, he pronounced Berlin "a splendid place" and recommended the city's fabled creative energies if one "wanted to get work done." Urged on by Auden's superlatives, the writer Christopher Isherwood followed his friend to Berlin, moving into a depressed neighborhood around Nollendorf Square, once proud Prussian buildings now subdivided into "pretentious slums." The people Isherwood encountered in his building became the cast of his *Berlin Stories,* later made famous by the stage play and film *Cabaret.* Stephen Spender was another of Auden's circle of Oxford friends drawn to Berlin's perverse, eclectic energy. During his visits to Isherwood's flat, Spender later recalled, "one or another of the characters of his as yet unwritten novels would dart out of one of the rooms . . . perhaps Sally Bowles would appear, her clothes disheveled, her eyes large onyxes fringed by eyelashes like enameled wire, in a face of carved ivory."

Beyond the bright lights, fashionable shops and packed theaters and cabarets of the newly restored Ku'damm lurked Berlin's dark side. "There was a sensation of doom to be felt in the Berlin streets," Spender later wrote. "The feeling of unrest in Berlin went deeper than any crisis. It was a permanent unrest." It was an explosive mixture: "the poverty, the anger, the prostitution, the hope and despair thrown out on to the streets. It was the blatant rich at the smart restaurants, the prostitutes in army top boots at corners, the grim, submerged–looking Communists in processions, and the violent youths who suddenly emerged from nowhere into the square and shouted, 'Germany awake!'"

Dora auditioned, but no one hired her. The classical style that she had learned was now out of fashion. With the unlikely triumph of *The Threepenny Opera,* the spectacles of Max Reinhardt and the "spiritual theater" of Louise Dumont lost ground to gritty works of social realism. The adaptation of Englishman John Gay's *Beggar's Opera* (first performed two hundred years earlier) was created by Bertolt Brecht—who went from being a radical leftist to a convinced Marxist while working on the piece—and an avant-garde composer, Kurt Weill. The play's nihilistic and unscrupulous hero, MacHeath, also known as Mack the Knife, illustrated the class conflict from a pointedly proletarian point of view. The production opened to "howling applause" and established a new standard for expressionist theater. Night after night, the wealthy and upper middle classes—the only ones who could afford the ticket prices—flocked to the theater to watch themselves ridiculed and denounced. The idea that drama could be a medium of revolution was born, setting the scene for what the Nazis later termed "cultural Bolshevism," using the arts to promote a revolution.

The revolution in the theater took to the streets. That summer in Moscow the official newspaper of the Comintern in Germany, the Communist International, published an article recommending "great attention be paid to the 'battle for the streets'" by reaching the masses through propaganda and agitation in an escalating struggle against a dangerous and aggressive antagonist, the brown-shirted storm troopers, or SA (Sturm Abteilung), which had been founded two years earlier, in 1927. The SA, under the direction of Joseph Goebbels, was part another revolutionary party, the NSDAP, the National Socialist German Workers Party. The party's leader, Adolf Hitler, had been released from jail early following his failed "Beer Hall Putsch" and had published his memoirs; he appointed Goebbels head of the Berlin district. Since arriving in Berlin in 1926, Goebbels had streamlined the party, organized and built the army of storm troopers, and concentrated on winning the battle for the streets of Berlin by first attacking "the Marxists."

Dora was in the middle of it all. At first she concentrated on trying to find work, but she couldn't find a job, any job. As conditions worsened around her, Dora grew angry and frustrated at the injustice and inequality evident among the socialists who were running the government. Her roommate, Eva Frietsche, was "a very active Communist, who from time to time, took me to a cell meeting," Dora later reported. She attended political rallies and read political literature, and was increasingly moved by the "overwhelming accusations made by Communism against bourgeois society, an accusation not only against all its institutions but also reaching deep in the individual soul." Dora, like many knowledgeable, educated, intelligent people of the time, was impressed by concrete communist plans for social and economic improvement for all people. Before long, she was convinced of the rightness of their cause.

Until the autumn of 1929, Dora had talked freely about Kafka. "How convinced and happy people are when I talk to them of Franz, some are actually changed," she said. "The floodgates open up in me, the more I tell. So I must, after all, have to some extent the means and ability to impart something of Franz. I even suspect that I show, in such moments, a kind of likeness to Franz, because the people listening to me have something similar in their expression as those who listened to him then."

That fall, Dora became embroiled in a public literary spat that taught her a painful lesson about giving interviews to reporters and speaking publicly about Kafka. It all started with an article in a respected Berlin newspaper, *Vossische Zeitung,* by a regular contributor, Ehm Welk. The article, published at the end of September, extolled the creative genius of Kafka's work but sharply reproached Max Brod for having published it, for having "breached the trust of a dying friend."

Dora jumped to Brod's defense. Deeply disturbed by the unfairness of Welk's article, Dora contacted Ehm Welk and went to visit him at the newspaper. Dora thought their meeting went very well. "I explained to Mr. Welk that he had based his opinion on an entirely false foundation; after a short conversation, he agreed to my most important objections," Dora reported. "He admitted that his behavior towards Brod was grounded in a misconception. He mentioned that he had become aware of this already through reading Max Brod's afterword, which indicated that his accusations perhaps might not be legitimate. In the end, he asked me what I thought he should do. I told him I would appreciate it if he would withdraw his accusations against Max Brod, which he now considered wrong. Mr. Welk promised to do this and even added that he was glad to see the case in the right light now, especially since he had always held Brod in such high esteem." Dora said she was "sincerely glad" and truly admired Welk's "honest and brave willingness to openly admit his mistake."

Before Ehm Welk could publish his "retraction," Brod himself responded to the attack in a long letter to the editor of the *Vossische Zeitung* on October 24: "Heavy conflicts arise when you deal with a work to which future generations have rights, even if the author himself wants its destruction," Brod said, pointing out that he dealt with these "complicated considerations" in his afterword to *The Trial.* "Welk knows this afterword, because he quotes it," Brod wrote, adding, "without this afterword no one would know of Kafka's wish of destruction." The final evidence Brod offered as justification for his actions was that had he not published these works, Ehm Welk would not now be able to criticize Brod for having saved them.

One week after the publication of Brod's letter to the editor, Welk published his response: "In Reply: A Conversation." His answer to Brod was a page of the edited transcript of his conversation with "Mrs. Kafka." Instead of constituting an apology for his earlier remarks, Welk's selected questions—and worse, Dora's answers to them—strengthened his original complaints against Brod. He had used Dora's own words to back up his condemnation. Dora was furious when she read her answers printed in the newspaper on November 10. She had no idea when she was talking to Welk that she was "on the record."

The spat became a brawl as public reaction mounted and more accusations were hurled at Brod. Four days later, Dora wrote her own letter to the editor of the *Vossische Zeitung*, saying that these attacks on Brod evidenced a "personal hostility," and that she was forced to respond to correct the "distorted presentation that Mr. Welk gives of our conversation." First, she pointed out, Welk had not asked, nor had she given her consent, to publish what she understood was "a private conversation." She didn't deny the correctness of the quotes Welk used. But the questions and answers he chose to publish "showed a certain consent between him and me, whereas he did not mention any of the fundamental areas where our opinions differed widely. In this way, he brought about the opposite of what I—had I ever considered a publication of the conversation—would have wanted to cause."

To definitively answer Welk and "all the others who made a mistake here," Dora stated for the record that "the accusations towards Max Brod were founded on a superficial observation and a lack of information." She lauded Brod's motives and intentions, emphasizing that there could be absolutely no doubt of his friendship, loyalty and respect for Franz Kafka, or the works entrusted to him. The argument would have horrified Kafka, and she would not allow him to be used in this manner. "Franz Kafka is perhaps not the most suitable object to be misused as an arrow in this not really very honorable fight," she concluded. Dora wanted to put an end "to the conflict of the Public vs. Brod. But just in case that this dispute should continue," Dora warned, "I am inclined not to say another single word in this matter. Quite the opposite, I am ready to ask pardon in advance for every word that might be regarded wrong, if by this I can prevent the continuation of this degrading and fruitless argument."

Dora couldn't quite end the letter there. There was something "fundamental" that remained to be said, no matter who else she might insult or infuriate: "There is much (unfortunately too much) talking and writing about Franz Kafka. Should not those who are starting to speak in order to acknowledge his personality and his work—before they do this—first ask themselves whether they do it out of an external cause, or out of a motive that is worthy of the person and writer Franz Kafka? To examine oneself in this respect is the heartfelt request of all those who are close to Franz Kafka."

The end result of the Ehm Welk affair for Dora was a painful break in her friendship with Max Brod—it would be many months before he spoke to her again—and the beginning of Dora's long public silence on the subject of Kafka. It would be nearly twenty years before she would give another interview about Franz Kafka to a member of the press.

At the end of October, an event took place that would soon change the world completely. The New York stock market crashed. Dora and other Berliners saw the headlines but failed to grasp their meaning. Few understood what effect the stock market in faraway America had on their everyday lives.

BERLIN, JANUARY 1930

The depression hit Berlin very quickly, and Dora was one of the hundreds of thousands immediately affected. There was now no hope of finding a job in the theater or out. When Wall Street crashed in October 1929, there were 1.75 million unemployed in Germany, nearly half of them in Berlin. Two months later, by January 1930, the number had doubled and kept climbing each month. As American and foreign investors started calling in their loans, Germany was immediately ensnared in what would soon be a global depression. According to Egon Larsen, a journalist who covered Weimar Berlin, "a vicious circle was in operation, reminiscent of that of the inflation; exports dwindled quickly as all industrial nations were caught in the crisis, foreign investments in Germany stopped, and as a result factories and companies went bankrupt by the hundreds, throwing their workers and office staff out into the streets."

The royalty checks Dora was still receiving from Kafka's estate were keeping her alive and allowing her to fill her days working for the rights of poor workers. She helped produce and hand out leaflets and helped organize strikes, rallies and demonstrations. She listened to the horrors and abuses suffered by the workers and grew enamored of the glorious plans for the "Communist Internationale," the anthem they sang together, faces glowing under the red flags:

O comrades, come rally, and the great fight let us face.
The Internationale unites the human race.

At the end of 1929, Dora applied for membership in the KPD, the German Communist Party. After a short period as a KPD candidate, in January 1930 Dora was admitted to the Charlottenburg street cell 218 and was given a "passname." For safety, party members were given aliases to keep their true identities secret. Dora's passname was "Maria Jelen." Along with her roommate, Eva, she continued to attend cell meetings. Seven years later, the section leader wrote a letter to the Russian Comintern in Moscow, answering a request for information about Dora's activities and commitment to the party, confirming suspicions that she was never a truly committed communist:

I know Comrade Maria Jelen (Diamant) since the year 1930. During that time, approx. one half year, she was active and took part in the everyday party tasks. I have no further knowledge about her party activities. About her personal circumstances I know that she received financial support from the estate of her first husband (Franz Kafka) from the leftist bourgeois Zionist writer Max Brod.

At the beginning of May, Dora received a royalty payment from Brod but no accompanying letter, not a single word, not even a greeting. In Franz's memory, she couldn't allow the situation to continue another moment, and she sat down to write a long letter to Max, an attempt to explain her position, both to him and to herself. "I thank you, but am very sad," Dora began. "The saddest part is that I know the road that led to this, but feel desperate, because of my awkward inability to untangle this misunderstanding. Because that's all it really is," Dora assured him. She apologized for not clarifying her negative feelings about the posthumous publication of Kafka's books before Brod read about it in Welk's article. Even now, trying to explain was impossible. "But how else are you supposed to believe me?" Dora wondered. "It is absolutely hopeless," Dora wrote, before pressing on: "Yes, you've just got to believe me when I say that I fully approve of all of your activities on behalf of Franz and his work, even if I myself would not have the strength to act accordingly. But this is a diagnosis of our different strengths, and I'm at a disadvantage."

Dora said she understood perfectly why Brod wanted to publish his works. "But then Franz was actually my teacher in all the things that I now have access to. Only with Franz's eyes, did I get to know you, which certainly excludes any error from the very beginning. . . . Dearest Max, it is completely impossible for us to hold even a shadow of suspicion against each other. To judge the magnitude of what you are doing for Franz, this I can only do with the help of Franz's gaze. By myself I am inadequate."

There was another, very difficult issue between them, but Dora was not ready to admit that she still had in her possession Kafka's last notebooks, as well as his thirty-five letters to her. She wondered if Max still believed she had burned all twenty notebooks, as he had written to Martin Buber. "I am rather honest on the whole, and that anything at all connected with Franz must be surrounded by truthfulness." But to that, she added the following disclaimer: "For myself, measured solely by my own standards, I can and should not judge."

Dora was beginning to realize the selfishness of her motives, yet she clung to them. "For even though in great love, I am a small, possessive woman," she explained. "As long as I was living with Franz, all I could see was him and me. Anything other than his own self was simply irrelevant and even ridiculous. His work was unimportant at best. Any attempt to present his work as part of him seemed to me simply ridiculous. That is why I objected to the posthumous publication of his writings. And besides, as I am only now beginning to understand, there was the fear of having to share him with others. Every published statement, every conversation I regarded as a violent intrusion into my private realm. The world at large does not have to know about Franz. He is nobody else's business because, well, because nobody could possibly understand him. I regarded it—and I think I still do so now—as wholly out of the question for anyone ever to understand Franz, or to get even an inkling of what he was about unless one knew him personally. All efforts to understand him were hopeless unless he himself made them possible by the look in his eyes or the touch of his hand. And this, of course, he can no longer do. All well and good what I am saying here, but it doesn't amount to much, as I have recently come to realize."

As Dora solidified her thoughts in the letter to Max, it dawned on her that she was just beginning to understand Kafka. Only now were pointless gestures he once made in a conversation becoming clear to her. He had to cope with some things alone, she realized, things that she had no idea about back then.

"Only in love, and earlier, the belief in God, had I any notion of the Absolute, the Infinite. It was Franz who gave me an idea of what it was, in other things, and in everything. And this notion, this idea is still developing; after such a long time it has yet to ripen, if indeed I will ever be able to have more than this vague perception of it. But it is this awareness which allows me to have perhaps more than an inkling of your innermost relationship to Franz." Dora stopped, frustrated. "Has any of this said anything?" she wondered. "I would believe that I had said everything if I knew that you understand me. Since this is exactly what I don't know, I am in great anxiety. Farewell, and do accept my most heartfelt greetings, Dora."

Dora's acting talent and theater skills did not go unrecognized by Berlin's KPD leadership. Agitprop theater groups had been springing up spontaneously around the country for several years, and the popularity of proletarian street theater groups was at its height. By the summer of 1930, Dora moved to the KPD agitprop department and was put in charge of training actors for the street plays. It wasn't the career on the legitimate stage that she had imagined for herself, but at least Dora was able to use her skills and talents.

Agitprop theater had evolved from its beginnings in Russia into an art form and weapon. In 1847, the year the League of Communists was founded, Friedrich Engels wrote a one-act political play to be performed by workers, and the concept of using theater as a weapon for revolutionary change had grown to include hundreds of agitprop groups with thousands of members. Of the many political parties struggling for control of the Weimar government, the KPD was the most underfunded, representing as it did the lowest echelon of income producers. The Nazis and the Social Democrats were rich by comparison, financed by industrial cartels and foreign investors and increasingly supported by the bourgeoisie, the middle class. Since the KPD couldn't compete through the mass media, it needed new and inexpensive ways to reach the public, to explain the complex economic dangers and political realities of capitalist greed and fascism. Their strategy was to develop agitprop troupes, which sprang up all over the country.

Proletarian writers and directors such as Bertolt Brecht and Erwin Piscator wrote effective agitprop skits and revues characterized by wit and biting sarcasm. Walter Langhoff, whom Dora knew from the Düsseldorf Playhouse, formed his own company from factory workers and the unemployed, who put their energy and anger to work, memorizing KPD songs, chants and marches. He later called these the best days of his life. They performed at festivals and in factories, halls, courtyards and wherever public space could be secured. They traveled the countryside to villages to perform songs and scenes, to pass out or sell literature, to spread their message through the entertainment they provided free of charge. The results were impressive. In one month before the July elections, agitprop troupes reached a total audience of 180,000 and recruited more than 1,120 new members.

It was a boisterous and heady experience for those involved in producing this form of revolution. They built their own program of songs and short skits, each scene being wrested from personal anguish and experience. The troupes designed and made their own costumes, which were more like uniforms, often trousers with blue blouses and red neckerchiefs or scarves. Because of the inexperience of the performers and the changing nature of the repertoire, which reflected current events, rehearsals were held daily, with performances usually scheduled for every weekend.

Dora joined the RGO (Revolutionary Trade Union Opposition) group Film and Stage at the height of agitprop activity in Berlin. The German press warily reported on their successes, noting that the performances illustrated "the proletarian struggle with the most revolutionary realism possible." The police were watching, too, and reported that "the KPD supports the agitprop troupes and with good reason. There is hardly any Communist event or meeting held without a performance. Troupes have caused a considerable growth in the numbers of people attending meetings and brought about a substantial increase in Party membership. . . . Short cabaret scenes, sketches, one-acts, etc. . . . are much more apt to convince the audience of the correctness of communist principles than the most effective speeches. Nothing has such an inciting and stirring effect. In the interest of the state itself and to protect the public the state must use all its powers against . . . the agitprop troupes."

Frightened, the ruling class agreed. Under the Weimar Republic's constitution, theater censorship was not allowed, so the Social Democrats passed new emergency security measures with names such as "For the Defense of the Republic" and "The Law to Fight Political Excesses," and changed the constitution. All agitprop performances were placed under the supervision of "uniformed officers who could break them up or dissolve them at any moment if they thought the content was subversive and against the interest of the state." As the influence of agitprop performances continued to grow, an even stronger measure was passed that banned all agitprop performances in Germany.

BERLIN-ZEHLENDORF, FEBRUARY 1931

Dora moved to Zehlendorf, not far from where she and Kafka had lived during their last six weeks in Berlin together. Exactly seven years had passed since that rainy February 1, when they had splurged on the taxi to take them and their baggage from the apartment on Gruenwaldstrasse to their new and final lodging at the home of the Widow Busse, on Heidestrasse. Seven years seemed a lifetime ago.

According to her own account in her Comintern autobiography, Dora rose quickly and smoothly through the party ranks. "After Charlottenburg, I worked for a short time in Zehlendorf, first as cashier, then organizer, then section leader, according to where something was needed. In my house in Zehlendorf, the ten-day school for course trainers of the MASCH (Marxist Workers Evening School) took place, in which I was also a student." Dora didn't mention any conflicts or problems within the party. Despite her commitment to helping others and her desire to work as part of a collective, however, her individualism and love of freedom prevented her from toting the Marxist line completely. One of her comrades remembered that while he was working in the office of the Charlottenburg district office, "she was accused of inactivity in her street cell."

Dora met her future husband, Lutz Lask, in her apartment in Zehlendorf, when she opened it for the ten-day courses in Marxist theory offered by the Berlin-Brandenburg Agitprop Department. Every evening, classes in history, economics and agitation techniques where taught to KPD leaders cut by experts in those fields. At first glance, there was little to suggest that Dora would soon marry the quiet young economist who taught the Marxist economic theory classes in her living room. Besides their political affiliation, they seemed to have little in common. Ludwig "Lutz" Lask was five years younger than she, an assimilated nonreligious German Jew, with a recent degree in economics from the World Economics Institute in Kiel. He had returned to Berlin at the beginning of the year; unable to find employment and encouraged by his mother, he began to work on behalf of the KPD. In July he joined the Lichterfelde-Ost cell, the same cell to which his mother and younger brother already belonged. The more involved he became in teaching the classes at the Marxist Workers College, the more the party work began to dominate his life. Dora probably had something to do with it, too.

Little is known of the courtship between Lutz Lask and Dora Dymant. He fell in love with Dora, probably seeing her as an exciting, attractive, experienced older woman, although he didn't know how much older. In his Comintern autobiography he noted that his wife, "the comrade Dora Dymant, was born in 1900," two years after the actual date. Slightly built, with a gentle manner, he had soft brown hair and large dark eyes. His face was long and narrow, and his lips, his best feature, were curved and full. In family photographs he is always dressed neatly, wearing a starched white shirt, striped tie and light-colored suit.

In many ways, he was Dora's opposite: reliable, quiet and calm where she was spontaneous, lively and outspoken. But he was very intelligent, well-read and educated. He could read Greek and Latin, as well as French and English. He studied law for five years at universities in Berlin and Freiburg, but after reading the first volume of Marx's *Das Kapital* in the summer of 1925, he changed his field of study to economics. After graduating with his diploma in economics in 1930, he published a study for the Kiel Economics Institute on the influence of the tax system on exports.

One of Lutz's greatest assets was his large, loving family. At the heart of it was his mother, Berta Lask, famous for her revolutionary zeal and idealistic leadership. Dora loved Berta, who, twenty years older than she, was a true mother-figure. Born on November 17, 1878, in Wadowice, then part of Galicia (not far from Dora's own birthplace), Berta was one of four children born to a well-to-do German-Jewish factory owner. When she was six, the Lask family moved to Mark Brandenburg, so that the children would grow up in Germany. The Lasks were politically liberal (though not socialists) and sent their two daughters, Berta and her older sister Helene, to a "school for better-class daughters" until the age of fifteen, when they were expected to prepare for marriage.

In 1901, at the age of twenty-three, Berta made a brilliant match when she married Dr. Louis Jacobsohn, a Berlin neurologist and brain researcher who served on the medical faculty at Friedrich-Wilhelm University. He was fifteen years older than she, with a great brown beard and pince-nez glasses. In family photographs taken in 1904, Berta Lask was a beauty, tall and slender, with large, brown, wide-set eyes, gently curving full lips, and a long, graceful neck. Five years later, four children had been born: the eldest, Ruth, was born in 1902, Lutz in 1903, Hermann in 1905, and the youngest, Ernst, in 1906. The family moved frequently to accommodate the growing family until settling into a large rambling house on Mittelstrasse (today called Bassermannstrasse) in Steglitz in 1914, a short walk to the Lichterfelde-Ost S-Bahn station.

After World War I, the German government enacted a new law allowing women who had lost brothers during the war to legally take back their birth names and give them to their children, in order to perpetuate their family name. According to Berlin-Steglitz civil records, in 1919 Berta and Louis took the name "Jacobsohn-Lask" and the last name was shortened to "Lask" for all four children. Unlike his wife, Louis was a political moderate, a member of the SPD. Despite disparities in age and politics, the Jacobsohn-Lasks enjoyed a committed and loving relationship that lasted despite many obstacles.

BERLIN-LICHTERFELDE, SPRING 1932

According to her Comintern file, Dora moved from her flat in Zehlendorf and joined the street cell in Lichterfelde-Ost, the cell to which the Lask family belonged. She rose to organization leader right away, working on the production and distribution of propaganda leaflets and newspapers, handing out the handbills and selling the newspapers at trade union meetings. She helped organize demonstrations and set up secret meetings. She and Lutz worked side by side, fighting for not only human rights and freedom but their lives.

Dora was thirty-four years old. She loved children and longed for her own. Her great regret was that she had not had a child with Kafka. She was tired of being alone. Behind the tall wrought-iron fence, the Lasks' large brick and stone house on Mittelstrasse was *heimelig*, warm and welcoming, filled with the vitality of an extended family of children and grandchildren, friends and comrades. The oldest daughter, Ruth, had married a French

Jew named Ernest Friedlaender, an engineer, and they had an adorable, curly-haired three-year-old named Frank. Hermann, Lutz's middle brother, had married Alice Mueller in May, and their daughter, also named Ruth, was born that July. Both Lutz and his youngest brother, Ernst, now twenty-six, were living at home, and the house was usually full of people, passionately involved with life, arguing economics, culture, philosophy and politics, and loving one another despite their differences. Before long, Dora lived there, too.

The number of unemployed now stood at over 6 million, one-third of the German workforce. The Weimar Republic was on the verge of collapse. Rumors abounded of "a military dictatorship, and of a general strike, and of civil war—but nothing happened." The Social Democrats still held the majority in the Reichstag but in recent elections had lost parliament seats to the Nazis and communists. Field Marshall Hindenberg, the president of the Weimar Republic, was eighty-four years old and increasingly feeble and senile. His seven-year term was nearly up, and Adolf Hitler was leading the race for the presidency in the upcoming elections.

Many notable Berliners read the signs of impending doom and left. Marlene Dietrich, already established in Hollywood, "came back to her native Berlin in 1932, took a careful look at the political warfare, and then decided to return to America for good." Albert Einstein and his wife, who owned a villa on a lovely lake near Potsdam, witnessed the growing anti-Semitism and the political direction, which "filled him with despair." When Einstein returned to the United States to teach another semester at Cal Tech in 1932, he told his wife, "Before you leave the villa this time, take a good look at it." When she asked why, Einstein answered, prophetically: "You will never see it again."

Dora was not without hope. From her point of view, things were already improving. In Berlin the communists were gaining a solid lead over the Nazis. In the July 1932 elections, the KPD won in Wedding, Friedrichshain, Neukolln, Prenzlauer Berg and Mitte, the same neighborhoods that fell under Soviet control when the city was subdivided after World War II and later became East Berlin. In the November elections in Berlin, the communists made gains while the Nazis received less than 25 percent of the vote.

In May, Dora officially withdrew from the Berlin Jewish community. It was a financial and political decision; she didn't think much about the greater significance of her action at the time. Dora had little contact with the Jewish community these days, but as a registered member of the Jew-

Dora Diamant, c. 1924
The best known photograph of Dora. One of only two known to exist until the discovery of the Lask Collection in Berlin in 1998. Dora gave this photograph to Hanny Lichtenstern. Photo reprinted by permission of Hanny Lichternstern and the Diamant family of Israel.

Franz Kafka, c. 1917
This was Dora's favorite photograph of Kafka. She took two framed copies with her to Israel and left them with family and friends. Photo reprinted by permission of Archiv Klaus Wagenbach, Berlin.

Postcard of Pabianice, **Poland c. 1910**
Dora's birthplace. The market square overlooking the sixteenth-century
Renaissance mansion and public school, which now houses the Pabianice
Museum. Photo reprinted by permission of the Muzeum Miasta Pabianic.

**Bedzin, Poland
c. 1910**
View from the river.
To the left is the
castle; to the right is
the large synagogue
built in the 1880s.
Photo courtesy of the
private collection
of Jeffrey K. Cymbler.

**Hebrew Class for
Women and Girls
c. 1916**
Although forbidden b
her father, Dora (first
row, right) was a stud
in Zionist Hebrew
classes for women an
girls in Bedzin. Dora'
teacher, David Malet:
stands in the back ro
Reprint credit: *Pinka*
Bedzin, Tel Aviv, A.S.
Stein, Editor, 1959.

Dora Diamant, c. 1925
Written by hand on the back
of the photo: "Dora circa
1925." Photo by permission
© 1998 Lask Collection.

**Sanatorium Kierling, view of the second floor
balcony room where Kafka lived his last weeks.**
Dora and Kafka lived here from mid-April until Kafka's death on June 3,
1924. He spent his days "lying half naked" sunbathing on the balcony, part
of the prescribed treatment for tuberculosis. Photo by Stefan Staengle.

13 Grunewaldstrasse in Berlin-Steglitz
The house where Kafka and Dora lived from November 1923 to January 1924 is the only one of their three residences that remains standing. A plaque on the wall between the two downstairs windows commemorates his stay there. The local park where Kafka and Dora met the little girl who had lost her doll is across the street. Photo by Felix Pahl.

Kafka's tombstone, Straschnitz Cemetery, Prague
Franz Kafka is buried with his parents, and a single tombstone commemorates all three. Herrmann died in 1931 and Julie in 1934. The memorial plaque at the foot of the obelisk commemorates Kafka's three sisters, who were murdered by the Nazis. Ottla died at the death camp at Auschwitz and Valli and Elli and their husbands were killed during the liquidation of the Lodz ghetto. Photo by author.

Robert Klopstock, the young physician who abadoned his medical studies to help Dora take care of Kafka in the last weeks. After Kafka's death, Klopstock wrote to Kafka's family: "Who knows Dora, only he can know what love means." Photo reprinted by permission of Archiv Klaus Wagenbach, Berlin.

Kafka's hairbrush

One of the only personal items of Kafka's known to exist. Dora kept the men's military style hairbrush, made by G.B. Kent & Sons (established in England in 1777), until leaving it with the Maletz family at the En Charod Kibbutz in Israel. Photo by author.

Max Brod, c. 1903

Kafka's best friend and literary executor. Without Brod, Kakfa's novels would never have been published. Brod and Dora remained friends after Kafka's death for the rest of her life. Photo reprinted by permission of Archiv Klaus Wagenbach, Berlin.

Dora, c. 1928

Resume shot. May have been used for her professional head-shot. (Note cropping lines.) Photo by permission © 1998 Lask Collection.

The Jacobsohn-Lask Family, Berlin, October 1903
Louis and Berta with Ruth and three-month-old Ludwig; the earliest photo of Dora's future husband. Photo reprinted by permission of Stiftung Archiv der Akademie Der Kuenste, Berlin.

Ludwig (Lutz) Lask (communist passname: Hans Eiler), c. 1933
An idealistic German Communist Party member and editor of *Die Rote Fahne*, the banned KPD newspaper. Lask remained a fervent believer in communism, despite the torture he endured under Stalin. Photo by permission © 1998 Lask Collection.

Dora with Marianne, Berlin, summer 1934
Outside the Lask family home at 11 Mittelstrasse in Lichterfelde Ost.
Photo by permission
© 1998 Lask Collection.

Dora and Marianne, Berlin, c. early 1936
Part of a series of photographs taken by Dora and Dr. Jacobsohn-Lask in Berlin before leaving for Russia. Photo by permission © 1998 Lask Collection.

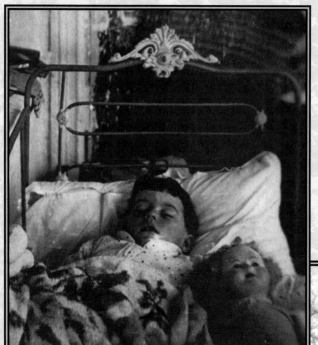

Marianne Lask, sleeping with a doll, Russia, c. 1938
Photo by permission
© 1998 Lask Collection.

Dr. Jacobsohn-Lask holding his granddaughter, Marianne, Berlin, 1936
One of almost a dozen photos taken of Marianne and her grandfather between 1936 and 1938.
Photo by permission
© 1998 Lask Collection.

Dora and Marianne, Crimean Peninsula, Soviet Union, 1938
Photo taken in Yalta Park, before Dora and Marianne left for Switzerland.
Photo by permission © 1998 Lask Collection.

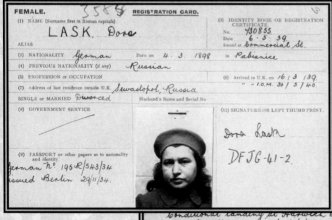

Dora Lask, May, 1940, Enemy Alien registration card, Isle of Man (front)
With Dora's German passport number, the date of her arrival in England. Dora's claim to be divorced was not true.

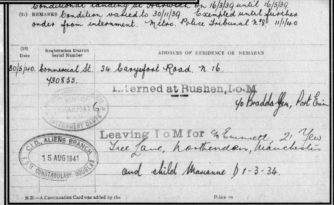

Registration card (back)
Completed in 1941.

David, Branka, and Zvi Diamant, Munich, 1949
Dora's older brother, David, age fifty-two, with second wife, Branka Besserglick, and their two-year-old son, Zvi. Although their spouses and children were murdered, David and Branka survived Dachau, where they met and married in the release camp after liberation in 1945. Photo by permission of Zvi Diamant.

Dora's brothers David and Avner, Passover, Munich, 1949
Dora's half-brother Avner, the second son of Hershel's second wife, Gitle, was one of only three surviving sublings. Avner remained hospitalized in Germany and died of tuberculosis in the early 1950s. Photo by permission of Zvi Diamant.

"Who knows Dora knows what love means." Zvi Diamant and his aunt's new tombstone, London, August 15, 1999
When Zvi learned that Dora was buried in an unmarked grave, he took immediate steps to rectify the situation. More than seventy-five people, including Dora and Marianne's family from Israel and Germany, attended the stone setting held on the forty-seventh anniversary of her death. Photo by Dvir Diamant.

Marianne Lask and her father, Lutz Lask, 1956
Marianne's reunion with her father in Berlin after two decades of separation.
Photo by permission © 1998 Lask Collection.

Berta Lask with her granddaughter, Marianne Lask, Berlin, 1956
In another snapshot taken that same day, the two walk arm-in-arm through Treptow Park. Photo by permission © 1998 Lask Collection.

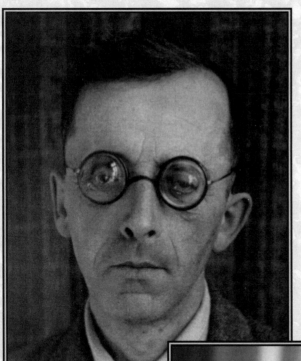

Lutz Lask, c. 1953
Released after eight years
exile in far eastern Siberia,
Lask was physically broken
and nearly blind, having
lost his right eye in an
industrial accident and
with only 3 percent vision
in his left. Nevertheless, he
claimed to be still capable
of being a productive
worker for the state.
Photo by permission
© 1998 Lask Collection.

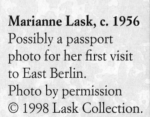

Marianne Lask, c. 1956
Possibly a passport
photo for her first visit
to East Berlin.
Photo by permission
© 1998 Lask Collection.

Marianne Lask on Oulton Broads with Hanny Lichtenstern, summer 1970
As an adult, Marianne (right) traveled with Hanny and Paul Lichtenstern on weekend getaways. Photo by permission © 1998 Lask Collection.

Ruth Lask Friedlaender and Lutz Lask, London, 1973
In Hanny's garden room, brother and sister met again after a forty-year separation. Photo courtesy of Hanny Lichtenstern.

Dora with stars of the Yiddish stage, April 1946
(l-r) Anna Tzelniker, Meta Segal, Dora, Yiddish writer H. Leivick, and Meyer Tzelniker. Tzelniker's portrayal of Shylock the Jew in a Yiddish production of Shakespeare's *The Merchant of Venice* earned Dora's highest respect. Photo reprinted by permission of Guido Massino, from his book *Fuoco Inestinguibile* (Rome: Bulzoni, 2002.)

Dora with Yiddish poet A. N. Stencl at the English seashore, 1950
Dora's friendship with Stencl spanned a quarter century from their first meeting in Berlin after Kafka's death until her death in London. Stencl never married and died in London in 1983 at the age of eighty-six. Photo by permission © 1998 Lask Collection.

Dora with Ruhama Maletz, En Charod Kibbutz, 1950
Ruhama was the second wife of David Maletz, Dora's Hebrew teacher from Bedzin. Dora stayed with the Maletz family at En Charod for two months. On the back of a framed photograph of Kafka, which Dora had given her, Ruhama wrote: *"Dora Dymant returned to England with the assumption that she would immigrate soon to Israel. She left her suitcase . . . [at] the guest house that then existed in En Charod. She left the picture of Kafka and his hairbrush, which he always kept with him, in our home. Ruhama Chazanov-Maletz, May 1990."* Photo courtesy of the Maletz family.

Hanny Lichtenstern in her garden room in North London, 1990
Hanny met Dora and Marianne on the bus from London to Liverpool, on the way to the Women's Internment Camp on the Isle of Man. Outside the glass window, the redwood tree grown from a seedling Marianne brought back from California is visible. Photo by the author.

Marianne Steiner, 1950
On back: "Photohouse Prio, Tel-Aviv, Allenby." At the end of June 1950, Max Brod's secretary Ester Hoffe wrote to Dora about meeting Kafka's niece: "*We were very happy with the visit of Marianne Steiner. She is a fine, intelligent and congenial person. Max sees a lot of similarity with Kafka.*" Photo courtesy of Michael Steiner.

Kafka's niece, Hampstead, London, October 1990
Mrs. Steiner's coincidental reunion with Dora in London after twenty-five years, "was the strangest thing that ever happened to me," Mrs. Steiner said. She died in November 2000 at the age of 86. Photo by the author.

Page 9 of Dora's "Cahier," her Kafka diary, begun on her birthday in 1951, after she learned she was dying. The "Cahier," which Dora's daughter gave to Kafka's French translator Marthe Robert after Dora's death, remained unknown, among Robert's private papers, until its discovery in Paris in the summer of 2000.

Partial translation: "Insertion: It is time to say at this point, that . . . my notes on Franz will be better than they have been up until now. I let them stand, only in case I might be prevented for some reason to be able to complete them. They bear about the same relationship to what I have envisioned as Franz's writings to that which _he_ envisioned. . . . All exaggerations in this journal are, from my point of view, genuine. Therefore I leave them, in case I don't succeed in finding a better form for what I want to say—but in no case do I wish that what I have said be made public in this form. . . ."

ish faith, she was still required to pay an annual religion tax. In the KPD, religious affiliation was superfluous—or worse. As a KPD member, she was also required to pay regular membership dues. Communism was not Dora's new religion, as it was for many others. For her, it was a matter of practicality: she couldn't afford to pay for both.

Dora's expectations for her life had become, as she said later, "less ambitious." She knew she would never again love anyone as she had loved Franz Kafka. She was happy among the Lask family, and Lutz was a decent, good man. In the midst of the turmoil and uncertainty surrounding them, their marriage was an act of pure optimism. They had a quiet civil ceremony, without religious symbolism or ritual. On Thursday, June 30, 1932, the registrar of marriages recorded the marriage of "the economist Ludwig Johann Lask of Berlin-Lichterfelde and the actress Dwojra (Dora) Dymant of Berlin."

It was, in many ways, a happy time. But the reality was grim. Outside Dora's narrow world, in the rest of the country, Hitler's anti-Semitic, anti-socialist message and the terror produced by his storm troopers—now numbering 300,000—was steadily growing. The result of the election that fall, which had so depressed Einstein, was the NSDAP's overwhelming victory. It was now the largest party in the new Reichstag, and Hitler was poised to become president.

15

EXODUS FROM BERLIN

Do not let Evil make you believe you can have se-
crets from it.

—Franz Kafka, *Blue Octavo Notebooks*

BERLIN 1933

On the last day of February 1933, five days before her thirty-fifth birthday, Dora became a criminal, subject to death for her illegal activities as a member of the KPD. The day before, the Reichstag building, the German seat of parliament, burned up in a mysterious and horrific fire. The Nazis quickly blamed the communists for the terrorist attack. As the flames shot out of the shattered glass dome, the symbol of the Weimar Republic, Hitler screamed to the head of his political police force, soon to be renamed the Geheime Staatspolizei (Gestapo): "Now we will show them! Anyone who stands in our way will be cut down! Tonight, all Communist members of the Reichstag are to be hanged, all Communist sympathizers must be locked up—and that goes for the Social Democrats, too!"

There were no mass hangings that night, but the next day Hitler announced an "Emergency Decree for the Protection of the People and State," which obliterated the Weimar Republic's constitutional freedoms and civil liberties. Under the new emergency decree, citizens no longer enjoyed freedom of speech and assembly. Police no longer needed search warrants or legal authorization to confiscate private property. Any action deemed to "endanger the state" was punishable by death. Mass arrests and arbitrary executions of well-known communists and other political opponents of Nazism began.

The German populace was stunned. Few had imagined how quickly the Nazis would seize control of the German government and transform it into a dictatorship. Since his reelection in spring 1932, President Hindenburg had refused to install Hitler—who openly stated that he wanted to "restore order" in Germany by expelling "all Socialists, Communists, and Jews"—as his chancellor. Less than six weeks before the Reichstag fire, Hindenburg was still telling his officers: "Gentlemen, surely you do not think that I would appoint this Austrian corporal Chancellor of Germany!" Nevertheless, on a wintry late January morning, the aging, exhausted Hindenburg capitulated to behind-the-scenes political intrigue, and Hitler was sworn in as the parliamentary leader of Germany.

On January 30, 1933, a two-word headline, "Hitler Reichskanzler!" covered the front pages of special editions of German newspapers. Radio reporters broadcast live the dramatic victory parade held that night in Berlin. Thousands of storm troopers and Nazi supporters began meeting at the Tiergarten in the afternoon and, as darkness fell, began to march to the Chancellery building. They were joined by ordinary German citizens caught up the jubilant hysteria. Brandishing torches, the triumphant mob marched up Charlottenburger Chaussee to the Brandenburg Gate. In front of the French embassy at Pariser Platz, the military bands stopped and defiantly played a World War I song, "We Aim to Defeat France," to the roaring approval of the crowd and the frightened eyes of witnesses viewing the spectacle from the windows of the legendary Hotel Adlon.

According to one German historian, "the first reaction to his victory was surprise, then bewilderment, then fear." Most citizens did nothing, waiting for the storm to pass. The only major political party to take action was the KPD, whose leadership immediately mobilized the membership to prepare for a general national strike, designed to cripple the new government before it could take hold. But the Social Democrats and trade unionists refused to cooperate, not wanting to be associated with the communists. One SPD official told a *New York Times* reporter that "he wouldn't be seen dead in their company." The SPD followed its official party policy: "Nothing hasty should be done."

In early March, Hitler allowed general national elections to be held. The Nazis won an unprecedented 44 percent of the vote, but not enough for a parliamentary majority. So Hitler cast away the last remaining pretense of democracy. He banned all communist delegates and ordered his storm troopers to march on the Kroll Opera House, where the German

legislature was meeting in makeshift quarters. The belligerent mob surrounded the opera house, "bellowing threats." Finally the cowed legislature agreed to "an enabling act" that gave Hitler dictatorial powers.
"After that," one historian noted, "there was no need for any more
elections."

At first the question was whether to run away or stay and fight. Thousands of communists, moderate and left-wing socialists, artists, writers, actors, civil servants and politicians, Jews and anti-Nazi Catholics were fleeing the country while the borders were still open. Others delayed, not
believing the new regime could last.

Lutz and Dora decided to stay and fight. In early March, the KPD
made Lutz responsible for organizing the illegal publication of the major
communist newspaper, *Die Rote Fahne,* for the entire Steglitz area. The official communist press, like most left-wing and socialist newspapers and
publications, had been shut down by the Nazis. But hundreds of small
printing presses, tucked away in attics, basements and backrooms, secretly
continued to crank out the newspaper and emergency handbills, urging a
national general strike, which they hoped would paralyze the country.
Most German communists, many of them idealists like Dora, believed it
was still possible to stop Hitler. Even Dr. Jacobsohn-Lask, a Social Demo-
crat, passed out anti-Nazi handbills to colleagues. A Gestapo letter reporting on his activities noted that the seventy-year-old physician was "suspected in 1933 of distributing documents against the State."

By the end of March, the Gestapo had arrested four members of the
Lask family. Lutz was arrested for the first time on March 23, 1933, according to a Gestapo report, "on suspicion of being involved in the production and distribution of the illegal communist paper *Die Rote Fahne.*"
After four days of interrogation and torture, Lutz refused to admit or reveal anything. The Gestapo, seeking more names and proof, raided the
Jacobsohn-Lask home on Mittelstrasse. The subsequent report noted that
"a substantial amount of highly treasonable written material was found."

The Gestapo found nothing relating specifically to Lutz's KPD activities, and the charges against him were eventually dropped. His younger
brothers, Ernst and Hermann, were arrested and held "on suspicion of
having taken part in a secret meetings of the illegal KPD." Both were
eventually released. They immediately applied for admission to the Soviet
Union and began making plans to leave.

The Gestapo found incriminating evidence against their mother on her
desk, in her notebooks and on her bookshelves. In late March, the Gestapo

came for Berta, a fifty-five-year-old grandmother, as her husband and family watched helplessly. The Gestapo noted that Berta Lask remained in "protective custody" for one month before she was released.

During one of these raids on Dora's living quarters, according to Kafka biographer Ernst Pawel, Gestapo agents "confiscated every scrap of paper they could get their hands on." Carried away in the bundles of evidence was Dora's secret treasure: her collection of Kafka's letters and notebooks. Dora was, Pawel reported, "disconsolate and hysterical with remorse."

Dora faced a difficult ethical decision: if she kept her mouth shut, if she never admitted her lie to anyone, no one would know, no one would blame her for the loss of Kafka's work. But if she did nothing to help recover Franz's writings, then she would be complicit, even guilty for the terrible loss. Finally, in the third week in April, after both Lutz and Berta had been released, Dora sat down to write a letter to Max Brod in Prague, admitting her lie and begging for his help in recovering Kafka's letters to her. Since the mails were no longer safe, Dora used a false name and return address: "Klopstock, Boot-Sommerfeld, Osthavelland."

Dora's letter to Brod, dated April 20, 1933, is missing, and its complete contents are unknown. The entire collection of Dora's seventy letters written to Max Brod over a twenty-five-year period has been missing since the mid-1980s, after being catalogued in Switzerland among the papers that Max Brod left to his longtime secretary, Ester Hoffe. The assistant to Hoffe's lawyer, who examined and catalogued Dora's letters, listed the four-page letter in the contents of "File 14: a grey-green file folder." Because of the importance of this particular letter, he quoted three sentences that Dora had written: "Franz's things are gone. Letters, pages from his diaries, and everything else, that I had. The lady from whom I rent a room was house-searched. . . ." The last sentence implies that the raid did not occur at the Lask home or possibly that Dora had not yet told Brod about her marriage to Lask.

According to Pawel, on receiving the news from Dora, Brod "immediately mobilized the Prague poet Camill Hoffman, at the time the cultural attaché at the Czech embassy in Berlin." Hoffman, who was one of Kafka's old friends and also Jewish, "did what he could, but was informed by the Gestapo that the mountainous stacks of paper confiscated in those first days of Nazi rule had already reached such monstrous proportions as to defy all rational attempts at locating a specific document."

Four years later, Brod reported for the first time on the tragic loss of Kafka's literary estate in the German-language newspaper *Aufbau*, published in New York in 1937. Brod did not mention Dora's role in the loss, saying only that "a portion of the manuscripts remained in Berlin after Kafka's death and was later confiscated by the Nazis. Although the Czechoslovakian legation, especially Camill Hoffman (who has now also become a Nazi victim) energetically tried to intervene, these writings were never discovered. Perhaps they lie today in some stack-room or other."

A quarter of a century later, in her first public interview on Kafka, Dora explained what happened to Kafka's last writings and his thirty-five letters to her. "In spite of all attempts," she said, "no one has succeeded in finding them again." Despite the finality of that statement, Dora did not believe that Kafka's letters to her were lost forever. She was not alone in maintaining hope that someday they might be recovered. In the 1950s, Max Brod attempted another search for Kafka's confiscated writings in the "mountainous stacks of paper" with Kafka scholar Klaus Wagenbach. That search ended unsuccessfully at the Iron Curtain. "For all we know," Pawel wrote in 1984, "those mountains are still there, as indestructible as the secret police itself, being sifted, indexed, and filed in the bowels of some bomb-proof archives beyond the Berlin wall, and may yet disgorge further incriminating evidence in the trial of one Franz Kafka."

Lutz Lask survived his ordeal at the hands of the Gestapo and jumped back into his work as editor of the illegal *Rote Fahne* with renewed fervor and commitment. Later he had "difficulty recalling all of the details of this work," but remembered that "up until the summer of 1933 we were able to distribute a large number of editions." Since his arrest and the raids, Dora and Lutz were careful to cloak their activities and changed residences frequently, staying ahead of the leather-jacketed Gestapo agents.

On April 1, the danger escalated. To be both Jewish and communist, as Kafka's niece Marianne Steiner later observed, "you couldn't have it worse." The official government campaign against the Jews began with a three-day boycott of Jewish shops and businesses. Armed SS and SA troops guarded entrances and posted signs reading, "Germans! Do not buy from the Jews! Jews get out!" One week later, the Reichstag passed the first of four hundred laws that would be enacted against the Jewish people. The Law for the Restoration of the Professional Civil Service, passed on April 7, called for firing all Jewish and non-Aryan civil servants. Thousands of Jewish judges, lawyers, clerks, state prosecutors, teachers and university professors were forced to resign. The SA set up interrogation and torture chambers in basements of apartment buildings throughout Berlin. In Dachau, near Munich, the Schutzstaffel, or SS, opened its first concentration camp. Legal attacks on the Jews, fraught with euphemism, mounted inexorably. On April 25, the Law for Preventing Overcrowding in German Schools and Colleges was passed, barring many Jewish schoolchildren from classrooms. Students of all ages were affected; Jewish doctoral candidates with completed dissertations were informed they would not be receiving their degrees.

The following month, a series of conflagrations took place throughout Germany. Beginning at midnight on May 10, the sky over central Berlin glowed red. Forty thousand people gathered to hear Goebbels, the new minister of propaganda and public enlightenment and leader of German culture, proclaim the "cleansing of the German spirit" and condemn the literary works of Jews, liberals, leftists, pacifists, foreigners and others who were "un-German." Libraries were ransacked and tons of books were pulled from shelves—works of fiction, poetry, science, social and economic theory and philosophy—and carted to the square across from the state library between Humboldt University and the Opera House on Unter den Linden. As torches kindled the flames, gangs of Nazi youth screamed, "Burn Karl Marx! Burn Sigmund Freud!" and danced wildly around the bonfires of classic literature and modern science. Among the books burned that night were the diverse works of Albert Einstein, Jack London, Upton Sinclair, Helen Keller, Margaret Sanger and H.G. Wells. Kafka's own books were spared that night, too little known to be banned. But the books of others whom Kafka knew, including Max Brod, Thomas Mann and Franz Werfel, went up in smoke. The conflagration spread quickly. Eight days later, book burnings had taken place in almost every major city and town in Germany. One of the authors whose work was burned that week was one of Kafka's favorites, Heinrich Heine, who had once written, "Wherever they burn books, sooner or later they will burn human beings also."

Berta Lask was the first of her family to escape from Berlin. On the first day of July, according to a Gestapo report in the Landesarchiv in Berlin, Berta "cancelled her registration and travelled to Prague." In Prague, Nazi informers were still watching her, reporting on her activities back to the Gestapo in Berlin. They noted Berta received support from an emergency refugee bureau set up for the "care of democratic refugees" until she was able to find work writing for several emigrant newspapers, including *Counter Attack,* an illustrated communist newspaper.

Dora was pregnant. For the remainder of the summer, as new life swelled within her, Dora continued to work for the KPD. She and Lutz moved frequently, living in tiny flats and rented rooms in Lichterfelde, Steglitz, Lichtenberg, Wilmersdorf and Friedenau. "In each residence," Dora later reported to the Comintern, "I was in contact with the Party and carried out tasks as I was instructed: Production and distribution of leaflets, newspapers, meeting point duty, demonstrations." For weeks they managed to elude the Gestapo, which was systematically hunting down all known communists, especially those in roles of influence and leadership.

Dora's life with Lutz Lask came to an end in the early hours of August 8, when Gestapo agents burst into their one-room furnished flat at 13 Pariserstrasse in Schöneberg, ransacked it, and arrested Lutz. He was allowed to take one suitcase. A few days later, Dora received the battered suitcase. Inside, she later told a friend, "she found his underwear stained with blood. She thought he was dead."

Dora retreated to the big house on Mittelstrasse, where Dr. Jacobsohn-Lask and a few other members of the family still resided. She continued to pay her KPD dues but was exempted from all further party duties and forbidden to contact any of her comrades. For the time being, because of the critical importance of his neurological work, Dr. Lask was allowed to keep his job at the university for the purposes of research, but he was not permitted to lecture or have any interaction with students.

Imprisoned in Columbiahaus, Lutz resolutely withstood Nazi torture. Although "beaten constantly," he never revealed any information or implicated another comrade. Not one member of his cell was arrested on his account. According to a KPD comrade imprisoned with Lask at Columbiahaus and also at the Brandenburg concentration camp, "Comrade Lutz exhibited an impeccable attitude" he reported, noting that because of his "Jewish descent," Lask was "subjected to increased terrorization by the guards."

"During the first days of the interrogation," Lask later wrote in his autobiography, "I was not able to ascertain whether or not the Gestapo knew anything concrete about my illegal activities for the Party. I said that I was a member of the KPD but had not taken part in any illegal activities. In the end, a party comrade from the street cell Lichterfelde West was brought before me and testified against me." Lutz remembered him, having once gone to see him about using a printing machine buried in his garden. Despite the comrade's damning testimony, Lask continued to deny everything and stuck by his original statement to the Gestapo. The beatings continued, but as Lutz said, he "suffered no permanent injury."

In October, Lask was informed that he had been sentenced to eight months "preventive detention" and was taken to the concentration camp at Brandenberg. Three weeks later, Lutz was back at Columbiahaus, accused of having smuggled out reports of the inhuman conditions at the prison. Lutz denied it. The Gestapo beat him and threatened further torture in the medieval dungeon known as "the Cellar." When he didn't talk, they threw him into solitary confinement, where he stayed for the remainder of his sentence, six months.

That month, Lutz's older sister Ruth, her husband, Ernst Friedlaender, and their four-year-old son, Frank, left Berlin. They arrived safely in Holland on October 9 and registered in the Parish of The Hague, beginning the long process of applying for admission to America.

BERLIN, 1934

On Thursday, March 1, three days before her thirty-sixth birthday, Dora gave birth to a beautiful baby girl, whom she named Franziska Marianne Lask. From the moment her daughter was born, Dora became, above all else, a mother with one purpose in life: to keep her child alive and safe. For the first time since Franz, Dora had a life entirely in her hands, an infant whose survival depended solely on her.

Dora had not heard from Lutz in six months, although word filtered out that he was alive. Comrades imprisoned at Columbiahaus at the same time occasionally caught glimpses of him and reported back to the family on "his brave, upright attitude." Someone had seen him in the exercise yard, and once or twice in the corridor. So far Lask had escaped the fate of other comrades, whom he occasionally heard being taken from their cells in the middle of night and shot.

On March 26, twelve days before he was to be released from prison, Lutz Lask was summoned to an office and told that the Gestapo had received a desperate letter from his wife, Dora, which had moved them to grant him an early release. "Due to the life-threatening illness of my wife," Lutz later reported, "I was to be given leave from prison." If Dora was indeed ill, she recovered shortly after Lutz's homecoming.

Photographs from the first months of Marianne's life capture happy moments and reveal doting parents and a smiling baby. Lutz's wide grin as he holds his daughter is proud and sweet. Pushing herself up from a baby blanket on the lawn, lit by a warm summer sun, Marianne's tiny face is alive with curiosity. As Dora holds her daughter, the dark-haired mother and child smile at each other, laughing, an intimate family moment frozen in time. On August 6, when Marianne was six months old, Lutz and Dora registered their daughter's birth at the district registry office in Berlin-Dahlem.

Marianne was the only bright spot in conditions of increasing hostility. Lutz was still "under police protection," required to report daily to the local police station. By May, his obligation to register was reduced to twice a week, but they refused to release him entirely. His KPD leader, known only to him as "Walter," wanted to meet with him until he learned of the continuing police surveillance. "Walter" then distanced himself from Lask but let him know that "should I want to emigrate out of Germany that he would approve my application to the area leadership." Lutz ignored suggestions to leave the country while he still could. It took several months before he was ready to admit that his only hope to save his family was to leave them behind in the care of his father and go ahead to prepare a new home in Russia, the workers' paradise.

On October 28, Lutz illegally crossed the German border in the Sudeten Mountains of Czechoslovakia, arriving in Prague just as Berta was preparing to leave for Russia. To be allowed to immigrate to Russia was a great privilege and coveted honor. Applications were approved only after a thorough examination of the applicant's party record and testimonials from comrades. Even with Berta's early and unwavering commitment to the party and her stature as a KPD leader, it had taken the Central Committee in Moscow over a year to approve her application. Once accepted, though, she was given the post of librarian at the State Library in Moscow. Berta said good-bye to her oldest son at the train station in Prague and promised to do everything in her power to expedite Lutz's application.

Four months later, Lutz Lask received permission to go to Russia. He arrived in Moscow on February 28, 1935, two years to the day after Hitler's seizure of power. Granted the status of "political emigrant" with all the benefits of Soviet citizenship, he was assigned work as a "junior academic assistant at the Marx-Engels-Lenin Institute."

Shortly after Lutz left Berlin, Dora began to take steps to go, too. On November 11, 1934, she applied for and was issued a new German passport, number 195R/543/34, in the name of Dora Lask. She was told the waiting list to emigrate was very long, especially for wives and children. Few KPD members or families were being admitted to the Soviet Union without strong party recommendations.

To many people, Russia seemed a utopia to Jews and a paradise for workers. Wondrous advances had been reported since the October Revolution of 1917. A great collective was reportedly rising from the crushing poverty long suffered by the masses. Soviet industrial production had tripled its prewar levels, and the mostly agrarian Russian economy had been completely restructured. Production was now socially organized and owned by the state, rather than set up strictly for the profit of a few. While the Western world was locked in the deathly grip of a global depression, wages in the Union of Soviet Socialist Republics increased by almost 70 percent. To Dora, Marxist economic theory had been proven correct.

Most important to Dora, the socialist ideals she had believed in were being actualized. The Soviet Union was the first country to introduce equal pay and equal voting rights. Communal kitchens, nurseries and child care centers had freed women from their traditional responsibilities and encouraged them to pursue an education and a profession. The revolution was spreading, though not as quickly as fascism was. Even in the fervently capitalist United States, socialist gains had been made. Franklin D. Roosevelt had been reelected with his New Deal, which included government-sponsored work programs and a minimum wage. In 1935, social security insurance was signed into law.

Trapped in Berlin, awaiting permission to leave, Dora dreamed of working again as a professional actress. It was possible in Russia, where the Jewish theater was thriving with great acting companies, such as the State Jewish Theater in Moscow and the traveling Habima Theater. Dora had no way of knowing it, since the negative aspects of the revolution went generally unreported in the world news media, but her hopes and dreams faced a harsh reality. In Russia, a ferocious weed had taken hold of the Communist Party and had strangled the socialist ideals and the idealistic revolutionary spirit that had captured Dora's loyalty. By the end of 1934, Joseph Stalin had gained control of the Communist Party, grabbing absolute power with brutal tactics, in much the same way Hitler had done in Germany. In the bloody massacre known as the "night of the long knives," Hitler had purged his own party, killing hundreds of Nazi SA, eliminating potential enemies along with longtime friends and loyal colleagues. The same thing was happening in Russia. The leading architects of the Bolshevik Revolution, who could have kept the socialist dream alive, were dead or gone. Lenin died in 1924 and Leon Trotsky was forced into exile in 1929. At the end of 1934, Sergey Kirov, the party boss in Leningrad and one of Stalin's most popular rivals in the Politburo, was mysteriously assassinated. As Hitler used the burning of the Reichstag, Stalin used the Kirov assassination to begin the Great Purges—a bloody reign of terror in which tens of millions would die.

Waiting for permission to join her husband in Russia, Dora lived quietly with her father-in-law, devoting herself to Marianne's care. She stayed in touch with Stencl, the romantic Yiddish poet who had once loved her. Dora had joined Stencl's Polish-Yiddish literary group, which still met, though now in secrecy.

On September 15, Dora first heard the news that filled Jews everywhere with despair. Anti-Jewish legislation had been passed at the annual Nazi Party Congress held that year in Nuremberg in southern Germany. Effective immediately, the Nuremberg Laws, as they came to be known, legally stripped Jews of their German citizenship, deprived them of their human rights, and expelled them from every arena of life. Marriage and extramarital relations between Germans and Jews was now forbidden.

The Nuremberg Laws defined who was a Jew: anyone with a Jewish parent or grandparent. There were three categories: *Voll Jude* (full Jew), *Mischling* I (mixed breed I—one Jewish parent), and *Mischling II* (mixed breed II—one Jewish grandparent). Conversion to the Christian faith made no difference. To the Nazis, as Holocaust historian Lucy Dawidowicz noted, "A Jew is a Jew is a Jew."

The answer to Dora's prayers arrived in the form of a letter from the Soviet Ministry of Health, delivered through the Soviet embassy in Berlin and addressed to Dr. Louis Jacobsohn-Lask. Berta had used her influential position in Moscow to rescue her husband and the last of her family members. Although he was not a communist, Dr. Jacobsohn-Lask received a highly unusual invitation to come to the Soviet Union, with the offer of a faculty seat at the University of Sevastopol to continue his research. The miracle for Dora, whose application for admission to Russia still had not been approved, was that she and Marianne would be allowed to accompany her father-in-law on his journey to Russia. They prepared to leave as soon as possible. Dora packed her suitcase with her remaining treasures: the library of Kafka's published books she had saved from destruction by the Nazis and the golden-bristled hairbrush, the only personal item of Franz's she still possessed.

BERLIN, FEBRUARY 10, 1936

It was Dora's last night in Berlin. Stencl described the meeting in an article published in a Yiddish journal in Warsaw. A Jewish restaurant had been rented for a "*tnoim*-celebration," the traditional Jewish celebration of the signing of the marriage contract between the bride and bridegroom. The engagement party was a cover-up for the real event: a joyous and clandestine celebration of the hundredth birthday of Mendele Mocher Sforim, the grandfather of modern Yiddish literature.

"At the head of the table, Dora Dymant, a professional actress, the friend of Franz Kafka—was the 'bride' and I was the 'bridegroom,'" Stencl reported. "Around us, there were a few dozen members of our now non-existent cultural club who were still in Berlin, and a few other lovers of Yiddish." Standing at the head of the table, Dora read a favorite chapter from Mendele's beloved story "Vintsh-fingerl" (The Wishing Ring). Then Stencl gave a talk he had written about Mendele, which moved and delighted Dora. "We all sang Yiddish songs, made merry and rejoiced that even we, a group of persecuted Jews in Nazi-Germany, still managed to participate in the centenary of our great classic writer."

The next morning, Stencl saw Dora off. "I brought Dora to the railway station with her one-year-old child, Marianne. Accompanying someone leaving for Moscow was a venture, which had just as strong a taste of danger as the disguised Mendele celebration the evening before," he explained. As they were saying good-bye, Stencl said, "Dora took out all the silver coins from her purse. She had more than the ten marks which one was permitted to take." She pressed the coins into his hand and said: "Have your talk on Mendele printed!" The money was enough, Stencl said, "to publish the Mendele essay on parchment paper, bound with a gold thread and dated 'Berlin 1936.' There was a drawing of Mendele on the cover."

With ten marks in her pocketbook, the maximum amount she was allowed to take out of Germany, and her almost-two-year-old daughter Marianne on her lap, Dora sat beside her father-in-law as the train pulled out of the station for the long journey east to Moscow. As they left, Gestapo agents were watching them. The report on the Lask family stated that "the noted Jewish professor and brain researcher Dr. Med. Louis Jacobsohn-Lask departed on 11 February 1936, going initially to Moscow and then later to take up a seat at the university of Sevastopol. The fact that he went into service for the Soviet State in order to act in the interests of the Bolshevik government is to be regarded as an especially serious break in loyalty to the German Reich." As an example of "the position enjoyed by this Jew in the Soviet Union is the fact the Russian newspaper *Pravda* (3.20.36) drew public attention to his arrival."

The Gestapo meticulously recorded the political and personal details of each member of the Lask family, listing birthdates and places and other vital facts. Amazingly, there was one item that the Nazis got wrong, a fact that Dora somehow managed to hide from the Gestapo's otherwise careful documentation on the Jacobsohn-Lask family. In their observations of "Ludwig Lask and his wife, the Jewish actress Dora Dymant," the Gestapo reported that "as far as can be ascertained, no children have resulted from the marriage."

16

THE WORKERS' PARADISE

*The Revolution evaporates, and leaves behind
only the slime of a new bureaucracy. The chains
of tormented mankind are made out of red tape.*
—Franz Kafka, in *Conversations with Kafka*

THE SOVIET UNION, WINTER 1936

The journey from Berlin to Moscow, from despair to hope, took forty-eight hours. As the train rolled east through Poland's snow-covered fields and forests, ancient villages and modern cities, Dora pointed out sights to Marianne, who spent the short daylight hours with her little nose and fingers pressed against the cold glass window. She was an adorable child, with round dark eyes that sparkled under a mass of feathery curls. Dora doted on her, and so did her grandfather.

Dr. Louis Jacobsohn-Lask was seventy-two years old and starting life over, leaving behind everything he had worked for. After a fifty-year career in medical research and a lifetime of hard work, he had nothing to show for it. He was a kind and dignified man, impressive with his long white beard and shock of wavy hair. He wore glasses, dressed formally in three-piece suits and smoked a pipe. When his own children were young, Dr. Lask spent little time with them. Forced into inactivity by the Nazi regime, he had come to know and enjoy his little granddaughter, who adored him. She was too young to remember her father, who had fled Germany when she was only seven months old.

Marianne's collection of family photographs includes several snapshots taken of the three of them on a snowy winter day outside their house, shortly before they left. In one photo, Marianne stands up in a buggy, exuberant in a white rabbit-fur coat. Dora, in a dark coat and hat, stands behind the buggy and smiles. Marianne was clearly an active child that day. In one photograph, she has dispensed with her coat and toddles down the snowy sidewalk. After Dr. Lask gathered his runaway granddaughter in his arms, Dora snapped a picture of him, in a heavy overcoat and fedora, holding her on his hip.

As the train left Germany and Poland, Dora had no way of knowing she would never return. Dora had returned to Bedzin to introduce Marianne to her family, but she would never go home again. Poland, too, was in the grip of the fascists, who were spreading anti-Semitic hatred across Europe. The movement had started in Italy at the end of World War I, when a right-wing nationalist named Benito Mussolini formed a party called the "Fascio de combattimento"—the fighting band—which became the inspiration for the Nazi Party. Within months of Dora's arrival in Russia, civil war erupted in Spain between the parliamentary government and fascist rebels, supported and financed by Hitler and Mussolini.

The moral decay and cultural breakdown was not limited to Germany, Dora pointed out: "All of Eastern Europe rolled up their skirts and joined the dance." It was a terrible time, she said, "when in Europe the name 'Jew' was identical with injustice and inferiority and, saddest of all, with brotherly betrayal." The Soviet Union offered Dora the only place "where the frenzy had to stop, where it had no visa to enter."

On the morning of the second day, the train reached the Russian frontier. Polish soldiers boarded and inspected everyone's passports. After a long wait, the train slowly began to roll through a "no-man's land toward Niegoreloye, the first station in Soviet Russia," where they would stop for a more thorough passport and luggage inspection. As the train came into the station, armed NKVD, the state police force and precursor to the KGB, checked under the train to make sure no one was trying to enter the country illegally by clinging to the underside of the cars.

At Niegoreloye, passengers were ordered to detrain and proceed with their baggage to the customs house. Dr. Jacobsohn-Lask produced his papers with the letter of invitation from the Soviet Ministry of Health, which gave permission for his daughter-in-law and granddaughter to travel with him. Dora was nervous. Printed materials were treated with the greatest suspicion and she was worried they might confiscate her Kafka library. She thought it a good idea to offer the customs official a small bribe, hoping he would "close an eye during the inspection." The official yelled at her in rough Yiddish: "A curse on your father's father!" Dora marveled at the sounds of the words. She had not heard her *mameloshen* spoken officially in public for three years. It was the first sign that she was no longer living under anti-Semitic rule or in a capitalist society. In the Soviet Union, one did not have to tip or bribe a worker to do his job.

After clearing customs—with Dora's collection of Kafka books intact—the three weary travelers boarded a Russian train for the fifteen-hour journey to Moscow, where Berta, Hermann and his wife, Alice, and Ernst awaited them. Dr. Lask's final destination was in the warm, sunny Crimea. Berta, at fifty-eight, nearing retirement age, was hoping to go with him to Sevastopol and live with her husband for whatever time they had remaining. Since arriving in Moscow two years earlier, Berta had lived at the Lux Hotel on Gorky Street, home to foreign leaders of the Communist International, the Comintern. Berta had her own room on the second floor, where the prominent German Communist Party leaders and officials lived, including Walter Ulbricht, who would become the first president of East Germany a decade later, and Wilhelm Pieck, head of the KPD.

Lutz was looking forward to being reunited with his wife and child. In anticipation of his family joining him, he had managed to get his own room in an apartment near the American embassy. He had a good job with the prestigious Marx-Engels-Lenin Institute and had willingly surrendered his German passport in exchange for Soviet citizenship. As a Soviet citizen, Lask was no longer entitled to the special benefits foreign workers received in Russia, but he was more than compensated by the knowledge that he was taking part in one of the most extraordinary experiments in human history.

"Despite what it turned into," observed one historian, "the Russian Revolution was a transcendent historic event: It advanced the demands of the French Revolution for liberty, equality and fraternity." Another historian, who covered Russia for the UPI, noted that just as the French Revolution put an end to the divine rights of kings, the Russian Revolution—which also degenerated into violence and bloodshed—signaled the end of "the divine rights of capital." The Russian Revolution had led to a bloody civil war, won at the cost of 7 million lives and the very reason behind it. The revolutionary dream of liberty and equality was crushed in the inhumanity of war and its aftermath. Moral corruption reigned in the emergence of a new bureaucracy, the "slime" that Kafka predicted. As the Bolsheviks struggled to govern and control the surrounding nations that composed the Union of Soviet Socialist Republics, "the bureaucracy was able to grow inside the state and the party, supporting and being supported by Stalin." By the time Dora arrived in Russia, the majority of the people, particularly the peasants, were living "under the heel of arbitrary power again, terrified by teeming threats: loss of bread ration, loss of passport, loss of their squalid 'living space.'"

It would be months before Dora discovered the true state of affairs in Russia. Foreign visitors and journalists, such as Gene Lyons of the UPI who later wrote a book about his experiences, witnessed the effects of the forced collectivization and the devastating famine it caused, the arrests of innocent people, the betrayal of the original revolutionary goals. Like many others reporting from the Soviet Union, Lyons focused on the significant positive gains the country was making under Stalin's leadership. Official censorship prevented international reportage of the brutality, but so did idealism and faith in the possibility of a better world. The real tragedy of the "Russian debacle," Lyons wrote in 1937, was that it could undermine "the value of all social striving" and that "by mocking ideals it threatened idealism."

MOSCOW, MARCH 1936

At first, Moscow seemed like a magical dream to Dora. Standing under a neon sign of enormous illuminated Hebrew letters that towered over a large theater building, Dora stopped and stared. Could this be the city, she wondered, "the land from which their best people had come for decades on pilgrimage to Western Europe to study in their tabernacles the laws of humanity, light and beauty? The tabernacles are now despised, contemptible, and here: 'Jewish Workers Theater!'"

In many ways, the Russian capital was still a sprawling ancient village on the banks of the Moscow River, with horse-drawn taxis and quaint wooden houses, but it was changing quickly. Under Stalin's second five-year plan, the city was being modernized with electricity, running water and sewage systems. Hundreds of streets had been paved and widened as cobblestones gave way to concrete pavement. The first line of the Moscow Metro opened in 1935, with thirteen stations from Sokolniki to Gorky Park. The stations were magnificent, described as underground palaces. Designed by prominent Russian architects, artists and sculptors, each station was unique and featured an assortment of marble, granite and other natural stone materials mined from across the country.

Days after her arrival, Dora's friends took her to see the famed Jewish Russian actor and director Solomon Mikhoels play King Lear at the State Jewish Theater. It was a night she never forgot. It was not merely Mikhoels's brilliant and legendary performance, but the entire scene that astounded her, as she wrote in an essay for Stencl's Yiddish journal many years later: "Try to imagine if you can, the effect of what I'm about to describe, on a person like myself, escaped from Germany, from the Nuremberg laws—how pale and innocent it seems now, compared to all that was to come, that no one could have dreamt of in their darkest nightmare. . . . We travel there, come out of the Metro, walk to the theater. Opposite, on the other side of the street, looms a large building, and high above it, in illuminated Hebrew letters: 'JEWISH WORKERS THEATER.' Above that, a bit higher, a little smaller, in Russian letters: 'Yebraiske Gosudarstveni Teater.' I stand and stare, I cannot take it in." Here in Russia, the birthplace of pogroms, Dora stood astonished on the street corner, her heart warmed by the sight of "glowing Hebrew letters on the whole bewitched building, which makes miles of Moscow happy and bright."

A crowd was lined up in front of the theater waiting to buy tickets. "Not only Jews," Dora marveled, "but descendants of all races, speaking all languages." The vision of people "standing for hours on a frigid winter's night, hopping from one foot to the other to keep warm, waiting patiently, hoping to be lucky enough to get a ticket to the Jewish Theater, for a Jewish performance of the great English drama, *King Lear*," defied belief. "If you can visualize all this, every bit of it," Dora wrote, "I envy you your power of imagination. I have to this present day, not been able to take it all in, make sense of it. Even now, I think, like on that Moscow night, that it has all been but a dream."

Dora didn't write about the production itself, since "volumes" had already been written; "it was praised and discussed in the theater chronicles of the world," she said. Instead she wanted to write about the man behind it all, who had founded the theater with a partner in 1920 and served as its lead actor and director. "The soul of all this awe-inspiring splendor was the Jew, Solomon Mikhoels," Dora wrote. "He carries it all on his shoulders, supported by a congregation of students. To see Mikhoels among his friends, pupils and just ordinary people, you start imagining that doves flutter around his head, bred in the warmth of friendship, belief and trust of all the people around him. It is not possible not to love Mikhoels," Dora concluded passionately. "It is not possible not to give him your trust with all your heart."

"It is not pleasant to feel your hope changing inexorably into despair," wrote Gene Lyons, the United Press International correspondent in Russia from 1928 to 1934. At first, almost everyone believed (or pretended to believe) whatever Stalin and the Communist Party said. There was no free press to report the truth. The NKVD, the all-powerful secret police, arrested those who criticized Stalin or the state, and fear kept others from talking. All private, independent thought was outlawed, while cheerful slogans endlessly repeated the party line. According to the party line, the sudden, unexpected arrests of suspicious comrades were necessary to preserve what they had fought so hard to achieve. The prevailing belief—at least in 1936—was that those who had been arrested had indeed partaken in counterrevolutionary sabotage and must be removed for the security of the society. Any note of criticism against the State was considered "anti-patriotic" and an example of "cowardly defeatism."

On February 25, 1936, Dora filled out the official form to transfer her party membership from the KPD to the Communist Party of the Soviet Union. She answered all the questions on the first page truthfully. She said her nationality was German, she was married to the Comrade Hans Eiler (Lutz's party name), had one child, and had last lived in Berlin-Lichterfelde on Mittelstrasse. She had joined the KPD six years earlier, in 1930, and worked with the agitprop group RGO Film and Stage. Dora came to the Soviet Union, she said, to join her husband.

Asked for exact names and addresses of "all comrades in Germany who can confirm the information given or who can give further details on political past," Dora listed only one name, with no address: "Comrade Rothschild (currently in prison)."

On the reverse side, Dora was instructed to write a detailed autobiography, with social background, general education, party training, activities and many other details. "I was born in the year 1898 in Poland," Dora began. "My parents are Jewish lower middle class people. Up until the war, they were small entrepreneurs, then independent craftsmen." She didn't mention her father's factory, nor the numbers of workers, tailors and seamstresses he had once employed. "My upbringing was very religious, the intellectual horizon of my childhood correspondingly reactionary. The war then changed it all. I came into contact with circles that belonged to the forbidden KPD, but I myself was without any political orientation. In 1918, I experienced, for the first time as a thinking and conscious person, the bloody persecutions of Jews in liberated Poland. I developed a strong nationalist opinion and leaned towards the factions that fought for Polish independence. In 1919, I left Poland. I came to Germany with the intention to study. I lived in Breslau for two years and in Berlin beginning in 1921. In the beginning I earned my living as a maid, then in a children's home, as a house seamstress."

In "1923," Dora wrote, "I married the German-Czech writer, Dr. Franz Kafka, who then died in the year 1924. 1926–28 I studied at a drama academy in Düsseldorf and in 28/29 I worked at the Rheinische Städtebundtheater. During all these years I stayed away from political life." In 1928, Dora reported, "I met people in Düsseldorf who introduced me to the beginnings of Marxism. The Communist Wolfgang Langhoff, with whom I was at the playhouse in Düsseldorf, told me that the communists have a different attitude towards Marxism than did his circle," which was, as far as she could remember, "a Sternberg group." At the time, Dora admitted, "I didn't understand what this meant."

Dora related how Eva Frietsche, her roommate in Berlin, took her to cell meetings, about her application for KPD membership in late 1929 and admittance in early 1930. She detailed her party activities in the Charlottenburg cell 218, which she first joined, and her later work as a member of the Lichterfelde cell. She named her section leaders, her work with the agitprop troupe, her participation in strikes, involvement in organizing meetings and distributing leaflets and propaganda, and frequent changes of address during the period of illegality. "In each residence I was in contact with the party and carried out tasks as I was instructed: Production and distribution of leaflets, newspapers, meeting point duty, demonstrations up until August 1933, the day of the second arrest of my husband." Dora explained that she had been exempted by the party from all duties and in fact "was forbidden to have contact with comrades. At the time, I was expecting a child. From then on until my emigration from Germany, I was only in occasional contact with the Party, and was only able to pay my dues." On the last eight lines of her autobiography, Dora expressed her gratitude to the Communist Party and her hope for her future in Russia, in the terms she thought they would most appreciate: "I want to continue to work as an actress here. I ask for admission to the Bolshevik Party because I want to be utilized again as an active worker in the workers' movement and in the building of Socialism. I owe my own liberation, my development as a conscious person, to the Party, which has the right to demand the commitment of all my energy to serve it, which I pledge to fulfill at any time with the most sincere willingness."

Before Dora submitted the form to the Central Committee, her attention was distracted by Marianne, who had fallen ill with scarlet fever, a deadly strep infection. The illness had started on the journey from Berlin with an inflamed sore throat that worsened in Moscow. A red rash appeared on Marianne's face and neck and soon covered her little body. For days, Marianne burned with a dangerously high fever, as Dora sponged her hot forehead and limbs with cool baths to keep her temperature down. By Marianne's second birthday on March 1, the fever had broken. Her temperature returned to normal and the rash faded and peeled, but little Marianne remained listless. The longer Marianne remained ill, the greater the danger of serious long-term damage to her kidneys and heart.

Penicillin, the miracle drug discovered by bacteriologist Alexander Fleming in 1928, too late for Kafka, could have cured Marianne. Unfortunately, it was not yet available in Russia. Russian medicine was making significant advances in the area of theoretical research—Dr. Jacobsohn-Lask's invitation to the Soviet Union was an example of the government's commitment to fund the advancement of scientific medical discoveries. But after the nation's entire resources had been poured into buying machinery, raw materials and technical expertise necessary for industrialization, nothing was left "to buy the elementary drugs and equipment for fighting disease."

The fear was that Marianne would have to be hospitalized. As Dora soon discovered to her horror, the glowing reports about socialized medicine were not based in reality. Gene Lyons had experienced the sad state of affairs firsthand when his wife was hospitalized in Moscow and wrote that "the gaping gulf between abstract research and practical application, between grandiose planning and messy execution, ran through every department of Russian life, but it seemed particularly horrifying in relation to medicine." The hospitals in Moscow were the worst that Lyons had ever seen: "Except under unusual circumstances, bed linens were changed once a week. The blankets were not washed but merely disinfected, so that they were crusted with the dirt and vomit of previous patients." Because of the proletarian principle that all share the same equal level of treatment, "the rules prohibited the bringing of linens, blankets or other accessories from outside."

In April, Dr. Jacobsohn-Lask and his wife, Berta, left for Sevastopol, and Dora and Marianne went with them. The hot, dry climate would be immeasurably better for Marianne, and Dr. Lask had access to the hospital facilities at the university. Lutz had to remain in Moscow. As a Soviet citizen, he was completely controlled by the state, which deemed his work too important to the state for him to leave. It was yet another blow to their marriage, which had already suffered from long separations. The conditions that had brought them together, as well as the heightened passions sparked by the danger surrounding them, had changed, and they were little more than strangers to each other now. They both loved their daughter, however, and Lutz readily agreed to let them go.

SEVASTOPOL, SPRING 1936

One thousand miles due south of Moscow, on the southwestern corner of the Crimean Peninsula on the northern shore of the Black Sea, Sevastopol was an Eden, compared to Moscow, with a warm subtropical climate that rarely dipped below fifty-five degrees Fahrenheit. The lush landscape featured "undulating forests, blue-green water, turbulent coast and the Crimean Alps," in the words of one travel writer who visited shortly after the turn of the century. Sevastopol, an important strategic naval station, had a rich and colorful history dating back to its founding as a Greek colony in the fifth century B.C. Located on a spectacular, naturally deep harbor, the city was famous for its seaside sanatoriums and health resorts. In the spring, Lutz was granted a vacation to Sevastopol for several days. Lutz reminded Dora that she had not yet turned in her autobiography and urged her to answer the letters that Central Committee had written to her, requesting a reference on a friend, Elizabeth "Ula" Wimmler. For months, Dora had simply ignored the mandatory requests for information, too concerned about Marianne to think about anything else. In fact, Dora possessed what could be considered incriminating evidence on Ula Wimmler but hesitated to put it into writing.

"Comrade Hess, please excuse my delay," Dora wrote to the Central Committee. She had postponed meeting with him "due to the severe illness" of her child and because, she explained, "I wanted to talk to you personally. Now I send you my autobiography along with the following statement, which was the reason why I wanted to call on you." Dora's information on Ula was damning—for both of them, although in her naïveté Dora didn't realize it.

"Comrade Ula Wimmler was a friend of Anatoli Becker," Dora wrote. Dora knew Becker through his wife, Carola Neher, a young German actress. Originally from Bessarabia, Becker had come to Germany and joined the KPD in the same year as Dora. He escaped to Prague, where he met and married his wife, and had come to the Soviet Union after the Nazi takeover in 1933. The Beckers had a son Marianne's age. Although Carola was not a member of the Communist Party, she found work in Moscow as a professional actress, working with the famous agitprop theater group Kologne Links.

Ula had attended drama academy in Düsseldorf with Dora and had behaved strangely after their last meeting. In these times of treachery, Dora couldn't ignore the possibility that that Ula was a counterrevolutionary. The Soviet newspapers were filled with reports of hundreds of "class enemies, saboteurs, and double-dealers" who had been uncovered through the "vigilance of loyal citizens." Dora knew too well how the Nazis worked undercover, and Ula did have Nazi ties. If Ula was working to undermine the state, Dora believed she must reveal the truth. Dora had last seen Ula when she returned to Berlin in 1935 from the Soviet Union. "In the past, she used to correspond with an acquaintance of mine, who lives in Berlin. This acquaintance, Hedwig Wittekind," Dora unwisely revealed, "came from a Nazi family and was a member of the NSDAP, the Nazi Party, until she began to sympathize with us. I spoke to Ula Wimmler when she stayed in Berlin last year and gave her instructions and small things to take with her to acquaintances in the Soviet Union. When she visited my acquaintances here, she denied categorically having seen me in Berlin. Since then, no one has heard anything from her. This is strange, to say the least, considering the other potential interrelations." Fear and suspicion permeated all social interactions and friendships, and Dora was not immune to the paranoia. "In case it should prove important, I could, if necessary, find out one thing or other," she offered.

Dora incriminated herself and others with each name she mentioned, thinking she was doing her part as a good Soviet citizen. Within the month, Anatoli Becker was arrested for treason. That September, Carola was also taken by the NKVD in the middle of the night. She was held at Lubyanka Prison for several months before being sentenced to ten years hard labor in a camp. No one knew what became of their son.

On June 30, thirty-year-old Ernst Lask, Louis and Berta's youngest son, died on an operating table in a Moscow hospital. The bravest and most headstrong of their children, Ernst had joined the KPD in 1929 and was arrested in 1930 as a suspect in the murder of a Nazi who was shot to death outside a bar in Wilmersdorf. Ernst escaped Germany in 1934, first to Warsaw, where he married twenty-four-year-old Mira Landsmann Lose, a bright young Berliner who had studied economics and German literature. They were admitted to the Soviet Union at the end of the year and granted Soviet citizenship. Living in Moscow, Mira enrolled in classes to earn a Soviet diploma as a teacher, and Ernst, despite a heart condition, continued to fight against the Nazis. Berta later blamed his death on "an exhausted heart after hard illegal party work."

To deal with her grief, Berta picked up her pen. Among her personal papers in her Nachlass, or literary estate, at the Archive of the Academy of Arts (Archiv der Akademie der Künste) in Berlin, was a poem, "To My Son Ernst," written after his death. "I now know, since death has forcefully spirited you to a strange distant place, how the soft tone of your voice is woven in everything, vibrates through everything," she wrote. Hearing a young man sing "of struggle and victory, full of tempestuous wild strength, the jubilation in his voice bore the passion of *your* deeds, too." Ernst's life, so abruptly burned out, remained branded on life itself, in everything and everyone she saw and experienced: "It shines from every child's face, it says hello with every friendly handshake. It stays in the strides of the young people who are victoriously building a happy future. It breathes quietly in the evening wind. It glows, where the sky is blue." His spirit had reentered her body and was once again a part of her own blood, and yet diffused, spread "wide in the world, through which it made its tracks."

Marianne's health slowly improved, although she still required bed rest. Surrounded by loving adults who spent long hours reading to her, Marianne's innate intelligence was nurtured, and she developed communication skills beyond her years. With its warm climate and healthful sea air, Sevastopol was clearly the best place for her. But there was nothing for Dora to do in Sevastopol. Marianne was getting plenty of attention and care from her grandparents, and after discussing it with her in-laws, Dora decided to return to Moscow, to rejoin the socialist struggle and find productive work in the theater. Perhaps if Dora lived with Lutz again, the marriage might be salvaged.

Moscow, August 1936

Dora returned in August, the month that the first of the infamous "show trials" was held in Moscow. The courts-martial of two top Bolshevik leaders, Gregory Zinoviev and Leonid Kamenev, old heroes of the October Revolution, were highly publicized. After hysterically confessing their guilt, they were condemned to death for treason. It was the first of four sensational trials of the old opposition groups. Before the show trials ended in Moscow, more than sixty once top-ranking generals and party leaders, the surviving core of the old Bolshevik party, were tried, convicted and executed. The fear of counterrevolutionaries, even among trusted comrades, was pervasive.

A few days after Dora returned to Moscow, Hans Schreiber, Lutz's friend since childhood, reported on Dora's activities to the security police of the NKVD. On August 29, Comrade Chernomordik reported to Comrade Kornilev: "Schreiber informs us that several days ago Dora Lask returned from Sevastopol to Moscow. She lives at 2 Boulevard Novinsky, apartment 4, with Eiler. Speaking with Schreiber she said that she knows from Anatoli Becker himself that his brother was earlier an active member of the White Guard." Although Dora didn't know it, Becker and his wife had already been arrested. By talking with Schreiber, Dora had unwittingly helped seal his fate. Becker's association with the White Guard, the anti-Bolshevik forces of the revolution and civil war, was further ammunition in the case against him. Becker was condemned to death and shot the following year.

Schreiber, whose real name was Hans Altmann, had been a leader of the German Communist Party in the northwest area of Berlin. Although he had been a loyal and fervent communist for ten years, Schreiber was under suspicion, although he may not have realized it when he reported on Dora, or perhaps his spying on Dora was meant to prove his loyalty. He stated that he had talked with Dora on several occasions in her husband's room. He had known her for six years. From the beginning, he said, he doubted her party commitment and loyalty. "He took her for a sympathizer and learned only later that she was a member of the KPD," Chernomordik wrote. Schreiber charged that while he worked with the Charlottenburg street cell in 1931, Dora "was accused of inactivity in her street cell." The accusation was unfair. Dora was no longer living in Charlottenburg at that time but in Zehlendorf, where she had opened up her flat for the KPD to use. She never returned to the Charlottenburg cell, being transferred to the Lichterfelde-Ost cell with the Lask family. Schreiber reported that during discussions, Dora "got into strong opposition to him and, in addition, expressed utterly senseless opinions." Schreiber's betrayal of Dora didn't help him. By the end of the year, he was arrested and sentenced to ten years in prison.

Moscow, December 1936

Dora wanted to protect her collection of Kafka's books. She had been thinking about what to do but had made no decision until she received terrible news from her in-laws: Marianne had taken a turn for the worse and was very sick. Dora had to return immediately to Sevastopol.

Dora took the small library to Moscow because she couldn't bear to be parted from it, but also because she wanted to share his work, to offer his wisdom to the great collective. Since Kafka's novels and the first four volumes of his collected works had been published in Germany, Dora had come to a new appreciation of their relevance as art. Beyond their value to her, beyond any material cost, the first edition books in Dora's possession were growing in rarity and could soon be among the few original copies left in Europe.

Kafka's work was now forbidden in Germany. After Brod published new editions of Kafka's collected stories in 1935, a German reviewer was "amazed that such anti-fascist books could be published right under the nose of the Gestapo." Kafka's work was promptly banned as a "degenerate Jewish influence." Nevertheless, Kafka's fame was spreading in Europe, England and America. In 1930 translators Willa and Edwin Muir (who was a respected poet) convinced an English publisher, Secker and Warburg, to publish the first English translation of *The Castle*. Later that year, Alfred A. Knopf published the translation in America. By 1936 *The Trial* already had been translated into French, Norwegian, Italian and Polish.

An Italian communist in Moscow, code-named Lenari, had expressed great interest in Kafka's books. Dora first met him when he visited a health resort in Sevastopol for physical therapy for his prostheses. A victim of Mussolini's torture practices, Lenari had lost both legs and a hand in a fascist prison in Italy. During the three months Dora lived in Moscow that autumn, she visited Lenari at his apartment several times to discuss Kafka and his books. "Because he seemed very knowledgeable in literary matters, " Dora said, "I conferred with him whether the works of my late first husband Franz Kafka would be of value to the Soviet Union." Lenari was very enthusiastic, Dora said. "He explicitly affirmed this and wanted to speak to the appropriate authorities himself to arrange it."

As she was packing to return to Sevastopol, Dora made her decision about Kafka's books. She knew her position in Russia was precarious. She had not received a response on her application for membership to the Communist Party of the Soviet Union, and her prospects were growing dimmer with each new arrest or disappearance of a long-time friend and trusted comrade. Foreigners were increasingly under suspicion for "fifth column" infiltration and other treasonable activities.

Dora had failed to protect Kafka's writings in her possession from the Nazis, a nagging and persistent regret that still tormented her. She was determined not to let it happen again. Before leaving Moscow, Dora bundled up her beloved library of first edition copies, wrote "Dymant-Kafka" inside each one, and took them to Lenari's apartment in Moscow for safekeeping. It was a painful sacrifice, but one she believed she must make to ensure Kafka's books were preserved for future generations.

Sevastopol, Spring 1937

On March 1, Marianne celebrated her third birthday. Her appearance shocked Dora when she first saw her. She had gotten taller, but she had lost weight. Her cheeks were hollow and her eyes enormous. She looked just like Franz had looked. It wasn't merely Dora's imagination. In a photograph of Dr. Lask holding the emaciated Marianne in the bright sunshine outside the university hospital, the similarity between Kafka and Dora's daughter is striking.

Marianne had suffered permanent damage to her kidneys and possibly her heart, and had been diagnosed with "children's tuberculosis." Other possible long-term complications included bronchopneumonia, meningitis, brain abscess, sinusitis, as well as the hair loss that she had already experienced. In the opinion of the physicians, Marianne's case was incurable, at least in Russia. The only hope was to get Marianne treatment by foreign specialists, where she would have "to live uninterruptedly in a sanitarium under constant strict medical supervision for several years."

It was impossible to leave the country without permission and permission, Dora learned, was impossible to obtain. Ignoring everyone, Dora petitioned the Narkomindel, the Ministry of Foreign Affairs, asking to take Marianne out of the country. Ideally, Marianne should go to a sanitarium in Switzerland. The medical services in Switzerland were said to be the most modern and best-equipped in Europe, but the cost was a problem, since it was forbidden to take foreign currency out of the Soviet Union. If Switzerland proved too expensive, then Marianne would have to go to Berta's sister Helene, who still lived in Germany and had promised to help take care of Marianne.

In her single-minded determination to save her daughter's life, Dora absolutely believed that she would be given permission to leave to get medical care for Marianne, and that her daughter would eventually recover. She would not let herself think anything else. Before she received an answer to her request from the Narkomindel, Dora learned that in addition to the required permission from her registration office, she also had to obtain a visa from the Swiss embassy, which was possible only with written permission from the Central Committee of the party in Moscow. Dora still had her German passport. She had managed to keep it, although it was illegal to do so and she could have been arrested and shot for that offense alone. Had she relinquished her passport on entering the country as many foreigners mistakenly did, she would not be able to leave under any circumstance.

Dora's letter to the Central Committee requesting permission to leave Russia is preserved in the files of the Executive Committee of the Comintern in the Central Archives of the Communist Party in Moscow, now renamed the Russian State Archives for Social and Political History. Written in 1937, during a period of time when thousands of disillusioned foreign communists were not only being denied permission to leave but placed under suspicion of treason simply for asking, Dora's blithe request "to be allowed to travel abroad for 8–10 days" was aggressively optimistic. Dora related the full story of Marianne's illness and the fatal prognosis if she remained in Russia, repeating the doctors' recommendation for treatment abroad by foreign specialists. She outlined options for getting Marianne to a Swiss sanitarium, contingent on the state of her child's health. She wasn't giving them much advance notice, but she had only recently learned that she needed their permission to go. She requested an answer as soon as possible. She wanted to take advantage of an upcoming opportunity. "Assuming that we get the permission from the Narkomindel," Dora explained, "we want to go to Turkey, to entrust the child to the old aunt. Or, if the state of the child should require it, I will have to bring her to Switzerland, because the aunt herself is ill and can't make the long journey with a severely ill child on her own." In case it proved necessary for Marianne to be placed in a sanitarium in Germany, Dora wrote, "we want her to be adopted by a distant relative, whose name is Wolff." Otherwise, Dora pointed out, in Nazi Germany Marianne would be "exposed to great danger as the child of Ludwig Lask and the grandchild of Berta Lask. She signed it: "with Communist greetings, Dora Lask."

SEVASTOPOL, SUMMER 1937

On June 9, the Executive Committee filed its report in the case of Dora Lask (Maria Jelen), protocol number 2245, regarding the transfer of the comrade from the German Communist Party (KPD) to the Communist Party of the Soviet Union (KpdSU). The committee's decision summed up Dora's personal and political history and the combined reports on her by comrades, reaching the following conclusion: "Because the activities of Dora Lask could not be confirmed, her contacts with the arrested Wimmler and Anatoli Becker could not be elucidated, her political development is weak and she was absolutely passive during the last years of the illegality, apparently had almost no connection to the party at all, transfer to the

KpdSU (B) is currently out of the question and her membership in the KPD since 1930 is merely confirmed."

As a foreigner without party protection, Dora was in extreme danger. She never received an answer to her repeated and urgent requests to take Marianne out of the country, nor did Berta Lask receive permission to visit her sister. Dora began to make other, private, plans to leave.

The news coming from Moscow was terrible. The purges had become epidemic. No one was safe. That summer, every foreigner working at the Marx-Lenin-Engels Institute was fired. Lutz continued to maintain his faith in Stalin and blamed the mass dismissal on what he called "the deterioration of the international situation." Because of a party recommendation, he could still work as a proofreader for a Moscow publishing house, Iskra Revolutzii. With party permission, he was also allowed to work as a freelancer for the publishers of foreign language dictionaries. Without work, he would lose his ration card, his living quarters, his way of staying alive. A month later, Lask received an official party reprimand from the German section of the Comintern for his "long term friendship with Heinz Altmann, known in the USSR as Heinz Schreiber," who had been arrested the year before.

Dora was devastated by the news that Lenari had been arrested in Moscow. No one knew anything about the books she had left with him, and no one was willing to ask the authorities on her behalf. Despite her best intentions, Dora had failed to protect Kafka's work again. Her decision to take action was both bold and foolhardy. On August 13, Dora wrote a letter to the NKVD. "Some months ago I learned of the arrest of the Italian comrade Lenari, and in connection with this I want to make a statement," she began. She explained how she met Lenari and how she came to give him her books by Kafka, and then made the following plea:

> Kafka's works are forbidden in Germany. Everything that was in publishing houses has been pulled out and pulped down, and they haven't been published elsewhere. Due to the increase of fascism it is not to be expected that they will soon be published anywhere else. The copies that are in Lenari's flat belong among the few that still remain. The value of these works is undisputedly acknowledged by the entire literary world. Therefore I would be every grateful, not only out of personal interest, if I received help to reobtain the copies located there.

Dora's letter was never answered, and she never learned the fate of her treasured books.

SEVASTOPOL, MARCH 1938

Marianne defied the dire predictions of the doctors and lived to celebrate her fourth birthday. Her hair had begun to grow back, although it was still short, cropped like a boy's. She was well enough later that month to accompany Dora on a trip to Yalta for a meeting of the Communist International. Several photographs taken that day remain in the Lask Collection. One is a picture of fifty comrades grouped around a reflecting pool in Yalta Park, with Dora smiling at the far right edge of the crowd. The rest are of Marianne, looking surprisingly healthy in a little Greek shirtdress in a garden with stately cypress trees.

Three days later, on March 26, Lask was arrested by the NKVD in his Moscow apartment and charged as a spy. For months it was impossible, even for Berta, to get information. He denied everything and maintained his innocence, waiting for a court hearing that never came. Three months later, after Hermann and Alice were also arrested, Lutz was informed that by "a 'Special Consultation' of the NKVD, he had been sentenced to five years imprisonment in a work and reform camp on suspicion of spying." There was no trial, and no defense or appeal was possible. Four months later, at the end of October, Lutz was shipped to a labor camp on the Kolyma River on the Arctic Circle in far eastern Siberia. Dora never saw him again.

The greatest mystery still remaining about Dora's life is her escape from the Soviet Union in 1938. There are no records documenting how or when she and Marianne left, and Dora never talked about it. What is generally agreed is that she accomplished the impossible. As Ernst Pawel noted, "If it took a miracle to cure the child, it took more than a miracle, at the height of the Stalin Purges, for the Polish-born Jewish wife of a convicted German Trotskyite saboteur to be allowed to leave the Soviet Union with her six-year-old daughter. What it took was Dora."

"Unless one had the permission of the NKVD, it was technically impossible to leave," stated social historian and researcher Bernd-Rainer Barth in Berlin in 1998. An expert in the foreign victims of the Stalinist terrors in the Soviet Union, Barth offered an intriguing theory: Dora could only have been allowed to leave if she agreed to do "special work," as it was called, for the party. "Because of the small number of intelligence sources outside the Soviet Union, spies were recruited from those foreign communists who wanted to leave. Almost all the communists who were allowed to leave were intelligence cases, sent out to gather information."

The most successful Soviet spies in the 1930s and 1940s were Eastern European, usually Polish, Jews. Barth cites the case of Leopold Tepper, a Polish Jew who was head of the Soviet spy network known as the Red Orchestra in occupied Europe during World War II. "Polish Jews were chosen because they had learned to live in different milieus," Barth said. "Many spoke three or four languages, and were better equipped to start a new life and a new identity than the Russian communists, workers or peasants, who had never worn a tie, or had any idea of how to behave in society. It wasn't called spying, but rather doing 'special work' for the party."

Dora's training as an actress, her age and destination all point toward this theory, he contends. At forty, "Dora was the right age to be sent out. The Soviet intelligence services wanted to place those who would be good sources for future information. Dora said she wanted to go to Switzerland, and the Swiss-Soviet intelligence networks were the most developed in Europe. The information sent to Moscow through these networks helped to win the war." In Barth's opinion, Dora's exit from the Soviet Union was most likely the result of a deal she made to act as an espionage agent of the Soviet Union. "Here is a woman who will do anything to save her daughter. She fits the profile of who they were looking for perfectly."

Another, less intriguing, possibility exists. When husbands were arrested by the NKVD, their families were cut off from society completely. They lost their previously protected status as foreigners or party members, as well as the vital necessities of housing, passports and ration cards. For many women, the arrest of their husbands led to their own arrest and death. Some of the children died of starvation, or were adopted by Russian parents. Women who managed to survive until 1939 were turned over to the Gestapo when Stalin and Hitler signed the nonaggression pact. But some, a very few, Barth concedes, were "kicked out of the country." Since Dora had wisely held on to her German passport, it is possible that her husband's sentencing and deportation may have freed Dora and her daughter to leave the Soviet Union, to save their lives, before Europe once again exploded into war.

17

THE GREAT ESCAPE

*"Alas," said the mouse, "the world is growing
smaller every day. At the beginning it was so big
that I was afraid, I kept running and running,
and I was glad when at last I saw walls far away
to the right and left, but these long walls have
narrowed so quickly that I am in the last chamber
already, and there in the corner stands the trap
that I must run into." "You need only change
your direction," said the cat, and ate it up.*

—Franz Kafka, "A Little Fable"

En Route Through Europe, October 1938

Dora's options were limited. If she returned to Germany, she would be
arrested. Her name was posted on at least three separate lists at border
inspection checkpoints throughout the Third Reich, which now included Austria and the Sudetenland, the border region of Czechoslovakia. The most recent list had been issued in January 1938 as "Appendix
II of the Confiscation/Loss of Nationality Order," issued by Dr. Werner
Best, a noted architect of Hitler's SS. The list was sent to all police stations in the Third Reich, the Ministry of the Interior for Outer Prussia,
the Reichkommissar for the Saar region (which Hitler had annexed in
1935, in his first expansion of Germany's borders), Gestapo headquarters in Berlin and all border inspection guards, ordering personnel at "all
local border crossing control points to immediately arrest all such persons should they attempt to cross the border."

Dora was identified as "Lask, Dora, born Dymant" with her correct birthplace and birthdate, and her old address on Pariserstrasse, where she had lived with Lutz during the early part of her pregnancy until his second arrest by the Gestapo. Typed beneath Dora's name was that of her niece, "Ruth Lask, born July 12, 1932." The Nazis need not have worried about the child. Hermann and Alice's daughter had died two years earlier at the age of four.

The safest and fastest way to Switzerland from Sevastopol was the southern route by steamer across the Black Sea to Istanbul, and then by train to Sofia in Bulgaria, to Belgrade in Yugoslavia, across the Balkan kingdom to Trieste on the Italian border. From there they would be able to travel across northern Italy to Milan, going either north into the Alps and crossing the Swiss border at Lugano or continuing west through France up to Geneva.

With a transit visa, Dora would be able to travel across the borders of Bulgaria and Yugoslavia, still ruled by kings, through Italy and France without having to get visas for those countries. But they would have to stay on the train for the entire journey. Through-passengers on transit visas were forbidden to leave the train until they reached their final destination. At major stations, the cars carrying passengers traveling on transit visas were separated, and guards were posted to make sure no one disembarked. The cars waited on the tracks for hours, even days for the next train.

After days, possibly weeks (no one knows), they reached the Swiss border. Very few people ever knew that Dora had once lived in the Soviet Union, and no one knew how she escaped. Years later, Dora told Kafka's niece, Marianne Steiner, that "she decided to go to Switzerland to have her child seen to by Swiss doctors." According to Mrs. Steiner, "when Dora and Marianne arrived at the Swiss frontier, they were turned away. The war was imminent, and the borders had been closed."

About the same time Dora and Marianne were being turned away at the Swiss border, a Jewish teenager walked into the German embassy in Paris and shot a German diplomat. The next day the minister of propaganda, Joseph Goebbels, called for revenge against all Jews. The next night, November 10, one thousand synagogues burned to the ground in a government-sponsored pogrom of destruction and murder known as *Kristallnacht*—the night of the broken glass. In Berlin, Munich, Vienna and dozens of other cities, angry mobs torched Jewish homes and businesses, smashed windowpanes and looted stores and destroyed synagogues. Thirty thousand Jews were arrested and sent to concentration camps.

Terrified Jews queued up in front of foreign embassies, desperately trying to find some country that would accept them, but immigration quotas in most western countries were already full, with long waiting lists. A bill introduced in the U.S. Congress to allow ten thousand German Jewish children into the country did not pass, although thousands of families had eagerly offered to adopt the children. According to a 1938 *Fortune* magazine poll, 83 percent of Americans responded no to a bill that would "open the doors of the United States to a larger number of European refugees than now admitted under our immigration quotas." As one opponent of the measure said, "If we are going to keep our country the way it is and not lose our liberty, we have got to keep not only these children out of it, but the whole damned Europe."

Holland's borders were still open. With the possibility that her brother and sister-in-law, Ernst and Ruth Friedlaender, might still be there, Dora decided to go to the Dutch capital, The Hague. What Dora did for money, how she paid for train fares, food and necessities during the long journey remains unknown.

THE HAGUE, WINTER 1938

Ruth Lask Friedlaender was overjoyed to see Dora and to meet her brother's child, Marianne, who had been born after Ruth and Ernst left Berlin. Ruth had feared she would never see her family again, and she was nearly right. She had heard nothing in years. Dora had to give her the bad news about the death of her brother Ernst and her namesake, Ruth, and the arrests of Lutz, Herman and Alice.

Dora and Marianne could stay with them. Ernst and Ruth Friedlaender had lived in a modern brick four-story apartment building at 234 Thorbeckelaan Street after moving to The Hague as refugees in 1933. Their names had been on a waiting list at the American embassy for five years. The visas might come any day.

"After Switzerland, England was her next choice," Mrs. Steiner reported. English doctors were reported to be excellent. There was a large Jewish community living in London's East End with organized relief service agencies for refugees.

Talk of war was escalating. Hitler had not been appeased by the British and French "betrayal at Munich." The surrender of the Czech democracy by British Prime Minister Neville Chamberlain and French Prime Minister

Edouard Daladier, hailed by western European countries as a "peace with honor," had failed. Hitler was now demanding new territory, new "living space" for Germans. It was only a matter of time before the German army attacked Czechoslovakia. If war broke out before Dora could reach England, the borders would be closed and they would be trapped in Holland.

After resting for a few days, Dora and Marianne said farewell to the Friedlaenders and left for the Hoek van Holland to take the ferry across to England. The trip to Harwich took about four hours. But when they arrived at the English port, they were turned away and forced to return to Holland. "With her German passport and Russian family, she was entirely too suspicious for the immigration officers to give her an entry permit," Mrs. Steiner explained. "With her sick child, she was sent four or five times across the Channel because England didn't want to let them in, either."

But Dora kept trying. Between failed attempts to get into England, they returned to The Hague and rested in the Friedlaender household until Marianne was strong enough to make the journey again.

Prague, March 1939

In the course of one day—the Ides of March, 1939—Czechoslovakia disappeared from the map. Although Hitler had solemnly promised in the Munich Agreement to annex only German areas of the industry-rich Sudetenland, he had already violated those borders. On March 15, German panzers and armored vehicles rolled into the country and completed the occupation of the western Czech provinces of Bohemia and Moravia. The spoils were divided: Slovakia seceded and remained intact as a puppet state of Germany. Hungary consumed the easternmost province, which included the Carpathian Mountains, and Poland grabbed control of the neighboring Czech city of Teschen.

In Prague, thousands of Czechs and displaced Jews from Austria and Germany who had fled to Prague to escape Hitler lined up at foreign embassies and consulates, seeking visas. It was impossible; immigration quotas were full. The British consulate, through its administration of Palestine, "grudgingly issued 1,000 Certificates, a drop in the bucket for the more than 50,000 Jewish refugees whom the government . . . kept urging to leave as fast as possible." Desperate to escape, thousands left illegally in a Zionist rescue operation that transported Jewish men, women and children to Rumanian ports on the Black Sea, where they embarked on "wretched ships, setting out on a journey fraught with hardships and dangers to the shores of the Promised Land."

A prominent Zionist, Max Brod received one of the thousand certificates, which allowed him to emigrate legally from Czechoslovakia to Palestine. On the night of March 14, unaware of the advancing German army just hours away, Brod left Prague for the last time, bound for Tel Aviv. His was the last train to cross the Czechoslovakian frontier before the Germans closed the borders. In his hand luggage he carried Kafka's last remaining unpublished manuscripts, diaries and letters.

Time had not dulled Max Brod's passion for publishing Kafka's work and for sharing his literary gifts with the world. In addition to publishing a collection of Kafka's writings, Max had written a book, *Franz Kafka: A Biography,* published in 1937 by a small Prague publisher. Dora didn't read the book until after she returned to Europe from the Soviet Union. When she finally got her hands on a copy, she learned what Max truly thought of her. Despite all her fears, he had described her glowingly, almost reverentially. The last chapter was about her almost as much as Kafka. Brod told the story of their love affair, beginning with the meeting on the Baltic Sea. He described Kafka's happiness with her, how she had suited Kafka "quite marvelously," and how their relationship had "perfected him." Brod painted an unforgettable picture of Dora's loving and self-sacrificing care for Kafka with the story of the trip to the clinic in Vienna in April 1924: "The only car to be had for the journey from the sanatorium to Vienna was an open one," he wrote. "It rained and blew. The whole journey through Dora stood up in the car, trying to protect Franz with her body against the bad weather."

In Brod's book, Dora was a young romantic figure who brought fulfillment to Kafka's life and awakened "all his vital energies." Brod got one major fact wrong, but Dora never corrected it and in fact perpetuated it. Max had written that Dora "must have been nineteen or twenty" when she met Kafka. From then on, Dora dropped those six years from her age, and for the rest of her life she maintained Brod's version of the story, at least as it related to her age, in the public record.

While Dora waited in Holland to make another trip across the channel, she met with a celebrated Dutch writer and critic, Menno ter Braak, who had written an earlier essay on Kafka. More than sixty years after his death, ter Braak is still considered "the first and most important Dutch theoretician of film." He is known as a brilliant and incisive writer who helped define the interrelationship of art and modern society.

In the 1960s, the editor of ter Braak's letters wanted to know more about Dora's first meeting with the Dutch critic. The meeting took place, according to ter Braak's desk calendar, at the Friedlaender home on February 17, 1939, at eight in the evening. When questioned about it, Ruth Friedlaender remembered only that Dora and ter Braak "spent several hours in animated discussion." She could no longer recall whether Dora wished "to speak to the writer because she was so enthusiastic about his essay—or because it contained statements with which she vigorously disagreed and which she thought she could correct from her own knowledge of Kafka."

Dutch Kafka scholar Niels Bokhove maintains that Dora wanted to meet ter Braak because she agreed with him about Kafka's importance as a writer, the influence of Judaism on his literary style, and "the congruence of humor and seriousness in his irony [and] his attitude towards his illness and religion." Dora's subsequent meetings with ter Braak point to agreement—and a growing friendship: Dora's name appeared on his calendar five more times over the next six months, scheduled between Dora's failed attempts to be admitted into England.

In early March, after being turned away at Harwich for the fifth time, Dora came up with a new plan. According to Mrs. Steiner, "after being returned yet again to the Dutch port, Dora asked the immigration officer to ring up her sister-in-law. 'If you ring her up in The Hague, I'm sure she will come and collect my child, and take care of her,' Dora said. The authorities agreed to this arrangement, and the sister-in-law came, taking Marianne with her. Dora went again across the Channel two or three more times, before the British eventually let her in."

On March 16, one day after German forces marched into Prague, Dora was admitted to England on a "conditional landing." Her permit allowed her to stay for two months. Dora made the most of it. She quickly found a place to live and began to take the necessary steps to get permanent papers as a resident alien. Ten days before her conditional permit expired, Dora registered at the police station on Commercial Street and received her identity book, number 430855. Her address was listed as 34 Carysfort Road, N16, her current nationality was German, her previous nationality Russian. Under the category "single or married," Dora had written "divorced." Because her papers were in order, Dora's conditional status was extended for six months, until November 30. With the necessary documents in hand, Dora left England, returning again across the English Channel to Holland to collect her daughter.

THE HAGUE, AUGUST 1939

Marianne was too ill to travel, so Dora had to wait until she improved. While Dora waited, more or less patiently, she met again with Menno ter Braak, both at the Friedlaender home and at his office. Her name appears on his calendar on July 5 and July 12 and again on August 4.

With every day, the danger of being trapped in Holland increased. That summer, Hitler turned his sights on Poland and began ranting about German rights to Polish territories. The British and French were forced to abandon their failed policy of appeasement and promised to protect Poland's borders. On August 23, Stalin and Hitler signed their infamous nonaggression pact. In essence, Stalin promised not to protect Poland from Germany and was offered a share of the spoils of war in return.

Two days later, on August 25, Dora knew she couldn't wait any longer. Saying a tearful good-bye to the Friedlaenders, Dora and Marianne left for the Hoek van Holland and the ferry for England. Their papers were in order, and they landed on English soil, safe at last. Exactly one week later, on September 1, the German army attacked Poland. The governments of Britain and France declared war and all international borders were closed. World War II had begun.

BEDZIN, SEPTEMBER 1939

Dora's father, Herschel Dymant, died during Passover 1938. He was spared the horrible experiences suffered by the rest of Dora's family, her stepmother and ten siblings and their children. Bedzin, near the German border, was one of the first cities captured. There was no place to escape; enemies now surrounded Poland on all sides. Many went to the main synagogue of Bedzin to pray. At midnight on September 9, the Germans sprayed petrol on the synagogue, filled with hundreds of Jews who had sought sanctuary there, and burned it to the ground, killing many of them and destroying more than fifty nearby houses. Bracha Plotkin, a survivor of those terrifying days now living in Israel, said that after the fire, the Jews took stones from the burned synagogue to secretly make menorahs from

them. Another survivor of the Nazi destruction of Bedzin, Dasha Werdy-
gier Rittenburg, who later immigrated to New York, remembered that
within a month of the German occupation, a strict curfew was established;
anyone using a light at night would be shot. To manage the town's population of over 27,000 Jews, the Germans created a Jewish Council composed
of the local Jewish leaders. They established workshops owned by Germans and having a Jewish workforce laboring under the lie that by doing
essential work for the Germans, the Jews of Bedzin would be saved.

Throughout the next months, shouts of "Juden raus!" echoed in the
streets of Bedzin as German soldiers banged on all the doors, ordering
Jews out for a "selection." As the people lined up in the square near the
train station, soldiers picked the youngest and healthiest for the labor
camps. The first from Dora's family to be selected was seventeen-year-old
Sara, Dora's youngest—and most religious—half sister. Sara was sent first
to Chebina, a transit camp, to await transport to Germany. At Chebina,
her family sent her packages, the contents of which she clearly remembered sixty years later: her "nice warm blue coat with an expensive fur collar" and her photo album, a memory book with photos of friends and
loved ones who wrote her messages and inscribed their names. Among
Sara's photos were two of Dora, one with Marianne as a baby. One month
later, Sara was deported to a labor camp in Germany where she lost all
contact with her family. For the next six years, Dora heard nothing from
Sara or any other members of her family.

LONDON, WINTER 1940

One week after her return to England, Dora was classified as an "enemy
alien." With the outbreak of the war, the British Home Office ordered all
aliens with German and Austrian passports to appear before police tribunals,
where they were placed into one of three categories, A, B or C: Class A enemy aliens were considered dangerous and "a potential security risk." They
were arrested and immediately interned. Those classified as "B" were "aliens
about whose loyalty the tribunals were not absolutely certain and who for
one reason or the other should be kept under a form of supervision." They
were allowed to remain free but were subject to certain restrictions. Class B
aliens could not go beyond a five-mile radius of their homes without police
permission and had to surrender any items that could be used in espionage,
such as cameras, maps and binoculars. Class C aliens were left entirely free
and were classified as "refugees from Nazi oppression."

On January 11, 1940, Dora appeared before Metropolitan Police Tribunal, number 8, and was classified as a "B." She was "exempted until further order from internment" and allowed to go free, with restrictions, for the time being.

LONDON, MAY 1940

By spring of 1940, Denmark and Norway had fallen to the Germans. On May 10, the Wehrmacht rolled through Holland and Belgium on the way to France. Less than one month earlier, Ruth and her family finally received their visas, and on April 15 the Friedlaenders boarded a Holland-America ocean liner to begin a new life in America.

On May 14, with Rotterdam in flames and the Nazi army advancing on The Hague, Menno ter Braak, aged thirty-eight, committed suicide. He was not a Jew, nor was his name on a list of those wanted by the Germans. He sought death, his biographer concluded, "because he thought a life under a German occupation would be unbearable."

On the same day that Hitler launched his blitzkrieg into Holland, British Prime Minister Chamberlain resigned. His replacement was Winston Churchill, who had always argued against the policy of trying to appease Hitler. Churchill's attitude toward the refugees hardened as reports of German behind-the-scenes infiltration came pouring across the North Sea. One day before the Dutch resistance collapsed, Churchill called for "a very large round-up of enemy aliens and of suspected persons in this country. It would be much better that all these persons should be put behind barbed wire," he said.

That day, May 15, all male Class B aliens between the ages of sixteen and sixty were arrested. When the Home Office Secretary, Sir John Anderson, announced the roundup in the House of Commons, many politicians felt he had not gone far enough. As one member of Parliament asked, "Is the female of any species not generally more dangerous that the male?" Members of the House of Lords concurred that "women spies were much more dangerous than men." Their conclusion was that "we should immediately put out of harm's way all the aliens together with all the communists, fascists and pacifists."

Public opinion had turned against the 70,000 German and Austrian refugees in Great Britain. While a few Nazi sympathizers were among those arrested and interned, the overwhelming majority of Britain's feared "enemy aliens" were Jewish refugees like Dora—now suspected of being

Nazi spies and collaborators. Newspaper headlines fueled the flames of fear and hatred, inciting a "rampant anti-refugee paranoia." Even Oxford University, with its long tradition of tolerance, issued the following official statement: "All aliens are a potential menace and should be interned."

By May 20, the German army had reached the English Channel. Four hundred thousand allied French, British and Belgian soldiers were pushed back to a French village called Dunkirk, near the Belgian border. Four days later, a secret memorandum went out from the Home Office to all chief constables in Britain, advising that "internment of all 'B' women between the ages of sixteen and sixty" would begin on Monday, May 27 at 7:00 A.M.

Early that morning, as the evacuation of trapped Allied forces began at Dunkirk, the police knocked at Dora's door. Accompanying the police was a member of the Women's Voluntary Services, who would have informed Dora to pack a suitcase. As her room was searched for "any incriminating material (such as plans for assisting the enemy)," Dora quickly packed the bag with Marianne's clothes and medicines. The one treasure left in her possession from Kafka, she tucked away in her purse.

With hundreds of other German-speaking women and children, Dora and Marianne were led through the grim gates of the forbidding Holloway Prison for Women in North London, where they were locked in a large cellblock. The first day they were given only tea and biscuits. Dora tried to complain. Because of her kidney condition, one of the complications from the scarlet fever, Marianne needed plenty of fresh water and raw vegetables. Other women complained too, but the prison guards paid no attention to their pleas.

Not once in three years as a Jewish communist in Nazi Germany, nor in two years in the Soviet Union at the height of Stalin's purges, had Dora been arrested or incarcerated. She had escaped from both Hitler and Stalin to the safety of England—to end up a prisoner. Two days later, the women were taken out and loaded onto buses for Liverpool. As the buses drove through the streets, British citizens vented their fears on the refugees, hurling insults along with the occasional rotten egg.

The buses were crowded, and Dora and Marianne were forced to stand. A young woman noticed the dark-haired child and said, "Here, come sit on my lap." Looking first to Dora for permission, Marianne climbed onto the woman's lap. Thus began a lifelong friendship.

Johanna "Hanny" Metzger Lichtenstern was twenty-four years old and a new bride. A singer who had come from Berlin to London in the summer of 1939 on a permit to work as a domestic, Hanny had fallen in love with a Jewish musician, Paul Lichtenstern, a refugee from Austria. They had been married two months earlier. When the bus arrived in Liverpool, Hanny lost sight of Marianne and Dora in the crowd as they boarded the large steam freighter owned by the Isle of Man Steam Packet Company. On the night of May 29, the ship packed with women and children enemy aliens left England's western shore, transporting them across the stormy Irish Sea to a dark and uncertain future.

18

THE ISLE OF MAN

*Believing in progress does not mean believing
that any progress has yet been made. That is not
the sort of belief that indicates real faith.*
—Franz Kafka, *Blue Octavo Notebooks*

PORT ERIN, ISLE OF MAN, JUNE 1940

For Dora and Marianne, the crossing from Liverpool to Douglas was a
nightmare. A late spring storm roiled the Irish Sea, and many of the three
thousand women and children packed into the ferry of the Isle of Man
Steam Packet Company were sick. Locked in small cabins, they were also
frightened, not knowing what would happen to them in the morning.

As the ferry steamed into Douglas, the island's capital on the eastern
coast, the sea calmed and the day dawned through the clearing clouds. As
the ship entered the wide harbor, passing the ancient stone fortress at its
entrance, the Isle of Man seemed like a paradise, if not for the barbed
wire. Surrounding the row of Victorian hotels and boardinghouses lining
the harbor's promenade, a sturdy barbed wire fence separated the quay
and promenade from one of the men's internment camps.

Since her arrest in London four days earlier, Dora knew she was being
deported to the Isle of Man. The tiny island in the center of the Irish Sea
between England, Scotland and Ireland was only thirty-three miles long
and thirteen miles wide. An independent isle, with its own government,
currency, stamps and language—Gaelic Manx—the Isle of Man was
"shrouded in myth, legend and fairies" according to its tourist brochures.
It was known as a holiday destination, dotted with colorful Victorian hotels and guest houses, blessed with a spectacular natural landscape of

rolling moors, rocky cliffs, protected harbors and sandy beaches warmed by the Gulf Stream.

Once again in its dramatic 10,000-year history, with alternating conquests by Vikings and Celts, the Isle of Man became home to a sort of penal colony: It was the main internment center in Britain for enemy aliens in May 1940. Two weeks before Dora's arrival on the Isle of Man, the British Home Office asked hotel and boardinghouse owners in the villages of Port Erin and Port St. Mary "if they would be prepared to accommodate internees in return for payment of three shillings per person per day." With war declared in Europe, tourism, the island's main source of income, was certain to wane that summer and the proprietors "were happy to agree." Within days, the women's internment facilities at Port Erin and Port St. Mary were hastily set up and named Rushen Camp, after the peninsula on the southwest corner of the island where the secluded villages were situated. Surrounded by barbed wire, the new camps were placed under the control of a "tough old commandant," Dame Joanna Cruikshank, a former military nurse who had served as an officer in World War I and had risen to the rank of "matron-in-charge" of the British Red Cross Society.

The first shipment of enemy alien women and children docked at 8:30 on Thursday morning, May 30. They disembarked at the Douglas Ferry Terminal and walked in single file, lugging suitcases and bundles containing their worldly possessions past hostile Manx natives who had gathered to witness the spectacle. They marched for a quarter of a mile to the steam railway station, enduring catcalls, shouts of "bloody Germans" and worse, before they were loaded into the carriages of an old steam train for the hour-long ride to the southern end of the island. The single-gauge tracks ran alongside the steep coastal cliffs and then inland past rolling moors, dotted with wildflowers and emerald fields. While some of the women slept, depressed by their ordeal and exhausted from the sleepless night journey, others sang songs, spirits lifted by the lovely views outside the train windows.

At Port St. Mary, the last stop before the end of the line in Port Erin, the women were divided into two groups. Approximately half of the thirty-two hundred women and children were ordered from the train. Dora and Marianne were in the second group and remained on the train for the short remaining journey. In Port Erin, Dora was registered, photographed and issued an identity book. From the receiving center, Dora and Marianne walked the length of Port Erin's promenade, lined with large Edwardian hotels and small boardinghouses. The road curved above the shoreline, past the lighthouse and the hotels lining the promenade, up the hill to a holiday camp situated at the top, overlooking a lush green glen.

The women had been assigned to their hotels and boardinghouses in haste, without rhyme or reason, two to a bed, four to a room. Dora and Marianne were quartered at the Bradda Glen Hotel. Huge flowering hedges of wild fuchsia surrounded the spacious grounds and overlooked the cliffs of Spaldrick Bay's village and harbor below. Perched at the very end of Bradda Head, its access blocked by rolls of barbed wire, stood a strange solitary Victorian tower. The women were not allowed to walk out to the point, but it remained, a dramatic and unforgettable sentinel shaped like a giant lock cartridge, jutting at the cliff's edge into the sea.

Years later, Hanny Lichtenstern remembered few details of the journey. She was allowed up on deck and wasn't seasick, but the trip from Douglas to Port Erin was a blur. Exhausted, she "tumbled in, and then tumbled out" of one conveyance into another. She took no notice of the scenery. A young newlywed separated from her new husband, Hanny felt both "betrothed and dismantled," as she wrote in her diary. She asked for and was given a small single attic room with a narrow dormer window on the fourth and top floor of Snaefell, one of the larger hotels facing the Port Erin harbor.

Hanny encountered Dora and Marianne living not far from her own hotel. It was only a short walk from Snaefell along the cliff path and past the sycamore and beech trees to Dora's room at Bradda Glen. Hanny was drawn to Dora's enthusiasm for life and insight into human nature. Hanny also liked Dora's six-year-old daughter. "Marianne is a born actress with an incredible instinct for both seriousness and humor. So original," she noted.

As the women and children settled in to their new quarters, the eyes of the world were focused a few hundred miles south on the English Channel, where one of the most dramatic events of the war was unfolding. Four days after the first shipment of women and children arrived on the Isle of Man, the evacuation of the British army from Dunkirk in France ended. The Allied forces were in full retreat. The German army now occupied the entire channel coastline and was poised to attack Britain. Soon the German bombing of Paris began. Then Belgium and Norway surrendered to the Nazis. In Italy, Mussolini succumbed to the "temptation to share the spoils of Germany's triumphs" and declared war on both France and Britain, and Italian troops swarmed into the south of France. By June 14, Paris was burning under German occupation.

On June 16, a Nazi collaborator, Marshal Petain, was installed as the new prime minister of France. The entire British Empire, including the internees of Rushen Camp, participated in general national prayers held that day for France. Dora and Hanny, along with two friends from Berlin who were also internees, Eva Nathan and Erica Stein, walked to the hill and sent their own prayers for the French Jews and foreign refugees who had been rounded up by the French government and interned in camps at the outbreak of the war. Now thousands of those innocent internees were being conveniently handed over to the SS and shipped to concentration camps in Germany and Poland. If the Germans reached England, the women knew that this would be their fate, too.

To deal with her feelings of helplessness and fear, Hanny began to write. Her diary, quoted for the first time, provides the only account of this period in Dora's life. Dora never talked about the experience afterward, and few ever knew it happened to her. Because of the stigma attached, Dora told Marianne she should never mention it, just as they never mentioned Russia, ever, to anyone. Many Kafka biographers wrote about Dora in the last chapters of Kafka's life, and most knew she had ended up in England, but none were aware of this interlude in her life.

In assessing life after two weeks in the camp, Hanny decided that "THE event here—for me—up till now is Dora Kafka." At first, Hanny thought Dora must be Kafka's wife because of the frequency and passion with which she talked about him.

Sixteen years after his death, Dora was still talking about Kafka and the story of their life together, winning converts to his inimitable view of the world. She often talked about "his love for all that is genuine, pure, truly great." Hanny thought Dora was still in love with Kafka. "I believe that she is still—or perhaps more than ever—with him, bound to him, and surely she has learned to think as he thought, to feel as he felt."

Hanny often sought out Dora's company when she needed cheering up: "Dora exuded warmth and she loved to laugh." They talked about many things, mostly "about religion, Jewishness and consciousness." Hanny admired Dora's insight and opinion so highly that she wanted to "ask Dora for an honest, unsparing critique about myself," she wrote in her diary. Instead, she decided to "leave that alone and WORK."

In the beginning there was little to do. There was nothing to read, no magazines or newspapers, no radio, so the women walked until they reached the barbed wire and were forced to return. The terrain surrounding Port Erin was beautiful. In the distance, gentle hills sprouted green fields, lush meadows and moors. A rocky beach lay at the bottom of the glen. There was a rushing stream, natural waterfalls and pools, and nature paths teeming with wild orchids, fuchsia, roses and exotic plants and birds. At first the nearby golf course was open to the internees, and several women had their golf clubs sent to them and played every day.

With the country in peril, the British politicians who had earlier argued for internment now condemned the Home Office for "the specially favorable conditions" enjoyed by the women internees on the Isle of Man. Was it right, one member of Parliament asked, "that these persons should be kept in luxurious idleness?" There was "considerable public resentment" as one MP argued, because "alien women interned in the Isle of Man were fully provided for by the government in hotels and boardinghouses at the payment of twenty-one shillings a week and are to be provided with swimming baths, tennis courts and golf links, while the wife of a private soldier in the army gets an allowance of seventeen shillings a week plus seven shillings deducted from her husband's pay?"

For internees with money, life was not bad. Luxuries like good soap and fresh fruit and vegetables could be purchased in town. But for those who had no money and no way of earning it, life was more difficult. After a while, the women were allowed to take domestic jobs in the hotels that earned them money from the Home Office. Later, an elaborate work-barter system was established. Dora went to work helping in the kitchen of the hotel. In addition to the six pence she earned per day, she became friendly with the cooks in the other hotels, who helped her squirrel away fresh raw vegetables and fruits, like cauliflower and apples, that Marianne needed. Hanny knew that Marianne was not well, but the child didn't seem to be really sick, certainly not so frail that she couldn't run around and play. If Marianne fell ill again, there was a small hospital set up in a little house off the main road, run by an interned female physician from Vienna and overseen by a one of the island's medical officers.

When Hanny was lonely or unhappy, she turned to Dora for advice and solace. "Dora Lask provides, again, calm and thoughtfulness," Hanny wrote on learning of France's humiliating surrender negotiations, news that "falls like a hammer on one's head." Alone in her attic room, Hanny wrote, "Foul, decaying Europe—everywhere one steps into bogs—if only one could wipe it off one's feet. Dora is absolutely right when she says we Jews were a warning when we left—and still leave—in droves. [The Jews] felt the ground beneath them tremble and destruction threatened, as they had always felt it."

The next afternoon Dora, Hanny and Eva took Marianne to see a new movie. Hanny reviewed *The Wizard of Oz* that night in her diary: "Technically admirable, contents full of ideas, witty, exciting. Delightfully colorful, splendidly acted, musically too enchanting." Marianne was also taken with the film and had things to say about each of the characters, beginning with the role of Glenda. "The good fairy," Marianne said, "is so blond, that one forgives her everything."

Marianne remained fascinated with the movie, obsessed with improving the story and its characters. One day she and Hanny acted out the *The Wizard of Oz* to a happy end. Hanny was impressed by Marianne's acute sensitivity to the suffering of others. It was unusual, especially in child of six years. "The death of the bad witch moves her to deep pity and so to sympathy with her," Hanny said. Marianne was "frightened to tears by my terrible, too realistic portrait of the witch and from then on, takes over this delicate part herself." Marianne decided to portray the witch as capable of change. "Finally, she changes, then crosses out the death of the witch, lets her promise to become 'good', then showers her with gifts and love."

In the warm evenings, Hanny walked with Dora and Marianne across the meadow or down in the rocks by the sea. Dora was often "delightful and in high spirits, which makes her incredibly young," Hanny said. One evening in mid-June, Dora spied "such a dear horse on the meadow," exclaiming "one absolutely *must* bring him some bread."

Although many women complained bitterly about the unfairness of their internment, the inadequate food, the loss of productive work and the close living quarters with the true Nazi sympathizers in their midst, Dora was very happy with the situation in which she had landed. She recognized her great good luck, compared to so many others whose fates she worried about incessantly. What was happening to her family, her friends? How were Kafka's sisters doing? As another internee at Port Erin explained, "Separation from family of course meant suffering. But how can one compare this to the humiliation, torture, slave work, killing, in the concentration camps. Even in prison, I felt safe, escaped from the Gestapo."

Not all of the interned women at Rushen Camp were Jewish or anti-Nazi. Several German women were outspoken in their hatred of Jews and secretly sewed Nazi swastikas onto banners to greet the victorious invaders when they arrived on British soil.

News of the war was limited, and rumors regularly flooded the camp. One rumor that proved true concerned the deportation of interned enemy aliens to Canada. The 12,000 German and Austrian enemy aliens under the joint control of the War Office and Home Office were draining the country's resources, and Churchill wanted to ship them all out of the country. On June 19, the Canadian prime minister announced that "Canada was ready to take interned aliens and German prisoners of war from Great Britain." The idea of deportation to Canada, in the New World, far from the threat of Hitler, was received in the camp with mixed reactions. In her diary, Hanny reported that "Eva is quite tearful about the Canada idea, poor dear. Dora is happy about the possibility. . . ."

Two weeks later, another terrible rumor washed ashore: a German submarine had torpedoed the *Arandora Star* in the Atlantic Ocean off the west coast of Ireland on the ship's second day out from Liverpool, en route to Canada. A former luxury liner that had once featured a kosher cuisine, the ship had been requisitioned by the War Office to transport German and Italian enemy aliens, mostly Jews, along with some bona fide Nazis and fascists, to Canada. The ship sank and six hundred internees died. Weeks passed before the women learned whether their husbands or sons were aboard.

In late June, a furious storm raged in the Irish Sea for three days, keeping everyone indoors. "It rains and then pours for hours and hours. . . . This wild, constant, icy storm is terribly tiring . . . it whistles through you as if you were a sieve." Crowded together with strangers, the women found little relief from the monotony and constant fear of worsening news of Hitler's conquest of Europe. Dora often had to listen to arguments and bickering among the women, who fought constantly in the hothouse atmosphere. Friendships that had started on the way to internment turned into terrible hatreds. "My head feels quite empty and not even shaking helps it," Hanny said. "What did help was the little Manx cat without a tail which ran towards me on the stairs and which I took into my room to play with."

To combat boredom, community activities developed quickly. "Very soon, Rushen camp was buzzing with schemes," wrote one of the chroniclers of Britain's internees during World War II. Within a few weeks, a school set up along "modern lines" by a "noted educationalist" was established for the children, who ranged in age from infancy to sixteen. Two Fröbel-trained teachers established a kindergarten. Older children were prepared for matriculation and offered vocational classes, while afternoon sessions for younger children were devoted to singing, games and handicrafts.

Many of the internees had previous theatrical experience, and numerous shows and concerts were organized in the different hotels. Hanny's mood improved greatly one afternoon after attending a "very mixed, very funny 'Variety Show,'" she wrote. She had "screamed with laughter and cried tears, laughing. It was like a refreshing shower and produced a cheerful mood even afterwards."

Bradda Glen had a large ballroom and a stage that was ideal for performances. Dora immediately got to work organizing shows, Yiddish poetry and play readings, recitals and musical concerts. Eva Nathan drew the posters, which were displayed in Snaefell, the Hydro, the Ballequeeny and other hotels. Other women worked on making costumes out of crepe paper. Dora was doing what she could to raise spirits, to help keep everyone entertained and creative. From the beginning, she encouraged Hanny, a singer with a lovely trained voice, to work on her performance skills.

Dora began coaching Hanny with acting techniques to help her deliver the songs. Over the next weeks and months, Dora taught Hanny movement and expression, how to perform the song and how to find her own voice. Dora assigned exercises and "emphasized the importance of consonants in speaking and singing." By the third week in June, Hanny was feeling better and admitted that "this diary and night breathing exercises are beginning to teach me some discipline."

July 3 was Kafka's birthday. If Kafka had lived, he would now be fifty-seven years old. The day was spent in a way Franz would have approved: in rehearsal for a show, with Dora helping Hanny on a performance of Shubert's "Lilac Time." In her diary, Hanny wrote: "And Dora! What she's made of this 'Song of a Seagull.' The intensity and creative power and the colors she produces are stunning, deeply moving proofs of a great skill—or even better—of a great character. I must learn so much, all I can possibly absorb."

When Dora was busy in rehearsals, Hanny sometimes looked after Marianne, who, like her mother, was a gifted natural performer. Once Marianne sang a little German song, a popular tune, "Hanschen Klein," "about a little child separated from its mother," Hanny remembered years later. "Marianne sang with such emotion, it brought tears to my eyes. She was one in a million, that child."

One Sunday, Marianne brought out her collection of family photographs. They were enchanting pictures of Marianne as an infant, cradled in her mother's arms, as a toddler running down a snowy street, a four-year-old asleep with her doll. For each photograph, Marianne had a story to tell. There were several with her grandfather, whom she loved very much.

Dr. Jacobsohn-Lask had recently died at the age of seventy-seven in Sevastopol; the news had not reached Dora yet. No news of any Lask family members had come out of Russia in the months since they had gone. After Lutz's arrest, there had not been one word from him. Dora and her daughter could only wonder—and try not to think—about his fate.

As the war raged on, new internees kept arriving. In the first week of July, 250 more women arrived, further crowding the camp and straining its resources. These internees were quite old, Hanny noted, between sixty and seventy years, and some were very ill. All arrived, she said, "without stockings. They'd spent a month in Holloway prison."

When Dora wasn't working in the kitchen or helping Marianne with her lessons, she spent her time producing and directing, as well as helping others rehearse and perform for the productions held at Bradda Glen and other venues. Occasionally Dora performed too, reciting poems, stories and favorite monologues and scenes. She concentrated on Yiddish songs and plays. It was a way to participate in the war against the Nazis, to combat the silencing and censuring of the Jewish culture she loved, to build pride and hope in Jewish hearts. Dora's strong feelings and commitment infused each performance. "She was excellent, a wonderful Yiddish actress," Hanny said.

Dora's friendship with Hanny grew as they kept busy with rehearsals, which often went on for weeks, followed by a single performance, maybe two. The point was to be creative and stay occupied. During a rehearsal for Goethe's famous poem "Gretchen at the Spinning Wheel," set to music by Franz Schubert, Dora did something Hanny would never forget. "Dora knew the poem by heart," Hanny later recalled, "and she acted the entire song out for me, showing me exactly what the young girl was expressing in her song. Then, she made me say it, without singing, so I could get the right feeling into it."

That summer, the Battle of Britain began. With the collapse of five European nations in less than eighty days, Britain stood virtually alone against the Nazi military machine. The United States remained steady in its decision not to get involved in another European war, but in June, President Franklin D. Roosevelt declared that the United States would "extend to the opponents of force the material resources of this nation." The Lend-Lease Act, passed the following year, allowed Britain to "borrow" military equipment and munitions from the United States.

The dogfights and air battles over the English Channel started in early June. In mid-July, Hermann Goering's Luftwaffe made its first full-scale daytime air raid on England. In August, the German bombing offensive shifted from ports near the English Channel to inland airfields and radar stations in the interior of Britain. For days in August, fifteen hundred German bombers and fighter aircraft darkened the English skies daily. In September, the British retaliated and bombed Berlin. German fighters began bombing civilian as well as military targets. Air raids continued, day and night, throughout the fall and winter of 1940–1941. The Blitz destroyed large areas of London, Southampton, Bristol, Cardiff, Coventry, Liverpool, Manchester and almost every major city in England as the German bombardment by air continued for months.

Grim reports of German bombings came through the grapevine. No one knew whether the stories were true or were just rumors. The Nazi internees grew more confident and began sneering at the Jewish refugees in the streets and mocking them with straight-armed salutes. After the blackout one night, a group of Nazi women were found using flashlights to signal out to sea. The camp remained in a state of panic after rumors circulated that a German invasion would arrive any day by sea.

PORT ERIN, ISLE OF MAN, NOVEMBER 1940

Dora was worried about Hanny. She'd lost so much weight that her bones poked through her skin. The younger woman was like a little sister or even another daughter to her, a "little half-pint" Dora once called her. Despite her pleasure in music and singing, Hanny was being worn down by constant fear and stress. Dora and Eva put their heads together to figure out how to help her and decided to fatten her up. On November 21, Hanny reported to her husband that her friends were taking very good care of her. "Dora made me a jarful of *schmaltz,* which tastes wonderful and which I eat with gusto."

Dora had insisted on a good margarine that was available at the canteen. She also arranged for the camp doctor to prescribe a bottle of cod liver oil for Hanny. "I felt just like a baby, but it's really quite nice to be treated this way," Hanny admitted.

Letters to and from the internment camps were censored and restricted. Hanny's husband, Paul, who had been interned in a men's camp on the island, was allowed monthly visits, but only in public. Between those visits, two letters of twenty-four lines each were allowed per week. Since Dora had no one to write to, she gave her letter allotment to Hanny, who was able to write two extra letters per week, with Dora's return address and last name.

Hanny's last performance in Port Erin was on January 25, 1941. She kept the poster announcing the program at Dandy-Hill School at 3:30 P.M. The program was billed as "Jewish Folksongs and Anecdotes; motives from 'Dybbuk'; Chassidic melodies (Nigunim); directed by D. Lask, performed by J. Metzger and R. Salinger." J. Metzger was Joanna Metzger—Hanny's maiden name. Eva Nathan provided the poster artwork: a religious Jew with earlocks, his eyes gazing upward, his arms open wide to the heavens. At the end of January, Hanny was released.

The previous summer, internees who could prove that they were "useful" to the British war effort were allowed to apply for release. A special advisory committee heard the cases, and those who were deemed completely safe as well as useful could be upgraded from B category to C. By February 1941, over 10,000 refugees had been released from the camps, including Paul and Hanny Lichtenstern. They returned to London to try to find a place to live, a daunting task for the largely reviled German refugees without money or family. Many homes and apartment buildings had been destroyed, and thousands of homeless people were living on the streets. Finally they found a room that they shared in Lady Montague's sister's house with another couple, a rabbi and his wife. Hanny continued to write to Eva and in March 1941 sent a package of gifts to Dora and Marianne. Dora had also been upgraded but still couldn't leave.

In a one-page letter-envelope addressed to Mrs. H. Lichtenstern, 36 Porchester Terrace, London W2, and postmarked "15 April 1941, Women's Internment Camp, Isle of Man," Dora wrote to thank Hanny for the parcel. It is the only letter that remains from Dora's fifteen months of internment. She began on a lighthearted note with a made-up endearment: "Dear sweet Kolibri." In the first eight lines, Dora played with words and peppered her sentences with Yiddish. Hanny's humor was *bechaint,* and she was, Dora said, "the oh, so able *balebosste* who has darned all fifty (or was it ninety?) pairs of socks."

Dora demanded assurances that Hanny was happy. "I miss you very much, you dear one," Dora wrote. "Actually I should be a little cross, because you don't write, but if one sits in a glass cage as I do, one must refrain from throwing stones. So, only because of this, I shut up." Had Hanny yet sung any of the Yiddish songs, Dora asked. What about the

"Ave Maria?" Hanny had once performed the sacred Catholic hymn for a church service in Port Erin. When Dora heard Hanny singing it, she later said, "it seemed to me as if a mystic was singing 'Shir Hashirim,' Solomon's Song of Songs." It was then that Dora began working with her, teaching Hanny the Yiddish songs, too. Now Dora wrote that Schubert's song "is just as perfect as some of the Yiddish ones, and with it you are on equally firm ground. I don't mean the subject matter. Well, you know what I mean."

"How lovely," Dora continued, "that with you I'm not so much afraid of being misunderstood. I suffer much from this fear in my relationship with people. To understand there must be, even before intelligence, good will. And this is a difficult thing, for it presumes the ability to submerge one's own critical view. Holy Cow! How did I get here? I only wanted to tell you, I'm not afraid of you, because you are good and honest. And here I made such a *Simmis*. Ah well, there's still five lines to go."

Dora wanted to know if Hanny had gotten in touch with her friend Stencl yet. She hadn't heard from him, or anyone else, in such a long time. "Will you, at some time, be able to write to my sister-in-law?" Dora asked. After spending another line wondering if she shouldn't wait to send the letter until she'd heard from Hanny, Dora had reached the last of the twenty-four lines allowed. "All the best and love, Dora," she wrote. There was still half a line left, not to be wasted, so Dora added: "Marianne is better."

Dora had one more thing to say, the underlying reason for the letter. Although she was out of space, she squeezed in a twenty-fifth—and officially illegal—line, a hint in tiny letters: "Have become a 'C,' would be released if I had someplace to go. . . ."

19

FRIENDS OF YIDDISH

*The crows maintain that a single crow could de-
stroy the heavens. There is no doubt of that, but
it proves nothing against the heavens, for heaven
simply means: the impossibility of crows.*
—Franz Kafka, *Blue Octavo Notebooks*

NORTHENDEN, MANCHESTER, AUGUST 1941

Once again, Kafka's influence helped Dora. In the summer of 1941, a
young Polish refugee living at the home of a lecturer in philosophy of religion at Manchester University was writing her master's thesis on Franz
Kafka. The refugee, Ilse Sarwitz, learned about Dora in Brod's biography.
In the course of researching Kafka for her paper, she discovered that Dora
was interned as an enemy alien on the Isle of Man, and that she could be
released if she had someplace to go or someone who would take her in.
Ilse went straight to the woman who had saved her own life.

Dorothy Emmet had been involved in saving Jewish refugees from Nazi
persecution since coming to Manchester three years earlier, in 1938, at the
age of thirty-four. Unmarried, without a family to take care of, she was able
to sponsor a number of German and Polish refugees, allowing them to emigrate to Britain. She opened her home to Ilse and several others until they
were able to find their own places. As many testified at a memorial service
in Cambridge in 2000, Professor Emmet practiced what she taught. The
philosophy she preferred, as one longtime friend and colleague put it, was
"connected to the real world and could make a difference."

As a young woman, Dorothy had witnessed the hatred against Jews.
Traveling through Germany on her own in the 1930s, she stumbled on a

Nazi Party rally in Nuremberg. In a characteristic spirit of adventure, she decided to investigate, following the crowds to the stadium, where she heard Goering speak and saw "a motorcade with Hitler standing in an open car. Everyone was giving the Nazi salute," she wrote in her last book, *Outward Forms and Inner Springs*, published in 1998, when she was ninety-four years old. "I kept my hands in my pockets and was glad to think I had a British passport."

When the war broke out in 1939, Dorothy and her younger sister, Margery Wilson, had been working with Quakers (the Religious Society of Friends) to facilitate entry of refugees into Britain and help them once they arrived in the country. After two years, Ilse Sarwitz still lived with her sponsor and with her help was completing her master's degree.

Dorothy Mary Emmet, born in London in 1904, lived an extraordinary life, especially for a woman of her time. The daughter of a country vicar and Christian scholar who was appointed dean of University College at Oxford shortly before his premature death, Dorothy graduated at the top of her classes at Oxford, with firsts in Classics and philosophy. After listening to a speech in Parliament by R. H. Tawney supporting poor Welsh miners in the General Strike of 1926, she underwent "the nearest thing I ever had to a conversion experience," she said. It changed her life. She went to live in the Rhondda valley, where she worked in the poor mining communities as a tutor for the Workers Educational Association, teaching Plato's *Republic* to unemployed miners and their families. The experience made her a socialist and, at the same time, drew her more deeply into philosophy in a search for understanding the human condition and spirit. When Dorothy was twenty-two, she read a book by Alfred North Whitehead, a former Cambridge mathematician and philosopher who was teaching at Harvard University, and her life took a new direction. She accepted a fellowship at Radcliffe, the women's college at Harvard. There she worked with the eighty-year-old Whitehead and became a family friend. Whitehead was famous for developing a metaphysical connection unifying space, time, matter and events. "Nature is a structure of evolving processes," he wrote. "The reality is the process."

Dorothy returned to Britain in 1928 as a research fellow at Oxford and continued her work with miners. In 1932 she published her first book, *Whitehead's Philosophy of Organism*. By the time she was appointed lecturer at Manchester University in 1938, she was already a "senior and well-published philosopher" whose interests ranged from philosophy of religion to metaphysics, ethics and social responsibility.

In the summer of 1941, when Ilse told her that "Kafka's Dora was at the Isle of Man Women's Internment Camp, and couldn't we have her here," Dorothy responded simply: "I said, of course."

It was a generous act of hospitality. The townhouse on Yew Tree Lane was cramped, three small bedrooms, a living room and a tiny kitchen, but they all managed to get along, despite the uncertain and frightening circumstances under which they were living.

"It was the time of the air raids," Dorothy recalled almost sixty years later in an interview she gave from her nursing home in Cambridge in the summer of 2000, shortly before her death. "I can still remember the three of us, Dora, Marianne, and myself, crawling together underneath the big steel table in the living room during an air raid, and waiting there together until the sirens ended." The Morrison shelter, as the reinforced steel tables were called, after government minister Herbert Morrison, had been issued to all homes for protection against aerial bombing attacks. They took other precautions as well. Curtains had to be lined with black fabric that blocked in all light. In addition, gas masks from World War I had been issued to each person in the household. The rubber masks were horrifying in themselves, and when worn, they created a claustrophobic, surreal world in which everyone looked like a creature from an H. G. Wells novel.

Dora and Marianne stayed in Northenden with Dorothy throughout the fall and winter. Once a small village on the river Mersey with ancient origins, Northenden was a community of Victorian and Edwardian homes, built for Manchester's industrial upper-level management. Incorporated into the city in 1931, Northenden was quiet and peaceful with tree-lined country lanes that dated back to Roman times.

Manchester was reminiscent of Lodz—for centuries it had been the textile center of the country, and it was filled with Victorian red brick factories and smokestacks. In fact, Lodz was often called the "Polish Manchester." Less than two hundred miles northwest of London, Manchester had the second largest Jewish population in the United Kingdom. The city offered great music, art galleries and fascinating old libraries to explore, such as the famous Chetham Library founded in 1653, one of Europe's first free public libraries. In one of the library's arched stone alcoves, Marx and Engels had met to discuss their revolutionary ideas.

Dora never talked about her communist past. During the years that Dorothy knew Dora, she had no inkling that Dora had lived in Russia before coming to England. "When Dora and Marianne were with me," the ninety-six-year-old professor emeritus reported, "she never let on about these other sides of her life. I only knew that she had been with Kafka and had come to England and been sent to the Isle of Man."

At the time, Professor Emmet couldn't understand Dora's apparent lack of interest in finding her missing husband. "Dora didn't answer her letters properly," Emmet said, a hint of disapproval in her voice. "The Red Cross was trying to put her in touch with Lask, but she muddled it up, she didn't reply in time." The professor had no idea that Dora's missing husband was a communist who had been imprisoned in a labor camp in Siberia, or that Dora herself had once joined the German Communist Party. Without that information, she had concluded that in regard to finding Lask, "Dora was very vague and scatterbrained."

Dorothy enjoyed the company: Dora was a "marvelous cook. She made very good soups, which were quite welcome in wartime," Dorothy recalled. She characterized Marianne as a special child, unusually thoughtful and serious: "I became especially fond of her."

Marianne was seven years old and should have been in school. Most of the local schools had closed during the Blitz, when the government recommended that all school-age children be evacuated to the country outside the cities. Dora wasn't ready to let Marianne go, nor was Marianne willing to be separated from her mother. Following the trauma of her illness, the long, difficult journey from Russia to England, and internment, Marianne had grown very shy. Until she knew someone, Marianne remained silent, her dark eyes surveying the situation while she hid behind Dora's skirts.

Dorothy Emmet arranged to get Marianne—and Dora—accepted at Yealand Manor, a country estate house built in the nineteenth century that now housed a private evacuation school run by the Quakers. Since the outbreak of the war, Dorothy's sister, Margery, worked and lived at the school with her two children, who were about Marianne's age. "Here's a girl who will benefit from the school and a mother who can help," Dorothy told the school's headmistress, Elfrida Foulds, who had made a practice of extending accommodation to all deserving children, regardless of religion or ability to pay.

YEALAND MANOR, NORTH LANCASHIRE, 1942

The school at Yealand Conyers in the peaceful countryside north of Carnforth, fifty miles north of Manchester, was already overcrowded when Dora and Marianne arrived. Set up in a Georgian manor house at the center of natural park and woodlands, the school had rooms that were "spacious, with the lofty ceiling proper to its period, but all the living rooms were used for at least two purposes, and the bedrooms were packed with children and adults. Both dining rooms served as classrooms in between meals, so that as soon as the pupils had put away their work, they had to collect crockery and cutlery, and lay the tables."

Dora knew very little about the Religious Society of Friends, but was very comfortable with those who addressed each other, regardless of rank or wealth, religion or race, nationality or gender, as "Friend." The sect had begun three centuries earlier in England as a religious reform movement based on what its founder, George Fox, believed to be the true spirit of Christianity. Dora was able to witness the religion in action: the school at Yealand Manor practiced the Quaker principles of peace, equality, community, simplicity, integrity and truth. The history of the school, in operation only during the war, was recorded by its headmistress, Elfrida Foulds. It was, she said, as it had been envisioned by its founders: "A place where as many children as possible might be gathered together during the war years, and trained, however imperfectly, to live in that spirit of which George Fox wrote, the spirit that 'takes away the occasion for all wars.'"

When the Home Office arranged the evacuation of all school-age children, Yealand Manor filled up with Quaker children from Manchester and surrounding areas. As the school's reputation for academic excellence and a healthy, safe environment grew, non-Quakers and foreign refugees also wanted to send their children, and the school began accepting applications from "a very wide range of people." There were "children who had been spoiled and children who had been neglected, children who had seen and remembered far too much of the welter of horror on the continent, and children who had been happily settled at Yealand ever since September 1939." It was, Elfrida Foulds said, "a healthily mixed brew."

At first, the mothers of the Quaker students provided the staff for the school, but as the war continued, "the basis of recruitment broadened very considerably," Elfrida Foulds said. Before long, the staff included some truly gifted teachers. The school developed a reputation for a "happy family life, for its good scholarship results, and for its apparent success in dealing with 'problem children.'"

At first, Marianne Lask was one of these problem children. Uprooted from the warm, cozy home in Northenden, forced from her mother's bed to sleep in a crowded dormitory room, Marianne revolted. For the past four years, Dora and Marianne had not been separated for more than an hour or two. Marianne's education had come naturally, on Dora's lap. She had been tutored by loving family members and adults, gifted teachers from her grandfather to Dorothy Emmet.

When Marianne first arrived at the school, Elfrida Foulds said, "she was subject to dramatic outbursts of fury which at first did not fail to attract the attention of which the poor child subconsciously felt that she had been deprived. She was a brilliant, handsome, delicate little girl, with an outstanding dramatic talent which found full vent in her temperamental tantrums, as she raged and screamed and spat."

Dora had not realized how much she had overcompensated for the fear and suffering in her daughter's life. Dora was concerned about Marianne's behavior but could not do anything. In fact, the less she did, the better. "The more these demonstrations were ignored, the less they were indulged in," Foulds pointed out. Failing to get the desired results, Marianne tried a new tactic: "There was a phase in which she would always take the blame for any wrong-doing in the school, thus again attracting interest, and always acting with such consummate skill that nobody knew whether to believe her or not." It took a while for Marianne's fears to abate. "Friendship, affection and understanding provided the medium in which she could develop. She was a deeply thoughtful child, appreciative and loving, and her sensitive nature must have suffered much," the headmistress concluded.

Dora kept her eye on Marianne from the school kitchen, where she often helped out. Dora's presence in the kitchen lingers in the memory of the children who were there at the time. "Dora was a cook of character," remembers Anthony Wilson, whose mother, Margery, Dorothy Emmet's sister, also worked at the school. Wilson, who was one year older than Marianne, remembered the mother more clearly than the daughter. The children knew that Dora was a woman with a past, although they didn't really know what it meant. Elfrida Fould's second daughter, Carol Shaw, remembered Dora through her reputation. "We were told that Mrs. Lask was 'Kafka's Dora,' which meant nothing to me at the time."

YEALAND MANOR, JULY 3, 1942

Dorothy Emmet came to the school to visit her family and to see Dora and Marianne. On the first Friday in July, she took Marianne on a long walk in the countryside. As they walked, Marianne announced, "Today is my first father's birthday." Dorothy knew she was talking about Kafka. The precocious child often talked about Franz Kafka, referring to him as "her first father," Dorothy remembered. "We picked some wild flowers and laid them in a stone circle and thought about him."

That same day, the Germans took Sevastopol. After a month-long siege, the Germans captured the Crimean port and began their drive north to Stalingrad. Dora read the headlines and worried. She had no way of knowing that Berta Lask was safe in Moscow or that Dr. Lask had passed away the year before. It was impossible to think about what Lutz might be suffering if he were still alive. His chances were not good. In the gulag, every day another of his labor camp compatriots died of the inhumane conditions. The situation was worse in Poland, where her family in Pabianice and Brzeziny had been rounded up and herded into the Lodz ghetto. In June, the Final Solution, the mass murder of Jews by gassing, was begun at Auschwitz, a town twenty miles from Bedzin.

LONDON, 1942

Marianne settled into the secure structure that the school provided and began to thrive academically and personally. Everyone grew fond of her, especially the headmistress. As time went on, Marianne Lask, Elfrida Foulds said, "became one of the most helpful children in the school, and one of the most loyal to the ideals for which it stood."

With Marianne safe at Yealand Manor, Dora returned to London to find work. What she found in the bombed-out streets of Whitechapel, in the remnants of the once vibrant Jewish East End, was a new purpose, a cause to which she could dedicate herself: the survival of the Yiddish language. Dora found her friend Stencl in Whitechapel, where he was very busy editing and publishing a Yiddish journal, *Loshn un Lebn* (Language and Life). According to those who knew him, he was a "humorous, charismatic, always interesting man." Dora said that "only two authors existed for him: Kafka and Flaubert. He didn't read anything else."

Before World War II, Stencl started a literary and cultural group, Friends of Yiddish, modeled on Stencl's Yiddish Circle in Berlin, of which Dora had been an early member. At that time, more than 100,000 Jews lived in the East End of London. It was in Whitechapel that Stencl found "his first permanent home," living on Greatorex Street, "refusing to move beyond the frontier of the East End" for more than fifty years until his

death in 1982. His passion had become his love of Yiddish and his obses-
sive "campaign to preserve Yiddish as a vibrant language," a flame that he
also ignited in Dora.

"Immediately after her arrival she associated herself with our work,"
Stencl wrote in an article in *Loshn un Lebn*. "She held lectures at the Shab-
bat afternoons, read from Yiddish literature, especially the classics. Dora
Dymant's readings of portions of Yiddish stories, for instance the poem
'Monish,' was always a '*Yontif*,' a Holy day at the Yiddish literary Sabbath
afternoons."

Arriving in England as a young refugee from Lodz, Majer Bogdanski
first met Dora when he participated in Friends of Yiddish meetings as an
audience member. Fifty years later, Bogdanski still recalled those magical
Saturday afternoon meetings he attended after the war, when "each meeting was an event." He would press himself against the wall at the back of
the room to see Dora Dymant at the front of the hall, as he said, "the star
of the show." After Stencl's death, Bogdanski took over the leadership of
the group, which has survived to the twenty-first century. Now frail in his
nineties, Bogdanski still regularly attends and performs poetry and prose
readings at the Friends of Yiddish meetings, which, although smaller, are
still held every Saturday afternoon at 3:00 P.M. at Toynbee Hall in Whitechapel. Bogdanski's performances are an amazing experience even for
those who speak no Yiddish but understand, as Kafka said, instinctively,
the great humor, pathos and ancient, nearly lost emotions of another time
and world.

According to her friends, Dora worked at many different jobs during
the war. She would try anything. Among other things, she worked as a
dress designer and opened a restaurant. "She was quite capable and very
tough; she could fend for herself," Marianne Steiner said. "While she had
no training as a dressmaker, she had the courage to give it a go. She was
not a caterer, but she ran a successful restaurant. She had the gift of the
East European Jews, to find some foothold and to earn a living in every
situation."

Little is known about Dora's restaurant in the East End, other than that
it was a success, as Mrs. Steiner said. At one point, Dora told her "it flourished so much I had to get rid of it." Mrs. Steiner asked what she meant.
"It was too much money," Dora said. "I couldn't bear it."

Stencl introduced Dora to Mosheh Oved and his wife. Oved owned a
little jewelry shop, Cameo Corner, on Museum Street between Great Rus-
sell Street and Bloomsbury Way. Oved also wrote poetry and helped

finance Stencl's publication by advertising his shop, Cameo Corner, as "Buyers and Sellers of Interesting Old Jewels." The advertisement was illustrated with an elaborate crest and the wording "By Appointment: Dealer in Antiques to H.M. Queen Mary" and appeared on the back cover of many issues. Occasionally Stencl would publish one or two of Oved's poems.

Mosheh Oved had done very well for himself. Born in Poland in 1885, he had come to England when he was eighteen to seek his fortune. Through wheeling and dealing, with a sharp eye for diamonds and rubies and other "baubles," as Dora called them, he moved from the Jewish East End of tenements and soup kitchens to the best part of London. He married a British woman who hired Dora to do clothing alterations. Soon Dora was designing Mrs. Oved's dresses. "Her designs were extraordinary," Hanny Lichtenstern remembered, "the designs were very imaginative and she got very well paid for them."

Dora's circle of friends grew as she connected with people in London's Yiddish literature, theater, arts and culture. She knew Sala and Joseph Leftwich, a wonderful couple who were deeply involved in Jewish relief work. Joseph Leftwich was a journalist, poet and author who had grown up in the "golden age" of London's Jewish East End. The most important translator and editor of Yiddish writers and poets of his time, he published several anthologies of Yiddish prose, poetry and essays. He translated many Yiddish writers into English for the first time, making their stories available to world literature. He translated both Stencl and Max Brod, and included one of Kafka's stories in *Yisroel: The First Jewish Omnibus*, a compendium of "the best Jewish writing of the Nineteenth and Twentieth Centuries." Ironically, the book was published on May 10, 1933, the day the Nazis began burning books. But even in London, Leftwich's book was not safe from Hitler's hatred of "degenerate Jewish writers." During the bombing of London, a German firebomb destroyed the bookstore and warehouse that housed all the copies available for sale.

When Mosheh Oved turned sixty, Dora helped organize a party in his honor and published a tribute in *Loshn un Lebn*. The three-page essay began innocently enough. "When I was busily occupied considering what I should say about Mosheh Oved at his great celebration organized by Friends of Yiddish, I suddenly realized that I don't have to ponder at all. It all lies clear, and ready, a real rich man's Sabbath plate—just help yourself," Dora wrote. She hoped, with all the choices to discuss, that "nobody will be offended if I select what is most to my taste, and say a blessing over it."

What Dora liked most about Mosheh Oved was his "playfulness, his childlike holiday-mood. Mosheh Oved will never become an adult," she wrote. "Even in the thievish world of business—there is no other world of business—he stays at least with one foot, one ear, and with one eye outside. . . . In his little world, one always walks with Simchat Torah flags," Dora said. "In short," she said, after elaborating on this theme for some time, with Mosheh, "it's always the Sabbath."

Although she praised his ability to "free the weekdays and turn them into festivals," Dora was not completely impressed with his literary artistry. "At some occasions, it happens that speeches are given about the great Mosheh Oved, about the greatness of his work. I must say that I always feel somewhat embarrassed during those speeches," Dora admitted. "I don't know if what he produces is great." His poetry, Dora decided, after giving examples, "is not a uniformly beautiful pearl, selected and placed one after the other. It is a string of beads, sparkling, all colors twinkling, clashing, found and collected while playing about and strung up while sitting somewhere on the back porch of the world." Dora gleaned some greatness in everything he did and concluded, "for just this strange string of beads, Mosheh Oved, may you be blessed for ever."

LONDON, 1943–1944

The war raged on. On Dora's forty-fifth birthday, the newspapers carried headlines about the first major daylight bombing raid on Berlin. The city that had meant so much to her was in flames. Dora lived in a middle-class and largely German Jewish neighborhood in West Hampstead. Her apartment at 59 Broadhurst Gardens was on the second floor of a Victorian building, not far from the Finchley Road tube station.

Marianne stayed on at Yealand Manor. After the worst of the Blitz in 1941, many children evacuated from the public schools returned to London, but classrooms were badly overcrowded. Many school buildings had been destroyed in air raids, and there was a shortage of teachers. Although Dora missed her, she knew that Marianne was safe at Yealand and was receiving more personalized medical attention than Dora could provide for her in London. Marianne's health, as predicted by Russian doctors five years earlier, was failing. Serious problems developed with her kidneys, and she was hospitalized before being released back into the care of the doctor on call at Yealand Manor.

In February 1944, the Germans renewed their air attacks in a series of quick bombing raids on the city, dropping one or two high-explosive incendiary bombs on London's suburbs every night for the entire month. April and May were quiet, but in June a V-1 flying bomb fell on Stepney in East London. For the next eighty days and nights, thousands of flying bombs rained on London and its suburbs. One bomb could shatter windows a half mile away and damage as many as fifteen hundred houses. In the first two weeks, nearly 400,000 buildings were destroyed or damaged. By the end of nearly three months of daily attacks, tens of thousands of homes and buildings were destroyed and over a million homes were damaged. Thousands of people died. In September 1944, the first V-2 rocket fell. The death toll and damage estimates climbed throughout that fall and winter.

Dora's home on Broadhurst Gardens was hit. During the months of the air attacks, along with almost half a million other Londoners, Dora slept at night in the underground tube station and wasn't home when her building was bombed. While repairs on her flat were being made, she moved into another flat in Hampstead, on Glenloch Road, at the bottom of Haverstock Hill. Her neighbor was a young Jewish wife and mother of two, Ottilie McCrea. Dora introduced Ottie to Hanny Lichtenstern, and they all became good friends.

LONDON, 1945

When war in Europe ended on May 8, 1945, Dora's euphoria and relief were mixed with growing horror of what had taken place in the Jewish ghettos and concentration camps of Eastern Europe. Through the Red Cross, Dora sent postcards to her family and friends, letting them know she and Marianne had survived the war and hoping to hear the same from them. It was almost a year before she received an answer to the letters sent to Poland or Prague. In the meanwhile, as time passed without a word from anyone, she feared the worst.

On May 28, 1945, twenty days after the German surrender to the Allies, Dora sent a telegram to Palestine, to Max Brod, who was working with the Habima Theater Company in Tel Aviv. She had written to him in March, a four-page letter, in answer to one he had written to her. When there was no response from him, on June 11 she sent a second telegram. As with almost all of Dora's correspondence with Max Brod, the content of these telegrams and letters is still unknown.

It is likely that Dora needed money. Marianne was hospitalized at Paddington Green Children's Hospital, where the doctors said she would have to stay for quite some time. At least Dora didn't have to worry about Marianne's education. Even in the hospital, Marianne was an excellent student and kept up her studies. In July Marianne wrote to Elfrida Foulds saying she had passed the scholarship examination to secondary school.

Dora was known as a gifted Yiddish actress, although she never acted on London's legitimate Jewish theater stage. The reason, according to Stencl, was that Dora couldn't compromise her ideals. "She rehearsed in the Yiddish Theatre for a short while, but her professionalism and her deep understanding of the art were difficult to combine with the standard of our theatre here." As a critic, Dora remained intimately involved with theater, especially Yiddish theater, although it was fading, withered by the Nazi destruction of her people, language and culture.

In 1945, Dora began writing, probably at Stencl's urging, and published her first theater review in *Loshn un Leben.* Over the next four years she wrote a half dozen articles and essays in the journal. Two of Dora's translations of Stencl's articles for German publications have been saved in an archive in Frankfurt, Germany. The German articles, written in the 1930s, include an essay on "Yiddish Theatre" and a review, "Ludwig Hardt Reads Sholem Aleichem," with a German translation of a poem, "Teyve the Dairyman." The article was published with a note: "For Hardt, with thanks for your reading."

Dora's articles written in Yiddish, collected and translated for the first time, reveal her concern for the future of the Yiddish theater and her deep desire to keep Jewish culture alive. Dora's expectations were very high. She had come of age when the three founders of modern Yiddish literature, Mendele Mocher Sforim, Sholem Aleichem and I. L. Peretz, were still writing their classics. She grew to womanhood amid the full flowering of Yiddish literature. She had witnessed the finest moments ever produced in the Yiddish theater, the majestic performances of the great artists of the Moscow Habima, now based in Palestine, and the Vilna Troupe, now in America.

What Dora described as the "impoverished" Jewish theater of London was one aspect of the Holocaust. More than one-third of the Yiddish-speaking population had disappeared, taking with them the future and promise of the language. This realization fueled Dora's desire to keep her culture alive, to prevent it from being murdered, too.

From the moment she saw "the first signs in the street" (as she called the posters advertising the I. L. Peretz story "The Three Gifts" on the Yiddish stage in London), Dora "waited for weeks with hope and impatience for the production. It was evident that all concerned devoted themselves to the work with the seriousness which Peretz as well as the stage demand. Those who had watched for years the hopeless state of such an important institution as the Yiddish theatre, started to hope again."

Dora's review of the play, after first welcoming its production wholeheartedly, asked, "Does this first attempt actually deliver—to some extent—those expectations?" Yes and no, Dora concluded. "From the mixture of feelings and impressions on the first night, there developed finally, slowly, a picture—similar to the soul on Judgment Day. The scales stayed in the middle, between good and bad." On the positive side, she said, there were "splendid single acting moments [singling out the work of Shlomoh Cohen] but no uniformity, no ensemble. What was missing was a firm grip on the idea," she said. The best part of the production was the casting—with one notable exception—and the excellent actors, whom she praised individually while pointing out the production's deficiencies at the same time. "Shlomoh Cohen," Dora reported, "possesses that rare charisma, that even the dreariest, amateurish set comes to life with an atmosphere to match when he steps on to the stage." Another actress fulfilled Dora's longing to hear her mother tongue used beautifully. Of actress Fela Feld's performance, Dora said that "her splendid, beautiful Yiddish refreshes like an oasis on a desert journey."

"It was therefore a pity," Dora added, "that the actual main part, the Soul, turned out not to be such a successful match." The actor, Dora granted, "has an excellent voice, he had moving moments, and his great effort to learn such a part in Yiddish—which is evidently not his language—is certainly to be admired. But one must unfortunately say that he did not represent a Jewish soul."

A great number of the actors, Dora glumly noted, and all of the younger ones, didn't speak Yiddish. Although Dora offered these actors her "full-hearted praise" for the great effort required in memorizing enough Yiddish to speak their parts, she asked, "Is this enough to wake up the Yiddish theatre? Why have we alone such a contemptuous attitude to ourselves, to our language, to our culture? How can we expect, with such an attitude, to awaken respect in others? One may think what one will of the Whitechapel Jews regarding their demands in Art," Dora concluded, "but concerning Yiddish, there is no difference of opinion: on a Jewish stage in Whitechapel, one must talk a Yiddish Yiddish."

In the end, Dora decided, it was a good beginning. "There remains the principle—the will to create a good Yiddish theatre," she pointed out, carefully drawing "a sharp dividing line between what the new Yiddish theatre strives for and that which it has already achieved."

After this first review, Dora's style became more direct in her criticism, although she never lost her sense of humor, nor was she ever cruel to an actor. Even in the worse cases, she looked for the silver lining in each actor's performance. When she discovered something she liked, her appreciation knew no limits. When the famous Yiddish actress Dina Halpern came from America to perform a series of Yiddish plays in London in the summer of 1946, Dora was ecstatic to "see real Yiddish dramatic art of great distinction."

"After so many years of being fed second to tenth-rate dramatic art— often below any rate altogether—one had gotten used to it," Dora wrote. "One had begun to doubt one's memories of a better theatre in years long past, since they came from the decayed manure heap of an over-civilized Europe on which the last scum, the Nazi monster, had unloaded itself." After lamenting in further detail the sad state of the London Yiddish theater, Dora concluded, "The most important effect that Dina Halpern achieved with her appearance was that it made a hole in the rubbish. The smallest worm felt a fresh little wind and a ray of light, showing that there are still riches in the world. How deeply—literally like a bomb shell— Dina Halpern impressed was shown when she performed for weeks, night after night, before a fully packed house, received with such admiration, fascination and love as only hearts long starved of beauty and truth can feel in their overflowing gratitude."

Dora bestowed her highest praise on an unlikely production: a Yiddish performance of Shakespeare's *The Merchant of Venice,* long controversial for its portrayal of Shylock, a bloodthirsty Jew who is the cruel, greedy villain of the play. "I have seen Shylock performed eight or ten times," Dora said. "The greatest of them, Rudolf Schildkraut, earnestly endeavored to create a great tragic figure. But after each one of those performances, I came away battered and violated, robbed and dishonored, unable to comprehend what had driven a mind like Shakespeare's to give us such a vicious kick in the ribs. I envied the non-Jews who had no difficulty in giving themselves wholly to the pleasure and enjoyment that emanates with such sensitivity from every verse of the play. They could enjoy the beauty with which the comedy rings. But as Jews, we feel that the splendid verses such as 'On such a night as this,' and others, similarly enchanting, are given to us mixed with venom. I could not forget for a single moment that the canvas on which this whole sparkling magic is woven, is a knife wound, filth and insult for the whole Jewish people. The formula: *L'art pour l'art*—art for art's sake—has never suited the Jewish soul, however 'European' or assimilated we may have been. The root that nourishes the Jewish people's soul is ethics, not aesthetics."

The idea that a work could achieve high artistic merit without regard to whether or not it was moral was "a contradiction," Dora argued. "If a work offends in its essence against simple, natural justice, it is perforce inartistic. Our first level—and nothing is higher—is: 'Be a man to a man.' Even our rebellious, jealous God stepped aside at this command and contented himself with second place. However artistically outstanding all the Shylock performances may have been, we must, as Jews, reject the play categorically, because both the author and his interpreters have desecrated art by using it to glorify blind hatred, robbery and violation."

But after Dora saw the Yiddish translation of the play and a great Yiddish actor playing the title role, she began her review with a biblical quotation in Hebrew: "Our hope is not yet lost!" Astonished by the production, Dora "danced with joy, convinced that one had always known that there are good, even very good, and perhaps even outstanding talents in the New Yiddish Theatre. But this—Shakespeare!!! And "the Merchant of Venice"! And in a new translation by Meisels. The idea alone, and the courage to undertake it, deserves admiration. How Shakespearean can one speak and behave in Yiddish? Friend Meisels, there are no words to express the respect which your work deserves."

Meyer Tselniker's performance of Shylock was "the most moving, shocking Shylock" she had ever seen. "I found myself seriously thinking about the fairness of my negative attitude to the drama, and became a little unsure," she admitted. "But only a tiny bit. It really needs a little more to shake such a self-imposed position. Meanwhile, one thing, however, is clear. Every other part in the play can be acted by anyone, even a corpse— but Shylock must be portrayed by a Jew from back-home, if the role is to be redeemed."

In this Yiddish production directed by Robert Atkins, "the hatred was at the right place, without anger at Shakespeare. Meyer Tselniker has lifted the play from the palm of the marksman where it is to be found to the present day on all stages of the world, and led it out to the path of conciliation. It is the most masterly creation that I have ever seen from Tselniker (and he has on his list quite a number of masterworks.) It is one of the rare, convincing triumphs by an actor in this role."

The direction also earned Dora's high regard. Not everything pleased her, though, especially the actors who portrayed the lovers. The actress was, Dora noted, "as lovely as gold and full of charm, and proves to be talented as well, but unfortunately she murdered the Hebrew reading to such an extent that one didn't know where in the world one was. If they'd only thought of giving her a partner with good Yiddish. I mean: Arnold Kalline as Lorenzo? One cannot judge. They suffered, we suffered."

After acknowledging the work of the remaining actors and congratulating the ensemble as a the whole, Dora turned her focus to the younger actors, whom she saw slipping away, lured to more professional and lucrative opportunities on other stages. "A strange and very disturbing phenomenon has shown itself for some time: A kind of extinction—heaven help us—of young talents. As soon as a young acting talent is discovered—and one barely has a chance to taste it—and already we've lost the child. Be very careful, London Jewish Theatre directors," Dora warned, "that a ship—not with sour milk, but actually with cream—will sail away from you. Pinje Goldstein, our most talented, original comedic character actor, may go to America. This has happened with the very gifted Tamara Solomov, now with the Habima in Palestine. So it has been with Fela Feld—and what about our Shlomoh Cohen? How many Shlomoh Cohens does the Jewish stage have?"

SOMETHING INDESTRUCTIBLE WITHIN

Man cannot live without a lasting trust in some-
thing indestructible within himself.
—Franz Kafka, in *Franz Kafka: A Biography*

LONDON, JANUARY 1947

For years after Yealand Manor closed, Elfrida Foulds continued to send the annual newsletter to former students and staff. In 1947 she wrote that "Marianne Lask is doing well at South Hampstead High School. She has had a busy time at home, as her mother has not been at all well. Dora Lask has been able to locate two of her brothers in Germany and a half sister: it must be a great joy to her to know that they are safe after all these tragic years."

Joy and grief walked hand in hand. The news of one life saved brought unbearable news of the tortured deaths of countless others. Dora was overjoyed to learn through the Red Cross that her siblings David, Avner and Sara were alive and living in displaced persons (DP) camps near Dachau, outside Munich. Of Dora's eleven brothers and sisters, only these three had survived. Dora's older brother David had lost everything. His wife, Gittel, and his three children were dead, murdered. At the age of fifty, David Diamant had nothing left, not even his belief in God. "The Nazis took that away," he told a friend. Dora's younger half brother Avner was very ill, confined to a hospital with tuberculosis. Unlike David, Dora's youngest sister, Sara, now twenty-four years old, had survived the ordeal by holding fast to her faith.

When the war ended on VE Day, after all of the concentration and labor camps had been liberated, between 7 and 9 million people were "displaced." One of the first concerns of the postwar era was repatriation—

getting all persons back to their country of origin. The massive operation to repatriate "displaced persons" was under the control of Allied military authorities, but care of the displaced persons was entrusted to the United Nations Relief and Rehabilitation Administration (UNRRA). By the beginning of 1946, millions had been successfully repatriated, mostly those from the western European countries.

It was a different story for the Jews of Eastern Europe. Many, like Sara, who tried to go home again only found more horrors. When the Russians liberated Gerlitz, the last of the six forced labor camps she had endured, Sara's first thought was to go home to Bedzin to find her family. She was terrified of the Russian soldiers, who, she had heard, "often raped the girls." So she asked a fellow survivor, a man she knew from home, to take her with him back to Poland. Abraham Baumer, whose sister had married Sara's older brother Nathan, was on his way to Sosnowiec to find his wife and three daughters. There was no public transportation available, so they hitchhiked with Russian troops. At one point, they were separated and Sara rode in another vehicle where a Russian soldier attacked her. "I've liberated you, now you have to give me a present," he demanded. She screamed and fought him off. He beat her but didn't touch her again. Instead he opened her hand luggage, looking for an easier present, and discovered a copy of *Mein Kampf*. The Russian soldier accused her of being a Nazi spy. Sara tried to explain that she had come across a copy of the book after liberation and wanted to read it out of curiosity, "to see what was in it." The soldier didn't believe her and turned her over to Russian officers when they arrived in Katowice. One of her interrogating officers was Jewish, although he didn't say so. After Sara told him about the past six years in the camps, she was released. Abraham Baumer was waiting for her. When they reached Bedzin, Sara went straight to her house and knocked on the door. Strangers answered. Poles now lived there, and they refused to let her in.

When her own front door was slammed in her face, Sara collapsed. Throughout the years of hell, she stayed alive by thinking of her loving family and imagining their reunion. She kept with her, hidden of course, a small memory book with family photos of her sisters and their children: Nacha with Friedale and Dora with Marianne. "Those photos made it possible for me to believe that maybe one day, I will somehow meet my family again," Sara said.

Abraham Baumer took her to the community building in Bedzin, where the names of survivors were posted. She found only her own name from her family. Until she learned that David and Avner had survived, she thought she was the only one left. Her beloved mother, Gitle, murdered. Gone too were Nacha and her baby, Friedale, born during the war. Her brothers Nathan, Pinches, Matis, Arie, Avraham, as well as their families, were all dead. David's wife, Gitle, who had moved into the family home with her children, Helusha, Tuvia and Frania—all lost.

There was nothing left in Bedzin for Sara. When Abraham Baumer went on to his neighboring town, Sosnowiec, Sara went with him. No one from his family was listed among the survivors. His wife and three children were missing and presumed dead. Baumer, too, found his home occupied by Poles who refused to let him in. With no place else to go, they went to another town in Poland, where they knew people and tried to start over, but it was impossible. Although the Nazis were gone, anti-Semitic hatred among the Poles was alive and festering, and the Jews who returned to their homes were attacked, beaten and killed. On July 4, 1946, in Kielce, a town north of Krakow, the Polish residents attacked returning Jews, maiming and killing more than one hundred concentration camp survivors.

Sara and Abraham had no choice but to go back to Germany, where they could find shelter, food and relative safety in the DP camps. Thousands of East European Jews were forced to flee in the face of continuing widespread attacks, and the number of displaced persons doubled in 1946. By the end of that winter, a quarter of a million displaced Jews were living in DP camps in Europe.

"Repatriation of Jews, of course, must be considered as out of the question." This conclusion was reached by UNRRA, Central Headquarters for Germany, and printed in the April 1946 report from Displaced Persons Operations. It created a new question: Where would all these Jews go?

When Sara and Abraham arrived at the DP camp at Dachau, the situation was terrible, not much better than life under the Germans. In 1945 President Truman sent a mission led by Earl Harrison, dean of the Law School of the University of Pennsylvania, "to inquire into the conditions of the Jews in the DP camps in the American zone in Germany." Harrison was shocked by what he found: "As things stand now, we appear to be treating the Jews as the Nazis treated them, except that we do not execute them." He reported that the vast majority of Jewish DPs "overwhelmingly wanted to go to Palestine" and strongly recommended that the British be asked to "issue, without delay, one hundred thousand entry permits, without waiting for an overall settlement of the Palestine question."

The "Palestine question" was an explosive one. The British had controlled the region since the end of World War I. In the thirty years since the Balfour Declaration had promised to secure the establishment of a national home for the Jewish People, a miracle had taken place in the desert. Through the back-breaking labor of two generations of Zionist pioneers, the deserts and swamp lands had been reclaimed, and successful communal farms and cities were growing up out of a wilderness. It was exactly as Theodore Herzl had imagined it fifty years earlier. The new city of Tel Aviv glistened, a white jewel on the Mediterranean Sea, the first Jewish city in the modern world. The British hoped that the Arabs would come to appreciate the new development, which meant increased wages and a higher standard of living for them. It didn't happen. The problem was, as one historian pointed out, "the Arabs of Palestine felt that any influx of Jews at all produced, in itself, an inadmissible effect on their civil and religious rights."

The vast majority of displaced Jews wanted to go to Palestine. But Jewish immigration to Palestine had been strictly limited by white papers issued by the British government in 1922 and 1939. The British were responding to pressure from the Arab countries, whose oil and loyalty the British needed, especially with the threat of war. Egypt, Saudi Arabia, Syria, Iran and Iraq, which opened its first oil pipeline in 1934, angrily protested any proposal to partition Palestine into two separate states and resented a large Jewish presence in their midst. To mollify the neighboring Arabs, the area of Palestine east of the Jordan River originally designated as part of the Jewish national home was separated from Mandatory Palestine and renamed "Transjordan." It gained full independence, as the Hashemite Kingdom of Jordan, in 1946.

The Jews felt betrayed by the British. In addition to the legal rights they had been granted to build their country, they also believed they had a historic right to the land. After centuries in exile, their daily and most holy prayers referred to their return to Jerusalem. Just when it was crucial for the European Jews to have someplace to go, the British White Paper of 1939 proposed limiting immigration to only 75,000 Jews over a five-year period and then cutting it off entirely. When the white paper was issued, David Ben-Gurion, who as a young man had worked in the fields of Carmel, who had helped form the Jewish Legion to fight on the side of the British against the Turks during World War I, declared, "We shall fight Hitler as though there were no White Paper, and we shall fight against the White Paper as though there were no Hitler."

After World War II, Jews would no longer stand aside and allow their rights and lives to be taken from them. They would no longer tolerate abuse and life in exile. The centuries-old Jewish practice of dealing with racial hatred with "simple, discreet and modest" behavior had led to the annihilation of 6 million. Enough was enough. When the war ended, the Jews began to fight back.

By 1947 Palestine was a battlefield of terrorist attacks between Arabs and Jews; Jews also fought the British. For a decade, the British government had done little to stop Arab attacks on Jews. In response, Jews formed their own army, the illegal Haganah, to protect Jewish lives on Jewish land. Since the beginning of the Zionist movement in Palestine, Jews had been buying land from Arab landowners to develop their collective communities and settlements. The white paper of 1939 severely limited further Jewish land acquisition because the British were concerned about the problem of a "landless Arab population." Unless Jewish immigration was halted, the British warned, "a fatal enmity between the two peoples will be perpetuated, and the situation in Palestine may become a permanent source of friction amongst all peoples in the Near and Middle East."

Life improved in Germany's DP camps after the Harrison Commission, which led the first U.S. mission in 1945, and other independent reports on the DP camps brought reforms. Jews were allowed to move to their own camps, set up in requisitioned apartment buildings, and form their own governing system. International Jewish aid organizations sent emissaries to the camps to assist with mental, physical and occupational rehabilitation. The human urge to live, to reproduce life, to fill the void of what had been lost was bearing fruit—and lots of babies. Thousands of marriages took place in the DP camps, and thousands of Jewish babies were born.

In 1946 Sara Dimant married Abraham Baumer. By the beginning of 1947 Sara was pregnant, and the couple relocated to a DP camp in Hesse, near Frankfurt. By the time Sara saw David again, he had married Branka Besserglick, a Polish survivor of the camps at Dachau and Bergen-Belsen. Branka's husband had been killed by the Gestapo and her twelve-year-old daughter murdered in the gas chambers. Zelig Besserglick, Branka's youngest brother, a survivor of seven concentration camps, was the only family member to attend the wedding. On July 4, 1947, Branka presented David with a son, Zvi, Dora's only living nephew.

That September, Dora took out an ad in the personal column of *Loshen un Leben* proudly announcing the birth of her niece, Gitle Tova Baumer, with the headline, *Mazal Tov!*: "A hearty Mazal Tov to my only sister, the survivor Sarah'le, and my brother-in-law Abraham Baumer on the birth of their daughter Gitale in Hesse, Germany. May this new life born help you rekindle your extinguished happiness, and may it grant you the power to believe in a brighter future. Your loyal and loving sister, Dora Dymant."

As Elfrida Foulds reported, Dora had been ill for months. Like Marianne, she had developed kidney problems. Her face and legs were very swollen and she required long periods of bed rest. She managed to earn some money working from home, sewing for a firm that produced ladies dresses and taking in boarders. From her bed, she read the newspapers and followed developments in Palestine. Amid growing international pressure to partition Palestine into two separate states, the British continued to hold a tight rein on the immigration quotas. Under the British, fewer than 20,000 Jews were allowed to enter Palestine each year. At that rate, it would take a decade or more before everyone who wanted to go could be admitted.

America had loosened its quotas, allowing 100,000 Jews (with priority going to orphans) to immigrate to the United States over a five-year period. But thousands more waited in the camps, determined to go to Palestine or die trying. The waiting lists were long, and many left illegally, desperate to begin new lives. Sara and Abraham remained on the waiting list for legal immigration to Palestine for two years before they were allowed to go.

As Dora's health improved, Marianne's declined. Every Saturday, she was required to go by train to the hospital in Luton for injections. "Dora was very worried about her," said Ottilie McCrea, Dora's upstairs neighbor from Glenloch Road who stayed in touch with Dora and Marianne. When Dora was sick, Ottilie, who now had two small girls of her own, took Marianne under her wing and helped look after both mother and daughter. Ottie remembers seeing Marianne off at the station for her solitary train trips to the hospital at Luton. Off she went, resolutely, with a book or a bundle of socks to darn that Dora had given her to keep her occupied.

With the reissue of Kafka's books in Germany after the war, arguments brewed among literary critics, each of whom proclaimed a different Kafka, "a strange and disconcerting genius," "a religious humorist," and "an existentialist." Ten years after its first publication in 1937, Max Brod published a second edition of his biography of Kafka, with a new chapter to address the sometimes acrimonious academic debate over Kafka's works: "One can hardly survey the gigantic essay literature that is concerned with Kafka," Brod observed. "This literature contains, alongside isolated moments which are correct, very many absurdities and contradictions." Brod pointed out that "only the externals of Kafka's methods have been imitated or analyzed, but not his essential endeavor." Brod suggested that Kafka's approach to writing was "beyond the reach of some who write so much about him and his art." He admitted not even his own biography could claim to have effectively explained Kafka's personal and literary aims, which he said were directed towards an "inner perfection, toward a stainless life." According to Brod, Kafka "was wholly occupied with striving for the highest ethical pinnacle a man can attain."

One of those newly fascinated by Kafka was Josef Paul Hodin, a forty-four-year-old student of expressionism who had learned about Kafka through the reminiscences of a painter living in London. The painter, who had known Kafka in elementary school in Prague, was one of those who contributed to the caricature-like picture of Kafka that was developing in the public psyche, what Brod called "the inevitable distortion of his image." After reading his work, this painter, who had known Kafka only slightly, decided that Kafka suffered from "a sexual development that is by no means normal" and that "he hated reality." The painter's memories of Kafka as a schoolboy were fading, but that did not lessen his confidence in his authoritative take on Kafka's psychological makeup: "Concerning the characteristics of Kafka's work, I should like to say that it shows all the signs of a deformed imagination," he said in an interview he gave Hodin about Kafka. While he acknowledged that Kafka was "honest and did not care about worldly success," the painter asserted that he was no genius: "Kafka's mind was basically corrosive and analytic. Why is analysis as an end in itself not a mark of genius?" he asked himself and then answered, "because it has no real content. It has no real meaning." Another Kafka expert had been born, another monster created, a monster that assumed, more and more, the features of Franz Kafka.

Despite his efforts and best intentions to make Kafka's work accessible to the world, Max Brod was criticized by the new Kafka experts and scholars. One suggested that Brod was too close to "the never-ending debate" about Kafka's work. He pointed out that Brod had been one of "a small group of initiates, those who had known him in the flesh. To a greater or lesser degree they shared his background and the experiences which had inspired him to tell his tales. They formed a sect, an intellectual conspiracy, and an elite."

In the midst of this brewing controversy—or *tsimmes,* as she might have said—Dora claimed her rightful throne as the reigning queen of

Kafka's elite inner circle. Not since the disastrous Ehm Welk affair had she discussed Kafka with any of the dozens of journalists, writers or "experts" who wanted insight into Kafka's unique vision. When Hodin contacted her in late 1947, Dora decided that the misconceptions surrounding Kafka had grown too grotesque, that it was time to end her long public silence.

Hodin's article "Memories of Franz Kafka" was published in English translation in the British journal *Horizon* in January 1948. Although Dora's command of English was excellent, she insisted that the interview be conducted in German, the language in which Kafka had written and the only language Dora felt was adequate to discuss him. Hodin's article appeared in the original German in *Der Monat* in June 1949, part of a tribute to Franz Kafka on the twenty-fifth anniversary of his death.

When Hodin rang the doorbell at 59 Broadhurst Gardens, Dora welcomed him and led him up the narrow stairs. In the small, sparsely furnished living room, he waited as Dora went into the kitchen to fix refreshments for them. "From the mantelpiece over the open fireplace," Hodin wrote in his notebook, "Kafka's eyes looked out searchingly into the darkening room from the last photograph that he had had taken in Berlin."

Before Dora began to talk, she asked Hodin to preface her interview with a disclaimer, a request he honored: "I have spent many hours with Mrs. Dora Dymant, talking about Kafka and those last months of his life. I am indebted to her for all that she told me so simply, warmly and candidly. Before I begin to quote it, it must first be said, as she herself emphasized: 'I am not objective, and I cannot be. It is more than twenty years since Kafka died. But in the end, one can only measure the passage of time against the weight of one's own experiences. Even today it is often difficult for me to talk about Kafka. Therefore, it is not the facts which are decisive, it is rather a pure matter of atmosphere. What I am about to tell has an inner truth, and subjectivity is a part of that.'"

Dora began the story of her life with Kafka with the story of their first meeting, in which certain facts, such as her true age, gave way to the atmosphere that Dora found so decisive: the feelings, the colors, the impressions it created. She built on the portrait that Max Brod had first painted of her, a decade earlier. The floodgates within her opened, the memories came rushing back, never far from the surface, as if it were only yesterday:

> I met Kafka for the first time on the Baltic, in the summer of 1923. I was very young, nineteen, and was working as a volunteer in the holiday camp of a Berlin youth hostel. One day on the beach I saw a family playing—

parents and two children. I was particularly struck with the man. I could not shake off the impression he made on me. I even followed them into the town, and later met them again. One day it was announced in the hostel that Dr. Franz Kafka was coming to supper. At that time I was in charge of the kitchen. When I looked up from my work—the room had grown dark, someone was standing outside the window—I recognized the man from the beach. Then he came in—I didn't know then that it was Kafka, and the woman with whom he had been on the beach was his sister. He said in a soft voice: "Such tender hands, and such bloody work for them to do!"

The essential characteristic of his face were the very open, often wide-open eyes, whether he was talking or listening. They were not staring in horror, as it had been said of him; it was more an expression of astonishment. . . . When he spoke, they lit up; there was a humor in them; but it was not so much irony as mischievousness—as if he knew something that other people didn't know . . . Kafka was always cheerful. He liked to play; he was the born playmate, always ready for some mischief.

It was the time of the inflation. Kafka suffered badly under the conditions . . . Whatever might happen around him, he had no right to shut himself off from it . . . The trip to town was always a kind of Golgotha for him. He could stand in queues for hours, not only with the intention of buying something, because blood was flowing, and so his must flow, too. In this way he experienced communion with an unhappy people in an unhappy time . . . I can see it clearly as the theme of *The Trial,* where he condemns K. because he tried to shape his life differently from a life of crucifixion. But there is no life except in crucifixion, and nobody is acquitted by the highest court of all.

Why did Kafka make such an impression on me? I came from the East, a dark creature full of dreams and premonitions, who might have sprung from a book by Dostoyevski. I had heard so much of the West— its knowledge, clarity, style of living—I came to Germany with a receptive soul, and it gave me much. But over and over again I had the feeling that the people needed something that I could give them. After the catastrophe of the war everyone expected salvation through the intermediary of the East. But I had run away from the East because I believed the light was in the West. Later I became less ambitious in my dreams: Europe was not what I had expected it to be, its people had no rest in their innermost being. They lacked something. In the East one knew what man was; perhaps one could not move so freely in society and could not express oneself so easily, but one did know the consciousness of the unity of man and creation. When I saw Kafka for the first time, his image corresponded to my idea of man. But even Kafka turned to me attentively, as though expecting something from me.

Kafka had to write; he had to, it was his life-breath . . . I don't think depressions were a dominant characteristic of his, except before he began to write . . . He would walk around, heavy and uneasy, before he began to write. Then he spoke little, ate without appetite, took no interest in things, and was very sad. He wanted to be alone . . . At other times he showed a great intensity towards even the most ordinary things. But on such days that vanished completely . . . Later on, he liked me to stay in the room while he was writing.

Once he started to write after supper. He wrote for a very long time, and I fell asleep on the sofa. The electric light was on. All at once he was sitting at my side: I woke up and looked at him. A palpable change was visible in his face. The traces of the spiritual tension were so obvious that they had changed the face utterly. He often read to me what he had written. He never analyzed, he never explained . . . . Time and again he said, "Well, I wonder if I've escaped the ghosts?" . . .

He wanted to burn everything that he had written in order to free his soul from these "ghosts" . . . He was as though possessed by this idea; it was a kind of sullen obstinacy . . . I respected his wish, and when he lay ill, I burnt things of his before his eyes. What he really wanted to write was to come afterwards, only after he had gained his "liberty" . . . I have been reproached for burning some of the things that Kafka wrote. I was so young then, and young people live in the present and perhaps in the future, too.

To Kafka, literature was something sacred, absolute, incorruptible, something great and pure . . . Kafka felt unsure of most things in life and expressed himself very cautiously. But when it was a matter of literature, he was unapproachable and knew no compromise. There he was concerned with the whole. Everything was interwoven with cosmic cause and effect, even the most everyday things. One finds this awareness in the East, too, a longing for the wholeness of life. If one is to live, there are spiritual matters which have to be fulfilled unconditionally. Kafka felt that. The West has forgotten it. That's why all the things could happen that we have experienced. Therein, so I believe, lies one of the reasons for the interest in Kafka: the consciousness that God has abandoned us.

Hodin didn't have to ask any questions. Once Dora started talking about Kafka, she was unstoppable. The hours passed quickly. As the light faded from the room, Hodin scribbled notes about Kafka's difficult relationship with his father ("he hated his father and felt guilty because of it! I assume that he often murdered him in his dreams"), his feelings about Prague, ("he really didn't hate Prague; he spoke of it as a European speaks of Europe") and the stories and details of his life. Underneath the minutiae of the things he loved—the shopping, walks, his pocket watch and the paraffin lamp she had assembled for him ("he loved its soft, living light and always wanted to fill it up himself; he would play about with the wick and continually found new virtues in it)—and those he didn't ("he didn't take a kindly view to the telephone. He was always distressed when it rang. I had to answer it")—was the awareness of the sublime:

> He experienced life as a labyrinth; he could not see the solution. He never got further than despair . . . In Berlin, he believed for a time in the possibility of saving his life, in a personal solution for the inner and outer confusion. He wanted to feel like an average human being, with only a few wishes and needs . . . In Berlin, Kafka believed that he had liberated himself from the tyranny of his past. But the earlier problems were too tightly bound up with his life. As soon as one touched even a single string of it, all the others vibrated, too. His inner life was of unfathomable depth and unbearable.

Dora described how Kafka would read to her for hours, from Grimms' and Andersen's fairy tales, E.T.A. Hoffman's *Kater Murr*, Goethe's *Herman and Dorothea*, Kleist's *The Marquis of O—*, and Hebel's *Schatzkästlein:*

> There was the story of the miner's sweetheart who accompanied her lover to the pit and never saw him alive again. They brought the bodies out into the daylight, but her lover was not among them. Her life passed away; she grew grey and old. Then one day his body was found in a shaft, quite unharmed, preserved by the gases. She came and embraced her lover; she had waited for him all these years and now it was a wedding and funeral in one.

She talked about his visitors, Willy Haas, Rudolf Kayser and Franz Werfel, who was now making a name for himself in Hollywood. She described the incident in which she saw Werfel leave their apartment in tears. "Anyone who put himself into Kafka's hands either had the most encouraging experience or despaired. There was nothing in between." But, she pointed out, "Kafka never made other people feel uneasy. He attracted everybody, and whoever came to him did so with a kind of solemnity. They walked as though on tie-toe or on soft carpets."

For the first time in public, Dora mentioned the thirty-five letters Kafka wrote her and revealed their tragic loss: "They were taken from me by the Gestapo, together with his diaries, and in spite of all attempts no one has succeeded in finding them again." Dora recounted their moves from hospital to sanatoriums, and his last stay in Kierling, where "he lived in a wonderful, permanently sunny room with a balcony!" Finally, she spoke of Kafka's dying and death. "The uncanny thing about Kafka's mortal illness was its outbreak. I felt that he had brought it about by downright force. It was like a deliverance for him; the decision was taken out of his hands. Kafka positively welcomed the illness, even though in the last moments of his life he once more wished to live."

Dora description of Kafka's death was brief. She did not—could not, even now—dwell on it. She ended her interview with a final statement:

Years later I often read Kafka's books, always with the memory how he read aloud from them himself . . . I felt then that the German language was a hindrance to me. German is too modern a language, too much of the present day. Kafka's whole world longs for an older language. It was an ancient consciousness in him, ancient things and ancient fear. His brain knew finer nuances than the modern brain is capable of grasping. He is no more the expression of an age than he is the representative of the fate of a people. Nor is it everyday life that his realism represents; it is an absolute, compressed logic, in which one can live for short moments only.

LONDON, SPRING 1948

Marianne Steiner, Kafka's niece, had met Dora only once, at the funeral of her uncle, when she was eleven. Now she was thirty-four and married with a ten-year-old-son. She and her husband had survived the Nazi occupation by escaping from Prague to England when her son, Michael, was less than a year old. She was tall and slender, her hair dark and full, still bearing traces of the "ravishing beauty" she had been in prewar Prague, when George Steiner first courted her. In many ways she resembled her uncle. Those who knew her said "she shared his honesty, his clarity, his passion for truth. She was noted for her wit, her courage and her tolerance. Her personal warmth was tinged with the wry sobriety that enabled her to thrive even in exile."

Marianne and George Steiner returned to Prague in the autumn of 1945, hoping to rebuild their lives, "soon realizing that it was a naïve and wrong decision." For three years, until they fled the Communist putsch in February 1948, they made the best of it, becoming "great friends" with the poet Edwin Muir and Willa Muir, Kafka's first English translators. When Edwin Muir was posted to Prague as director of the British Council, designed to promote British culture with a library, lectures and performances, "it occurred to him that there might be someone of the Kafka family still alive."

With the exception of Kafka's nieces, everyone was dead. Kafka's parents, Herrmann and Julie, died in 1931 and 1934, respectively, and shared a grave with their son. Kafka's three sisters were murdered by the Germans. Valli and her husband, Josef Pollack, and Elli and Karl Hermann were arrested in October 1941 and deported to the Lodz ghetto in Poland. They survived that miserable existence until the late summer of 1944, when they were "liquidated" along with the entire ghetto. Of Elli's children, Gerti "simply vanished" and years passed before her fate was known. Kafka's nephew Felix died in a concentration camp in France.

Ottla's children, Vera and Helene, survived because their father was not Jewish and because Ottla had convinced him to divorce her in order to save their daughters. When the Germans occupied Prague, Ottla voluntarily registered as a Jew. In doing so, Ottla "demonstrated once again the courage, selflessness, and stubborn idealism that Kafka had so admired in her. . . . Because she was the wife of an Aryan, she was exempt from the deportation law, but for her this was itself proof of how absurd the law was. She was still a Jew, and if Jews were suffering, she would not avoid sharing their fate on a technicality. Beyond that, she felt that to hide behind her marriage was to corrupt it." Ottla was arrested by the Germans in August 1942 and sent to Theresienstadt, a concentration camp outside of Prague, "where she spent the next year doing her best to help and console the other prisoners."

In the fall of 1943, Ottla volunteered to escort a group of Polish Jewish orphans from the Bialystok ghetto. According to camp authorities, they were being sent to Denmark or Sweden, but the transport went directly to Auschwitz. In the records of the museum of the death camp at Auschwitz, Ottla's name, "Ottilie David," appears sixth on a transport list of fifty-three volunteers who accompanied 1,260 children leaving Theresienstadt on October 5 and arriving at Auschwitz two days later, on October 7. The designation "special transport" meant that the same day they arrived, the entire trainload of passengers was directed to the gas chambers.

On a rainy October afternoon in 1990, Marianne Steiner talked for the first time at length about her relationship with Dora, which had a great impact on her life. Their coincidental meeting, she said, was "the strangest thing that ever happened to me." Once in Prague, in a conversation with the Muirs, she mentioned that she had known "Kafka's last friend, Dora Diamant, who I had met only once, when, after his death, she came for a short visit to Prague. I told Mr. Muir that I had no idea what happened to her after that. He was astonished: 'So you do not know that she lives in England?' He told me that Dora had gotten in touch with him and they had met several times. She even visited him once with her little daughter, Marianne. He said that Dora lived under very strained financial circumstances."

After returning to London in 1948, Mrs. Steiner went to see Kafka's English publisher, Secker and Warburg. "I knew that there were royalties accumulating abroad for the heirs," she explained. "I knew that Dora was living somewhere in England, and had very little money. I was determined to find her and offer her financial help." After meeting with the firm's director, Roger Senhouse, and discussing the royalties with him, she asked "by any chance whether he knew Dora." He said he did and rummaged through a "chaotic" pile of papers on his desk looking for her address. Finally he gave up and promised to find it and mail it to Mrs. Steiner at the boardinghouse where she and her family were living temporarily.

"A few days after my discussion with Mr. Senhouse, a real estate agent who was to find a flat for us rang up and said that he had found a convenient flat. I agreed to come right away with a friend. At that very moment, the postman brought me a letter from Mr. Senhouse with Dora's address. Reading the address, I saw that she lived only a stone's throw from the agent we were going to meet. Being in a hurry to keep my appointment with him, I decided to ring up Dora after my return. I went with my friend to the agent's office and talked to the man who had rung us up some thirty minutes before, when suddenly a woman entered, and began to talk to another employee at the opposite end of the room. I couldn't really see her, I only heard her voice. She had a scarf on her head. She was small, and rather plump. Yet somehow I knew from that very moment that it was Dora.

"I turned to my friend and told her that this woman was Dora. She laughed at me: 'You just saw that address and now every woman you meet you think is Dora.' I, too, could hardly believe it. So I listened to what the woman was saying and I overhead her say that she wanted to let a room in her flat. The employee noticed that I was listening in and frowned at my indiscretion. But I had to know if the woman in the scarf would give the address that I had in my pocket. And she did. It was Dora! In this huge town, Dora had come to the agent's office at the same minute as I. And I recognized her even though I had met her only once in 1924 when I was eleven.

"Since that day I have believed, and it's a very consoling thought, that there are more things between heaven and earth than we realize. I believe that I was meant to be in that office at precisely that moment. In my life there are many coincidences. I like them, and they like me. But this meeting with Dora was quite extraordinary. It still gives me a shiver up my back each time I think of it, standing in the middle of the office with quite a few people there, everyone noticing that something strange was going on.

"I went up to her and said, 'You are Dora.' She nodded, and I said, 'I am Marianna.' This didn't mean anything to her, so I added, 'Valli's daughter.' She looked at me without understanding. I said, 'Franz's sister Valli's daughter.'

"Then she understood. She trembled, tears ran down her face, and we stood there in the middle of that room, amazed. We couldn't believe that it was not a dream."

21

THE PROMISED LAND

Splendor forever lies in wait about each one of us in all its fullness, but veiled from view, deep down, invisible, far off. It is there, though, not hostile, not reluctant, not deaf. If you summon it by the right word, by its right name, it will come. This is the essence of magic, which does not create but summons.

—Franz Kafka, *Diaries*

Tel Aviv, May 1948

At dawn on the Sabbath of May 15, 1948, a new flag, a white field with a blue Star of David at its center, was raised for the first time over a new nation. For Dora, and for millions of Jews worldwide, a long cherished dream had become a miraculous reality. For the neighboring Arab countries, it meant war.

Six months earlier, the United Nations had passed a resolution calling for partition of Palestine into two separate nations, an Arab state and a Jewish state. The part of Mandatory Palestine east of the Jordan River had been separated from it in 1921 and given by the British to the Emir Abdullah, a British ally from the Hejaz (now part of Saudi Arabia). In 1946 the British unilaterally gave Transjordan its independence, and its name was changed from the Emirate of Transjordan to the Hashemite Kingdom of Jordan. The part of Mandatory Palestine lying west of the Jordan River was divided between Jews and Arabs, and the capital city, Jerusalem, was declared international territory. The Jews welcomed partition and accepted their state, with rejoicing, singing and dancing in the streets. But a day of celebration for 600,000 Jewish Israelis was a day of mourning for millions of Arabs in neighboring countries. Palestinian Arabs rejected partition and rejected the state offered to them.

As the sun rose for the first time on the new Jewish state, the combined regular armies of Egypt, Lebanon, Iraq, Jordan and Syria attacked Israel's new borders in a declared "war of extermination." The Egyptian army invaded along the coastal plain to the south, heading for Tel Aviv. The Syrians attacked the oldest kibbutz in the Galilee, Degania. The Lebanese army took Nazareth, and the Jordanian army cut off Jerusalem. On the day of its birth, Israel's fight for its existence had begun.

Despite the ongoing war for independence, Jews continued to pour into Israel. In the summer of 1948, Sara, her husband and daughter sailed toward a new life in Tel Aviv. They settled in the tiny upstairs apartment of a square two-story house built on the sand in the narrow streets of Neve Tzedek, the old quarter of the city built by Jewish settlers in the late nineteenth century. It bordered on the old Arab port of Jaffa. David had prospered in Germany while working with the Americans, and he had to be convinced to move to Israel. He agreed the following year, and in 1949, David Diamant, Branka and their two-year-old son, Zvi, left Munich. They settled in Jaffa in a subdivided house formerly occupied by a high-ranking British official.

LONDON, MAY 1948

Ever since she could remember, Dora wanted to go to Eretz Yisroel. The Zionist dream of a Jewish homeland was born a year before Dora, and throughout her life, she felt the magnetic pull of the ancient land she believed to be her true home. Now that Israel existed and her family was there, Dora more than ever wanted to go. But it was impossible.

Dora was well again, but Marianne's health continued to decline. Her kidneys had deteriorated to such an extent that she now needed daily treatments. She had to withdraw from her classes at South Hampstead High School and was sent to Pembury Hospital near Tunbridge Wells in Kent, thirty miles south of London. Everything Dora earned went for monthly expenses and Marianne's treatments. There was nothing left over at the end of each month. Still, Dora dreamed of going to Israel.

In 1947 Solomon Mikhoels came to London from Russia as chairman of the Jewish Anti-Fascist Committee, a Soviet propaganda organization composed of prominent Jewish scholars, artists, poets, writers and social and political leaders, to talk about the "gruesome events" of the German occupation of Eastern Europe and Russia. The famed Yiddish actor and director of the Moscow Jewish State Theater, whom Dora had seen on stage as King Lear in the winter of 1936, "trembled as he described how the Germans danced on the Torah Scrolls." In Dora's eyes, Mikhoels was "a fighter for all mankind," who spoke with "a passionately beating Jewish heart, which bleeds with every drop of our spilled blood." She saw Mikhoels as a man "who still takes his spiritual nourishment from the roots of his people, and who grew organically from it. Only such a person can feel so united with his own humanity."

When Dora pondered her own relationship to Judaism, which she no longer practiced but which continued, perhaps more than ever, to define her, she said there always appeared before her "two sentences from Psalm 1: the first, *'Ashre ha'ish'* (Blessed be the man), and the second, *'Lo chen hareschoim'* (Not so the evildoer)." When Dora thought of Solomon Mikhoels, she thought of the first sentence of the book of Psalms: "Blessed be the man." He symbolized to her "the unquestioned certainty of natural law: as the branch of a tree sprouts and is warmed by the tree in the spring sunshine, trembles and sighs with it in the cold and storm, and goes up in smoke with it when the wood is on fire. . . . You know he will not betray you because he has never betrayed himself and his world."

In January 1948, the Soviet press reported that Solomon Mikhoels was killed in a tragic car accident. In fact, he was assassinated on orders of Stalin, who had begun his own campaign against the Jews. In the February issue of *Loshn un Lebn*, Dora published a tribute entitled "Solomon Mikhoels, The Jew." In his memory, Dora revisited her own spiritual questions concerning her assimilation into Western culture and her unwillingness or inability to move forward, to leave the past behind her. Since the end of the war the question had arisen again for Dora, the "constant thought" that had plagued her for years: "No to assimilation? Yes to assimilation? There must be at last an end to it!" she cried.

LONDON, 1949

Yealand Manor's annual newsletter came out in the spring, with the following news item: "Marianne Lask was still in hospital (Pembury Hospital, H2, near Tunbridge Wells, Kent) at Christmas, having been there since last June. She writes very pluckily and happily, and says that the doctors and nurses are all very kind. The children have a tutor, so that they are able to keep up their education, and they are provided with plenty of handicraft materials."

Dora visited Marianne in Kent every week. On Wednesdays, Ottilie and her husband took Dora to Penbury in their car. She now had two little daughters of her own, Doreen and Pamela. Occasionally the whole family went with Dora to visit her daughter in the hospital.

Marianne was fifteen years old but was, in many ways, as innocent of the world as a child. She remained hospitalized in Kent for two years, entering adolescence and then womanhood in her hospital bed, her narrow, sheltered existence a comfort to her, a refuge with limited outside contact, a safe place to explore the world through its literature, which she read constantly.

Dora's life was permeated with sadness and loss, as well as the constant fear of losing her daughter. The Yiddish world of "Jewish art" was vanishing before her eyes, unable to survive the postmodern world, which had been born in the apocalyptic end to the war. A discontinuity brought about by the cataclysmic events of 1945 had changed the very composition of the universe. With the birth of the atomic age, the old world of Yiddish had dimmed and was dying. Dora saw herself as "engaged in a bitter struggle to preserve that bit of honesty and purity that we possess."

The birth of a Jewish nation had not helped the Yiddishists' cause. Israelis spoke Hebrew, the revived and updated ancient language of the chosen people, as the language of the future. Yiddish was scorned by the Israeli literati, shunned as the old-fashioned jargon of a victimized people.

In the dark performance halls of Whitechapel, Dora continued to fight "against forgetting." She implored the Jewish community to greater creativity and artistic expression. Dora never gave up the struggle to keep the language alive, according to Marthe Robert, who later became famous as Kafka's French translator. Dora produced and directed "conferences, meetings, readings, shows in which she dressed up and read several parts—reciting, miming, singing, encouraging her audience to sing, deploying in front of a public to whom ancient, almost forgotten emotions had to be recalled. It was a reasoned passion, motivated by the disappearance of the Jewish Poland she had fled in her youth, but which, nevertheless, had never left her."

Dora had undertaken a difficult task, Robert said, "a task which might one day no longer be necessary, but was imperative at the time: to save the

Yiddish language from the death which threatened it. In her eyes, Yiddish poetry and literature were only part of the truth which she was able to preserve and to transmit."

It was dispiriting and disheartening to see the Yiddish audiences grow older and dwindle as no new artists appeared. But, as Dora reflected, "What can you do? Out of great need and misery you take what is given—and you shrug your shoulders. One must, after all, keep the soul alive. So you give in. However, this 'giving in' is the saddest part of our hopes and struggles."

Three years later, in Tel Aviv in 1952, two men strolled along the beach in Tel Aviv, discussing Dora and explaining how they both knew her. One of the men, a Yiddish writer named Mendel Mann, had met her in order to write a story about her. The other man claimed to have spoken to her about one of Kafka's manuscripts and had seen her once on a stage in Whitechapel. His description of the scene was melodramatic:

She stood, confined by a dark curtain, and read an entangled one-act play. In the half-empty hall sat old Jews from Whitechapel. Dreaming Jews in dark suits with big waistcoats. Women, double-chinned, with veils. One man in the first row took out a large pocket watch with Roman numerals on the dial and held its face close to his eyes. The silver chain jangled and fell silent. Her voice was swallowed up the dark ceiling, the heavy benches, and I could not catch the full meaning of her speech. I left in the middle of her reading. My steps echoed in the half-empty hall. In the dark corridor, I looked around and had the feeling that something was trying to hold me back so I would not be able to get out of the darkness.

Despite young men fleeing the halls, Dora continued to organize lectures, concerts and performances, and write opinion essays and reviews for *Loshn un Lebn*. One concert she was particularly pleased to review was held in January 1949 at the People's Palace. Hanny Lichtenstern, using her stage name, Hannah Metzger, performed a selection of Yiddish folk songs, which, as Dora noted, earned her "the wild enthusiasm of the audience." Dora happily admitted that her review would "dwell extensively" on the talents of Miss Metzger, whose "development in the sphere of Yiddish folk songs" Dora had "followed from the very first beginning." In fact, Dora had planted the seed in Hanny, which she now proudly saw in full bloom.

"She didn't know Yiddish, and musically she was trained in the classical school," Dora wrote. "Yet while working with her I could not stop being amazed at the ease with which she got into and became familiar with the Yiddish sounds, Yiddish gestures, Yiddish words: it was as if an old instrument with a rich sounding-board, which had stood forgotten by its master for a very long time, was suddenly brought to life, to sound and ring with its old splendour as its master's fingers glided over it. Some kind of archaic process of nature has brought her back to her origins."

Dora and Hanny rarely saw each other. Hanny was a mother now, with a five-year-old son, David, and was kept busy with her singing and teaching, as well as accompanying her husband at the Belsize Square Synagogue, where he was the organist. Another reason they weren't as close as they had been was jealousy on the part of her husband. "Paul was jealous of Dora," Hanny admitted in 1990, "because I spent too much time with her, and thought so highly of her opinion. When I told her so, she said that Paul had a very possessive love for me. But she was wonderful. She backed off gently. She understood human nature, and made allowances for all."

Dora's friendship with Marianne Steiner developed quickly after their first emotional meeting in the real estate office. The first time the Steiners came to Dora's house for dinner, it was winter, Mrs. Steiner remembered. "It was very cold in that poorly furnished room. There was a stove, which was red hot, yet the room was absolutely icy." Dora didn't seem to mind. "Keep your coats on for a while, soon it will get very warm," she said. They did keep their coats on—"we couldn't have helped it," Mrs. Steiner said, but the room remained freezing cold. "I noticed that one of the windows was open. I thought that perhaps the glass was broken, and Dora didn't have money to have it repaired, and so I didn't say anything. And so we sat shivering for at least an hour, when Dora suddenly exclaimed, 'I forgot to close the window!' That was so typical of her. She was so animated and stimulated by this meeting that she never thought of shutting the window."

The Steiners enjoyed Dora's company. "She was very lively," Mrs. Steiner said. "Tears and laughter came very easily to her. She was extremely generous. When a cousin of mine who lived in Canada came to visit us, Dora immediately gave her one of the dresses she was making for a living. Although she had so little money, whenever she invited us to her home, the table would be laden with sandwiches, pastries and fruit."

When Mrs. Steiner offered Dora money from the Kafka estate, Dora accepted it for two reasons. Marianne would have what she needed, and Dora could begin saving for a trip to Israel.

In Israel her brother, David Diamant, was doing what he could to help her. David's brother-in-law, Dov Goldman, one of the founders of the kibbutz Mishmar HaSharon outside of Netanya, knew Mordechai Namir, a leader in Israel's powerful Labor Federation, who was the Israeli ambassador to the Soviet Union. David and Dov convinced Namir to invite Dora to come to Tel Aviv to speak about her perspective on Kafka, who was already well-known in Israel, his works having been translated into Hebrew. In the end, an invitation was issued to Dora to speak as a guest of the city of Tel Aviv, with an official reception to be held afterward.

Dora was going to Israel! She planned to leave in October or November and stay through the end of the year, maybe longer. Since the beginning of the year, Dora had been regularly, almost every month, corresponding with Max Brod. A single paragraph from one of her letters, written at the end of August, was published in a German journal in 1988 as a footnote to an article about Kafka's meeting with Dora at the Baltic Sea. How the author managed to see this letter to Max, part of the missing Brod Collection, is not known. "This whole business still appears very implausible to me," Dora wrote. "I was just realizing that I am indescribably happy to see you. I am so utterly longing for Franz. The longing of all these years is so concentrated that I become utterly helpless if I dwell on it. It was Franz's dream to have a child and go to Palestine. Now I have a child—without Franz, and go to Palestine—without Franz, but from his money I buy the ticket to go there. At least so much."

Israel, October-November 1949

In her eighties, Bracha Plotkin still remembers the disappointment she felt at not being able to attend the Tel Aviv reception held in Dora's honor. It seemed to her that at least fifty members of the kibbutz Mishmar HaSharon, located five kilometers from Netanya, were journeying south to Tel Aviv for Dora's lecture and reception. Dov Goldman had organized a group of people, originally from Bedzin, who had known Dora or her family before the war. Bracha hadn't known Dora, but she had known the family. As a girl, she had had a crush on Tuvia, David's first son, who was born the same year she was, in 1919. Tuvia was twenty when the Germans occupied Bedzin. During the liquidation of the Ghetto in 1943, he was taken to Auschwitz. Bracha's sister had seen him there. "He didn't have on his hat, which he always wore," she said. "His head had been shaved and his earlocks cut off." Later Bracha's sister "saw the selection ceremony, where he was selected to die."

Dora had left Bedzin before Bracha was born, but Bracha was brought up on tales about her, some of which she heard from David Diamant himself. "Dora wanted to become an actress before the war," Bracha said, repeating one of the stories she heard. "Her father, Herschel, didn't want her to go to the big city, so she took her small suitcase, and said she was leaving. Her father said that if she did, he would sit *shiva* for her, would tear his shirt, and mourn her as dead. She left anyway."

According to Bracha, David missed his sister Dora very much and wanted to see her again. "He felt he owed her a debt. He said he still regretted that he had not done anything to help her back then, to do something to make the situation better between her and her father."

In Israel, Dora felt she had come home at last. "Her visit made her feel like a human being again for the first time since the war," her daughter Marianne later wrote. Dora was deeply moved by the awareness and the depth of public feeling and understanding of Kafka in Israel. These Jewish immigrants, she told a French journalist, "reached the sunny country from the bottom of hells no less terrible that the one inventoried by Kafka." They saw Kafka differently than Europeans, who perceived him as "neurasthenic and discouraged." In Israel, Kafka was seen more correctly, Dora thought, "as an elder brother, who helped them through his courage and clear vision."

Kafka's friends in Israel—Max Brod in Tel Aviv and Felix Weltsch in Jerusalem—welcomed Dora warmly during her "all too brief stay in Israel," as Brod put it. In her honor he organized "An Evening with Dora Diamant at the Habima," the legendary theater of Russian origin, and gave the introductory remarks. Felix Weltsch wrote down "much of what she said in public and in private" about her life with Kafka, and wrote an article in French from his notes, entitled "Conversations with Dora Dymant."

While Dora was in Israel, Brod said, "she visited me often. During one such visit, I read to her from Janouch's manuscript." Max had received the manuscript from Gustav Janouch almost three years earlier, but it had lain forgotten and unread in pile of papers until his secretary, Ester Hoffe, "took it upon herself to look into the manuscript." Brod admitted to being "stunned by the wealth of new material I encountered—which plainly and unmistakably bore the stamp of Kafka's peculiar genius. Kafka's appearance, his manner of speech, his expressive and yet delicate way of gesticulation, the very movements of his facial muscles, were reproduced in the most vivid manner. I felt as if my friend had suddenly returned to life and had just entered the room. Once more I heard him speaking, saw his animated, shining eyes resting upon me, felt his quiet, pained smile, and was deeply stirred by his wisdom."

Dora's reaction to the manuscript was the same as Max's: "It affected her as it had me," Brod reported. "She too recognized Kafka's inimitable style and his way of thought in all the conversations that Janouch had preserved. She also was shaken by the feeling of having again encountered Kafka."

In Israel, Dora experienced the warmth of Kafka's reflected glow nearly every day, often from unexpected quarters. The man who repaired the roads stopped to talk to her about his love of Kafka. His cabin housed "his wealth—a beautiful collection of Kafka books." Another time, during a visit to a kibbutz, she found herself "surrounded by twenty-five Kafka enthusiasts, instead of the expected four or five family members." Ironically, the person who appeared to show "the greatest joy in seeing Dora again" was Tile Rössler. A quarter of a century had passed since Tile, as an unhappy teenager seeking Kafka's advice and love, had come to visit them at their flat in Berlin.

Dora was stimulated and excited by the vision of "men formerly reduced to compromise and to the worst downfalls, now asserting themselves as free men, authentically themselves." In them, she saw new possibilities for herself. It was not too late for her. Others, much older than she, were starting their lives over again in Israel. It would be good for Marianne, too, to feel a part of the strength of the young Israelis, who had committed their lives to restoring and protecting the land, who had become a part of it themselves.

Until David told her, Dora had no idea that her sister Sara lived in Tel Aviv, too. Since the birth of her niece in Germany, Dora had lost touch with Sara and told someone that she "had disappeared." Finding her only living sister alive in Tel Aviv made Dora's journey a complete triumph.

No words can describe the happiness Sara Baumer felt at finding her sister again. The photos she had hidden in her little memory book—Dora with Marianne and Nacha with her baby Friedele—had kept Sara alive in the camps. When she was reunited with Dora, hope was reborn in Sara's heart and soul. In a personal interview she gave in London in 1999 at the age of seventy-seven, Sara said, "The connection during Dora's visit was very deep. We grew very close in a short time. We felt our souls were united. We knew we should never be separated again, we would finish our lives together in Israel."

Dora loved Israel, Sara emphasized. "She was *ganz meshugge* for it. She loved everything about it. She didn't have a bad word to say. She talked all the time of coming back. She had to leave only because Marianne, her daughter, was still there. Dora returned to England to get Marianne and come back. She left with the thought of returning."

According to Sara, Dora's great regret was that she never had a child with Kafka. "Dora still had a great love for Kafka. She had so much to say about him. She really wanted his child. Dora told me while she was in Israel, that if she had had a baby with Kafka, the world would shine." When asked what she meant, Sara said, "Dora thought a child of Kafka would be a gift to the world."

Dora stayed with David and his family in the house they shared with another couple, Bulgarian immigrants, during her first month in Israel. Dora's nephew, Zvi, was a healthy, handsome, bouncing boy of two and a half. He was surrounded by loving family members from his mother's side, Branka's four surviving siblings and their children, his cousins, who all lived nearby in the same neighborhood in Jaffa.

David Diamant experienced difficulty adjusting to life in Israel. In Germany and Poland, he had been a successful businessman. In the four years in Germany after the end of the war, he had opened several business ventures, catering to the American military in Munich. His businesses, which included a restaurant with live music and dancing and a money exchange service, thrived. In 1947 he moved his entire extended family, which included Branka's two brothers and two sisters, plus a nurse for Zvi, into a spacious six-room apartment in Munich that previously had been occupied by a high-ranking Nazi official. Israel's economy was in a shambles as the country fought for its very survival, and David was not able to repeat his previous successes. He bought a van and began working as a vendor to grocery stores. He bought produce and food products, such as pickles, from the farmers and sold directly going store to store. Zelig sometimes went with him.

Zelig Besserglick came to Israel in 1949 from Munich with Branka and David, and lived with them before moving to New York in 1959, where he still lives in Brooklyn. In an interview he gave in 1999, he was happy to remember his brother-in-law. "From him, I learned to make business," Zelig said. "Everybody told him to buy a house: 'Oh Mr. Diamant, you should have a house.' 'A house I can buy later,' he said, 'but first I buy a business. I can't eat the four walls.'"

David was very intelligent, Zelig said. "Like a lawyer. Everyone went to him, and he would solve their problems. He knew how to deal with people. He was also a scholar. He spoke Yiddish, Hebrew, Polish and German. Everyone came to him to ask his advice—me, too. He was like a rabbi, but no more does he *daven* the Torah. I asked him why he doesn't anymore. 'The Nazis took that away from me,' he said."

Nevertheless, David continued to go to a synagogue every Sabbath. Zvi remembered his father, who died shortly before his bar mitzvah, taking him to different synagogues every Saturday. Even if he believed, as he told Dov, that "God is dead," David wanted to make sure his son had the experience of the Jewish rituals and knowledge of the religion, so he could make his own decision.

David was a good father to his only living child, Zelig said. "When Zvika wanted to go outside to play, David said no, first do homework," Zelig remembered. "He told me he taught Zvi to play the accordion. Why? So that when he grows up he can catch the girls!"

After staying with David and his family for one month, Dora moved to Sara's house, sharing a room with Sara's almost three-year-old daughter Gitele, known by her Hebrew name, Tova. As an adult, Tova remembered Dora's visit as if "suddenly a light emerged" from the feeling of "family orphancy." Dora's presence in their home dissipated the pain Tova felt acutely as a child, "not knowing what it means to have a grandmother, a grandfather, uncles, aunts, cousins, an extended family." In a speech she gave in 1999 at Dora's graveside, Tova remembered her "auntie," the warmth of her love and the optimism that she radiated. She remembered Dora telling her stories, singing lullabies and kissing her goodnight. She remembered walking hand in hand between her mother and Dora as they walked on the street to Max Brod's house.

Dora had told Max Brod about her sister, Sara, describing how, when she lit the Sabbath candles every Friday night, she mentioned in her prayers "all the names of each of her family members murdered in the Holocaust." He was very moved and wanted to meet her. One afternoon, Dora took Sara—with Tova—to Max's house, where they sat and drank coffee and talked about her family's terrible experiences in the Shoah.

After living with Sara's family for a month, Dora moved for a few days to a rundown wooden house in a courtyard off Yarkon Street, only steps from the beach. It was the home of the aged father of someone Dora had once known and loved in Bedzin. While she was staying there, she received a visit from a Yiddish writer named Mendel Mann. He wanted to write a story about her, and she agreed to meet with him. His darkly atmospheric essay, "Franz Kafka's Wife," first published in Yiddish and translated into English in 1969, was based on that one visit, the memory of which was sharply etched into his psyche and drenched in poetic self-consciousness.

When Mann opened the door of the wooden shack where she lived, he said, "the door creaked. The glass panes were loose and rattled. Against a wall covered with mildewy wallpaper there was an old man with a red beard lying in an iron bed." His ancient hand with its long yellow bony fingers twitched.

"I want to see Madam Dora. Is this the place?" Mann asked.

"Wait a few minutes, you've found it. She'll soon be here." The old man nodded his head reassuringly.

The old man looked at him "with large staring eyes," Mann wrote. He described the room, the brass candlesticks, the photographs on the table, an old black-framed mirror in which he could not see his own reflection but only the "yellow face of age dying." He heard footsteps, and a darkly dressed woman entered.

"She looked at me with a gray, gloomy face," Mann said. "It had become so still in the room. . . . Then she lifted her eyes and I saw the dazzling brightness of her large protruding pupils. She was carelessly dressed, her hair windswept, eyebrows untidy and tangled in her dark hair. Her round forehead was faintly lined. It was the face of a widow in her first weeks of mourning. She carried her grief as naturally as the clouds of the night carry the dim light of a setting moon."

He apologized for coming unexpectedly.

"No!" she said, "I was told that you would be coming." Mann thought "her voice was full of grief. The way people speak in rainy fields at late harvest time."

"You are Madame Dora?"

Dora smiled, her first smile since entering, and her appearance changed. "The light lines on her forehead disappeared, and I saw her suddenly pull herself together with that coquettishness which in an older woman almost approaches charm. An experienced woman's eye had waited for the least quiver of my face muscles."

Mann talked nervously about the heat and asked if she could spare a little time to talk to him. "She made another desperate attempt to smile," he wrote. "I felt a curious fear. It made me want to get away as quickly as possible. Yet at the same time, I felt drawn to this woman."

He didn't want to say Kafka's name. He wanted her to say it. But she didn't. After a moment he said, "Forgive me, permit me to pronounce the name and to talk openly." Dora nodded. "You are the wife of Franz Kafka?" Dora only "closed her eyes and the lines on her forehead moved nervously." Mann stood up, apologized, and started to go.

"You musn't do that, young man," Dora stopped him. "Just a minute, I'll be back soon." She left the room and Mann could hear her in the kitchen, preparing tea. Then he heard the creaking of a side door. After a few moments, she returned. She sat down in a wicker chair, facing him. She was wearing the same black blouse and dark skirt, but Mann noticed she now "had a white dusting of powder on her face, and she wore a silver brooch that looked like a spider's web of silver threads."

"I see you are surprised to find me living in this shack," Dora said. "I shall be staying here for a few days. The old man is the father of a friend of mine, who lives in a kibbutz. His son and I were close friends, first in Poland, then in Berlin. Then Franz came. But for that meeting, I would be living in Israel with my friend. He is in Galilee, a vine grower. We hadn't seen each other for years. His sudden departure from Berlin and my being here now are connected," Dora mysteriously added.

If not for that fateful meeting with Franz, Dora said, "everything would have been different. I often see myself in the fields of Galilee. But it all turned out somewhat different—a small room in a poor quarter of Berlin. A kerosene lamp burning on the writing table. Franz loved writing by the light of this oil lamp. You'd like to know how it started?" Dora asked theatrically, Mann thought, holding up her arm "as though to stop a galloping black coach in the street at night."

As if retelling a fairy tale, Dora began, setting the scene in a square where "sad chestnut trees grew." She cast herself as "a young Fröbel teacher surrounded by children. . . . Someone passing through the square stops, and the two look at each other—the Fröbel teacher and the young man. The witnesses at that meeting are the children and the just-beginning-to-bud spring trees."

Dora's monologue, as written by Mendel Mann, is an oratorical tone poem, a creation of Dora's metaphoric descriptions and Mann's unique perception of them:

That was the beginning. Everything was in that mutual glance: the germination and, at the same time, the forecast of the end. After that, I wandered with Kafka, was present at all the hearings before the judges of the eternal trial. I crept up narrow stairs, a tight squeeze between dark walls, in long endless dim corridors. We banged our heads on the

low ceilings. I poured oil into the lamp and burnt my fingers trimming
the wick. No, not only the wick was charred! I have never been able to
get away from the world that he created! That is a real world! So it is
to the present day. One wants to polish it, to decorate it. There in that
little room, by the light of the oil lamp, he discovered the real world. As
it is! Don't you see the confused people on the roads of all the towns on
this earth? Are you not confused yourself? I feel well here, in this little
room, with the brass candlesticks, the peeling wallpaper and the mirror
with the black frame. Such is the true face of the world! All the rest is
whitewash, dressed up lies of a cheap little traveling theater.

Dora crossed to the old man and took his hand. "My friend's father
comes from the East. Already, forty years in this country. When I look at
him, I see Prague. This is how Franz's father looked. Everywhere I go I
meet that gloom. I move in a labyrinth of stairs and doors, of narrow
courtyards."

Dora studied the younger man carefully, appraising him, drawing him
into the game by accusing him, mocking him: "I've seen you too somewhere before. Yes, perhaps you came to Kafka with a batch of your poems? Perhaps you bowed to us in one of the Prague streets? Didn't you
once stop in front of a frightened young man and stammer something
about beauty and eternity, at a time when everything is sinking into darkness? No? You mean to say it wasn't you? Never mind! It doesn't matter.
But I know you! As I know the chestnut trees that bloom and wither."

Dora laughed but Mann did not. "Don't be angry," Dora said, still
laughing. "I didn't mean to hurt you." She reached out to touch him. He
felt her cool fingers on his hand and withdrew from her. He felt offended,
as if she were treating him like a member of the audience. "This was not
the first time she was speaking these words," he wrote. "This was how
people speak on the stage, standing against the curtain. They love the
shadows that sway in the light of the lamps. It creates for them the illusion
of real people." He left shortly afterward and never saw her again.

En Charod, Jezreel Valley, Israel, January 1950

The great Jezreel Valley, the site of numerous biblical battles, identified in
the book of Revelation as the "stage for humanity's apocalyptic finale,"
looked nothing like Armageddon. When Dora first saw the lush, fertile

valley that had served for millennia as the main route between the Mediterranean and the Galilee, it seemed like heaven on earth. But it had not always been so. When the first group of settlers came to En Charod to start up the kibbutz at the base of Mount Gilboa, the area was a swampy, malarial marshland. David Maletz had arrived in the second group of pioneers, who worked long and hard for many years without electricity, running water or health facilities. Life was brutal for the settlers, and the kibbutz cemetery was completed before the first permanent buildings. The large dining room and kitchen, the heart of the kibbutz, was built in 1929. When Dora arrived at En Charod in 1950, she found a thriving, dynamic community of more than a thousand members, working, living, playing, growing together—the embodiment of the socialist ideal. Today En Charod kibbutz is still there, surrounded by six national parks and preserves and an expansive landscape of farmland.

Dora's reunion with David Maletz, her first Hebrew teacher from Bedzin, was warm and wonderful. It was as if no time had passed at all in their friendship, and their terrible losses receded for a moment. Maletz and his family had escaped the European Holocaust but not Jew hatred. His only son, Rafael, died in 1948 during Israel's War of Independence.

Half a century later, Dora's visit to En Charod was clearly remembered by the two daughters of David Maletz's second wife, Ruhama. Rena was fifteen at the time of Dora's visit and Noga was eleven. Fifty years later, both sisters, still living in Israel, talked about Dora's stay with them. They remembered two gifts she brought with her, two jersey blouses, which she had designed and made herself.

Dora made a deep impression on them. "She was our guest for six, perhaps eight weeks," Noga said in an interview at her home in 2000. "She was always so pleasant, cheerful and friendly. She was small, petite, and had a wonderful smile. Her skin was very pale, and beautiful. Her hair was light brown and matched her eyes. I loved her laugh, which was very young, like a girl's. She enjoyed everything. A light came out of her. There's a Hebrew word for it, *korenet*. She seemed to have glow, there was a brightness about her. Both my sister and I remember this."

What Noga appreciated most was the personal attention Dora gave her. "I felt like she was really interested in me. When I came home from school and my mother wasn't there, Dora would greet me at the door with a feeling of welcome, smiling, and ask me about my day." Although both girls spoke only Hebrew, they had no problem communicating with Dora, whose skill with the language was "natural and spontaneous."

Several families shared the small house, and Dora slept in the bedroom with the girls, occasionally staying overnight at the large, rambling guest house at the top of the hill. The kibbutz was a beautiful place, and Dora's days were filled watching the sun rise and set, surrounded by native acacia, olive and palm trees, cypress pines and huge flowering bushes of oleander, jasmine and bougainvillea. To help out, she occasionally worked in the communal kitchen.

The kibbutz had a very active literary club and reading groups, which Maletz had started several years earlier. While working on the tractors, before he became a teacher, he would wake up at four each morning to write, publishing several books and novels this way. As a teacher, he taught literature and philosophy before becoming headmaster of the kibbutz school. According to Noga—and Ora Fein, the archivist for En Charod since 1984—David Maletz was a truly extraordinary teacher who inspired learning and discussion. His first book, *Young Hearts*, a novel of modern Israel, was the first realistic portrait of life on the kibbutz. Highly controversial, it opened up public discourse in the areas of sex and interpersonal relationships. While sex was practiced freely, it wasn't talked about. "These subjects were close to pornography then," Fein explained.

One of the kibbutz members was a member of the first parliament of the Knesset and had the use of a car. He invited Dora to accompany him on a trip to the Galil, the hills above Lake Kinneret (Sea of Galilee); Ruchama, Noga and a young friend of hers went along, too. "Dora asked so many questions," Noga remembered. "She was much lighter in spirit than my mother. Dora loved to laugh."

In January 1950, a freak winter storm hit Israel, and the northern part of the country, including Jerusalem and Tel Aviv, was covered in deep snow for a full week. Ruhama Maletz was finishing up her master's degree in literature at Hebrew University in Jerusalem, where she had an apartment, and she invited Dora to stay with her. Ruhama was twelve years younger than Dora but much more serious. According to her daughter, Ruhama considered Dora a very disorganized person and frowned on her for not trying harder to find her missing husband. Nevertheless she enjoyed Dora's company and, despite her serious nature, often found herself laughing along with her.

Both sisters remember Dora as being very feminine, compared with the other women they knew. In those days on the kibbutz, "women didn't have cosmetics available, but Dora showed my mother and sister how to make their own," Noga said. "Dora had brought with her from England the ingredients. Rena helped her mash the cucumbers to make a face crème. They also made small soaps. Nobody on the kibbutz used cosmetics or cremes, it was not a part of the life style. But I remember Mother used it dedicatedly afterwards."

After almost four months in Israel, Dora had to go back to England. She was determined to return to Israel and bring Marianne back with her. In saying her good-byes to her family and friends, she vowed repeatedly to return soon. As a parting gift, Max gave Dora a copy of his latest book with the inscription "For your quick return." Dora was short of money, and Sara and Abraham helped pay for her passage home. In return, Dora left Max's signed book with Sara for safekeeping and gave her one of the two framed photographs of Kafka that she had brought with her to Israel. The photographs that she had chosen to bring had been taken in 1917, when Kafka was thirty-four, with a full head of raven hair, a slight smile and a searching look in his eyes, the way he looked when Dora first met him.

Leaving En Charod was painful. This was the place, she had decided, she wanted to live the rest of her life. She left a suitcase full of clothes at the hostel with the manager, who promised to keep it safe until her return, and left two items with the Maletz family. The first was a gift, the other framed Kafka photograph, identical to the one she left with Sara. The second item she left with them was her greatest treasure, the only possession of Kafka's that she had. When they took his letters from her, the Gestapo had ignored the hairbrush sitting on her dresser. She'd carried it with her to Russia and kept it with her through her long journey to England, during the year of internment. It had even survived the bombing of her home during the war. Now she was leaving it with them, as a talisman to ensure her return. By bringing Kafka's hairbrush with her, it was as if she had brought him to Israel with her. She wouldn't make him leave this paradise.

She held the hairbrush in both hands. The wood was light and smooth and the golden bristles worn away where his palm had once gripped the sides. She caressed it one last time and handed it to Ruchama, who promised to take care of it until Dora's return.

22

A MEMORY COME ALIVE

Anyone who grasps life completely has no fear of dying.

    —Franz Kafka, in *Conversations with Kafka*

PARIS, FEBRUARY 1950

Dora returned to England via France. Sailing from Israel across the Mediterranean Sea to Marseilles, she took the train to Paris, where she stayed for several days before crossing the channel to England. She had a specific reason for going to Paris: She wanted to meet Jean-Louie Barrault.

At the age of forty, Barrault was at the height of his fame. The French actor/director, who had built his theatrical reputation by playing Hamlet, was known internationally for his starring role as the mime in the 1945 film classic, *Les enfants du paradis.* After the war, Barrault formed his own acting company at the Theatre Marigny in Paris. One of his first productions was an experimental work, a dramatization of *The Trial,* with the adaptation of Kafka's novel by André Gide, the winner of the Nobel Prize for literature in 1947. Barrault cast himself in the role of Joseph K., the protagonist, who is arrested one morning without having done anything wrong. The play, as well as the many reviews written about it, enhanced Kafka's fame in France, but the production was, according to Kafka experts of the day, produced by "imitators rather than genuine disciples." What Barrault and Gide had achieved was "a melodrama" and "the most popular and most misleading corruption of a Kafka hero," stated critic and Kafka scholar, Heinz Politzer. "With Barrault, the Kafka hero became a withered dancer on the avenues of our sorrow, the charmingly evasive Hamlet of French existentialism after World War II."

Nicolas Baudy, a French essayist and writer, witnessed the meeting between Dora and Barrault. After that, Dora agreed to be interviewed, and granted "several long conversations" to Baudy. His six-page article, "Conversations with Dora Dymant," was published in a Parisian literary journal the following month, in February. Baudy began with the meeting of Kafka's last love and the legendary actor and director. "Last Friday, a hatless woman, whose rebellious hair had apparently always been exposed to the sun, wind and rain, wearing a long, shapeless, brick-colored coat made of a thick, rough material, crossed the foyer of the Theatre Marigny," Baudy wrote. "As soon as he was told, Jean-Louis Barrault received Dora Dymant and tried to answer her first question: 'Why did you make *The Trial* into a play?' He showed her photographs of the sets and the production. Dora agreed that the mask of K. . . . held a striking resemblance to Franz's face. She felt, however, that Barrault—who was the same age as Kafka when he died—was 'too young to interpret the personage.'"

Barrault accepted the criticism and then asked Dora a question: "Did you bring the two missing signatures?" According to Baudy, this wasn't exactly the question Barrault asked, but since his English wasn't very good, that was the question Dora heard, and the one she answered. The two missing signatures were those of Kafka's nieces, Vera and Helena, who still lived in Prague. Their signatures were necessary in order for Barrault to be able to collect the income from the Kafka play, which had been blocked by the Societe des Auteurs Dramatiques. Since 1948, Czechoslovakia had been under Communist control, behind the "Iron Curtain" that blocked the Soviet Union and its satellite eastern bloc countries from communication and interaction with the western world. Although Marianne Steiner, Kafka's niece in London, had already signed the contract transferring the rights, the current political situation made it impossible to obtain the signatures of the other two nieces. Dora said she "did not see how the situation could be resolved."

"A Kafkaesque situation," someone commented.

Baudy watched for Dora's reaction. "Such remarks have no effect on Dora," Baudy observed. "She now has sufficient experience of the many misunderstandings of all kinds that abound around Kafka. She has stopped calling attention to them, one by one: it would be impossible. After more than twenty years of silence, however, she has decided to help in reconstituting Kafka's true face, to open 'a pathway, however narrow, to the understanding of the person.'"

Dora wanted to correct the idea that Kafka was without hope. "I am convinced," she told Baudy, "that he would not have wished for young people who read his books to be imbued with a concept of the world such as it emerges from *The Trial* or *The Castle*. He went on his way—I only realize today the sufferings he went through—to arrive at the foot of a high wall that remained to be scaled. He would have been horrified that his testimony was regularly invoked to state that *The Trial* is final, that there could be no appeal. Nothing is more awful, more injurious to Kafka than to think of him as someone who passively—even with a dreamlike passivity—sanctions human failure. While K. was condemned at the trial, Kafka, having demonstrated the absurdity of the trial, never lost hope of reopening it. He led us, divested of lies, better armed to storm the great wall."

Dora related her story of Kafka to Baudy, much as she had told it to J. P. Hodin. "Dora does not wait for me to ask too many questions," Baudy wrote. "She has asked them all of herself. She does not elude any."

Baudy was fascinated by Kafka; he had read the novels and much of the commentary written about him and had discovered a wide gulf between the popular image of the haunted, lonely, alienated existentialist who believes in nothing but hopeless failure, and the man described by those who knew him. "His kindness and a sort of glow struck all those who approached him," Baudy said. "His friends, just like the strangers who knew nothing of him, came under his influence. All speak, more or less, of this experience. Dora Dymant, however, is especially arresting. One feels her taller, ennobled, definitively marked by the contact with an exceptional being. While listening to her, one can follow closely Kafka's efforts to find a direction for himself and for his life. An exemplary man, not satisfied with half solutions, pseudo-solutions, barely with the most advanced solutions was he able to reach through to the human condition."

"The word, 'saint,'" Baudy said to Dora, "has been pronounced about Kafka." Dora had heard this before. In Israel, Felix Weltsch had asked her why "a man who knows these things" said to him that Kafka was a "Mekubal," the Hebrew word for a high-level Kabbalist, someone highly advanced in the study and practice of the Jewish mystical tradition. Dora was uncomfortable with these questions. "Dora replied slowly and carefully, weighing each word," Weltsch reported: "I don't know anything about that. . . . But you could say that."

Dora responded to Baudy's comment by avoiding it: "He suffered intensely from the sufferings of others. He never thought of building a protected life for his own safety," she said. "This, however, did not make him pessimistic. Pessimism is a resignation. It tends to compromise. It abandons the fight. While Kafka had an inexhaustible source of vitality and of generosity."

Almost everyone who questioned her asked about Kafka's spirituality. It was one of the first things she talked about with Marthe Robert, a Parisian intellectual and socialist who wanted to translate Kafka's work. In an article she wrote after Dora's death, Marthe Robert concluded that "Dora had nothing final or new to tell those who interrogated her on Kafka. She was not able to answer the 'fundamental' questions she was regularly asked— Kafka's position on the problem of religion, for example. She would have not been like him—honest, scrupulous and prudent—if she had been able to answer these questions right away. When she was pushed too far, she was forced to disappoint the listener by telling him he was going the wrong way. I suppose that she not only surprised, but even offended some minds hungry for a truth easily absorbed."

Edwin and Willa Muir, Kafka's English translators, were fixated on Kafka's belief in God. Each time they met with Dora, they asked her, "Did Kafka have faith?" Dora invariably replied: "No." This was, Marthe said, "a scandalous reply, not without mischievousness, considering Kafka's deep obsession with this problem, but which, however, conveyed her warning: 'We cannot begin where he may have ended but can only take things where he saw them, in the dolorous and inevitable contact with humanity. Do not talk of God—where and when did he ever speak of him?— but look at his life, read his books, look at them with the purest attention, with the utmost accuracy, and if you can do it—it is hard, he would have said—you will not have an answer, but at least you will cease to turn your back on what you are looking for.'"

"If one would only listen, and ask only the questions she was able to answer, Dora became unstoppable," Marthe observed. "All remained to be said. She would never run out of new instances, things she had experienced with him but had not understood at the time. She told anecdotes, moments of everyday life, a particular phone call, the placement of a piece of furniture, a letter, which at the time she thought of as a game, but which had taken on new significance."

"The game, and the exaggeration of the game, were an integral part of what he had to say, and since I was really playing, I never knew if he was half-playing or if he was serious," Dora told Marthe.

"The anecdote she evoked was suddenly full of sense, of a density of sense equaling that of a page written by Kafka," Marthe said. "One would like to tell all the stories told by Dora. All hold a part of what Kafka meant to say in his life and in his work. All reveal a facet of truth."

When Marthe Robert met Dora in Paris in the winter of 1950, Marthe was thirty-four years old, beginning her brilliant career as an author and a translator of Kleist, Freud and Kafka. It took almost thirty years for her to complete her psychoanalytical biography of Kafka, *As Lonely as Franz Kafka*, which was finally published in 1979. When Marthe Robert died at the age of eighty-two in 1996, her Associated Press obituary ran in newspapers throughout the world, naming her an "award-winning literary critic and translator best known for rendering Franz Kafka's German works into French. A passionate student of language and psychoanalysis, Ms. Robert delved deep into the background of those she translated to remain as close as possible to their original work. By doing so, she was the first to establish how Kafka's writings were influenced by French author Gustave Flaubert and the Austrian pioneer of psychoanalysis, Sigmund Freud."

Marthe and Dora became good friends in the two years they knew each other. After Dora's death, Marthe Robert became the leading female Kafka expert in Europe, serving on the editorial board of the German Historical-Critical Edition of the Complete Works of Franz Kafka. Her extensive Kafka translations earned her France's highest literary accolades. "In translating an author, to be able to get at the heart of his phrase," she was quoted as saying after her last of her thirteen books was published in 1994, "it is necessary to know what he loved."

LONDON, MARCH 1950

As soon as she arrived back in London, Dora began "to prepare for her final departure to Israel," but Marianne was still in the hospital, too ill to travel. According to the Yealand Manor newsletter that year, "Marianne Lask is still in hospital (Hut 2 Pembury Hospital near Tunbridge Wells, Kent). She spent a very happy Christmas, with a lot of noise and laughter. If you've ever spent a Christmas in hospital, you'll know what I mean! She is now working hard for S.C. (School Certificate). Her mother has just returned from a three months holiday in Israel which she has enjoyed immensely."

As long as Marianne was ill, Dora had to remain in England. She and her daughter were still stateless refugees in the eyes of the British government, yet they were treated "very well indeed," Mrs. Steiner said, especially in regard to Marianne's education and health care. "Because Marianne was very intelligent, she was taught in the hospital by a teacher who came every day to prepare her for matriculation. She passed this exam in bed."

That spring, a new adaptation of Kafka's *The Trial* opened on the London stage and flopped. Dora had warned Max about her unhappiness with the production after seeing a rehearsal. After opening night, she wrote again giving credit wherever she could, trying to break the bad news gently, since it was Max himself who had written the adaptation. At the end of June, Dora received a letter from Max's secretary, Ester Hoffe. In trying to relieve Max from outside distractions, Ester had taken over his correspondence. She didn't flatter herself that she was a substitute for Max, and she expected people to be offended. Her letter was long and friendly, and talked about Max's passionate obsession with "his great new novel." It had been accepted by an American publisher and he was rushing to finish it. Ester wrote: "But you know such moods from the same kind of vantage point."

From her letter to Dora, written on June 20, 1950, it is clear that Ester felt a deep kinship with her. Although married to another man, Ester Hoffe loved Max Brod and believed him to be a truly great writer who needed her assistance and protection. Ester's letter was chatty, full of information. She included news about her two daughters, Ruthi and Chava, and reminded Dora: "Your sister hasn't yet picked up the package that Mrs. Steiner left with Max, with the little doll. Please write to her about it, or give us her address." Ester and Max hoped that Marianne's health improved soon to allow them to immigrate to Israel. They had been delighted to meet Marianne Steiner, who had gone to Israel following Dora's visit. Max found Kafka's niece to be "a fine, intelligent and sympathetic person," Ester said, and noted that Max had seen "a lot of similarities" between uncle and niece. In the margin of Ester's letter to Dora, Max wrote a brief apology for farming out the letter: "Please understand and don't be cross," he scribbled.

LONDON, JULY 1950

Marianne was allowed to go home on weekends. She was now sixteen years old, although she looked younger. She was excruciatingly shy around strangers. The children she had known in the hospital either got better and left or died. Except for her mother's friends, she had no friends of her own. Even around the Steiners, Marianne was unusually reserved and quiet. The only man she was truly comfortable with was Stencl, whom she'd known since she was a baby.

On Saturday afternoons when she felt well enough, Marianne accompanied Dora to the Friends of Yiddish meetings. On the first Saturday in July, they took the subway from Finchley Road Station to Aldgate East and walked the few blocks to the meeting room at Toynbee Hall. A smaller number of members had shown up that day, which was a shame, since a special guest from Canada, a well-known Yiddish poet and essayist, was scheduled to speak. Dora had met him twenty-five years earlier in a small town on the Polish-Russian border and wondered if he would remember her.

Melech Ravitch hadn't thought of Dora in years. After this second meeting, he never forgot her again. For his memoirs, *Stories from My Life*, he wrote about his two remarkable meetings with Dora. The story, "I Am Franz Kafka's Wife," was translated from Yiddish and reprinted in the literary supplement of the *Jewish Chronicle* in London in 1992, more than a quarter century after Ravitch's death.

"It is the Saturday afternoon literary get-together at the Jewish center near Whitechapel, organized by the poet A. N. Stencl," Ravitch began, describing the second meeting. "There are about sixty people in the audience, their combined age probably approaching the total age of the world, according to Jewish tradition. I am introduced to the audience. I tell them something about Jewish life in Canada. Some of my poems are read out, and the meeting is drawing to a close. A short, stocky woman comes up to the stage. Her face is devoid of color, except for the pallor of hardship. Her voice has no timbre, except the subdued quietness of pain and poverty. The woman asks if I recognize her: 'How quickly the years go by,' she says. 'It seems like we just met at Tomashov. . . .'

"I had so many friends in Tomashov," Ravitch countered. "How would I ever recognize them now? How can one remember? . . . "

"I am Dora Diamant," the woman said, "Franz Kafka's wife—do you remember?"

Ravitch remembered. "Dora Diamant, 'Franz Kafka's wife!' She asks my permission to read the audience one of my poems. I try to dissuade her. First, my poems are difficult to recite; second, people are already on their way out. She says she doesn't care about the audience. It is for herself and the poet she wants to read the poem. If people want to leave, let them. Of course I agreed. The poem she wanted to read was 'And it came to pass at the end of days.' Slowly, in a low, husky voice, she read. Softly, very softly, then loudly, very loudly, she went through it verse by verse, from the first verse—

I believe—Jewish people, believe in your mission,
True as I am the son of Hinda,
Daughter of Bleima.
I believe—Embattled as I am with all the other "I believes" of
     Rambam's flint-sharp mind.

—to the last:

And the first word of those new tablets—
the latest, washed and shined in blood—
Jewish blood—will still be I. But not Yahweh.
The next word written will be Man.

Melech Ravitch was astonished by Dora's reading, and profoundly moved. "If anyone ever read or recited one of my poems, not just read, but produced it from the depths of their soul, it was she: Dora Diamant, 'Franz Kafka's wife.' If ever a perfect rendering was given to my poems it happened then, that Shabbat afternoon. She got through to the poem's every word. Why she chose that one, I do not know. After the lecture she introduced me to her daughter and gently we wended our way together through the ruins of Whitechapel till she and her daughter came to the Underground."

For the next twenty-five years, until his death in 1976, Melech Ravitch continued to think about Dora. "Her soft, toneless voice echoes in the awesome silence of many of Franz Kafka's works written before he ever knew her. I still hear that toneless voice of hers telling me in 1925: 'I am Franz Kafka's wife'—and a quarter of a century later, words delivered in every possible shade of the human voice."

PLAISTOW HOSPITAL, JANUARY 1951

The last mention of Marianne Lask in the Yealand Manor newsletter appeared in 1951: "Marianne has come out of hospital, and has passed her School Certificate. Her mother is now in hospital, and Marianne suspects she has decided to try her luck there, as Marianne came out looking so well!"

Marianne and Dora were putting a bright face on it, but the news was grim. Dora was diagnosed with chronic nephritis, a rapidly progressive and fatal kidney disease. The early symptoms of weakness, fatigue and general flulike symptoms had been subtle, and Dora didn't realize how sick she was until it was too late. The inflammation of both kidneys had been progressing for well over a decade, destroying healthy cells and leaving scar tissue. By the time Dora saw a doctor, her kidneys were on the verge of failure. Her only hope of prolonging her life was to remain on complete bed rest and restrict protein and salt in her diet. There was no cure.

Dora was tormented by two thoughts. The first, "above all, that I leave Marianne so utterly unprovided for," Dora said. She had nothing to leave her daughter, no money, only the lease on the flat and a few pieces of furniture. Marianne knew nothing of the world outside of hospitals. How would she survive? What would become of her? Lying flat on her back, unable to move, worry and guilt consumed Dora. "I cannot remember ever having experienced such agony in life," Dora wrote. "These would be the torments which end in death, they go beyond every limit of what is bearable and comprehensible." The second thought, "if one could call this function thinking," Dora said, "I was plagued by the thought that I had not written what I wanted to write about Franz."

In the greatest favor Dora had ever asked of anyone, she talked to all her friends, asking them to help look out for Marianne. It was the Steiners, however, whom Dora asked to shoulder the greatest responsibility: to become Marianne's guardians, to make sure that she would always be taken care of, perhaps even with royalties from the Kafka estate, if Dora died before Marianne came of legal age. They consented, to Dora's enormous relief and gratitude.

Even before she had fallen ill, Dora had considered the benefits of British citizenship for Marianne and asked the Steiners for their opinion. They advised her to apply. "Our argument was that Marianne's English was perfect," Mrs. Steiner said. "She spoke German very well, too, but English was the language in which she was taught, and England was the country in which she would live." Dora applied to the Home Office for British citizenship. The reply came back that citizenship could be granted under one condition: "Dora would have to pronounce her husband, Ludwig Lask, as dead."

It had been over ten years since Dora had received one of the Red Cross postcards from Lutz, but that didn't mean he was no longer alive. She had done nothing to try to get in touch with him, for several reasons. One was the danger she and Marianne would be in if they admitted their communist past. The anticommunist sentiment and rhetoric in England and in America, especially, had grown ugly since the beginning of the Cold War in 1948. Even if Dora risked everything to find out about Lask, only to learn he was by some miracle still alive in a frozen labor camp somewhere in the Far Eastern Soviet gulag, what good would it do?

Dora and Marianne had to ask themselves another question: Could they declare him dead for their own convenience? They decided no. "Although it would have helped them so much," Mrs. Steiner said, "they said, 'no, on principle we can not, because he may be alive.'"

PLAISTOW HOSPITAL, MARCH 4, 1951

On her fifty-third birthday, Dora finally began to write about Franz Kafka. That same day, she wrote a three-page letter to Max Brod, telling him she'd "begun to systematically write down memories of Kafka." Across the red cardboard cover of the exercise book, Dora wrote in black ink: "To be given to Max Brod." Inside, she wrote her address: Ward Pasteur I, Plaistow Hospital, E15. Then she began: "The first step: free yourself—clear, purge the way to the 'Indestructible,' only then can one 'be.'" On this first page, which Dora later crossed out entirely, she tried to explain the intensity with which Kafka approached life. As an analogy, she described how Franz would painstakingly prepare a cup of tea for an expected guest. "Everything he did, even the most insignificant action was performed as if for someone that he revered or loved. This gave everything he did a pure religious intensity and tone. This final thoroughness, the demanding preparation claimed his attention so much, kept him so busy, that he didn't manage to put the cup of tea on the table. He used up all his strength in the preparation."

Dora filled several pages describing Kafka's preparations and similar themes in his writings before throwing her hands up in frustration: "I have already recognized that I cannot cope, I cannot come to terms with my battered thoughts. The time is too short, the breath is too shallow, the hand can only grab a pitifully poor little bit—a heap of crippled, wriggling, squeaking dwarfs." She stopped, realizing that Franz had said "just that, or nearly that" in one of his diaries.

Two volumes of Kafka's diaries, edited by Brod, had been recently published by Schocken Books. She received complimentary copies, which she mined for new understandings of Kafka. The diaries had been written long before he met her, but Dora found items that she thought applied to her. One that made her laugh had been written on October 9, 1911: "Should I reach my fortieth year, I will probably marry an old maid with protruding upper teeth slightly bared by the upper lip." Dora jotted down the coincidences: In addition to the fact that Kafka was just forty when they met, Dora noted, "I have a short upper lip which slightly exposes the upper teeth."

Through his diaries, Dora learned more about Kafka that substantiated her instinctive knowledge of him. She gained new insights through reading his innermost thoughts about his friends, many of whom she had known. For example, she better understood the scene she had witnessed between Kafka and Franz Werfel in Berlin in 1923. When Kafka was twenty-eight, he had written in his journal, "I hate Werfel, not because I envy him, but I envy him too. He is healthy, young and rich, everything that I am not. Besides, gifted with a sense of music, he has done very good work early and easily, he has the happiest life behind him and before him, I work with weights I cannot get rid of, and I am entirely shut off from music."

Dora copied Kafka's diary entries, originally written in his exercise books, into her own, with the reference dates and page numbers. In one entry, she says she has found "one passage among many that offers the key," to all who were fascinated by the question of Kafka's difficulty with women, or as Dora put it, "the supposed impotence."

Many people asked Dora about Kafka's sexuality, but she never discussed her sex life with Kafka. Even when she addressed the question in her journal, she was gracious but not very clear. One had to search deeply for the answer. "Since I will hardly ever say more about this, for those who often tried to question me (I never took offense at them) about this problem, I would like to point out this and countless similar passages." The passages she referred to came from Kafka's diary entry from October 3, 1911. "'A Hunger Artist' is also a help," she hinted, obliquely, "but not as revealing." Kafka was "sensuous like an animal—or like a child. Wherever does the assumption of Franz as an acetic come from?" Dora asked.

Often questioned by what she called the "searching psychoanalysts," Dora allowed that "some are to be taken very seriously, and have probably come very close. Their efforts remind me of the game, Cold—Warm—Hot. They were like an intelligent child, who through clever and proficient questioning and a lively imagination gets to warm, and even hot, in a flash, but who fails all the same, because the answer was hidden even more cleverly by the 'hider,' who had hidden it. . . . When I saw such truly serious people in these efforts, I was sometimes tempted to give them a little punch in the right direction. . . . But even if I did give them a little kick, out of sport, it would hardly be of any use. What they are looking for is in a region beyond their reach. They could perhaps just guess it, if they could move the analytical way of thinking out of the way and start searching *only* intuitively."

Even as Dora wrote her journal, she railed at the impossibility of her task. At moments, she felt "totally at home, walking on firm ground, surrounded by forces from on high. Even if I distort it, Franz will smile about it, mischievously amused. . . . So once again, there is no completion. What we perceive is a way, a becoming, a flow, movement. . . . Others have probably said that before me, dealt with it—I have just experienced it. So is Kafka's life, so his attempt to write. Franz is the substance we call life (stream of life, of being?). . . ."

Dora wrote primarily in German but switched to English, Yiddish or Hebrew when necessary to convey a certain mood or idea. It was a stream-of-consciousness method, except that she constantly second-guessed herself, crossing out not only words but also whole lines. She despaired over her inability to write down in words the thoughts and ideas she wanted to convey. "I want to say something essential here, or experience it. Must therefore definitely be on my guard. . . ."

Dora allowed her thoughts to flow from her pen without form or order, making up a word when she couldn't find just the right one in any of the languages available to her. At one point she mentioned the relationship between Kafka's sense of humor and that of the Chinese: they shared the same "dreamy, blossom seed-tiny precision." But then her fears rose up: "Have an unpleasant feeling that I am mimicking Tolstoy here. Well, I don't care about Tolstoy, I care about myself. Essential things cannot be achieved in such easy, dishonest ways." After pondering the problem, she decided that there was no other, more simple way to say what she had to say. She wasn't imitating Tolstoy or Kafka, for that matter:

With Franz, there is absolutely no imitation. If there is imitation it is possibly with my daughter, when she copies me. Absolutely no anxiety about that at all. (Just now I made, to myself, a face that Franz used to make when he was absolutely sure about something, even if all appearances seemed against it.) Radiant triumph, sparks flashing from the eyes, the mouth firmly closed, the hint of a smile playing on it, but held back, though with difficulty (because it would so dearly like to come out.) A thousand dancing devils in his eyes. To have seen that in all its earthly

and heavenly glory, one can die happy. I swear it by my love for Franz—
a million times greater than I am in my entirety—which is just as great
and incomprehensible as Franz, by this my love I swear that I mean
what I just said, each and every word. . . .

Dora now better understood Kafka's desire to burn his work. She filled
the next page with a promise and a disclaimer: "At this point, it's time to
say that my future notes on Franz will be better than what I've written so
far." Her scribblings were a long way from what she wanted to say, but
this, too, she shared with Kafka: "They bear about the same relationship
to what *I* have in mind, as Franz's writings to what *he* had in mind." Unlike Kafka, however, who wanted to destroy the evidence of his failings,
Dora would let them stand as is, partially in case something happened and
she was "unable for some reason to be able carry on with them."

"All exaggerations occurring in this exercise book are, in my point of
view, genuine. I will let them remain, in case I can't find a better way to say
what I want to say—but in no case do I wish what I've written be made
public in its current form. Max can read it, because he alone knows how
hard it is to find the perfect word, phrase or idea, completely adequate in
substance and style, to get the message of Franz over. . . ."

"Who is to gain from this writing! At best myself alone, in case I should
want to write again, and destroy the things already written again. But this
could repeat itself indefinitely. Every time I write something down, after a
few days, it is ridiculous and superficial, since by the act of writing it down,
and by thinking about it for several days, it becomes closer and clearer. I
would be thoroughly ashamed, if anyone saw it in this reduced state."

Dora noted that her attempts to write about Kafka were not complete
failures. "With each new attempt I found out, at any rate, how far the earlier attempts were wrong or not sufficient. Also concerning honesty, and
the courage to be honest, they are a help to me. Therefore, I don't consider them worthless. Even if I should not progress at all, they point to
something. . . ."

EASTERN LONDON, MID-MARCH, 1951

"Marianne is very ill," Dora wrote in her journal. "Must be operated on,
but must wait until a bed is available at the Hospital. I can do nothing because I am seriously ill in Hospital. Marianne is now helplessly alone at

home. It is winter. She cannot manage to drag coal up two floors, so she is in the cold. And she had just started to get better from her long-standing kidney trouble." Dora's friends, including Mrs. Steiner, Hanny and Ottilie, were checking in on her, but Dora still felt terrible at the thought of her little "Mariannchen," alone at night in the cold and the dark.

The day before Easter, Dora wrote in a letter to Hanny, "I spent the whole day, with great sadness, looking out the window, thinking about the poor people, millions, on the highways, in the villages, at the seaside." After such a bitter winter, the people were "starved for a ray of sunshine," and she thought it a terrible shame that their spring holiday was ruined in the never-ending "wind and rain and darkness."

Dora thought of others to avoid worrying about Marianne. There was an abscess in her neck, a further complication of the scarlet fever that required an operation and then radiation treatments, too. The immediate crisis had passed but had further damaged Dora's health and well-being. After several days, Marianne was admitted to the hospital, but for days Dora could get no news of her. When Dora learned that the staff had blundered and sent Marianne to the wrong hospital, her maternal instincts exploded in a total disregard for her own health. She sat up writing angry letters to Marianne's doctors and the kidney specialist—now Dora's doctor, too—demanding help for her daughter. Marianne was back in Queen Mary's Hospital, where she should have been all along, and Dora was receiving almost daily reports from her, as well as from her doctors and nurses.

On Easter morning, the clouds lifted. The day looked a bit more promising, and Dora made a concerted effort to cheer herself up by writing to Hanny. Because of the holiday, the ward had been awakened early. "Everyone had to be ready, washed and polished and pottied, beds made," Dora wrote, for a Communion service held at seven. By eight, Dora had been up for hours and was "quite ready for the Easter Parade." Next to Kafka's photograph on Dora's bedstand, the flowers Hanny had sent to her still stood, "though each day fewer. Now there are still six. I bathe them twice each day from top to toe, and cut them and encourage them."

Dora thanked Hanny for dealing with problems at the flat but insisted she stop. Dora's house had just been renovated and was full of painter's rubbish. Before she could rent out the room again, she said, "all the heavy cases would have to be schlepped from one room to the other." Dora was upset just thinking about Hanny doing it. "A little half-pint like you? You of all people . . . the thought that you would use the little time you can devote to your singing for things of very much less importance is really worrying." Dora was deeply grateful, however, for Hanny's "true act of friendship" in making inquiries on Dora's behalf about Marianne. "You see, that is something I would never refuse."

PLAISTOW HOSPITAL, APRIL 1951

On April 9, Dora was upbeat and cheerful. Marianne had survived the operation and was recuperating at Mrs. Steiner's house. Marianne had come to visit her in the hospital, and later that day Dora wrote a letter to "Hannichen." "In no way does she give the impression of being ill and I am much relieved," Dora said. "But the swelling in her neck is still there. She is being treated with radiation. Apparently it's working, and the swelling is receding."

Dora had improved to the point where she was allowed to sit up in a chair for an hour at a time. From her hospital bed, where she spent most of the day, she handled her correspondence and received visits from concerned friends, including Stencl, Hanny and her son David, Ottilie and her two little girls, the Steiners, the Leftwichs and others she knew less well, including Hanny's cousin, Gustav Metzger, an internationally recognized artist who remembered seeing Kafka's framed photograph on Dora's hospital bed stand. Until then, he had no idea of Dora's relationship to the famous writer. Mrs. Steiner sent Dora matzos and shampoo, along with a friendly letter on April 10. If Dora needed anything else, she wrote, please let her know.

Dora missed the annual meeting of the Friends of Yiddish. She was very sad; she had something important she wanted to say while she still could. She wrote a letter addressed to the secretary of the Friends of Yiddish, which was published in the April issue of *Loshn un Lebn*. The letter was a tribute to Stencl, something Dora wanted placed in the record about the extraordinary man who had been her friend for many years. She began by saying how much it hurt to miss the annual meeting and sent her greetings to the leaders of the circle, especially Stencl, its "spiritual leader," who had provided the impetus for the preservation of Yiddish. "It is thanks to Stencl's zealous faith that our enterprise continues to exist," she said. She admitted that doubts crossed her mind, but she always found herself running back to the meetings, anxious to arrive on time, to put her "trembling hand around the small flickering flame of faith in the cause which has been abandoned in the open desert winds." What Stencl was doing to keep Yiddish alive, Dora declared, was "a *mitzvah* for those in London, in Europe, and for all the Jewish people."

On April 10, Ester Hoffe wrote a second letter to Dora on Max's behalf. Dora's doctor had written to Brod, and Ester said the news had given them a "fright" and how "sweet and touching" it was that Mrs. Steiner was looking after Marianne "so lovingly." Mrs. Steiner had also written to them earlier about Marianne, describing her as "intelligent and original." Ester mentioned that Kafka's diaries, which had been edited by Max, were being published in Germany. At the end of Ester's typed letter, Max added a handwritten note: "I'm very happy that you're writing down your memories of Franz! When a part is finished I'd like to read it. Just now I've placed Janouch's memories with S. Fischer in German and in French with Calman-Levy in Paris."

With this encouragement from Max, Dora continued to pour her thoughts into her journal. When she opened the exercise book, she opened herself up at the same time. She approached the writing with excitement and enthusiasm. She would start out with an idea feverishly beating in her heart, which she always felt while thinking and dreaming of Franz, but the feeling evaporated once she tried to write it. After only a sentence or two, sometimes only a word, her excitement and certainty abandoned her. "It is much easier in letters," she lamented. "But this 'getting it down on paper' brings me close to despair. There is nothing to help me. How easily a pair of ears or eyes would extract it all from me." Instead of an eager audience urging her on when she spoke about Kafka, or the eyes she imagined hovering as she wrote her letters to Max, beneath the pages of her exercise book was only another page, "just as helpless and soundless." Dora forced herself to continue, to fill the pages. She crossed out words and added new ones.

The perfect honesty accompanies you, voluntarily, only for a short way, then you have to force it, and if even this doesn't help, one leaves it behind and carries on, utterly poor, instead of put up with it . . . only because one believes one must finish something, bring it to a conclusion. How much we have achieved gets lost in this way. Oh, Franz knew all about that! If not, why did he write only fragments? He set off with so much hope, so protected and secure, so safe—and then, all of sudden, everything became dark, abandoned. But he couldn't stop, he couldn't give up. He always had to try again. Because it was there! It was there in abundance. After all, one had so often truly experienced it, how could one now give in? One must try again—perhaps this time prepare oneself longer, discard more, perhaps primarily—no not primarily, this time exclusively—concentrate, and perhaps one will, in the end, get a step closer. And for each further step it was worthwhile. . . . He never gave up. He died from exhaustion.

In her deeply personal exploration of Kafka's significance to the world, Dora often waded into unknown, dangerous territory. She often got lost and had to abandon that particular approach. "One human being alone can not explain Franz," she concluded.

She had to be careful. "Sometimes, when I think of an occurrence or incident with Franz, I slip into fantasizing, which becomes just as real and intensive as the occurrence itself. And just as gratifying. . . . My fantasies and dreams are a clear, logical, organic development, a continuation of the experience. A living-on of the events. A continuing flow of the wave. Perhaps it would be better if I wrote a book . . . then I would not be bound to factual truth."

At times she felt guided—"taken by the hand by Franz"—when she got close to what was essential. At those times, she felt as if she walked, following him "on clean paths, which he had cleansed with his blood." This feeling she had now, "this being-taken-by-the-hand by Franz," was what he had longed for. "All his life he waited for this miracle." At the same time, she realized that "it would never even have occurred to him to take others by the hand . . . to act the redeemer." Based on that, Dora asked herself: "Do I believe that he got further than Jesus? Actually, I do believe that."

Dora knew precisely how horrified Franz would be by her words. "If such a thought ever found its way to Franz, it would be driven off with the most furious self-ridicule, or he would note in his diary that his insufficiencies, lurking in the background, have now really gone too far. . . ." Dora continued to follow his likely train of thought to its logical conclusion: his inevitable destruction. "In little things, I knew Franz as well as one can know anything outside one's own body," Dora wrote. "Like one's own child? More? Certainly not less."

Kafka had "a mandate," Dora said. "He knew if he couldn't fulfill it, no one could." In one moment, he was the "rushing, ardent, radiant messenger, filled to the brim with faith and hope, with strong arms, entirely conscious of his power, scattering obstacles." But as each new obstacle was cleared, new, more fearsome obstacles, previously unseen, reared up, ad infinitum, "so never, never will he overcome them."

As Dora thought about Kafka's mandate, she thought she better understood Jesus' mandate as it was revealed to him: "I am the life." Dora had "never come so close to these things" before, and she knew she was in dangerously deep waters: "I know so little about swimming and I dare to swim so far out." Nevertheless, she continued on to define the points she wanted to make about Kafka's mandate and its beneficial influence on others, especially on her. "It is like this," she said:

I. Whoever knew Franz, could do nothing else but strive for order. This, and the example of Franz's life, made it easier to do and say things in the best form possible, and in fact, for no other reason that this (now higher) form, now available to them, had already become their own. And so, one advanced from step to step, the longer and better one knew him.

II. Franz understood best how to say or do things. From this it follows, that what is done or said best, is actually part of Franz. (How much better Max could say that, instead of me here digging with a toothpick.)

Halfway through the journal, on page 19, Dora noted that "the writings in this exercise book have degenerated into diary. I will not fight it because this is the first that I ever wrote and it may also well be the only that I ever will write. So I will let it live. I won't suppress it. I am curious what will come out of it."

Dora's journal recorded her many painful attempts to explain something for which there was no adequate language. Yet it wasn't language itself that was at fault, she admitted, but her proficiency in any one language. "How sad it is," Dora said, "that I am so little at home in the German language. And since English is not my language, I am sentenced to eternal homelessness in this most important matter. My mother tongue, Yiddish, I left in the years decisive for an honest development. Now the gap is too great to be able to build a passable bridge back. Although it helps me, like a mother, in moments of need, it fails me in most things and I have to reach for the more helpful replacement, German."

Dora realized that she was not alone with this problem. "Even Franz, whose span stretches for generations, maybe even epochs (I do not grant Franz less space than Christ), even he complained about shortcoming and inadequacies in the language, which hindered him expressing matters fully. . . . Has anyone ever been able to say all that can be said in one language?" She thought of James Joyce. "He certainly knew what he was talking about when he refused to restrict himself exclusively to one language. He knew what was at stake."

"In the bed directly opposite me, a woman lies dying," Dora wrote in her journal. "An older woman. She's whimpering incessantly, trying to say something. The nurses are trying to understand what she says. Earlier on she cried. She lay quite still, and the tears flowed from her closed eyes down her face. A beautiful woman, fairly plump, cheeks a little pink, maybe she has a fever. What does she think? Does she know she is dying? She seems to be conscious. Then she certainly knows it. It is simply something one cannot overlook. I was not as far gone a few weeks ago, but still I knew exactly how things looked for me. What are her thoughts? What demands confront her? Exhortations? Calls? She is an Englishwoman, so at least she's dying in her homeland." Dora switched to Hebrew. "What is her punishment after death? Will they ask her, too, 'What is your name?'" (At birth, Jewish children are given a Hebrew name, a holy name, by which their spiritual acts are known.) "Will she, too have no answer?" Dora wondered. "Which unfinished tasks torture her now?"

Dora's reverie was interrupted when the doctor and nurse came in to examine the old lady, and her bed was screened off. "I think it is the end over there," Dora wrote. "It is difficult to think about anything else. Now and then one hears laughter from the other end of the ward. On the whole most are quiet, not depressed, although though they too think of nothing else, it seems."

As Dora and the others watched in silence, the whole ward was screened off, from one end to the other, including the entrance. "What happens now?" Dora wondered. All those on the other side of the room were moved to her side. "A woman next to me is crying very quietly. Men arrive, one sees them through the screen. Are they relatives? A husband? Sons?" Dora wrote. "All that is unimportant. What matters is the old lady and the secret over there. Now the screens are being removed, one after the other, only one, around her bed is left, close to the bed, not, as usual, with space left for the nurse or doctor. Now no one will come near the bed. They have carried her away. The screen remains standing around the empty bed."

It was the first death in the six weeks Dora had been in the hospital. Amazingly, considering the violent times she had lived through, Dora added, "And it was the first death of another person that I have ever witnessed." In parenthesis, she explained: "The death of Franz was my own experience of death."

Dora did not write again for several weeks. In mid-April, she suffered a serious setback. Overactivity and the shock of Marianne's illness were blamed, and Dora was ordered to lie flat on her back, not moving, for several weeks. When she was finally allowed to sit up again, she wrote her first letter to Marthe Robert, who had proposed coming to London to talk further with Dora about Kafka.

Marthe Robert's letter to Dora has been lost, but Dora's response, written on May 12, 1951, gives definite clues to its content. Dora's letter is one of fourteen letters she wrote to Marthe over the next twelve months. Dora's correspondence with Marthe Robert was uncovered in Paris in 2000 and is published here for the first time.

"What a lovely idea, to write me such a letter," Dora began. "It has made me feel all warm inside. Actually I shouldn't be answering it yet, but rather allow it to warm me some more." Dora encouraged Marthe to come to London and offered the hospitality of her own flat. "I know it's very hard now for visitors to find accommodation in London, and I have a spacious apartment and am always able to lodge a guest comfortably." Dora didn't mention that she would lose money by not renting the room out during Marthe's stay.

"About the way I see you—how could one see you other than the way you are. It's not chance that you love Kafka. It's not chance that you translate Kafka. Maybe it isn't even chance that we met." She added, in parenthesis, "Although generally I dislike these facile mystical maneuvers which so willingly present themselves." Since she had asked, Dora shared what she had jotted down about the Frenchwoman: "Marthe talks in a bright, open language, quite uninhibited, like I do in the safety of thinking. I never speak of Franz like this. I don't dare, there is no one to whom one can speak like this. I admire her courage and nonchalance. I don't even dare to listen seriously when somebody talks like this (with very big words and religious allusions). I even laugh about it sometimes, to show that I don't believe in such a thing. . . ."

Dora could barely finish the letter, since her arms were weak from not moving for so long. "The bloodless and muscle-less look of my writing makes me angry," she wrote. "I can hardly believe that a person can sink so low, become so destitute, that one is grateful to be able—once again— to slowly crawl along with the fountain pen for two and one half pages. If I could ask you a favor," Dora concluded, "it would be to accept all this as calmly as I do. I was very upset only in the first weeks. Then I had done nothing for my daughter and hadn't written about Franz. Now I have made it up somewhat to the two of them. Can therefore afford to indulge my fatigue, having thus obtained a degree of freedom."

23

"MACH WAS DU KANNST"

Beyond a certain point, there is no return. This
point has to be reached.
—Franz Kafka, *Blue Octavo Notebooks*

LONDON, JULY 1951

Dora was upset and annoyed. When the doctor learned that Dora's sister-in-law from America, Ruth Lask Friedlaender, was coming to London for a visit, he suddenly became "pig-headed" and refused to discharge Dora until he had spoken to Ruth. He wanted to make sure that Ruth, as Dora's houseguest, understood the seriousness of Dora's condition and the severe limitations on her activities. Now, Dora complained, there was no one to meet Ruth at the station, no one to welcome her at home. Just thinking about the "complete fiasco" Dora said, "one can get sick." Ruth's trip had been planned and the crossing booked long before anyone had any idea that Dora would still be in the hospital in July. Then, after months of good health, Marianne had gotten sick and was back in the hospital, too. Dora couldn't bear the thought of her dear sister-in-law, whom she had not seen for twelve years, traveling halfway around the world and arriving to an empty house. She was forced to ask for help.

"Hannychen," Dora began, in a letter to Hanny on Monday, July 2, "here I present you with a piece of wisdom. If one day somebody plants himself in front of you and, with a broad entreating gesture, puts the palm of his hand on the right side of his heart and says, with great pathos, 'No, I cannot accept that, it is too much! This one cannot expect from anybody, etc., etc., etc.'—there's only one thing to do, Hanny: *nemen di fiess off di plezyes* [take the feet off the ground] and run! Run, Hanny, run as fast as you can, without looking back, as if the fire of an English June sun were behind you."

After a few more warning paragraphs hinting at the climax ("does the heart suspect something?"), Dora finally "got down on her knees" to beg Hanny to "succumb to this sacrifice." The favor Dora needed was for Hanny to meet Ruth at the station, take her to the flat, spend an hour or two to get her settled, and give her directions to the hospital. Dora provided all the necessary details: Ruth's full name, a small photo of her, and a description: "Small, about my height, a tiny bit taller, thinner than I, but a little broader, very simply and conventionally dressed. No high heels. She will have a few suitcases. The ship on which she sails is the 'Niew Amsterdam' (Holland-America Line) which left New York on June 29, and arrives according to schedule on the 6th of July in Southhampton." Dora told her that the boat trains from America arrived at Waterloo Station at midday.

Dora included a second letter in the same envelope, this one written in English, to Hanny's son, David. Taking her lead from the letters that Kafka wrote to the little girl in Berlin, Dora composed a special letter to seven-year-old "Davy" with a true story about a little six-year-old girl on her ward.

"I suppose," Dora began her tale,

as a man of the world, you'll know a thing or two of a young lady's ways and habits, and I don't think, I can tell you much about it. But still, maybe there is one thing or another you didn't come across. And I'm sure, a little girl in hospital, is not a thing you just bump into everyday. So here goes: Entrance: Brenda: A wild, screaming bundle of goods, kicking, scratching, tearing-to-bits pajamas. Just plain cuckoo! The work in the ward stops abruptly. All available hands rush to save the life of the nurse holding this mad piece of arms and legs (you couldn't say which was which). This performance lasted for about ten minutes, when the tempest started subsiding, gradually, into regulated sobs and occasional sniffs, and then it was quiet again on the Eastern Front. Every peace-loving citizen could take up again her useful work, as there is: coughing, sneezing, moaning, grumbling, and looking holes in the air. And being so deeply absorbed once again in their daily tasks, they were suddenly startled by a peal of laughter, giggling, gurgling noises, emerging from that Far Eastern corner. Every one sits up with a jerk, or jumps to her feet (if she could). Great bewildered confusion: What's happened? Good Lord, what's come over her now? What do we see? It cannot be! Where is the downpour of tears? The wild despair and agony, where? Gone, gone with the wind! A cheerful little cherub instead, beaming at the world, a huge warming grin covering the face from one ear to the other. . . . All bright sunshine, not a trace of a clouds. . . . Her command over her watering system is really something to marvel at. She can turn on her water taps before you can say 'cuckoo' and turn them off again, tucking them away safely for the next occasion. That occasion presents itself every third day, when her arm is being pricked, and some blood taken. The screams lift the ceiling, the tears flood the ward, and the nurses have to put on armor. I asked her one day, whether it really hurts so much, when the blood is being taken.

'No, not really.'

'So why all the hullabaloo each time, as if you were being done in?'

'Oh that. It's because I want them to think it hurts, so they make a fuss of me. If I don't cry or scream, they'll think, it doesn't hurt and won't say nothing, and won't make a fuss of me. And I like to be made a fuss of. I like to make them believe things that ain't true, and if I know they ain't, it's great fun.'

"So," Dora concluded, "that's Brenda Brian of 90, Cuckoo Mansions, Riddle Road, born—I suppose—on February 30 (remember? Cuckoo Mansions, where all the inhabitants are all born on the last days of February.)"

After four months in Plaistow hospital, Dora was finally allowed to go home. Although she had to stay in bed, she was, to a very limited degree, able to play the hostess for the remainder of Ruth Friedlaender's visit. Marianne also recovered and came home. Their reunion was warm and wonderful. Marianne was so happy to see her Aunt Ruth, whom she remembered clearly. It gave her a feeling of family that she missed.

Ruth had not heard from her family in Russia and had no idea if any of them were still alive. Ruth and her husband now lived in San Mateo, California, in a big house with fruit trees in the yard. She encouraged Marianne to come to California to visit them. Marianne, who had never before considered such an idea, began to dream of going to America. She wanted to see for herself the vast and immense landscape of the American West.

Dora and Marianne still needed medical treatments. Since they shared the same doctor, every other Monday an ambulance came to take both of them to the hospital for treatment. Marianne continued to improve, and the doctors cautiously stated that she might be finally getting well. Dora's health held steady throughout the rest of the summer and the fall. Dora continued work on her Kafka diary but was feeling no closer to what she wanted to say.

In her last letter to Ester, Dora said she was very much in doubt if she wanted anyone to read her Kafka diary during her lifetime. There were many reasons, she said, "not least for the reason that I would not feel myself free. And if one is not free, one cannot be true either, and that is the first and last commandment in all things connected with Franz."

Marthe Robert had written from Paris about wanting to translate Kafka's diaries into French. She had not been able to interest a publisher but wanted to undertake the project anyway. Dora agreed that Marthe should do it. In fact she had an idea, probably "very silly and impractical," Dora said to Marthe in a letter written that summer, "but I believe deeply in its possibility. I even have grand visions. I suggest we look for the means to publish the diaries at our own expense. I'll be able to contribute some money. All the money I receive from the royalties from now on will be used to this end. As you know, I didn't want to accept it anymore. But for this purpose, I will. We could publish the diaries together with a portion of my book. Otherwise, I won't publish any of it while I am still alive. We could both use this opportunity to say once what is necessary to say in connection with Kafka. Everything. Without reservation. I have no doubt that it is right to do it this way. I see Ottla in front of me, her eyes wickedly flashing, as she gives us a keen nod of approval. It would be difficult to ask Franz, unpredictable how he would answer. . . ." Dora ended her letter to Marthe, her "dear, very dear girl," on an optimistic note: "Healthwise, I'm better. I think I'll get over it!"

On August 25, Dora wrote again, eagerly looking forward to Marthe's upcoming visit to London. "I am now significantly better," Dora announced. "Coming home was unimaginably good for me." The guest room for Marthe, she said, was being prepared at that very moment by two friends. Dora's excitement was palpable. She added three postscripts containing motherly instructions on not overtipping the taxi and the exact address to give the driver. Dora asked her to call from the station when she arrived. "But only if it isn't inconvenient for you—but what am I saying? Of course it's inconvenient! What with the luggage, the porters, with the buzz of the train or airplane in your ears. So, no phone call."

A few days later, Dora jotted off another quick letter to Marthe. "This is not a letter, just a key," Dora wrote. It was possible that Marthe might arrive on the day Dora was scheduled to go to the hospital for treatment, and Dora didn't want her to be locked out.

The details of Marthe's visits to Dora and the growing friendship between them is best told through Dora's following letters to Marthe, reprinted here with the kind permission of Marthe Robert's widower, Dr.

Michel de M'UZAN, who accompanied his wife on her visits to Dora in London.

59, Broadhurst Gardens
N.W.6
28 September

Dear Marthe, —Well, now you're gone, and that's a fact. But not as much as you think.

Almost every day traces turn up: Making my bed, I found two hairpins in it; today I found your watch, which had stopped at four o'clock (like the clock on the town hall spire in Prague, according to Brod); the Kafka volume; the burnt pot will remain as an eternal keepsake. . . . I'll keep it for January when I will see you again.

The parcel with the handful of things will go off tomorrow. That involved a dilemma: I wanted to have the cleaning lady wash the pajamas, then I noticed they were men's pajamas. And what audacious ideas that might give her—I don't even dare to think about it, so I'll send them to you unwashed. Other than that I have no worries. Only whether you arrived well and if everything worked out. I would have very much liked to observe your triumphal procession back to France, being welcomed and surrounded by your loyal subjects. Have you already received the Iron Cross? Actually you should have gotten it here. But they didn't foresee that you don't have one yet, they believed that you were an old battle-tried war veteran covered in decorations. But there people know of your first great, heroic deeds. So tell me about it, please. My admiration follows you like a shadow.

And now I greet you most very warmly, dear girl. . . . I thank you with all my heart for every single one of the eleven wonderful days.

Yours, Dora

9 October 1951

But Marthe! It seems to me that I have more reason to take the French Post Office to court for conspiracy against me. You had no letter from me? Two letters, Marthe, two long letters have I written to you . . . and the parcel I sent off about eleven or twelve days

ago. It worries me that you didn't have it by the date of your letter.
I received all your letters and you will, if you please, apologize to
my British Post Office. It is the most reliable Post Office in the
world.—I say, these foreigners!

I'm getting all dizzy from your breakneck successes and
prospects with the translations, am almost afraid to talk about it.
I'm waiting for the first decisive word. As soon as you have it,
please, don't let me wait a minute. If this herd would only grasp
what it would mean for you the make the translations, they would
fall on their knees before you and beg you to do it. It takes one's
breath away to comprehend this madness.

I'm sort of okay. The doctor seemed satisfied. But he won't let
me get up, and that's very inconsiderate of him, because I cannot
not get up. And you are naïve, too. How can I be in bed without
getting up if I'm alone twenty-two hours out of twenty-four? Of
course I restrict this to an absolute minimum, and I can't imagine
that the damage this might do isn't more than compensated by the
freedom, the comfort of being at home, and the much more precise adherence to the diet than in the hospital. So you shouldn't
worry needlessly.

Now I'm keen to hear whether and when this letter reaches
you.

Again, warmly, Dora

Marianne was released from the hospital again at the beginning of November, and now helped take care of Dora. At the beginning of December,
Dora wrote to Marthe, apologizing. "If I'm not ashamed before anybody
about myself, I am before you. But how serious it really is one can only
judge by the fact that even shame can't do anything about it." Until now,
Dora had not written to thank Marthe for the food parcels she had sent
several weeks earlier. "My gratitude knows no bounds. But please," Dora
begged, "don't do it again."

On the last Friday of December 1951, S. Fischer Verlag in Frankfurt
sent Dora a complimentary copy of Gustav Janouch's *Conversations with
Kafka*. One year had passed since Max had first read it aloud to her in his
office in Tel Aviv. Reading Janouch's book made Dora's Kafka memories
come alive again. "I got so excited, remembering the pleasure that he experienced," she wrote to Marthe. "How happy it makes me to think about
it. You have no idea how he could relish and enjoy life. Just as deeply as

suffering. Not an iota less! Oh dear Heaven, how I love this man. I can be completely happy with the slightest memory of that which I know brought him happiness. I collect these sparks like a treasure, and protect them, and am grateful."

The day after receiving Janouch's book, Dora wrote to Marthe to see if she had received a copy, too. "If you haven't yet received it, I will send you mine," Dora said. "You, above all, have to read it."

Dora asked what was happening with the translation of Kafka's diaries. Schocken Books, who owned the copyright to Kafka's works, was withholding the necessary permission. At Dora's urging, Brod had written to Schocken with his "urgent recommendation" on Marthe's behalf. Had Max been able to help, she wondered. "Well, it doesn't depend on him," Dora said. "On whom does it depend? Does anyone in the world know this with certainty?"

Dora mentioned that Miron Grindea had come to see her. Grindea was the cofounder, along with artist Henry Moore and poet Stephen Spender, of the International Arts Guild, which organized prestigious events, lectures, concerts, recitals and exhibitions. He also edited *ADAM,* an established international literary and art review published in London. Grindea was on his way to Israel, and Dora gave him a letter of introduction to Max Brod, whom he wanted to meet. Grindea suggested that the guild invite Max Brod to England to speak about Kafka. "I am in favor of this with heart and soul," Dora told Marthe, suggesting that an invitation to France should also be forthcoming. "I think this is the least that Europe owes him. He deserves its gratitude."

LONDON, JANUARY 1952

Something strange had happened. The news from Ester Hoffe about the publication of Kafka's diaries in Germany had shaken her, but not as much as she had imagined. Since receiving the books from the German publishers—Kafka's diaries and the book by Janouch—Dora "could not suppress the feeling of joy." Seeing Kafka's works printed, and reprinted, in German, the last vestiges of Dora's reluctance to see his work published disappeared:

> It now seems to me that all the time I really hoped that Franz would be published in Germany. This is a dreadful thing, the further I explore it.

I am of the firm belief that Germany can save itself through Franz. As the world once saved itself in monotheism. I am afraid I think that this is Franz's "mandate." I do not doubt that in the whole world nobody listens to Franz the same way as in Germany. All the storms around Franz will be like a small, gentle breath of wind compared to what will happen in Germany. It is the only soil ripe for this seed. . . . Germany was accorded the sad fact of being "the chosen" to prove with scientific thoroughness the horrors that which, although perhaps suspected, had not yet been proven. Thanks to their higher intelligence, they have fulfilled their task, leaving no doubt. . . . Does this seem grotesque? Seen superficially, probably, but not really. One can not see far enough to get an overall view. Franz probably could. For him, the connections were so close that he held them in the palm of his hand. He "saw" everything.

Dora had filled almost forty pages of the exercise book. She started over at the back of the book and began to write from the back to the front, in the Hebrew style. She quoted other writers on Kafka, including Pavel Eisner, Kafka's Czech translator, and the poet W. H. Auden, who had said that Kafka "bears the same relationship to our age, as Dante, Shakespeare and Goethe bore to theirs." She took issue with something Pavel had written about Kafka's "embodying the tragedy of the West European Jew." Dora did not think Kafka's isolation stemmed from his experience as a Prague Jew and an assimilated member of the Czech petite bourgeoisie. "Franz's isolation," Dora said, "began with himself."

After many years of denying the importance of Kafka's literary contributions to the world, Dora had finally come to realize that Kafka's mandate overcame any of her own personal, private objections to sharing her deepest knowledge and understanding of him. In her journal, she developed her own theories on the nature of his writing. Kafka seemed like a scientist in his writing, experimenting with man as an object of research. "He was (still?) at the stage of the dissections; cold, matter-of-fact, (writing with a sure hand at night in the dark). He trained himself on the human being. The writing itself was bringing the material, the point of view in order. Even then, the writing was still a work of dissection, therefore he could not leave it behind in that state. He did not manage to finish the research that might have taken him closer to resolving his task: to bring the world to purity. As a naked, torn body, spread out on the dissecting table with bulging entrails—that cannot be left behind as one's work. When one cannot get further, it's better never to let this unfinished work see daylight.

... The thought that this output will survive him is unbearable, for someone could actually believe and also announce—that to achieve 'this' was his 'mandate.'—Even worse: to believe and announce that in reality, this *is* the mandate. Cruel power of misunderstanding!"

59, Broadhurst Gardens, N.W. 6
Monday, January the 28, 1952

Dear Marthe,

Finally, Thank God! Poor you, what you had to go through. I shall write to Schocken, in order to speed up the signature thing. It's really time that you got some money. (But that I won't write.) —And you are coming! What else could one want? I've waited weeks for this news of your coming (hopefully, both of you.)

Marthe, for Gods' sake, send no more butter. I am not restored to health enough to open a butter shop. And what else I shall do with the heap of butter, I really don't know. I am only allowed a very little bit. I shall have to boil it up—otherwise it will get rancid. So please Marthe. —Of course I received your parcels. Wonderful. I stuffed myself with the pressed grapes and nuts. Many thanks, but please, no more. I am now really well supplied with food.

Listen, does your grey wool suit have short or long sleeves? I found a piece of cloth, could make you a second pair of sleeves, so that you'll have short sleeves for summer and long sleeves for winter. With my warmest regards,

Yours, Dora

PS. Oh, I forgot, about me: not much to report, fairly unchanged. My daughter is in hospital for the past four weeks, is (hopefully) coming home in two weeks. Did I forget anything else? Because of the butter-danger, I can't take time to think about it. The letter must be sent off today to prevent the disaster!

59 Broadhurst Gardens, NW 6
Maida Vale 1402
February 18, 1952

Dear Marthe,

That's grand! And to make it quite clear: you're staying with us. Our guest-room is ready for you and Michel. My daughter will be here, too, and I hope you'll be made more comfortable than your last visit.—

I am a bit better, too, and hope to make a better hostess.—

It's wonderful to think I'll be seeing you soon. Please don't bring any food, we've everything in plenty. All the best wishes for a good crossing,

Yours, with love, Dora

P.S.

When you ring our doorbell, please step back and lookup to our window to catch the key I'll throw down. I don't go down yet to open the door, and my daughter may just be out.—

Marianna would like very much to meet you at the station. So write, please, at what time you'll be arriving, and on what platform. She'll be wearing a navy coat and a red velvet cap.

LONDON, MARCH 1952

It was Dora's fifty-fourth birthday. It would be her last, and she knew it. She observed the day by writing her last will and testament. She produced two versions, one in German and another in Hebrew. Her last wish, she wrote, was to "be buried beside Kafka in Prague." She folded up the two pages and placed them in a small envelope, on which she wrote: "to be opened after my death." She composed a final, four-page letter to Max. On March 18, Max received the letter and the small envelope containing Dora's final wishes. According to the annotated list of Dora's missing letters to Brod, his records of correspondence indicate that he opened the small envelope that same day.

Marthe and Michel's second visit with Dora in March had gone very well. On March 25, Dora received another package from them with more food gifts. "It's your birthday," Dora wrote, "and I'm getting parcels. Please, Marthe, stop sending things. We're still drinking your coffee. Marianne, who loves you dearly, is very careful with it, so that she can keep on asking: 'From Marthe's coffee?'" Marianne prized the coffee that Marthe had brought with her as a gift and conserved it to such a point that Dora said, "she has grown used to weak coffee, which is much better for her." Dora admitted that she had been remiss in writing to Schocken. "I have a real fog, thick and impenetrable, in my head, from all the business stuff, and I don't think I'll finish the letter."

Dora's diary was also unfinished. Half the pages in the exercise book remained blank. She kept it close to her, behind the pillows on her bed, so she could pull it out at any time, whenever she had a thought worth jotting down. Sometimes she wrote only a line or two. On one page, Dora had written two unrelated sentences: "The writing, as it is now, is only a preparation for the 'mandate'—for the assumption of the mandate." Above that, Dora had written: "I am very grateful that I stayed alive."

Although bedridden, Dora still received occasional visits from those who wanted to question her on Kafka. One of the last of these inquisitors was Martin Walser, a twenty-five-year-old German writer who had written his dissertation on Kafka. Five years after his meeting with Dora, his first novel was published, and he later became one of Germany's foremost writers. In May 2002, Walser's seventh-fifth birthday was celebrated with a two-day international conference, sponsored by the Goethe Institute and German embassy, at the Institute for Germanic Studies in London.

Walser first came to England in 1952 to work on a joint project for the BBC and the Süddeutschen Rundfunk (Broadcasting Company of Southern Germany). Through his general manager, he met someone who knew Dora and recommended that they meet. Forty years passed before Walser was finally able to understand what he had missed: "There are few opportunities that I have wasted as completely as this one that afternoon, sitting in a chair next to the bed of the woman who lived with Kafka."

Walser learned about Dora through Brod's biography. He was captivated by two images of her, first, the description of her in the kitchen at the Baltic Sea as she scaled fish, and Kafka's first words to her: "Such tender hands and such bloody work." Equally unforgettable, he said, was Brod's portrayal of the drive from the sanatorium to Vienna, during which Dora was supposed to have "stood upright in front of Kafka during the whole journey in an open car, trying to protect him from rain and wind with her body."

Walser's description of their only meeting is haunting. "It was the darkest late afternoon in my life," he wrote. "In the staircase of the old apartment building there was a kind of night in comparison to which real night must be called day. I groped my way up along the banisters. Upstairs, a girl of thirteen, maybe sixteen, opened the door. She led me to Dora Diamant. . . . There was a minimal bedside lamp that wrested a little island of light from the room that appeared boundless in the darkness. Dora Diamant's hair, loose. Maybe just combed by her daughter, who led me to the bedside chair and then disappeared. Dora Diamant looked ill. But the real catastrophe for me was not her condition but my incompetence to do justice to this condition. As soon as I sat down, she reached under one of the many pillows, which she sat in front of, rather than lying on. She got out some kind of exercise book and started to read aloud from it. These were her records of Franz Kafka. But they were not about the Franz with whom I had occupied myself for the last six years, who had made me immune to nearly all other reading matter."

Walser was repulsed. "Her notes, which she penned after Kafka's death, didn't deal with *my* Kafka, but with hers. This was a founder of a religion who I didn't know and who I didn't want to get to know because of my literary narrow-mindedness. I was not capable of accepting this wholly religious experience of a woman coming from the Eastern Jewish tradition as the language of a Kafka experience. She spoke of Kafka as of a redeemer. The light in which someone appears to us always comes from ourselves. For me they excluded each other: religion and literature. Nevertheless, I should have heard the true origin of Dora Diamant's religious tone. But no, I felt repelled by this tone in which she religiously transfigured her Kafka. At least I should have remained curious. But no, I was the opposite: narrow-minded. Thus I ridiculously mucked up a unique opportunity. When I read the sentences of this woman in the edition of Kafka's letters, which so meticulously preserves Dora's involvement, I realized how close she was to Kafka, what a help she must have been to him. In this way I became once again aware of the extent of my previous failure. I let Dora Diamant sit in front of her pillows, and drove back from Chelsea to Piccadilly Circus and went to the theatre. Something with music.

"I only understood many years later what I had missed."

May 7, 1952

Dearest Marthe,
Your wonderfulness, Marthe: You apologize for not having written for such a long time. And it actually works. You almost manage to make me feel okay instead of having a bad conscience. Of course, your letters did arrive, as usual. They are always a dear event to us. My reluctance to write has no connection with them or with you.

The best (and most exciting) thing in your letter is the news about your coming. Would it be possible to let us know in advance? I rented out the small room. We needed the money. But I can have it back at any time for a short time, only I have to know well in advance. I am afraid that this news might put you off from coming or that you might perhaps stay somewhere else. That would be a great loss for us, and I want to have your reassurance that's not so. Let us know in time when you are coming and everything will be in order (or disorder).

Somehow I am sure that when you've finished the translation it will be published. The few French readers are really waiting for the diaries. They've come out in German and English, so why should they hesitate when they hold the translation in their hands?

All in all, it is a God-given miracle that the world appears as it does with all this going on. . . . It is no doubt under the protection of Providence, along with children and fools. . . . It is very likely the 'Indestructible something' which, each moment, pulls the world out of the mud, over and over again, and sustains it.

I feel fairly unchanged. Maybe a bit worse. I am very weak and I have many worries. I don't get around to writing. (That is probably a cause as well as the effect of the weakness). . . . I am sending you my best greetings, Michel as well.

Dora

[PS] Marianne conveys to you both the best greeting from her full loving heart. You can't imagine how much she likes the two of you. She'll write another time.

This was the last letter Dora wrote. Dora's last entry in her Kafka diary was the "God of Abraham" prayer, which she wrote out in Hebrew in its entirety. It was the prayer that Kafka had loved, which "he knew by heart, as a child knows the fairy tales which have been told to him countless times." Dora noted how every Saturday night, Kafka wanted to hear her recite the prayer. It had been a ritual between them. She remembered how he nodded his head in rhythm to the words: "God above us all: on you and on your grace do we all depend. . . . To you and to your grace do we all turn our hope. May the gates of Jerusalem soon and quickly stand open. Open shall they stand. Into it we shall go, into it we shall step. . . ."

PLAISTOW HOSPITAL, AUGUST 15, 1952

Dora was in a coma. Marianne rarely left her mother's side. She knew that comatose patients could still hear and smell and be aware of what was going on around them. She'd spent enough time in hospital to know about that. The doctors had recently pronounced Marianne cured from her kidney problems. She now had a future and decisions to make: she could get a job or perhaps go back to school. She had dreamed of working with books, perhaps becoming a librarian. For the past few weeks, the world had been wide open before her, but now it was collapsing.

"Unfortunately, I have to break some sad news. Last week, all of a sudden, Dora was taken seriously ill again," Marianne wrote a few days later to Dora's friend in Israel, David Maletz. When Hanny came to see her, Dora showed her tongue, which "was very dark, almost black," Hanny said. "It's not a good sign," Dora pointed out.

Mrs. Steiner also visited Dora during those last days. "We never spoke about her imminent death, but she knew and we knew that her end was near." When Mrs. Steiner arrived at Plaistow Hospital on the afternoon of Friday, August 15, she found Marianne sitting by her mother's bed. "Dora was in a coma, or heavily sedated, when suddenly she woke up," Mrs. Steiner remembered. "I said, 'Don't worry about Marianne, I'll look after her.' And Dora replied, '*Mach was du kannst.*' —Do what you can."

Those were Dora's last words. She fell back to sleep and Mrs. Steiner left soon afterward. At ten o'clock that night, with Marianne by her side, Dora released the ties that bound her to this world and passed into the next.

24

KAFKA'S DAUGHTER

*Man's embittered features are often only the pet-
rified bewilderment of a child.*
—Franz Kafka, in *Conversations with Kafka*

EAST HAM, LONDON, AUGUST 18, 1952

Dora was buried in the United Synagogue Cemetery on Marlowe Road in
East Ham on Monday, August 18. The cemetery stood in a vast treeless
field dotted with tombstones and granite monuments. Dora's grave was
some distance from the entrance in the far west corner, in the middle of
the fifteenth row of the XC section. Recent graves surrounded the gaping
hole in the rocky earth into which Dora's plain wooden casket would be
lowered, but no tombstones. In the Jewish tradition, one year must pass
before the memorial or tombstone is set.

"Dreadful storms threatened England that day," Marthe Robert said.
"Black silhouettes sank in puddles up to their ankles under icy cloud-
bursts. One could only move forward by pulling hard on each leg to tear
the feet away from the mud. The rain had only faces to batter in this treeless and naked field, nothing but faces already dripping wet, nothing but
this face, next to me, streaked with black from the dripping head-covering
made of newspaper, handed out at the cemetery door to serve as a hat."

"No writers or journalists attended her funeral," Marthe reported in an
article on Dora that was published in a French journal three months later.
"The news had not reached them; only those with whom Dora had
worked, played and sang were now crying openly under the rain in the big
East End Jewish cemetery." There was no better proof of Dora's importance, Marthe said, than the speed with which news of her death reached

the crowd now gathered at her funeral: "All those who knew her were aware of the importance of her presence, not only because of the great writer whose life she shared—for one brief year, or if one wishes, for almost thirty years. The figure of Dora does not come under literary history, not even for those who saw in her a reflection of Kafka's light. She spread her own light . . . she was still spreading it in the Jewish milieu of Whitechapel."

It seemed to Marthe that Dora "did not really live in London. With the most intense part of herself, the most inaccessible to change, she lived in Berlin in 1923, or rather . . . it lived within her. With all her energy, her love of life, her courage, and clarity, she lived in Whitechapel doing the only work she felt called to do: to save the Yiddish language from the death that threatened it."

Dora was buried in eastern London, Marthe said, "among 'her people' in the only place she can still call her own in this Europe, which she had tried to leave on two occasions and where, twice, she had been held back by death." Dora's hope of returning to Israel died long before she did. When she was diagnosed with nephritis, she quietly let go of her dream and never spoke about it again.

"Dora Dymant did not think she had to intervene in the debates that were opening up everywhere," Marthe said. "She would not, she could not expose new ideas; she paid attention to the discoveries of others. Where Kafka was concerned, she was full of curiosity, and resigned to hearing many errors. 'No matter,' she said. 'Franz has time.' Thus, she did not correct what she felt was wrong. She limited herself to tell facts with gestures, which created true details and unmasked the errors. Assuredly, the correctness of her tone came from Kafka. The influential position in her entourage came from her; she is the one who gave a strong basis to the generosity she gave to all things in life, which illness never diminished."

In her final analysis of Dora, Marthe concluded that "she was alone, in spite of all her activities, in spite of those around her. I can see what she gave to others; but what could one give to her? She had received the totality of what was hers twenty-five years earlier, and she needed all of her time to put order in this inheritance. She had just begun writing about Kafka when she became ill. Her notes represent a patient attempt to really understand what her great youth had allowed her to live in wonderment, without asking questions."

Max Brod never saw Dora's exercise book. After her mother's death, Marianne typed up a copy of the handwritten journal and gave both to

Marthe Robert, who quoted from it in her article, "The Unpublished Notes of Dora Dymant about Kafka." Marthe referred to Dora's unpublished journal as a *cahier*, the French word for exercise book, and translated selected passages into French for her article. "They offer little of a philosophical or religious nature," she asserted, "but one cannot ignore the effort they reveal nor the mark they carry."

In the summer of 2000, four years after Marthe's death, Michel de M'UZAN found Dora's *cahier* among his wife's private literary papers. One of France's leading psychoanalysts, Dr. M'UZAN, who made Dora's *cahier* and letters to Marthe available for this biography, had no idea why Marthe kept the *cahier*, why she chose not to send it to Max despite Dora's instructions written on its cover. Whatever the reason, Dora's diary remained in her personal files, forgotten and unread, for almost fifty years.

Six days after her mother's death, Marianne wrote to David Maletz at the En Charod kibbutz in Israel: "I am writing to you because I didn't want you to learn about it in a roundabout way. You know her from childhood, so I can understand how this will be for you. If you would like more details about her illness, then write to me please. Greetings, from Marianne Lask (Dora's daughter.)"

Dora's friends now rallied around Marianne. A collection was taken up for her and deposited in a bank account in her name. Everyone wanted to help her, to make her a part of their families. "Marianne stayed with us for a time," said Mrs. Steiner. "But eventually, she decided that she had to stand on her own feet, and she returned to her flat. My husband helped her with all the formalities. When we traveled with her on a bus, she was terrified because she thought there would be an accident. She had never before been to the Post Office, never to a restaurant, she was like someone who is suddenly put into another world. She only knew hospitals. It was pathetic. Nonetheless, she courageously decided to go back to the flat. We insisted that she again apply for British citizenship. The condition concerning Mr. Lask, which had been an obstacle for Dora, did not apply to the daughter. Her application was granted shortly."

Within the month, Marianne returned to the apartment at Broadhurst Gardens. She organized Dora's papers and typed a copy of Dora's *cahier*. It was a labor of love that took weeks. Dora's crossed-out parts were very hard to read in places, and Marianne's German was a little rusty. She painstakingly incorporated all of Dora's edits, indicating the marked-out words and sentences by typing over the words with Xs. The typed *cahier,* which Marianne titled "Die Aufzeichnungen des Quartheftes" (Notes from the Quarto Notebook), filled eighteen single-spaced pages. She made corrections to two dates that Dora had copied incorrectly from Kafka's diaries and signed her initials, ML, to the changes.

At eighteen, Marianne Lask was very attractive, a petite young woman with a round face like Dora's. Her pale skin was framed by dark, thick hair and punctuated by dark arched eyebrows. She had a widow's peak, like Dora's, and her eyes were large and dark, her lips full. Those who knew and loved her stated that she was a very difficult person to get to know. "She was intensely private and had so little confidence," Mrs. Steiner said. "The only person she was close to was her mother."

In the respected opinion of Dr. de M'UZAN, a Freudian psychoanalyst, "Dora and Marianne's relationship was too close, almost symbiotic. Marianne was very strange and phobic in many areas. It was clear that she was very clever, even more clever than her mother, but she was so serious for her age. She took everything too seriously, and had a deep preoccupation with philosophy."

There was always a photograph of Kafka in Dora's room. For years after Dora's death, Marianne kept the photograph on the mantelpiece in the living room, in honor of Dora and in memory of "her first father." Once Marthe Robert said something to Mrs. Steiner, which, when she heard it, rang true: "Marianne could have been, and indeed was, in many ways, Kafka's daughter," Marthe said. Mrs. Steiner agreed: "Marianne's nature was very akin to Kafka's." It was a biological impossibility, of course; Marianne was born ten years after Kafka's death. But there were similarities. In addition to the physical resemblance, which Mrs. Steiner noticed the first time she saw Marianne, Dora's daughter possessed, like Kafka, a keen intellect, acute powers of observation, extreme sensitivity, and a mischievous sense of humor. Perhaps, Mrs. Steiner suggested, "Franz had been so constantly on Dora's mind so that her child, though born several years after his death, had many of his characteristics."

A month after Dora's funeral, Marianne wrote a second letter in German to David Maletz in Israel, thanking him for his letter of sympathy, which he had written in Hebrew. "Mr. Stencl translated it for me," Marianne explained, "and he writes you some lines, which I enclose in the letter. He also gave me a book of his, so that I should send it to you. Dora probably told you about Stencl."

David Maletz had asked about Dora's papers and whether they would be published. "Unfortunately, there are only a few," Marianne informed him, "since she had neither time nor thought after some months in the hospital. She was too busy, arranging things with the flat for me. It would have been much more important if she had written instead; I would have managed; but a mother cannot change this. I am now copying the few notes she made."

Dora had urged Marianne to go Israel without her. "Her journey to Israel made Dora feel like a human being again for the first time after the war," she told Maletz. "And thinking of it, she still became happy. But I can't make up my mind to leave. At least, I have to try to live here; and to do a job for some years. Probably, then, it will be too late to leave. But I have to risk it."

LONDON, AUGUST 15, 1953

It was not just a matter of not having the money; Marianne said she didn't want a headstone. She was very firm and wouldn't even discuss it with Mrs. Steiner. To Ottie McCrea she only said, "Mother isn't there." According to Dora's friends, neither they nor Marianne ever returned to the cemetery during her lifetime. And so the first anniversary of Dora's death passed without any ceremony or stone setting at the cemetery in East Ham. For almost five decades, Dora's grave remained unmarked, an unknown and solitary rectangle of bare rocky earth between tall granite tombs and white marble slabs.

Dora's first *Yahrzeit* did not go by entirely unrecognized. A memorial notice appeared later in *Loshn un Lebn*: "This month, the eleventh of Av, is the first anniversary of the death of Dora Dymant. She was one of the founders of the 'Friends of the Yiddish Language.' At its inauguration ten years ago, she was voted the vice-president of the society. Dora Dymant belongs to the rare number of intellectual and gifted women, and not just here in our community in London. Immediately after her arrival she associated herself with our work. She held lectures at the Shabbat afternoons, reading from Yiddish literature, especially the classics. Dora Dymant's performance of Yiddish stories, for example, 'Monish,' was always a 'Yontif'—a good and holy day at the Yiddish literary Sabbath afternoons. She worked hard and suffered greatly, and to our great loss and great regret she died before her time. Her name will be remembered in the ranks of intellectual women in the struggle for Jewish spirituality."

EAST BERLIN, AUGUST 15, 1953

On the first anniversary of his wife's death, Ludwig "Lutz" Lask, unaware of his wife or daughter's fate, sat in the Berlin headquarters of the Central Committee of the Socialistische Einheits Partei (SED), the East German Communist Party, writing his life story, his official autobiography. It was the first step in the strange process of being "rehabilitated following his presumed death," party lingo for readmittance to the Communist Party following his expulsion in 1938.

Lask was fifty years old but looked like a broken old man. He had arrived in Germany from the Soviet Union with his mother on August 12, after a grueling eight-year-long battle that Berta waged on Lutz's behalf. In the secret SED archives at the Bundesarchiv in Berlin, Lask's files contain Berta and Lutz's first statements on arriving in Berlin, as well as the numerous letters Berta had written from Moscow to the East German Communist Party leaders Wilhelm Pieck and Walter Ulbricht, alternatively demanding and begging their help in getting her son released from imprisonment and hard labor in Siberia.

Berta Lask's letters are a moving testament to the inexhaustible persistence and unrelenting tenacity of motherhood. Beginning in 1945, Berta, who had moved back to the Lux Hotel on Gorky Street, wrote dozens of letters to influential comrades in the Central Committee of the Communist Party, asking that her sons, Lutz and Herman, both living in exile, be allowed to return to Germany. She reminded the Comintern of her writings against fascism and for the revolution. After three years, Herman's application was approved because as an engineer he had needed skills, and he and Alice were allowed to return to Berlin in 1948 with their son, Ernst, who was born in Arkhangelsk in 1937. It would take Berta another five years to save Lutz.

In his SED autobiography, Lutz Lask wrote down exactly what happened to him after his arrest in Moscow, about his life in a labor camp on the remote Kolyma River in the far east corner of Siberia, above the Arctic Circle, a story with a distinctly Kafkaesque flavor. "On the 26th of March I was arrested and charged with spying," Lask wrote. "However, there was no concrete accusation made against me. I claimed complete innocence. There was also no court case. In the summer of 1938, I was informed that I had been sentenced to five years imprisonment in a 'work and correctional camp.' All my applications for a review of my case were unsuccessful. As my prison term came to an end, I was informed that I was to be held until the end of the war. I was released from the camp in 1946."

He came out crippled. He lost his right eye in 1943 and had only 3 percent of normal sight in his left eye. With glasses, he said, he could still read and work. He was released from the work camp in 1946 but was not allowed to leave. He went to work in an auto repair shop in Magadan and began the interminable process of applying for repatriation to the Soviet-occupied zone of Germany, the DDR. But nothing happened. He lived, forgotten (except by his mother), "in eternal exile."

Between April 1946 to June 1948, from her room at the Hotel Lux, Berta wrote eight letters to the leader of the German Communist Party, Wilhelm Pieck, which are preserved in the SED archives in Berlin. In the first, Berta alludes to earlier, unanswered letters and says that she wants her son released. She was too old to be waging this battle: "I am sixty-seven years old, and in bad health." In a letter written four months later, Berta pointed out that "Ludwig has now been imprisoned for eight years and four months. . . ." Still she received no answer. Eight months later, in desperation, she wrote the following letter to the two highest ranking leaders in East Germany:

> Moscow, Gorky Street 10, Room 216, 15 April 1947
> To Comrade Wilhelm Pieck and Comrade Ulbricht
>   Dear Comrades!
>   This year, at the end of February, I sent a letter to you concerning my son, Ludwig Lask. Unfortunately, I remain, as always, without an answer from you. From my earlier letters you should know everything. Today I repeat only briefly that my son (with his eyes badly hurt, which could be cured by an operation in Moscow) is still in Magadan, that his general state of health is such that he spent sixteen months out of the last three years in hospital, and that, although he is free since as a free worker, meaning in his case that he is a nearly blind invalid, he has to stay there.
>   I have heard from authoritative well-informed sources that a request from you would allow him to be sent to Germany with me. This is why today I again repeat my request to receive orders to return as soon as possible, together with my son. I believe that my twenty-four year long party membership and the books I have written entitle me to this request. If you do not give the necessary orders, you will bear the responsibility for the pointless death of an old, still useful party member who has never done wrong. I am determined, though the current traveling conditions are enormously hard, to set out on the journey (that will take one and one

half months) to the Far East and to stay with my son indefinitely.
With my sixty-eight years and very weak heart, I will probably not
survive the cold winter there.

Expecting your reply with a heartfelt greeting,

Berta Lask

Three times, on June 2, June 22 and August 15 of that year, Berta wrote
again to Pieck about securing freedom for her son: "Often I have written
to you in the past two years . . . without any answer. Many letters get lost, I
don't know if you've received them." That August, Lutz Lask was allowed
to leave the frigid Far East for Novosibirsk, a drab industrial town in the
western Siberian lowlands, where he was assigned work in an auto repair
shop.

Two years later, in the spring of 1950, with Lutz still in Novosibirsk,
Berta began her letter-writing efforts anew. Berta had received permission
to leave Russia, but not Lutz. She refused to go to without him and let her
permission expire. Now she was trapped there, too.

In a letter to Ulbricht in April 1950, Berta Lask started over again, from
the beginning, to argue her son's case. She began with the date and place
of his birth, his studies in Kiel, his diploma in economics. She outlined his
party activities as a student organizer at the university in Kiel through the
dangerous period of editing the illegal party newspaper, *Die Rote Fahne,*
in Berlin, and his arrests by the Gestapo and imprisonment in Columbiahaus and the Brandenburg concentration camp. She wrote about her son's
escape from Berlin through Czechoslovakia to Russia, and his work at the
Marx Engels Institute, and his job as a proofreader after all the foreigners
were dismissed. She recounted his arrest by the NKVD "without any particular accusation or trial" and his eye injuries and sufferings in Magadan.
In Novosibirsk, where he worked at hard physical labor, despite the dire
warnings of the eye specialists, he was frequently hospitalized, Berta reported, "because of an almost deadly exhaustion." Despite everything,
Berta assured Ulbricht, "My son has not changed in any way. He is the
same unshakable, convinced and admirably steadfast Communist he used
to be. This is why I, as an old Communist, considered it to be my duty to
stay here and keep him alive until he can get permission to leave."

Three more years passed. Pieck and Ulbricht both recommended
Lask's release but nothing happened. Lask continued to file applications
to leave and was interviewed many times, but he never heard anything. Finally, on March 5, 1953, days after Stalin's death, Lask's final application,

addressed to Comrade Stalin, the chairman of the Council of Ministers of the Soviet Union, was finally granted.

Before signing his name to his six-page life story, Lutz Lask echoed his mother's assessment of his steadfast and unwavering faith in communism: "For the period of my imprisonment in the Soviet Union and the period following, my Communist convictions and my trust in the Party have remained unshaken. In the past five years I have tried to restore and further develop my knowledge of Marxist-Leninism. I have reread the whole of *Kapital* by Marx and Engels; and have read most of the works of Lenin and Stalin, and the history of the German Communist Party in the Soviet Union. I have read Hegel's *Logic, Encyclopedia and Phenomenology.* I have also studied the German translations of Lenin's *Aspects of Hegel's Logic,* as well as two of Stalin's works. I have read continuously Russian and foreign texts translated into Russian about political economics. Further I was a regular reader of *Pravda* and the newspaper *Bolshevik.* My only wish is to commit my entire energy and knowledge to the achievement of our great goal in the ranks of the SED."

Two months after Lask returned to Berlin, his application for a position as an economist at the MELST (Marx-Engels-Lenin-Stalin) Institute was approved, despite the fact, as noted in his file, that he "expressed the desire to be allowed to make contact with his wife or daughter, who live in England." Contact with the West was forbidden. Nevertheless, that November, he was granted full German citizenship, with restrictions. A note was placed in Lask's file on November 6, 1953, which read: "Comrade Lask will not travel to other countries, and not to West Germany."

That fall, Lutz finally learned what became of Dora. Reading an old newspaper, he found his wife's obituary, which reported that the last friend of Franz Kafka had died in London. The article mentioned a surviving daughter who lived in London. That October, a policeman knocked at Marianne's door with a letter from her father.

After getting permission from the East German Communist Party, according to Mrs. Steiner, Lask had written to the lord mayor of London "with a request to find his daughter for him." In a single moment, Marianne was no longer an orphan. Not only was her father alive and living in Berlin, but she had a family. Her grandmother, Berta Lask, was still alive, as were her Uncle Herman and Aunt Alice and cousin Ernst, who was about her age. In the more than fifteen years since they had seen her, the Lasks had wondered and worried about her, and they were happy and thrilled to find her. They all hoped she would write to them and tell them about herself.

LONDON, 1955

Marianne loved books and had always wanted to work around them. "Her wish was to become a librarian," Mrs. Steiner said. "We went together to ask her doctor's advice. He said it was out of the question: she was still not allowed to carry heavy books. At that time she had still to be extremely careful. It was several years before she was pronounced fully cured."

Marianne's first job was as a secretary for a company that produced bread for diabetics, where she received her secretarial training and improved her typing skills. According to Mrs. Steiner, "she worked there for a year or two, but still longed to have something to do with books."

She continued to live at Broadhurst Gardens and took in lodgers to help pay the rent. She still saw Dora's old friends, who had now become hers. She took holidays with the Lichtensterns to the English countryside. She had tea every Sunday with Ottilie and her daughters Doreen and Pamela, and she accompanied them on family trips and outings. "We all loved her very much," Hanny Lichtenstern said. "There was nothing Marianne could not do. Everything interested her. Her outstanding sensitivity caused her to suffer with all sufferers, to be always on the side of the underdog, to be so generous when she herself had so little."

EAST BERLIN, 1956

According to a note added to Lask's SED file, on March 14, 1956, "Comrade L. approached us today asking for the support of the party. His daughter, whom he hasn't seen in seventeen years, has now indicated the desire to visit both him and her grandmother, who also lives in the DDR. Comrade Lask informed me that he has made all the necessary arrangements with the Ministry of Foreign Affairs."

In her passport photograph, taken when she was about twenty-one years old, Marianne is a beauty. Her face, free of makeup, is young and fresh. Wisps of dark hair catch the light behind her, giving her an alive, almost electrified look. Her round dark eyes are wide open, her full lips pressed together, suppressing a smile, her dark eyebrows arched in surprise.

Twenty years after she left it, Marianne returned to the ruined city of her birth to meet her family. In Marianne's personal photo collection, there are more than a dozen photographs of Marianne's first visit to Berlin in 1956. The most touching pictures are of Marianne with her father and

grandmother. A series of snapshots show Lutz and Marianne talking together by a hedge. Marianne is animated. Lutz smiles down at her proudly.
In several pictures Berta and Marianne are together, walking arm in arm
along a broad Berlin street under the dappled shade of chestnut trees, sitting on a park bench and standing next to immense statues and the grand
architectural scale of Treptow Park.

Marianne was very fond of her grandmother, whom she remembered
with love. At seventy-eight, Berta was at the height of her writing career.
She was recognized as a German communist heroine and the beloved author of children's books. Throughout the long years in Moscow after the
war, she continued to write and published three novels in Russia. Since she
returned to Berlin, her earlier books had been reprinted, and she had written her "epic work," an autobiographical trilogy, *Stille und Sturm*, published in 1955. Two years later, in 1957, Berta received the prestigious
Clara Zetkin Medal on the hundredth anniversary of the birth of Zetkin, a
founder of the international women's suffrage movement.

Over the next fifteen years, Marianne returned at least twice to East
Berlin. She got to know her father and her cousin, Ernst Lask, and became
attached to her aunt, Mira Lose Lask, the widow of Berta's youngest son,
who died young in 1936. Berta had taken Mira under her protective wing,
and they lived together in Moscow and now in Berlin. Mira repaid the favor, working as secretary for the literary estate of her mother-in-law until
Berta's death in 1967 at the age of eighty-nine.

Marianne had always been intensely private, even before her reunion
with her family in East Berlin. As a small child in Nazi Germany and Stalinist Russia, she knew how to keep her mouth shut and understood the
universal wisdom of divulging as little personal information as possible.
While the worst of the red-baiting had passed, a deep fear and distrust of
communism remained. Most of Marianne's closest friends had no idea that
she had ever lived in Russia or that she had living family members who
were leading communists in East Berlin. Mrs. Steiner knew, of course, but
even she thought Marianne was "always morbidly guarding her privacy.
One always had to be on one's guard so as not to intrude."

En Route Across America, 1962

When Marianne was twenty-eight years old, she embarked on the greatest
adventure of her life. More than a decade after her Aunt Ruth had issued

the invitation, Marianne finally accepted it. On the last day of November 1962, she sailed from Southhampton on the Holland-America Line RMS *Rotterdam,* docking in New York on December 6. She thoroughly enjoyed the crossing. The food was "superb," she wrote to Hanny. She had to restrain herself with difficulty from "hogging" the complete seven-course meals. From the window of the club room, where she sat writing the letter as a "furious Bridge contest" raged around her, she watched "the rising, swelling, breaking sea. The sea is really beautiful in all its variations of tempo, rhythm and color. From a black granite base, the individual waves rise to a curling white peak and break into a churning cascade of green foam," she told Hanny. "By the time you get this, I will be on my way to Chicago."

One week later, she wrote a quick note on a postcard of the Wrigley Building at night, looking north on Michigan Avenue. A few days later she was in California. Although she intended to stay for only two months, Marianne actually spent more than four months with her Aunt Ruth and Uncle Ernest Friedlaender in northern California, taking occasional excursions to San Francisco and longer family trips with her cousin Frank, his wife and their children.

PALO ALTO, JANUARY 1963

"You poor frozen souls!" Marianne wrote to Hanny and Paul on January 18. She was sitting on the Friedlaender's patio, the sun slanting through orange and lemon trees. London was under snow, while Marianne was basking in the California winter, daily sunshine and afternoon temperatures ranging between 55 and 65 degrees Fahrenheit. "Everyone here groans at the unusually bitter winter, i.e. there has been frost at night," Marianne wrote. "Last week we had tea in the garden, and a mellow sun tanned my bare arms!"

Marianne adored San Francisco. "It really is an enchanting place, with steep, steep streets of delicately pastel-washed and brightly white two story houses, all glistening in the sun. The center has high, narrow buildings, quaint cobbled alleys and very smart shops." At the entrance of the Golden Gate Bridge, "a long magnificently designed bridge, painted bright red," she walked across about half a mile, admiring "the delicate tracery of the cables which stood out high and slender against a deep blue sky."

3rd April 1963
Palo Alto California

Dear Hanni and Paul,

Since my last note, we have all traveled 300 miles south, to spend a week in sunny Santa Barbara, which is on the coast, not far from Los Angeles. It is in a delightful setting against the Santa Ynez mountains; and is full of quaint old (and reconstructed!) Spanish adobe houses. On the way down we stopped at two of the towns where the original Spanish fathers built missions during their long, conversionary trek down the coast in the latter part of the 18th and early part of the 19th Centuries. One is a charming, simple white church built in 1772; the other, a classical Spanish affair, with a beautiful succession of arches, was built by "voluntary" (!) Indian labor in 1826. Needless to say, my cameras have been very busy!

California has had a welcome, though very late, fall of snow in the Sierra Nevada, so that we drove southwards amidst a riot of spring blossoms, carpets of wild flowers, and all this and the lush new grass, was set off against a background of snowy mountain peaks. Further south there was added to the spectacle, parched, semi-desert landscape, palm trees, and again, gaunt, snow-capped mountains. A weird and beautiful confusion of our accepted ideas of landscapes. To this must be added the incredible blue, pounding, foaming Pacific Ocean. It has a completely different rhythm from the Atlantic and the North Seas. I stood for ages in the evenings, on the little fishing pier at Santa Barbara, just listening to the stealthy rolling of the waves, as they crept quietly up from the depths of the sea before they crashed onto the beach with a resounding boom and broke in a woosh of foam. It is quite fascinating to stand and listen, and try to get the feel of it, and guess when the next wave will arrive.

We had hoped to visit a glacier park on the way back, but Ruth wasn't feeling too good, so we only got as far as Fresno, which is in the fruit growing San Joaquin interior valley. On the way we passed miles of semi-desert country, where a few cattle nibbled at the meager grass and left sandy patches at the end of each meal. At times we came to patches of aquamarine growth which we at first took to be lakes, so vividly did they shine out against the yellow and purple hills. On coming closer, we discovered that these were strips of weeds, planted to keep the shifting sands in place.

All the best Yontov wishes for Pesach, and a happy holiday
spent together. Please give my regards . . . of course, to David.

Kindest regards,

Marianne

In the third week of March, Marianne sent a postcard to the Lichtensterns from Santa Barbara, with best wishes for Passover. "While I would
love to be with you, I wouldn't miss this trip for the world!"

In April, rain fell "fairly steadily" throughout the entire month. On the
last Friday of April, her last in California, the weather "miraculously
cleared up," Marianne reported, "so we all piled into my cousin's station
wagon early Saturday (grandchildren, parents, grandparents and 'Auntie'—that's me!) and drove 100 miles down to Carmel, on the beautiful
Monterey Peninsula. There we had two glorious days of sunshine and
white sands. I had my first (and last!) toe-dip in the icy Pacific, and came
home with a bagful of pebbles."

Marianne mentioned that "if all goes well, I'll be in Berlin over July, to
comfort my poor old grandmother and congratulate my cousin and new
wife and perhaps become an 'Auntie—once removed' when their baby is
born." In Berlin, Marianne's cousin Ernst had married Dina Rosen. Their
first child, Peter, was born in March of that year. Their daughter, whom
they named Ruth, was born four years later, in 1966.

Marianne's next letter, written en route to Canada "from somewhere in
Northern California," was addressed to Hanny, Paul, David and Paddy
(the family cat), and also to Hanny's sister, Mady, her husband, Walter, and
their cat, Charlie. "Pitch dark outside, 10 PM, Monday, April 29," Marianne reported. "Well, I'm off again, wandering into the unknown. All
wobbles, blots, and blunders by courtesy of very rattling Southern & Pacific train. Just looked out the window and see landscape blanketed by
snow! At five o'clock we were sweltering in the spring sunshine in Oak-
land."

Marianne spent "a whole, wonderful week in Vancouver. I enjoyed
lovely walks round the several harbors and watched the sun rise and set on
the various beaches. In Stanley Park, which covers an area of about 1,000
acres at the tip of the town, I walked miles, through pine tree woods and
followed the rugged coastline. Every now and again I met a policeman
mounted on a horse, at the crossroads of the trails, watching to see that
man and beast were behaving themselves."

By mid-May Marianne was in Banff, Alberta. "The scenery is breathtaking," she wrote. "When I leave my house in the mornings, beautiful mountains soar away up above me on every side. In the valley flows the lovely clear green Bow River, which has many flashing rapids and waterfalls. On the higher slopes grow wild crocus, anemone and edelweiss. In fact, the whole scene is very reminiscent of Switzerland. . . . I have seen so much unusual wildlife on my walks, deer, elk, chipmunks, snakes, three kinds of squirrel, buffalo, and an enormous bear! This last blocked my path as I was sauntering down a lonely woodland trail this morning. I have never sauntered away so quickly and so silently before! Everyone asks me whether it was a black, brown or grizzly bear, but I didn't actually stay to investigate its species."

By the time she reached Montreal, before returning to New York and sailing to London, Marianne's head was spinning with the memories of her trip. The pebbles she had collected on the beach at Carmel, as well as "a dismaying collection of souvenirs," were now weighing down her luggage "and causing consternation among porters." Her heart sank at the thought of clearing customs in Southampton. "I shall end up at Carisbrook Castle, as a desperate smuggler, I'm sure." Among her souvenirs, Marianne was carrying four redwood tree saplings to give to friends in London as a gift: the potential growth of the largest life form on earth.

25

A REDWOOD GROWS IN HAMPSTEAD

You do not need to leave your room. Remain sitting at your table and listen. Do not even listen, simply wait. Do not even wait, be quite still and solitary. The world will freely offer itself to you to be unmasked, it has no choice, it will roll in ecstasy at your feet.

—Franz Kafka, *Blue Octavo Notebooks*

LONDON, 1963–1973

After her adventure across North America, Marianne returned to London and went back to work. She found a job that allowed her to work around the books she loved, as a secretary in a firm of printers and magazine publishers. "She never earned much money, but she could make ends meet," Mrs. Steiner said. She lived very quietly, spending weekends and holidays with friends. She never dated, never once going out with a man, but spent her free time and holidays with Dora's friends. "We all stayed close, and she became a part of all our families," Hanny said. Marianne accompanied the Lichtensterns on family weekend trips, including one to the Cotswolds. She spent Christmas holidays with the Steiners and McCreas, and celebrated Passover and Channukah with the Lichtensterns. Every Sunday, Ottilie McCrea said, "Marianne came for lunch and tea. Ours was a second home for her."

Marianne was interested in many things, from the mysterious history of Easter Island to crochet pattern designs. But according to Mrs. Steiner, "the theatre was Marianne's great love. Dora brought her up to appreciate acting. When she told us about a play that she had seen, she acted it out for us enthusiastically. It was fascinating."

Marianne took a keen interest in gardening, which was Hanny's love. The Lichtenstern house featured a glassed-in conservatory that opened onto a lush backyard garden. Only one of the four seedlings Marianne brought back from California took hold: the one Hanny planted in her backyard. Within a decade, the tree was taller than the Lichtenstern's two-story house. By the end of the century, before it had to be cut down (having undermined the foundations of Hanny's house), the California redwood towered over the entire residential neighborhood in Cricklewood, just north of Hampstead.

Like Kafka, Marianne loved nature. Her letters contained detailed, beautifully worded observations of the natural world. The photographs she took often depicted landscapes and plants growing around thatched-roof cottages or large estates. In Marianne's papers, Hanny found a poem that Marianne had written, probably about her garden, entitled "Green Spell":

> *This is the home of the plant soul.*
> *In vain the human hand seeks to contain:*
> *The garden ever more engulfs the house,*
> *Here vegetation reigns supreme.*
>
> *This is the home of the sprouting green.*
> *The stick of dead wood into leaf does prick,*
> *Stretching its ancient, red-tipped arms out wide*
> *In ritual exultation.*
>
> *And this is the home of the climbing green,*
> *Young tendrils lovingly entwine the sills*
> *Of windows and the posts of doors*
> *To meet with rapturous arm across the roof.*
>
> *This is the home of the spiky green.*
> *Its soul is mean and grudgingly does dole*
> *Inch by slow inch the little prickly growth*
> *To plump perfection in the pot.*
>
> *And this is the home of the trailing green.*
> *It spills ecstatically the tumbling rolls*
> *Of its young growth, which ever is renewed.*
> *There freshness clothes each lonely wall.*

This is the home of maturing green.
The sweet succulent firmly swells to meet
The onslaught of the burning sun's fierce rays;
And Africa glows on its pebbled bed.

This is the home of advancing green.
It never sleeps but softly creeps
Till its slow hug unwraps walls and roof around
And pulls them back into the ground.

In 1973, Hanny's garden room was the scene of a family reunion between Marianne's father, Lutz Lask, and his sister, Ruth Friedlaender. They had not seen each other in forty years. When he was seventy years old, Lutz Lask was finally granted permission to leave Germany to visit his daughter in London, and Ruth, who had left Germany during the Nazi takeover in 1933, came from California to London at the same time to see her only surviving sibling. Herman had died in 1959, and her mother had passed away peacefully in 1967 at the age of eighty-nine.

Hanny enjoyed meeting Ludwig Lask. She thought he was "a very pleasant, highly intelligent man with a fine sense of humor," and "someone you could trust." Mrs. Steiner was less impressed. "Lask was a clever man," she said, "but rather dry, argumentative, with little charm or warmth. He never renounced his belief in communism. He stayed only a few days, and shortly after his return he died."

On December 14, 1973, Marianne's father passed away in Berlin. Her cousin Ernst Lask took care of the cremation and burial. His death notice, the last item in Lask's SED file, announced that in recognition of Ludwig Lask's service to the working classes since 1931, he had been awarded the Fatherland Order of Merit in silver and an honorary medal for forty years of party membership.

HIGHGATE, LONDON, JUNE 6–8, 1977

Marianne was forty-three years old and had enjoyed remarkably good health in the twenty-five years since Dora's death. Except for smoking cigarettes and drinking coffee, she took care of herself. On June 6, 1977, two days before she moved out of her flat at 62 Cromwell Avenue in Highgate in north London, Marianne Lask drew up her last will and testament. As executors and trustees, she appointed Michael Steiner, an attorney, and his mother, Mrs. Marianne Steiner, of 4 Upper Park Road, Hampstead, London. The two-page legal document was witnessed by Mrs. Sala Leftwich of 2 Winchester Place, Highgate.

To her aunt, Mira Lask of East Berlin, Marianne bequeathed "all the Lask and Friedlaender Family photographs in my possession." These photographs included Marianne's baby pictures and many of Dora from the 1920s and 1930s. To her first cousin, Ernst Lask, she left "all my correspondence, with the exception of that specified in clause 3 below." Clause 3 gave "to Mrs. Marianne Steiner all correspondence relating to Dora Dymant and Franz Kafka, for her to dispose of or add to the Kafka Archives as she thinks best." Twenty-five years after Dora's death, Marianne still remembered Dora talking about the letters that Kafka had written to her, the precious letters that had been lost, confiscated by the Gestapo the year before her birth. Marianne, like Dora, and Max Brod, too, believed that Kafka's letters to Dora were lying in a secret warehouse or bunker somewhere in Eastern Europe, behind the Iron Curtain, waiting to be discovered.

Marianne bequeathed all her Hebrew and Yiddish books and periodicals, including the *Lebn un Loshn* journals with Dora's articles, to Jews College, London. The remainder of her books were to go to Mrs. Steiner. The few small possessions she had left she gave to friends.

In the quarter century since Dora's death, Marianne had come to regret that her mother's grave was still unmarked, without a stone or a plaque or memorial of any kind. In clause 8, Marianne instructed that any funds remaining in her estate after the payment of her debts and funeral expenses were to go first "to pay for the erection of a tombstone on the grave of Dora Lask in the Jewish Cemetery at East Ham." In regard to her own funeral, Marianne left her body "to the nearest teaching hospital, to use in any way that they wish, either for transplantation of organs, or for dissection purposes." She wanted her "remains to be cremated, and no memorial, service or ceremony to be held."

Two days after making out her will, Marianne moved into a new room in a subdivided house in Hackney, east of Islington. She sent postcards to her friends with an announcement: "Miss M. Lask wishes to inform all friends that as from 8th June, she will be at her new residence: 31 Church Crescent, Muswell Hill, London, N10, and hopes to see friends there at an 'at home' later in June."

HACKNEY, LONDON, 1979

Tova Baumer Perlmutter knocked on the door of Marianne Lask's room in Muswell Hill. "Who's there?" Marianne called out. "It's your cousin from Israel," Tova replied. The two cousins had never yet met. "She opened the door and asked me to wait while she got dressed. A few minutes later, I called my husband and we both went in and talked for a while. When I asked to use the bathroom, I had to go down the hall, where she shared it with someone." Born in a displaced persons camp in Germany, Tova had grown up in Tel Aviv; this was her first trip outside of Israel. When her mother, Dora's sister Sara, learned Tova was going to London, she made Tova promise to try to find Marianne.

Tova and her husband, Moti, went with Marianne to the South Bank and walked along the Thames, through theaters and art galleries, and then to a small café that Marianne said was the best place in London for tea and cakes. "We talked about books, theater, about my parents, my family," Tova said. "I didn't ask her personal questions. You could see she was a closed person, and I didn't want to shut her down." Although Marianne was gracious and pleasant to Tova and her husband, "she was not at all at ease," Tova remembered. "She was like a frightened mouse," Moti agreed.

Despite this, Marianne accepted the invitation extended by Sara and Abraham Baumer to visit Israel over the Passover holidays the next year, in 1980, when Marianne would be forty-six. The Baumers paid for her trip, and according to both Sara and Tova, Marianne had a wonderful time. "She was blooming," Tova remarked. But Tova couldn't ignore her cousin's strangeness.

LONDON, 1980

"When Marianne was in her mid-forties," Mrs. Steiner remembered in 1990, "we noticed a strange change in her behavior. Every Christmas I decorated a tree for children and the whole family came for a festive meal. Marianne was invariably present and many times I heard her say how she loved these traditional festivities. Then, quite unexpectedly, she informed me that she would not come, as she hated Christmas. Of course, we were very much taken aback, but did not dare to insist. She always got presents from every member of the family. Since she refused to come to us, we decided to bring the presents to her flat, next door to Mr. and Mrs. Leftwich, old friends of Dora. We rang the doorbell, saw the light in Marianne's window, but the door remained closed."

According to Ottie McCrea, Marianne had begun to hear voices. Spending the night at Ottie's one night, Marianne woke her up at three in the morning because of the voices arguing in the stairwell. "Can't you hear them?" Marianne asked. "I listened, but could hear nothing," Ottie said. "Nobody was there." Marianne was so distressed by the voices that she went to the police to tell them about it.

In early 1981, Marianne was found wandering in the streets at midnight. She was taken to a mental hospital and "kept there for several months," Mrs. Steiner said. "She became very attached to a social worker who looked after her, but when that lady told her she was expecting a baby, Marianne refused to see her again, her reason being that a woman in her condition should avoid such depressing work. Eventually she was discharged and seemed much improved. She invited my husband and myself for tea and offered us plates with elaborate sandwiches and pastries. She even played her new records and was friendly and cheerful. But it was only a temporary improvement. Soon she again refused to open the door to anybody."

Ottilie McCrea thought that Marianne was "diagnosed as schizophrenic while institutionalized. She was given medication, which she renounced. 'I'm not going to take those pills anymore,' she said." At one point, Marianne told her: "I don't want to live. I'll die before I'm fifty." Ottie was shocked and saddened by this statement and never told anyone about it.

Hanny and Paul watched helplessly as Marianne shut herself off from everyone who loved her. When Hanny told her she considered Marianne part of her own family, Marianne replied firmly and with finality: "I have no family!" Hanny kept all the letters that Marianne wrote to her over the long years of their friendship, even the disturbing and cruel notes that Marianne wrote in the last years of her life. In one, Marianne had written: "Dear Sir and Madam, Your further communication is acknowledged with thanks. Please excuse me if I don't ring or write as I used to—it is as much as I can do to look after myself. I'm not really much of a socialite. Yours, etc, etc, Marianne Lask." In another, she wrote: "Dear Mr. & Mrs. Lichtenstern, I acknowledge receipt of your letter sent recently. It is awfully good of you to remember me like this, but you are really wasting your time. I have nothing to say to you and shall never be a Zionist."

Hanny enlisted the help of social services and a doctor in trying to help her. On Chanukah Hanny said, "I called on her flat and kept on ringing her bell until at last she opened the outer door, by pressing a button. She stood on the far side of the entrance, in her nightdress, and said 'I can't ask you in, I'm ill.' I said I didn't want to disturb her, but as it was Chanukah I had brought her a few things—sweetmeat from the baker's, homemade potato latkes, which she used to love, and flowers. She thanked me and apologized, and I left quickly. Paul was waiting for me in the car, and I burst into tears when I told him what happened."

But Hanny didn't stop trying to reach out to her. In July, she wrote another letter to "Liebe Mariannchen," saying how much she missed her. "I want to know how you are, how you cope. . . . Could we two not meet if only for any hour or so?" The letter was returned, unopened, with a note on the back: "This letter has not been read. Please stop pestering me and attend to your own family and business. Any further communications will be handed to the police. M. Lask."

A glimpse inside Marianne Lask's private hell was contained in her personal papers. On Sunday, December 13, Marianne wrote a cryptic note in her pocket diary: "3–4 p.m. In bath. 2nd 'visitation,' as in Pembury in 1949, but with crackling and buzzing around me." On January 19, 1982, she wrote about "alien thoughts" being thrust into her brain. "Gremlins getting through again, this time in my brain, not on the phone or on tape. A kind of subliminal promotional effort." On February 10, she described another incident, which again occurred in the bath: "Suddenly felt the old nausea and cold grip me. Got dried and a dressing gown on, and then just lay down on the floor and passed out for a few minutes. Got up on regaining consciousness and felt better, but disinclined to go out shopping or do housework as I had intended. Not quite such a darkening in front of the eyes as in December, and instead tried hard to fight it off for a few minutes. Hardly any 'buzzing,' just a prickling, bubbling sensation."

London, August 1982

Marianne was forty-eight years old, penniless and in debt. On a small notepad she had listed her bills and current expenses, including the back rent for May, June and July, and her unpaid loans from friends. The total was over £1,000: an impossible sum.

Marianne had been unable to work for the past two years, but she would not accept anything from anyone, not even unemployment benefits she was entitled to or the restitution she was eligible for under the conditions of

Germany's surrender. In her last letter to Hanny and Paul, written on July 18 and addressed to "Mr. & Mrs. Lichtenstern," she apologized for sending them a card intended for someone else by mistake, "and must thank you exceedingly for its return. I will let you have the value of the stamps, too, as soon as possible. I still owe you £95.00! I don't know when I shall be able to remit this further and final payment, but keep this letter as evidence of the debt and then you can produce it should you be asked to come forward, (if you know what I mean.)"

Hanny didn't know what Marianne meant but already "feared that her sad life would end tragically. She had withdrawn from all who knew her, more and more until she did not communicate anymore, and gently but finally told the hospital doctors, social workers, that she did not want, did not need any help—all she wanted was to shrink out of existence, cease living."

On July 17, the day before she wrote her last letter to Hanny, Marianne received a letter from the representative of the building owners, advising her that her rent check had been returned from the bank unpaid, and that she was now three months in arrears. "Obviously we do not intend to allow this to accumulate over further months and we are placing the matter in the hands of our solicitors for payment of overdue rent and vacant possession of the flat." A stamped notice was added at the bottom of the letter: "We wish to advise that we have to increase your rent by £4.- per calendar month to cover increased costs of rates, water, house lighting, etc. This increase will become effective as from the next rent payment due July 1, 1982."

Marianne responded the next day, acknowledging receipt of their letter. "I owe you £232.00 for same, plus probably cost of replacing lock on door of flat and repairing window in kitchen and replacing red and black cushion cover on which I accidentally spilt some bleach. I should like, as a matter of form, to let you know that the overflow from the bath is faulty and water is spilling out at the back rather a lot." She also acknowledged "four week's notice to quit the premises and will endeavor to do so before the date specified, that is 14th August."

"Again she refused to open the door to anybody," Mrs. Steiner said. "The milkman noticed that she didn't order any milk and the other people in the boarding house became uneasy, too. The house had a communal telephone in the entrance hall and her room was nearest to it. Yet she would never pick it up when it rang. Eventually, one of the tenants would answer, and we'd ask him to knock on Miss Lask's door and they would come back and say that there was no answer."

Among Marianne's papers was a letter, dated August 23, 1982, from the office of the director of social services in Muswell Hill, addressed to Ms. M. Lask:

> You may remember that I wrote to you some time ago and you replied indicating that you felt you did not wish or need help from a Social Worker. I was informed today that the police were called to your flat last night (Sunday 22 August) due to concern expressed about you by your neighbors. I understand the police discovered that your electricity supply had been disconnected and they wondered if you needed some assistance with this matter. Please call in at the above address and ask for the duty social worker if you are having difficulties and feel we may be able to assist you overcoming them.

The last item found in Marianne Lask's personal papers was the September 1982 issue of *Exit,* the newsletter of the Voluntary Euthanasia Society.

In mid-September, the police were notified again by friends and neighbors. No one had seen Marianne for several weeks. On September 12, the police broke down the door and discovered Marianne Lask, "dead on the floor, in an advanced stage of decay."

The coroner's report listed the primary cause of death as "Left Ventricular Failure" brought about by "extreme neglect." Hanny identified the body and made Marianne's final arrangements. "We are heavy with guilt," Hanny wrote in her diary, "feeling desperately that this should not have happened—yet knowing that her illness made it almost inevitable—her illness coupled with the sensitivity and strangeness of her character! How would she have reacted, had one forced oneself upon her, invading her privacy and demanding contact??!! But to die so lonely, collapsed on the kitchen floor—did she cry out for help and wasn't heard? —It doesn't bear thinking—."

A memorial service for Marianne was held on October 19. "At 2:45, Marianne was cremated," Hanny wrote in her diary. "The tiny Bedford Chapel in Golders Green Crematorium had plenty of seats left. Just twelve friends were there: the Steiners, plus a niece from Prague on a visit, Ottie and Pamela, who was deeply affected, Mrs. Leftwich, and Stencl, all the way from the East End, looking frail and showing his age. . . . Straight ahead, as one enters, the opening in the wall, lit dimly, with the simple black coffin, holding what is left of Marianne Lask, forty-eight years young, hundreds of years old and wise, having lived too little and suffered too much."

EPILOGUE

There is always something unaccounted for.
—Franz Kafka, in *Conversations with Kafka*

Dora's story does not end here. It is still unfolding as new documentation of her life continues to be found. As recently as October 2002, Kafka scholar Klaus Wagenbach found a stack of papers written by Dora that had lain forgotten in his archive for almost half a century. As interest in Dora is awakened, other papers, still missing, may be found that can deepen our understanding of both Dora and Kafka, and reveal more details of their lives. If the seventy letters that Dora wrote to Max Brod or Kafka's thirty-five letters to Dora, as well as the final diaries and notebooks he kept during the last year of his life, are uncovered, new chapters of both their lives will need to be written. As a well-known writer and publisher in London noted, "Part of Kafka's legacy, and therefore that of world literature, remains untold in the absence of the documents." Despite the overwhelming odds that these papers will never be found, as one former East German philosopher put it, "the chance is not zero."

Following the fall of communism and the collapse of the Soviet Union in the 1990s, it became possible for the first time since before World War II to search once secret government archives and repositories in Eastern Europe and Russia. Rightful owners of Holocaust-era assets—gold, art, Swiss bank accounts, insurance policies and Jewish cultural properties stolen by the Nazis—could finally petition for their return. In Central and Eastern Europe, numerous deposits were uncovered, containing massive stacks of Third Reich–era papers and documents, carted out of Berlin during the war, stored in bags and boxes, untouched for more than fifty years. German archivists have estimated it will take at least ten years to sort, index and catalog the recently discovered materials.

In 1996 the Kafka Project, the first official search since the 1950s for Franz Kafka's lost papers, was established at San Diego State University. A petition was filed with the German government to search Nazi archives and records and a claim entered for the return of Franz Kafka's writings confiscated from Dora Diamant (Dymant-Lask) by the Gestapo. In September 1998, following a four-month search of Berlin archives, the Kafka Project found documentation of the confiscation of Dora's property, but no further leads. Future searches are merited, and with time the fate of Kafka's papers, if not the papers themselves, could very well be discovered. The Kafka Project's search for Kafka's lost papers in Berlin in 1998 had unexpected benefits. Other discoveries in Berlin made Dora's biography possible for the first time. It also led to the reunification of Dora's relatives in Israel and the Lask family of Berlin.

Zvi Diamant, the son of Dora's older brother David, had no idea that "Kafka's last love" was his aunt until 1996. Born in 1947 in the release camp at Dachau, Zvi moved to Israel with his parents when he was two years old. David died in 1960, shortly before Zvi's thirteen birthday and bar mitzvah, before his father had the opportunity to share with him "the remarkable story of his sister." Zvi first became intrigued with Dora when he received a yellowed newspaper article, with "this beautiful love story of Franz Kafka and Dora Diamant." Because of their shared last name, Zvi started to wonder if he might be related to Dora and began looking for more information on her.

"What happened to her after he died?" Zvi wondered. Did she survive the Holocaust? "Did she marry? Did she have children? Are any of her family still alive?" Zvi wanted to find out, to dispel the mystery shrouding Dora Diamant. "I was determined to find the answers to these questions," he said.

He turned to the Internet and found the Web site of the *Kafka Katern,* the journal of the Franz Kafka Circle of the Netherlands, where he posted an open letter requesting information about his Aunt Dora. The Webmaster, Kafka scholar Niels Bokhove, compiled a four-page timeline and bibliography on Dora's life for Zvi, including every published item he had found and his own personal research. From Bokhove, Zvi learned that Dora had married "a certain Lask" sometime "between 1926 and 1936" and had given birth to a daughter, Marianne. He learned that Dora had died on August 15, 1952, and was buried in east London.

Zvi wanted to find Dora's grave in London, but the Dutch scholar admitted he didn't know where it was. "He told me that many had looked for her grave, but nobody had found it." Zvi believed he had reached a dead end.

The next year, in late September 1998, Zvi telephoned me in Berlin on Yom Kippur Eve, in answer to a letter that I had written to him telling him about the Kafka Project and the results of more than a dozen years of in-depth research into Dora's life. When Zvi learned the sad news of Mari-anne's death and Dora's unmarked grave, he felt he must do something. Believing himself to be Dora's only living relative, he decided that he must "repair this wrong" and provide each of them a tombstone. We agreed on a date for the stone setting: August 15, 1999.

Two weeks after learning about the Lask family, Zvi flew from Tel Aviv to Berlin to meet them. It was a joyful meeting, Dora's nephew with the Lasks, who consisted now of Ernst's widow, Dina, and her two children, Peter and Ruth, Dora's great-nephew and great-niece.

The story of Zvi finding his long-lost Aunt Dora, Kafka's last love, and the reunification with the Lasks was published in Israel's largest daily newspaper, *Yediot Achronot*, on May 20, 1999. That same day, Zvi received a phone call from Tova Perlmutter: "I am your cousin," she told him, in-troducing herself. "My mother, your father's sister, is alive and lives in Tel Aviv." Sara Baumer's address was only ten minutes from Zvi's home in Holon.

"I was speechless for long minutes," Zvi said. "Is it possible?" he won-dered. "Until that moment I didn't know about any family on my father's side, and suddenly a sister of my father and a sister of Dora came into my life." He met Sara and Tova the next day and was overwhelmed with new information from his newfound family. He considered it "a miracle."

Three months later, on the forty-seventh anniversary of Dora's death, a memorial stone setting was held at her unmarked grave in the United Syn-agogue Cemetery on Marlowe Road in East Ham. From Berlin came mem-bers of the Lask family: Dina Lask, the widow of Marianne's cousin Ernst, and daughter Ruth Lask, the granddaughter of Berta Lask. Dora's *mis-poche* (family) from Israel included Zvi Diamant, his wife, Shoshi, and their four children, Dvir, Hadas, Idan and Shani; Dora's second cousin Etty Diamant and her husband, Hillel Schenker, and their son, Adi. Dora's sister, Sara Baumer, came with her daughter, Tova Perlmutter. Sara was seventy-seven years old and expressed two wishes before she died: "to see her father's grave in Poland and to visit Dora's grave."

Over seventy-five people—Dora's friends and family along with Kafka scholars and Kafka Project researchers and supporters from England,

Germany, Israel, Holland and the United States—attended the ceremony. The reception that followed at the Spiro Institute at King's College in Hampstead offered a moving testament to the power of the Yiddish language in a magical performance of a story by Dora's favorite author, I. L. Peretz, given by ninety-four-year-old Majer Bodansky. As a young man he had watched Dora perform the same piece for the Friends of Yiddish. Although the majority in the audience spoke no Yiddish, everyone understood the depth of emotion.

At the cemetery, Zvi recited the Kaddish and Sara read from the Torah, saying a prayer, in the Jewish tradition, for each letter of Dora's name. She read a short speech in Yiddish, remembering the joy Dora brought into her life when she came to Israel: "I was so happy to meet you, my only surviving sister. We hoped to live our lives together. Unfortunately you died so young, and our dreams for being together were prematurely interrupted. Your soul was pure and sacred, you had the heart to forgive all the wrongs inflicted on you. May you rest in peace, and may your soul join the pure souls in heaven."

Tova, Zvi and a few others also spoke on that bright, windy Sunday at the "informal yet dignified" ceremony in East Ham. Zvi remembered his father, "this kind, intelligent and knowledgeable man," who would have done exactly as he had done in providing Dora a tombstone. "Let him rest in peace and be proud with what I have done," Zvi said.

Marianne was not forgotten. Although her ashes are interred at Hoop Lane in Golders Green with a plaque in her and Dora's name, maintained by Hanny Lichtenstern, Marianne's name was included on Dora's beautiful white marble tombstone, which is engraved with both their names, along with a quotation by Robert Klopstock, written on the day after Kafka died: "Who knows Dora, knows what love means."

NOTES

Kafka's texts and Dora's published articles and unpublished letters and diaries, the collections in which they are housed and names are abbreviated as follows. (Private and personal collections are designated as PC.) All interviews, unless otherwise noted, were conducted by the author.

DD Dora Diamant (Dymant)
DE Dorothy Emmet
FK Franz Kafka
HL Hanny Lichtenstern
LL Ludwig "Lutz" Lask
MB Max Brod
ML Marianne Lask
MR Marthe Robert
MS Marianne Steiner
OD Ottla Davidova
RK Robert Klopstock

Briefe FK, *Briefe an die Eltern*
"Cahier" Dora's notebook diary (1951)
Diaries FK, *The Diaries, 1910–1923*
Letters to Friends FK, *Letters to Friends, Family, and Editors*
Letters to O FK, *Letters to Ottla and the Family*

ARCHIVES

AdK Stiftung Archiv der Akademie der Künste, Berlin
AKKA Archiv Kritische Ausgabe Kafka, Wuppertal
Bodleian Collection Bodleian Library, Department of Special Collections and Western Manuscripts, Oxford University
Bundesarchiv Bundesarchiv Stiftung Archiv der Parteien und Massenorganisationen der DDR, Berlin-Lichterfelde
DLA Dumont-Lindermann Archiv, Düsseldorf Theatermuseum
PRO Public Records Office, Kew
Russian Archives Rossiyskiy Gosudarstvennyi Arkhiv Sotsialno-Politicheskoy Istorii (Russian State Archives for Social and Political History, formerly Central Archives of the Communist Party), Moscow

TRANSLATIONS

Dora's *cahier* and letters were translated from the German by Hanny Lichtenstern and Stefanie Groenke. Yiddish articles and diary entries were translated by Hanny Lichtenstern. Additional Yiddish translations were supplied by Heather Valencia and Leonard Prager. Robert Klopstock's letters translated by Hanny Lichtenstern. German texts and archival material were translated by Stefanie Groenke, Johanna Hoornweg, Marcus Derham, Felix Pahl and Trudi Diamant. Marthe Robert and Nicholas Baudy's articles were translated from the French by Nicole Chapman and Anthony Rudolf. Sally Lecompte translated Felix Weltsch's essay on Dora; Stencl translations from Yiddish were by Heather Valencia; Hebrew translations were by Mitra Makbuleh and Zvi Diamant. Russian translations were by Yoram Mayorek.

CHAPTER ONE: THE THRESHOLD OF HAPPINESS

1   "I am a memory." Franz Kafka, *The Diaries, 1910–1923,* ed. Max Brod (New York: Schocken, 1948), 392, October 15, 1921.

1   "He had never wished." Max Brod, *Franz Kafka: A Biography* (New York: Schocken, 1964), 209.

2   "They waited so long." Franz Kafka, *Letters to Friends, Family, and Editors,* trans. Richard and Clara Winston (New York: Schocken, 1977), 419.

2   "The childlike, well-behaved virgin." Egon Larsen, *Weimar Eyewitness* (London: Bachman & Turner, 1976), 97.

3   *Shtetl:* A town or village composed mostly of Jews and insulated from outside the world, described by Sholem Aleichem in his Tevye stories, in which "Yiddishkeit entered a golden age." See Leo Rosten, *The Joys of Yiddish* (New York: Pocket Books, 1970), 373–376.

3   "Jewish People's Home activities." Dr. S. Lehmann, *Erste Bericht . . . First Report of Jewish People's Home* (Jüdische Gemeinde Bibliotek-Berlin).

4   "In the fields of Galilee." Mendel Mann, *Franz Kafka's Wife,* trans. Hanny Lichtenstern (London: Di Goldene Keyt, 1958), 2.

4   "If you will it." Theodor Herzl, *Der Judenstaat,* 1895; Elena Romero Scatello and Ureil Macias Kapon, *The Jews and Europe: 2000 Years of History* (New York: Holt, 1994), 90.

5   "To make the pilgrimage." Dora Dymant, "Shlomo Michoels: The Jew," *Loshn un Lebn* 97 (February 1948).

5   "An eager soul." J. P. Hodin, "Erinnerungen an Franz Kafka." *Der Monat,* June 1949, 91.

5   "A character springing." Ibid.

5   "The governess in the home." Eric Gottgetreu, "They Knew Kafka," *Jerusalem Post,* June 14, 1974, 16.

7 "He had to be a half-breed." Hodin, "Erinnerungen," 91.

8 "Such tender hands." Ibid.

8 "Was overrun with joy." Marthe Robert, "Notes inedites de Dora Dymant sur Kafka," *Evidences* (Paris) 28 (November 1952). Translated by Nicole Chandler.

8 "Perhaps the most anxious of all" through "Kafka could not be saved." Hodin, "Erinnerungen," 91.

10 "Through the trees." Franz Kafka to Hugo and Else Bergmann, July 13, 1923, *Letters to Friends,* 373.

11 "The only path." Franz Kafka, *Letters to Felice,* ed. Erich Heller and Jürgen Born, trans. James Stern and Elisabeth Duckworth (Middlesex, U.K.: Penguin, 1978), 500.

11 "As a little child." FK, *Diaries,* December 2, 1921, 397.

11 "Dora was with me, . . . a wonderful person." FK to Tile Rössler, August 3, 1923, *Letters to Friends,* 375.

11 "Truly more lovely, more varied, livelier and younger." FK to Else Bergmann, July 13, 1923, *Letters to Friends.*

11 "With both ears." Dora Dymant, "Cahier," TS 14-2, PC.

12 "Walked on tip-toe or as if on soft carpets." Hodin, "Errinerungen," 93.

12 "The indestructible." FK, *Blue Octavo Notebooks,* ed. Max Brod, trans. Ernst Kaiser and Eithne Wilkins (Cambridge, Mass.: Exact Change, 1999), 93. ("The indestructible is one; it is each individual human being and, at the same time, it is common to all, hence the incomparably indivisible union that exists between human beings.")

12 "Manifest disparities." Ernst Pawel, *The Nightmare of Reason: A Life of Franz Kafka* (New York: Farrar Straus Giroux, 1984), 439.

12 "It is easy to see why." Peter Mailloux, *A Hesitation Before Birth* (Newark: University of Delaware Press, 1989), 535.

12 "Suited one another quite marvelously . . . which she entered into easily and like a game." Brod, 208.

13 "After the catastrophe of the war." Hodin, "Memories of Kafka," 36–37.

13 "To test my transportability." FK to Hugo Bergmann, July 1923, *Letters to Friends,* 372.

13 "A short test run for the greater journey." FK to Else Bergmann, July 13, 1923, *Letters to Friends,* 373.

14 "If only it were possible to go to Berlin." FK, April 5, 1914, *Diaries,* 267.

CHAPTER TWO: A DARK CREATURE FROM THE EAST

15 "There is no one here who wholly understands me." FK, May 4, 1915, *Diaries,* 339.

15 "A man without a wife is not a man." Pawel, 264.

15 "Envy, nothing but furious envy." Pawel, 263.

16 "In July, something momentous." FK, *Letters to Milena,* edited by Willy Haas, translated by Tania and James Stern. (Great Britain: Vintage, 1999), 188.

16 "Dwojra Diament," from the official birth certificate, *Rzeczpolpoita Polska,* no. 51/1899/4, Citizens Registration Office (USC), Pabianice.

16 "Herschel" is the Yiddish version of the German word for deer, *Hirsch.* The Hebrew version of the name is Zvi.

18 "Not by their tastes, literary preferences, or style of dress, but by the character of their observance." Eva Hoffman, *Shtetl* (New York: Houghton Mifflin, 1997), 104.

18 *Shtreimel:* A black, broad-brimmed hat, trimmed with velvet or edged in fur, worn by religious Jewish men in Galicia and Poland. Today shtreimels are worn by the very orthodox and the Chassidim. Rosten, 377-378.

18 *Gabbai:* local religious leader.

18 *Stiebel:* prayer room or small house synagogue used by followers of a rabbi whose main synagogue and court are held in another city.

19 "Put his stamp." Raphael Mahler, *Hasidism and the Jewish Enlightenment: Their Confrontation in Galicia and Poland in the First Half of the Nineteenth Century,* trans. Eugene Orenstein (Philadelphia: Jewish Publication Society of America, 1985), 312.

19 "Inflexible and extreme conservatism." Ibid., 313.

19 "Plague of the Haskalah," "free thinkers." Ibid., 314.

19 "Highly structured symbolic universe." Hoffman, 97.

20 "Was capable of direct contact with God." Ibid., 152.

20 "Layers of doctrine." Ibid.

21 "Each side had suffered." Isaac Asimov, *Asimov's Chronology of the World* (New York: HarperCollins, 1991), 505.

21 "If I forget thee, O Jerusalem." Psalm 137:5.

21 "Next year in Jerusalem!" Rabbi Benjamin Blech, *Jewish History and Culture* (New York: Alpha, 1999), 272.

21 Available online at www.jewishgen.org/yizkor/bedzin/Bedzin.html.

21 "National language to the masses." Moshe Rozenkar, *The Blossoming of Hebrew Language Restoration in Bedzin,* ed. Pinkas Bedzin and A. S. Stein (Tel Aviv: Association of Former Residents of Bedzin in Israel, 1959), 294.

22 "Served as the foundation." Ibid.

22 "Were received with great love." Ibid.

22 "As a desecration of the holy language." Ibid.

22 "Student-trainee." Ibid.

22 "With favour the establishment in Palestine of a national home for the Jewish People." The Balfour Declaration: www.yale.edu/lawweb/avalon/balfour.htm.

23 *Takke:* something that is truly real or possible.

23 "The poorest will leave first." Theodor Herzl, *Der Judenstaat,* 1895; Scatello and Kapon, 90.

23 "To protect Jewish girls." Eetta Prince-Gibson, "Finishing School," *Jerusalem Post Magazine,* March 10, 2000, 18.

24 "She was supposed to study there to become a teacher in a religious ortho-dox school." Sara Baumer, interview no. 1, August 1999.

24 *Fröblerin:* a kindergarten teacher. F. F. Fröbel (1782-1852) was the Ger-man educator who founded the kindergarten system.

24 "Bloody persecutions of Jews." Dora Dymant, Comintern autobiography, file and document no. 495/205/1573/5, Russian archives.

24 "That it was not for her." Baumer, interview no. 1, August 1999.

24 "A pretty and intelligent woman . . . youngsters who might otherwise have gone into the assimilationist or left-wing camp." Gottgetreu, 16.

25 "Was intoxicated with Germany." DD, "Cahier," TS 18.

25 "To a very considerable extent." Otto Friedrich, *Before the Deluge: A Por-trait of Berlin in the 1920s* (New York: Harper & Row, 1972), 111.

26 "Continually menacing." FK to MB, August 8, 1923, *Letters to Friends,* 378.

26 "My own great fatigue." Ibid.

26 "Full of high courage." Brod, *Biography,* 197.

26 "Anxiety—ghosts, nothing specific." FK, *Diaries,* August 17, 1923.

26 "Read aloud the curses from Leviticus." Ronald Hayman, *Kafka: A Biogra-phy* (New York: Oxford University Press, 1982), 292.

26 "Borrowed the family's Hebrew prayer book." Ibid., 332 n. 22.

26 "A six-foot skeleton." Pawel, 434.

26 "Bright, sensitive, independent." Mailloux, 381.

27 "Humility and pride." Ibid., 133.

27 "Refusal to be bullied in any way." Ibid.

27 Objections of relatives and friends. FK, *Letters to Ottla and the Family,* trans. Richard and Clara Winston, ed. N. N. Glatzer (New York: Schocken, 1982), ix.

27 "The monastic cell of a real writer." Brod, *Biography,* 156.

27 "At almost every meal." Kafka, *Letter to His Father,* trans. Ernst Kaiser and Eithne Wilkins (New York: Schocken, 1966), 39.

28 "Too many counterforces." FK to MB, August 29, 1923, *Letters to Friends,* 379.

28 "Up a little, scarcely noticeable." FK to MB, September 14, 1923, *Letters to Friends,* 381.

29 "His life hung in the balance." Pawel, 372.

29 "Brave of heart, honest." FK to MB, February 6, 1919, *Letters to Friends,* 213.

29 "She probably put on a fancy blouse." FK, *Letter to His Father,* 107.

30 "Missed so much, never having learned devout praying, never having been taken to experience the profound devotion of a congregation." DD, "Cahier," TS 36.

31 "Berlin is a medicine against Prague." FK, September 1922, *Letters to Friends,* 361.

31 "Berlin, too, is almost beyond me." FK, September 13, 1923, *Letters to Friends,* 380–381.

CHAPTER THREE: A FREE LIFE IN BERLIN

32 "There is a point of no return."

32 "His frequent letters to her." The correspondence—or any record of it—between Kafka and Dora during this period has been lost, possibly taken along with the letters confiscated by the Gestapo in 1933. Given the fact that Kafka wrote to Dora up to three times a day when they were separated for three weeks in March 1924, it is likely that he wrote to her frequently during this first separation, too.

32 *Daven:* to pray rhythmically, swaying and bending back and forth, while reciting prayers aloud.

33 *Goyim:* plural of *goy:* a Gentile, someone who is not a Jew. Jews hired non-Jews to perform the work that they were forbidden to do on the Sabbath.

33 *Shofar:* a ram's horn that is blown in an elaborate ritual in the synagogue during the High Holidays.

34 "Fatness from Schelesen." FK, September 26, 1932, *Letters to O,* 78.

34 "I'm leaving tomorrow." FK to Robert Klopstock (RK), September 23, 1923, *Letters to Friends,* 382.

34 "Frightfully complicated packing." FK to Ottla, September 26, 1923, *Letters to O,* 77.

34 "People were capable of a greater degree." Alex de Jonge, *The Weimar Chronicle: Prelude to Hitler* (New York: Paddington, 1978), 182.

34 The revolutionary Spartacist movement, which had proclaimed its own new German government, evolved into the early German Communist Party.

35 "Police obliged to open fire." De Jonge, 182–183.

35 "Within the limits of my condition." FK to Oskar Baum, September 26, 1923, *Letters to Friends,* 382.

35 "His decision to cut all ties, get to Berlin, and live with Dora stood firm—and this time he carried it out inflexibly." Brod, *Biography,* 197.

35 "One of the very worst." FK, September 26, 1923, *Letters to O,* 77.

36 "She is charming." FK to MB, July 10, 1923, *Letters to Friends,* 371.

36 "Wonderfully helpful friend." Brod, *Biography,* 40.

36 "Knowledge of the world." Ibid.

36 "Unique in the history of literature." Pawel, 110.

36 "Mainstay of my whole existence." Brod, postscript to *The Trial,* trans. Willa and Edwin Muir (New York: Vintage, 1969), 330.

36 "Quite simply and baldly as a swindler." Brod, *Biography,* 43.

36 "Endless conversation." Ibid., 43–44.

37 "Simplicity and naturalness of feeling." Ibid., 44.

37 "At school I modeled myself." Ibid.

37 "Outward appearance was above all." Ibid., 43.

37 "Remarkably quiet, observant, reserved." Ibid., 48.

37 "Absolute truthfulness." Ibid., 47.

38 "While Kafka floated through college." Mailloux, 81.

38 "Energy and initiative." Ibid.

38 "Shamefaced lanky." Max Brod, *Streitbares Leben* (Munich, 1960), 245f. Translated in *Letters to Friends,* 426 n. 12.

38 "A key to unlock unfamiliar rooms in one's own castle." FK to Oscar Pollak, November 9, 1903, *Letters to Friends,* 10.

38 "A life-threatening curvature of the spine." Pawel, 113.

39 "If his subsequent promiscuous generosity." Ibid.

39 "An equality of rights was cheerfully acknowledged." Brod, *Biography,* 58.

39 "The most important writer of his time." Pawel, 112.

39 "In the evenings." FK to OD, October 2, 1923, *Letters to Ottla,* 78.

40 "The landlady is allegedly satisfied." Ibid.

40 "I had a severe fit of numerical obsessions." FK to MB, October 2, 1923, *Letters to Friends,* 383–384.

40 Prices were marked up 20 percent every day. De Jonge, 93.

40 "One billion paper marks equaled one gold mark." Richard Bessel and E. J. Feuchtwanger, eds., *Social Change and Political Development in Weimar Germany* (London: Croon Helm, 1981), 57.

40 "Rushed off to the shops." De Jonge, 95.

41 "Workers were paid once, then twice." Ibid.

41 "Deliberately let the mark tumble." Friedrich, 133–134.

41 "It was my first social occasion." FK to MB, September 28, 1923, *Letters to Friends,* 383.

41 "When conditions here." FK to RK, September 26, 1923, *Letters to Friends,* 382.

42 "Infinitely patient." Original source: Marthe Hofmann, "Dinah and the Poet: Franz Kafka's Correspondence with a Sixteen-Year-Old," *Die Österreichische Furche,* October 1954; Hans-Gerd Koch, ed., *Erinnerungen an Franz Kafka* (Berlin: Verlag Klaus Wagenbach, 1996), 168.

42 "Filled with a stunned gratitude." Koch, 169–170.

42 "All of these young people." Ibid.

42 "I'd give God knows what." Ibid., 171.

42 "Tenderest empathy." Ibid.

42 "Wait here a moment." Ibid.

42 "The kitchen supervisor." Ibid., 170.

43 "We do not have to discuss." FK, October 8, 1923, *Letters to Ottla,* 79–80.

43 "Wry and sometimes bitter sense of humor." Mailloux, 92.

43 "I have after all stayed longer." FK to Felix Weltsch, October 9, 1923, *Letters to Friends,* 385–386.

43 "I scarcely go beyond the immediate." FK to MB, October 16, 1923, *Letters to Friends,* 386.

44 "The real agony of the prices." FK to MB, October 2, 1923, *Letters to Friends,* 383.

44 "If it proves at all possible." FK to RK, October 16, 1923, *Letters to Friends,* 386–387.

44 "I don't want to return." FK to MB, October 16, 1923, *Letters to Friends,* 386.

45 "If I do not write." FK to MB, October 25, 1923, *Letters to Friends,* 387.

45 "In spite of all the difficulty." Ibid., 388.

45 "Diamant is her name." Ibid., 389, 392.

46 "A pound of butter cost six million marks." Larsen, 53.

46 "As much as anyone could want." FK, September 26, 1923, *Letters to Ottla,* 77.

46 "Please, do not exaggerate." FK to RK, October 31, 1923, *Letters to Friends,* 392.

47 "Tearing himself away from Prague." Hodin, "Memories of Kafka," 43.

CHAPTER FOUR: THE IDYLL IN BERLIN

48 "This is a place." FK, *Blue Octavo Notebooks,* 88.

48 "To have lived one single day with Franz." Felix Weltsch, "Entretiens avec Dora Dymant," unpublished, 1949–1950, PC.

48 "Taller, ennobled, definitively marked." Nicolas Baudy, "Entretiens avec Dora Dymant," *Evidences* (Paris) 8 (February 1950): 24.

48 "Kafka was always cheerful." Hodin, "Memories," 37.

49 "The content of my consciousness is entirely." FK, *Diaries,* January 24, 1915, 329.

49 "That way he could." Hodin, "Memories," 40.

49 "He loved to play." Weltsch, 3.

49 "With the state of his health." Ibid.

49 "There aren't enough words." Ibid., 2.

49 "When he spoke." Hodin, "Memories," 37.

50 "His voice was a hesitating, muted baritone." Gustav Janouch, *Conversations with Kafka,* trans. Goronwy Rees, 2d ed., rev. and enl. (New York: New Directions, 1971), 17.

50 "Depending on how much he was amused." Ibid., 33.

50 "Kafka speaks with his face." Ibid.

50 "The smiling Franz Kafka." Ibid., 196.

51 "From the front pages of the newspapers." FK to MB, October 25, 1923, *Letters to Friends,* 388.

51 "She appeared to be in complete despair." Anthony Rudolf, "Kafka and the Doll," *Jewish Chronicle Literary Supplement,* June 15, 1984, vii.

52 "Who met Kafka in the Park?" (Wen traf Kafka im Park?), *Tagesspiegel* (Berlin), May 18, 2000.

52 "Kafka had to write, he had to." Hodin, "Memories," 38.

53 "A form of prayer." Franz Kafka, *Dearest Father,* trans. Ernst Kaiser and Eithne Wilkins (New York: Schocken, 1954), 312.

53 "His day was strictly planned." Hodin, "Erinnerungen," 93.

53 "The elation that comes." Franz Kafka, "A Little Woman," in *The Complete Stories,* ed. Nahum N. Glatzer (New York: Schocken, 1971), 321.

53 "He wanted to feel like an average person." Hodin, "Memories," 40.

53 "He would pace." Hodin, "Erinnerungen," 93.

53 "Writing things and a lamp." FK, January 14–15, 1913, *Letters to Felice,* 272. Edited by Eric Heller and Jürgen Born. Translated by James Stern and Elizabeth Duckworth. New York: Penguin, 1983.

53 "She was an excellent girl." Hodin, "Memories," 42.

53 "The average: a comfortable home." FK, January 24, 1915, *Diaries,* 328.

54 *Alles ist in Ordnung:* "Everything is in order."

54 "His engagement was an attempt." Hodin, "Memories," 42.

54 "He, too, was moved by the love." Ibid., 41.

54 "In Berlin, he believed for a time." Ibid., 40.

54 "Yield not a particle." FK, *Diaries,* 328.

54 "Verve and passion." Baudy, 22.

54 "Well, I wonder if I've escaped the ghosts." Ibid., 22.

55 "Consult the calendar." Hodin, "Memories," 40.

55 "One moment can ruin everything." Ibid., 41.

55 "He attached great importance." Ibid., 40.

55 "What would I do if Prague rang?" Martin Walser, "Kafkas Stil und Sterben," in *Werke* (Frankfurt, 1997), 12:733.

55 "He loved Kleist." Hodin, "Memories," 41.

56 "No woman could read it without blushing." Thomas Mann, preface to Heinrich von Kleist, *The Marquise of O— and Other Stories,* trans. Martin Greenberg (New York: Criterion, 1960), 20.

56 "A masterpiece of succinct exposition." Ibid., 14.

56 "In M—, a large town in northern Italy." Ibid., 41.

56 "Finally she opened the door." Ibid., 78–79.

57 "To risk the ludicrous to achieve the sublime." Ibid., 33.

57 "Modestly—with trembling heart." E.T.A. Hoffmann, *Selected Writings of E.T.A. Hoffman,* ed. and trans. Leonard J. Kent and Elizabeth C. Knight (Chicago: University of Chicago Press, 1969), 2:9.

57   "Should anyone be so bold." Ibid., 2:11.

57   "O Nature! Sublime and holy Nature! How your raptures, your ecstasies fill my sympathetic breast!" Ibid., 2:13.

57   "Something is stirring marvelously." Ibid., 2:14.

58   "I am too weak for the practical classes." FK to RK, October 25, 1923, *Letters to Friends,* 389.

58   "It soon became quite clear." Koch, *Errinerungen an FK,* 167.

58   "I believe she had found out." Franz Kafka, *Briefe an die Eltern aus den Jahren 1922-1924,* ed. Josef Cermák and Martin Svatos (Frankfurt am Main: S. Fischer, 1990), 34–35. Beginning of November 1923.

58   "He loved its soft, living light." Hodin, "Memories," 40.

58   "My kerosene lamp burns marvelously, a masterpiece . . . but then we, too, are the same." FK to Valli Pollak, November 1923, *Letters to Friends,* 395.

59   "Spoiled . . . by the Steglitz air." FK, *Briefe,* November 20, 1923.

59   "A highly advantageous move." FK to MB, November 2, 1923, *Letters to Friends,* 393.

59   "Not far, two lanes further away." FK, *Briefe,* 35.

59   "This little woman, then, is very ill-pleased." FK, "A Little Woman," in *Complete Stories,* 317–324.

60   "Utterly taciturn.'" FK, November 1923, *Letters to Friends,* 396.

60   "Es ist bestimmt in Gottes Rat" (it is determined by divine decree) is the first line of a well-known poem set to music by both Mendelssohn and Schumann concerning the transitoriness of all things and the hope of meeting again in a better world. FK, *Letters to Friends,* 490 n. 66.

61   "Followed the two furniture movers to the stairs." FK, October 16, 1923, *Letters to O,* 118 n. 20.

61   "In the middle of breakfast." Dora Dymant, "Chronologische Initialien," Klaus Wagenbach Archive.

61   "If there is a moving men's school. . . ." FK, October 16, 1923, *Letters to O,* 83.

61   "I found an idyll." Brod, *Biography,* 197–198.

61   "Sleeping well—an unheard of novelty." Ibid., 198.

62   "Led by a short fellow." Larsen, 74.

62   "The national revolution has started." Ibid., 75.

CHAPTER FIVE: THE BURROW

63   "There I can curl myself up in comfort." Franz Kafka, "The Burrow," in *Complete Stories,* 327.

63   "The dirty Jewish streets of Berlin." FK to RK, July 24, 1923, *Letters to Friends,* 374.

63   "Literally 'drinking in' the words." Baudy, 22.

64   "A whole building of handsome lecture rooms." FK to RK, December 19, 1923, *Letters to Friends,* 403.

64   "I wanted to go to eat." FK, November 17, 1923, *Letters to O,* 85.

64   "H. Unger." Baudy, 25.

64   "He did not need such accidental puns." Ibid.

64   "Was very kind and friendly." FK, November 17, 1923, *Letters to O,* 85.

65   "Things in Berlin are not so bad." FK, *Letters to Milena,* 188.

65   The official exchange rate in Prague on November 10, 1923, was 1 trillion marks to 12 Czech kronen.

65   "It is expensive, of course." FK, November 20, 1923, *Briefe,* 42.

65   "The man who dominated through possessions." Hodin, "Memories," 39.

66   "Now I have repeatedly asked." FK, October 16, 1923, *Letters to O,* 82.

66   "The parcel arrived in excellent condition." FK, November 23, 1923, *Briefe,* 43.

66   "Dear mother, you need not worry." Ibid.

66   "Today Ottla is here, approving of everything she sees, I think." FK to MB, November 25, 1923, *Letters to Friends,* 399.

67   "The heavy overcoat." FK, October 1923, *Letters to O,* 83.

67   "When I sit just looking out the window." FK, October 14, 1923, *Letters to O,* 81.

67   "Moved heaven and earth." Pawel, 441.

67   "I have not been sick." FK to MB, November 25, 1923, *Letters to Friends,* 399–400.

68   "Unfathomable depth." Hodin, "Memories," 39–40.

68   "Whatever might happen around him." Ibid., 37.

68   "Every time Franz goes." Brod, *Biography,* 201.

68   "We too must suffer." FK, *Blue Octavo Notebooks,* 97.

68   "Blood was flowing." Hodin, "Memories," 37.

69   "He was often more than depressed." Ibid.

69   "With Kafka, no exaggeration is possible." DD, "Cahier," TS 24.

69   "Literature for him was something sacred." Hodin, "Memories," 39.

69   "Merely wavering reflections of the present." Janouch, 40.

69   "Felt unsure about most things in life." Hodin, "Memories," 39.

69   "I think we ought to read." FK to Oskar Pollak, January 27, 1904, *Letters to Friends,* 16.

70   "God doesn't want me to write." FK to Oskar Pollak, November 9, 1903, *Letters to Friends,* 10.

70   "Insisted that the job." Pawel, 173–174.

70   "The final thoroughness." DD, "Cahier," TS 1–2.

71   "A palpable change was visible." Hodin, "Memories," 38.

71   "Refuge in case of extreme danger." FK, "The Burrow," 327.

71   "I have completed the construction of my burrow." Ibid., 325.

71   "The most arduous labor." Ibid., 328.

72   "Periods of particular tranquillity." Ibid., 330–331.

72   "It is his castle." Mailloux, 546–547.

72   "An almost inaudible whistling noise." Kafka, "The Burrow," 343–359.

72   "Dangerous beyond all one's powers of conception." Ibid., 353.

72   "But all remained unchanged." Ibid., 359.

72   "He was working with pleasure." Brod, *Biography*, 198.

72   "Frequently experienced great happiness." Brod, postscript to *The Trial*, 326.

73   "Embittered struggles." Ibid., 326, 331.

73   "We use this opportunity." Kurt Wolff Verlag to FK, October 18, 1923, Archiv Kafka Kritische Ausgabe (Archive of the Critical Edition), Wuppertal.

73   "I am just being asked about my condition." FK to RK, November 23, 1923, *Letters to Friends,* 402.

74   "A refuge of peace in wild and woolly Berlin." FK to RK, December 19, 1923, *Letters to Friends,* 402–403.

74   "It's very good that you will be seeing Pua," "Another student wishes to enclose a greeting." Ibid.

CHAPTER SIX: THE KILLING WINTER

75   "You belong to me, I to you, we are united. What can harm us?" FK, "The Burrow," *The Complete Stories,* 342.

75   "I also took part." FK, *Briefe,* January 5–8, 1924, 50–51.

75   "Excellent . . . conjured up." Brod, *Biography*, 202.

75   "My nourishment, about which you ask." FK, January 1924, *Letters to O,* 90.

76   "Was so splendid." FK, December 5–8, 1923, *Briefe,* 50–51.

76   "Fifteen kilograms." FK, December 1923, *Letters to O,* 86.

76   "Looked down on Eastern Jewesses." Hayman, 297.

76   "Luckily he didn't come himself." Brod, *Biography,* 202–203.

76   "Later, D. negotiated it down." FK to MB, mid-January, 1923, *Letters to Friends,* 403.

77   "You must earn gold marks." Brod, *Biography,* 203.

77   "But the rise in prices." FK, *Briefe,* January 5–8, 1923, 50.

77   "Franz knew the 'Got fun Avrum.'" DD, "Cahier," TS 36.

77   "Our dear, holy, blessed Sabbath is passing." Ibid.

77   "May the gates of Jerusalem soon stand open. Open shall they stand." Ibid., 15.

77   "Into the gates we shall go." Ibid.

78   "He missed so much." Ibid., 17.

78   "What is Klopstock up to?" FK to OD, first week of January 1924, *Letters to O,* 90.

78   "Extraordinarily beautiful." FK, *Briefe,* January 5–8, 1923.

78 "We poor foreigners." FK, mid-January 1924, *Letters to Friends*, 404.

78 "The miracle of getting by on 1000 crowns." FK to OD, first week of January, 1924, *Letters to O*, 90.

78 "Must give up the struggle." Brod, *Biography*, 203.

79 "Really pursuing these studies, but only doing them for pleasure without the necessary groundwork." FK to MB, mid-January 1924, *Letters to Friends*, 405.

79 "Warm, well-fed Bohemia." Ibid., 404–405.

79 "If the creature were not so decrepit." Ibid., 405.

79 "Of course, I'll try." Ibid., 404.

79 "D. had a big cake baked." Ibid., 405.

79 "Dora knows Manfred Georg." Ibid., 406.

80 "At the moment we have apartment troubles." FK to RK, January 26, 1924, *Letters to Friends*, 406.

80 "A fine job." Ibid., 406–407.

80 "It's true that I write to you." FK to Felix Weltsch, January 28, 1924, ibid., 407.

81 "A magician," "powerful feeling of freedom." Janouch, 98.

81 "A servant of the word." Ibid.

81 "But sad to say." FK to Ludwig Hardt, February 1, 1924, *Letters to Friends*, 408.

81 "The other student." FK to RK, January 26, 1924, *Letters to Friends*, 406.

82 "Reciting the whole thing." FK to MB, mid-January 1924, *Letters to Friends*, 404.

82 "Dear Ludwig Hardt." FK to Ludwig Hardt, early February 1924, *Letters to Friends*, 408.

82 "Fräulein Dora Diamant." Ibid.

82 "His nature and his books." Koch, 196. Original obituary: Rudolf Kayser, *Die neue Rundschau* (Berlin) 35, vol. 2, no. 7 (July 1924): 752.

82 "In a Berlin suburb." Koch, 196.

83 "Anyone who keeps the ability to see beauty." Janouch, 30.

83 "Understand or appreciate each other's work." Mailloux, 135.

83 "The visit had been extremely difficult." Ibid., 539.

84 "When I entered the room." Hodin, "Memories," 41.

84 "Anyone who put himself." Ibid.

84 "I was so young then." Ibid., 39.

84 "What he really wanted to write." Ibid.

84 "At his instructions." Hayman, 296.

84 "After all, what one writes." Janouch, 41.

85 "Only in a jocular way." Brod, *Biography*, 203.

85 "He earned a few pence through his contract." Ibid., 201.

85 "It was impossible to shut one's eyes." Ibid., 203.

85 "Enervated evening orgy." FK to RK, February 29, 1924, *Letters to Friends*, 408–409.

86 "Strong Jewish commitment." Gottgetreu, 16.

86 "Her simplicity, originality and intelligence." Ibid.

86 "He was in a wretched state." Ibid.

87 "After the first step." FK to RK, early March 1924, *Letters to Friends,* 409.

87 "He loved this situation." DD to OD, early 1925, MS Kafka 50, fols. 51–53, Bodleian Collection.

87 "We very often amused ourselves." Hodin, *Memories,* 37.

87 "I am resisting a sanatorium." FK to RK, early March 1924, *Letters to Friends,* 409–410.

88 "Uncle proposed that I go." Ibid., 411.

88 "I might not finish." FK, *Briefe,* March 15, 1924, 65.

88 "To the home from which." Hodin, *Memories,* 41.

Chapter Seven: The Most Fearful Day of Disaster

90 "A man is only fully aware." FK, in Janouch, 44.

90 "I have to be careful." DD, "Cahier," TS 12.

91 "Technical errors." Hodin, "Memories," 43.

91 "Highwaymen had taken him." Hodin, "Erinnerungen," 95.

91 "I think I began to investigate." FK, *Letters to Friends,* 495 n. 20.

91 "No outward signs of his illness." FK to MB, April 1921, *Letters to Friends,* 274.

92 "Very ambitious." FK to MB, February 1, 1921, *Letters to Friends,* 259.

92 "Sublimely, childishly ridiculous." FK to RK, November 1921, *Letters to Friends,* 311.

92 "Whenever he drank certain beverages." *Letters to Friends,* 495 n. 20.

92 "Come tomorrow again at this time." Brod, *Biography,* 203.

93 "If anyone of us should speak to Dora." FK, *Briefe,* April 7, 1924, 67.

93 "The patient's condition is very grave." DD postscript, FK to MB, April 9, 1924, *Letters to Friends,* 412.

93 "D. is with me." FK plus DD postscript, April 9, 1924, *Briefe,* 67–68.

93 "Only medical matters." FK to RK, April 7, 1924, *Letters to Friends,* 411.

93 "Everybody drops into a shy, evasive." Ibid.

94 "I am being transferred." FK plus DD postscript to RK, April 13, 1924, *Letters to Friends,* 412.

94 "Obviously, I could not manage this." FK plus DD postscript, April 10, 1924, *Briefe,* 68–69.

94 "The most fearful day of disaster." Brod, *Biography,* 203–204.

94 "A little water." FK, conversation slips, *Letters to Friends,* 416.

94 "Most exquisitely painful." Pawel, 443.

94 "I am afraid of your codeine." FK to RK, April 13, 1924, *Letters to Friends,* 412.

94   "It is expensive." FK to MB, April 9, 1924, *Letters to Friends,* 411–412.

95   "Endless journey." FK, *Briefe,* 67.

95   "Most beautiful Laryngological Clinic in the World." Rotraut Hacker-müller, *Das Leben, dass mich stört: Eine Dokumentation zu Kafkas letzten Jahren, 1917–1924* (Wien-Berlin: Medusa, 1984), 106.

96   "I am very well taken care of." FK, April 11, 1924, *Briefe,* 69.

96   "From two to four Dora is always with me." FK, April 12, 1924, *Briefe,* 70.

96   "Herr Herrmann has just arrived." DD postscript, Ibid.

96   "A down-filled quilt." FK plus DD postscript, April 13, 1924, *Briefe,* 71.

96   "I am quite well." FK, April 15, 1924, *Briefe,* 72.

97   "Kafka was not shaken." Hodin, "Memories," 44.

97   "Dear Parents of Franz." DD to Hermann Kafka, MS Kafka 51, fols. 31r, 32r, Bodleian Collection.

97   "Extraordinary patience of the priest." Brod, *Biography,* 204.

97   "I've cried without reason." FK to MB, April 20, 1924, *Letters to Friends,* 412.

98   "A certain Werfel." Hackermüller, 118.

98   "The food in the clinic." DD to Frau Julie Kafka, April 18, 1924, Friday, MS Kafka 51, fol. 32v,r, Bodleian Collection.

98   "The weather has become very beautiful." FK and DD, April 16, 1924, *Briefe,* 73.

99   "Where he can have exactly the same treatment and be at the same time in absolutely the right surroundings." DD to Frau Julie Kafka, April 18, 1924, MS Kafka 51, fol. 32r, Bodleian Collection.

99   "Franz goes Saturday into the sanatorium." FK plus DD postscript, April 16, 1924, *Briefe,* 73.

99   "Professor Hajek maintained the only chance." Brod, *Biography,* 204.

99   "This happens with the agreement." DD to Julie Kafka, April 18, 1924, MS Kafka 51, fol. 32r, Bodleian Collection.

99   "Robert, dear Robert." FK to RK, April 18, 1924, *Letters to Friends,* 412.

CHAPTER EIGHT: THE BEST OF BEGINNINGS

101   "My life was much sweeter." FK to MB, July 4, 1922, *Letters to Friends,* 334.

102   "Between eleven and fifteen crowns." Hackermüller, 126.

102   "Felix Weltsch returned to Prague yesterday." DD to Elli Hermann (EH), end of April 1924, MS Kafka 51, fol. 49v, Bodleian Collection.

103   "I am building my hopes." DD to EH, April 23, 1924, MS Kafka 51, fol. 49, Bodleian Collection.

103   "Unfortunately we had to discontinue." Ibid.

103   "It is good." DD, end of April 1924, MS Kafka 51, fol. 28r, Bodleian Collection.

103   "Dearest Parents, the postal route to here." FK, end of April 1924, MS Kafka 51, fol. 28v, Bodleian Collection.

103   "My condition is bearable." FK to MB, April 28, 1924, *Letters to Friends,* 413.

104   "A sick old man." FK, June 2, 1924, *Briefe,* 82.

104   "I cannot travel now." FK to MB, April 28, 1924, *Letters to Friends,* 414.

104   "It is really a shame that Franz's recovery . . . prepare a meal yourself just the way you would like to have it." DD to Herrmann Kafka, May 1924, MS Kafka 51, fol. 29r, Bodleian Collection.

104   "I hope to thank you personally." Ibid.

104   "I need money." DD to EH, May 2, 1924, MS Kafka 51, fols. 49–50r, Bodleian Collection.

105   "Yesterday I was called to Kierling." Brod, *Biography*, 205.

106   "Nothing is changed." DD to EH, before May 5, 1924, MS Kafka 51, fol. 51r, Bodleian Collection.

106   "Has changed for the better." DD to Julie Kafka, May 7, 1924, MS Kafka 51, fol. 33r, Bodleian Collection.

106   "Dear, beautiful Ottla." DD to OD, May 6, 1924, MS Kafka 50, fol. 51r, Bodleian Collection.

107   "I am full of hope." Ibid.

107   "Klopstock's being here is favorable." Ibid.

107   "A little bit urgent." Ibid.

107   "Dear Madam!" RK to OD, after May 6, 1924, MS Kafka 51, fol. 51v, Bodleian Collection.

108   "Nobody should come!" DD to EH, prior to May 5, 1924, MS Kafka 51, fol. 51v, Bodleian Collection.

108   "Of course it would be terrible." RK, note in FK, *Letters to Ottla,* 121 n. 14.

108   "Good night to the Franzs." RK to OD, May 1924, MS Kafka 80, Bodleian Collection.

108   "There should now be a chapter about Dora." Ibid.

109   "Although he was not a practicing Jew." Brod, *Biography,* 208.

109   "To sit *shiva* for her." Bracha Plotkin, interview, Mishmar Ha-Sharon kibbutz, May 2001. *Shiva:* The seven days of mourning for the dead, in which ancient mourning rituals are observed. Mourners rend their garments at the lapel just before the funeral. It was not uncommon for a family member who had left the Orthodox fold to be banished from the life of the community and literally mourned as dead.

109   "No." Brod, *Biography,* 208.

110   "Telephone! Immediately!" Ibid., 207.

110 "While it is true." Ibid.

110 "In a remarkable fashion." Ibid.

110 "Franz had been quite fresh." Ibid., 208.

110 "Does my larynx hurt so much?" FK, conversation slips, *Letters to Friends,* 416.

110 "Tremendous amount of sputum." Ibid.

111 "Dora and Klopstock would then try." Mailloux, 554.

111 "How many years." FK, *Letters to Friends,* 419.

111 "No pretext would be so opaque that *his* gaze would not be able to penetrate it." FK, *Letters to O,* 121 n. 14.

111 "These two, Dora and Dr. Klopstock." Brod, *Biography,* 204.

111 "The bird of death." Ibid, 208.

111 "Whole existence took an unforeseen turn." Brod, postscript to *The Trial,* 331.

111 "Dora told me about how Franz cried for joy." Brod, *Biography,* 209.

112 "How many stations there are." Ibid.

112 "They often joked together like children." Ibid., 208–209.

112 "It is entirely due to Dora that Franz is now eating . . . of course he notices that the beer is not especially good, but he drinks it anyhow." FK, *Letters to O,* 120 n. 12.

112 "Of Franz's eager, sparkling and cheerful intellect." RK to Julie Kafka, May 17, 1924, MS Kafka 99, Bodleian Collection.

112 "For instance the day before." RK to Julie Kafka, probably May 13, 1924, MS Kafka 97, Bodleian Collection.

113 "The poor dear." RK to EH, probably May 5, 1924, MS Kafka 100, Bodleian Collection.

113 "You praise so arbitrarily." FK, *Letters to Friends,* 421.

113 "I'm only so sad." Ibid., 419–420.

113 "If it is true." Ibid.

113 "Over two pounds every day." Hackermüller, 132.

113 "I do have a guilty conscience." FK and DD, May 19, 1924, *Briefe,* 77.

114 "What an exchange of joys." DD to Herrmann Kafka, May 26, 1924, MS Kafka 51, fol. 30, Bodleian Collection.

114 "Please don't hold it against me." Ibid.

115 "The trouble is that I cannot drink." FK, *Letters to Friends,* 419.

115 "That is a pleasure." Brod, *Biography,* 207.

115 "It is as if I were drinking it." Willi Haas, "FK's Death," *Der Tagesspiegel* (Berlin), November 25, 1953, suppl. 1; Koch, 194.

115 "Why didn't I once try beer." FK, *Letters to Friends,* 423.

115 "How easy it was." Ibid., 422.

115 "Sensual like an animal." DD, "Cahier," TS 12.

115 "A bird was in the room." FK, *Letters to Friends,* 416–422.

115 "Gave orders for changing." Brod, *Biography,* 211.

115 "They have waited so long." FK, *Letters to Friends,* 419.

116 "With every limb as tired." Ibid., 423.

116 "That he sometimes cried afterwards." Mailloux, 558.

116 "When the doctors let it be known." DD, "Cahier," TS 6.

116 "I was called to the office." Ibid.

117 "Franz was feeling very well." Brod, *Biography,* 209.

117 "Dearest Parents, Now about the visits." FK, *Briefe,* June 2, 1924, 80.

117 "From which I see that Father doesn't." Ibid.

117 "Shock of the larynx business." Ibid.

117 "In spite of my wonderful helpers." Ibid., 81–82.

117 "I took the letter from his hand." Ibid.

118 "Franz is breathing badly." Brod, *Biography,* 211.

118 "And so the help goes away." FK, *Letters to Friends,* 423.

118 "Place your hand on my forehead." Ibid., 422.

118 "So brusque as he never was." Brod, *Biography,* 212.

118 "You have always been promising." Ibid.

118 "Don't cheat me, you are giving me an antidote," "Kill me, or else you are a murderer." Ibid.

118 "That's good, but more." Ibid.

119 "In the event of his death." Haas, suppl. 1. Also Koch, 194–195.

119 "The person who had the sad duty." Haas, suppl. 1.

119 "About the writer Franz Kafka, I cannot judge." Ibid.

119 "Kafka seemed to be completely unconscious." Ibid.

CHAPTER NINE: FUNERAL IN PRAGUE

121 "Prague doesn't let go." FK to Oskar Pollak, December 20, 1902, *Letters to Friends,* 5.

121 "The death of Franz was the experience of my own death." DD, "Cahier," TS 11.

121 "Never went anywhere without it." Ruhama Maletz note on back of Kafka photograph, En Harod, Israel, PC.

122 "My dearest, my love, my good one." Brod, *Biography,* 212.

122 "Alone in the dark, uncovered—O my God! My love." Ibid.

123 "Poor Dora." Ibid., 212–213.

123 "We still don't know what has happened." Ibid., 213.

123 "Dora's wish decisive." Herrmann Kafka, telegram, KL 1–4, AKKA, Wuppertal.

124 "Saw deeply into present-day social injustice." Mailloux, 561.

124 "Although one of these misspelled his name." Ibid.

124 "Dr. Franz Kafka, a German writer." Mailloux, 561.

125 "In a summer's light." Johannes Urzidil, *There Goes Kafka,* trans. Harold Basilius (Detroit: Wayne State University Press, 1968), 183.

125 "For the German literary artists." Ibid., 185.

125 "His death now tore the capstone." Ibid., 185, 190.

126 "I am convinced." Ibid., 186.

126 "Strengthening and affirming power." Ibid., 186–187.

126 "The clarifier and eternal stimulator." Ibid., 187.

126 "I would love Kafka so much more." Ibid., 188.

127 "Rode or walked, each in his own way." Ibid., 192–193.

127 "The saddest of the sad." Mailloux, 559.

127 "A penetrating and painful cry." Urzidil, 193–194.

127 *Kaddish:* the mourner's prayer, the most solemn and one of the most ancient of all Jewish prayers. The children of the deceased repeat Kaddish at the grave for eleven months after a death, and each year on the anniversary of the death. Rosten, 164–165.

127 "She fainted." Hayman, 304.

127 "Not a word was spoken." Urzidil, 194.

127 "When we got back to the house of mourning." Brod, *Biography,* 209.

CHAPTER TEN: IN MEMORIAM

128 "The real, independent life of the books." FK, *Letters to Milena,* 185.

128 "Great eulogy." Urzidil, 195–197.

128 *Shekhina:* "Divine Presence," "actual dazzling, radiant, shining Presence of the Lord himself." Rosten, 336.

129 "Josef K. was dreaming." FK, "A Dream," in *Complete Stories,* 399–401.

129 "The Emperor from his deathbed." FK, "An Imperial Message," in *Complete Stories,* 4–5.

129 "In whispers." Urzidil, 197.

130 "Too deeply hurt to fully realize." Baudy, 25.

130 "In the home of Kafka's parents." Ibid.

130 "Was a lovely woman, infinitely kind to me." Ibid.

130 "Console them on the death of their beloved and ever problematic son." Melech Ravitch, "Stories of My Life: I am Franz Kafka's Wife," *Jewish Chronicle Literary Supplement* (London), February 7, 1992.

130 "A mass of papers." Brod, postscript to *The Trial,* 327, 333.

131 "The most wonderful treasures, and measured against his own work, the best things he has written." Ibid., 332–333.

131 "Same truth to nature." Ibid., 333.

131 "Dearest Max, my last request." Ibid., 328.

131   "Dear Max, perhaps this time I shan't recover." Ibid., 328–329.

132   "Unclouded friendship." Ibid., 330.

132   "My last testament will be quite simple." Ibid.

133   "Without ever saying so." Ibid., 327.

133   "Ten large quarto notebooks." Ibid., 332.

133   "What unforgettable, entirely original." Ibid., 334.

133   "The very insidious lure of such scruples." Ibid., 332.

134   "The whole world doesn't have to know." Max Brod, *Der Prager Kreis* (Stuttgart: Kohlhammer, 1966), 112.

134   "Burned some twenty notebooks while Franz watched from his bed." Franz Kafka, *I Am a Memory Come Alive: Autobiographical Writings,* ed. Nahum N. Glatzer (New York: Schocken, 1974), xiii.

Chapter Eleven: Life After Kafka

135   "Begin to see who you are." FK. *Diaries*, August 27, 1916, 369.

135   "As the cemetery of my life." DD to EH, August-September 1924, MS Kafka 51, fol. 52r,v, Bodleian Collection.

136   "Unhealthy to repress one's impulses." Larsen, 98.

137   "You could always tell a Reinhardt actor." Friedrich, 250.

137   "Thin, ill-shaven, unkempt." Ibid., 245.

137   "A little drunk." DD to EH, August-September 1924, MS Kafka 51, fol. 52r,v, Bodleian Collection.

138   "As the wife of Franz Kafka." Ibid.

138   "It was very thoughtless of me not to go to see her." Ibid.

138   "Deep devoted earnestness." DD, "Chronologische Initialien," Klaus Wagenbach Archive.

139   "How I shall manage to write this letter." DD to OD, October 1924[?], MS Kafka 50, fol. 52v, Bodleian Collection.

139   "Felt like a criminal." Ibid.

139   "I am sitting wrapped." DD to OD, October 1924[?], MS Kafka 50, fol. 52r.

140   "Bohemian, hand-to-mouth, spontaneous existence." Heather Valencia Czeladz, "Berlin and Whitechapel: The World of Avrom-Nokhem Stencl," *Edinburgh Star,* May 1993, 27.

141   "Simply drunk with joy." Heather Valencia, "Yiddish Writers in Berlin, 1920–1936," in *The German-Jewish Dilemma: From the Enlightenment to the Shoah,* ed. E. Timms and A. Hammel (Timms, U.K.: Lampeter, 1999), 195.

141   "The most curious international mob." Friedrich, 148.

141   "From those fleeing from the pogroms." Valencia, "Yiddish Writers, 195.

141   "Dear Ottla! Are you cross?" DD to OD, early 1925, MS Kafka 50, fol. 53, Bodleian Collection.

CHAPTER TWELVE: BETWEEN TWO WORLDS

143 "The truth is always an abyss." Janouch, 154–155.

144 "Great bundle of papers . . . separating the finished from the unfinished chapters," "memory came to the aid of judgment." Brod, postscript to *The Trial,* 334–335.

144 "I was forced to do this." Written by MB on the bottom of a letter from Die Schmiede, Berlin, November 27, 1925, AKKA.

144 "Some considerable time ago." Ibid.

144 "The most joyous and painful emotion." Baudy, 22.

145 "Going back home." Ibid., 24.

145 "One should believe in something indestructible." Ibid.

146 *Mameloshen:* mother language or mother tongue. "Hebrew was the father tongue, since the holy books were in Hebrew, and only Jewish males were taught to read. Yiddish became known as the 'mother's tongue' the language of the home." Rosten, 222–223.

147 "Who is Kafka?" Ravitch, vi.

147 "In his reports to the company he would enumerate the eerie coincidences." Ibid.

147 "To help explain Kafka." Ravitch, iv.

148 "Not unusual for those 'wild' days." Ibid.

148 "When a writer came." Ibid.

148 "In a voice with no tone." Ibid.

149 "Could not talk." Ibid.

149 "Somehow I managed to give the lecture." Ibid.

149 "I took no questions." Ibid.

149 "They had never been officially married." Ibid.

149 "When I mentioned that I had heard." Ibid.

CHAPTER THIRTEEN: THE NATURE THEATER OF OKLAHOMA

150 "As long as you keep climbing." FK, "Advocates," in *Complete Stories,* 451.

150 "Very friendly." Betty Marcus Kuttner, interview by HL, London, August 14, 1995.

150 "Dora was very lively." Ibid.

150 "What beautiful hands Franz had." Ibid.

151 "To avoid anything." Malcolm Pasley, afterword to *The Castle,* trans. Mark Harman (New York: Schocken, 1998), 318.

151 "Something very like a breakdown." FK, *Diaries,* 398–399.

151 "Strange, mysterious, perhaps dangerous." FK, January 27, 1922, *Diaries,* 406–407.

151 "The existence of the writer." FK to MB, July 5, 1922, *Letters to Friends,* 355.

152 "It is like trying to dig a foxhole." FK to RK, end of March 1922, *Letters to Friends,* 322.

152 "The best writer since 1900." Mailloux, 563.

152 "To the wonderful couple." Niels Bokhove, *Kafka Katern* (The Netherlands) 3, no. 2 (1995): 39.

153 "The greatest injustice." RK to OD, June 10, 1926, Bodleian Collection, no. 113.

153 "She is incredibly wonderful." Ibid.

153 "Cooks splendidly." Ibid.

154 "Perhaps she will get an engagement." Ibid.

155 "It was one of the great chances in my life." Leon Askin Web site: www.askin.at/leon.askin/english.htm.

155 "A queen of antiquity." Ibid.

155 "Dwora Dimant." Stadtarchiv Düsseldorf Einwohnermelde-registratur, microfilm: MF 561.

156 "A three act comedy." *Die Opunzie* poster, DLA.

157 "Deeply stirred." Berta Lask, Kaderfragen, DY30, Bundesarchiv.

157 "Shrouded in mystery." EEK, *Welt am Abend,* July 1927, AdK.

157 "Leuna Prison." Ibid.

157 "The provocations of the factory's private police." Ibid.

158 "A social passion." Ibid.

158 "Radical antimilitarism." Berta Lask, Kaderfragen, DY30, Bundesarchiv.

159 "Since I have to travel." DD to OD, undated, SHD IV.2 9818.

159 "Two weeks' leave of absence." DD, letter to the office of the artistic director, Düsseldorf Theater, March 1927, SHD IV.2 9818, DLA.

159 "Herr Direktor." Bela Dimant to academy director, November 17, 1927, SHD IV.2, 9820, 1–2, DLA.

159 "Strong and individual." Gried/Everths to DD, May 23, 1928, SHD IV.2 9820, 1–2, DLA.

159 "Dear Miss Diamant, I hear complaints." Berthold Viertel to DD, September 29, 1927, SHD IV.2, 9819, DLA.

160 "Unbelievable ecstasy," "greatly inspired." Brod, *Biography,* 128.

160 "I know the autobiography of Benjamin Franklin." FK, in Klaus Mann, preface to *Amerika,* trans. Willa and Edwin Muir (New York: Schocken, 1962), xii.

160 "Financed by invisible but extremely powerful benefactors." Ibid., xvi.

160 "Within this 'almost limitless' theater." Brod, afterword to *Amerika,* 298–299.

160 "It was reported that you lingered." Letter to DD and Mia Bing, November 9, 1927, SHD IV.2 9819, DLA.

160 "Request for an explanation." Letter to DD and others, January 21, 1928, SHD IV.2 9819, DLA.

161 "Doris took a shine to me." Luise Rainer, interview, March 13, 2002.

162 "Dear Mrs. Dumont!" DD to Frau Dumont, undated, SHV IV.2, 9818, DLA.

162 "From the beginning, she was recognized." Letter signed by Greid/Everth, May 23, 1928, SHD IV.2, 9822, DLA.

163 "A storm of applause." Dr. T., *Gladbecker Zeitung*, October 4, 1928, DLA.

163 "Raised the creation of the princess." Ibid.

164 "The play is moving." "Rheinisches Städtebundtheater: Der Tor und der Tod," *Düsseldorfer Nachrichten,* November 4, 1928, DLA.

Chapter Fourteen: Description of a Struggle

165 "That which is possible."FK, *Diaries,* January 5, 1914, 251.

165 "Little Wedding." Richard Bessel and E. J. Feuchtwanger, eds., *Social Change and Political Development in Weimar Germany* (London: Croon Helm, 1981), 214.

165 "Would feel obliged to challenge the ban." Ibid., 224.

165 "A senseless rage." Ibid., 225–226.

166 "Berlin's art and artists." Larsen, 118.

166 "A splendid place." Friedrich, 304.

166 "Pretentious slums." Stephen Spender, *World Within World: The Autobiography of Stephen Spender* (New York: Modern Library/Random House, 2001), 133–134.

166 "There was a sensation of doom." Friedrich, 306.

167 "Howling applause." Ibid., 271.

167 "Great attention be paid." Eve Rosenhalf, "Working-Class Life and Working-Class Politics: Communists, Nazis and the State in the Battle for the Streets, Berlin 1928–1932," in *Social Change and Political Development in Weimar Germany,* 207.

168 "A very active communist." DD, Autobiography, Comintern file 495/205/1573/5, Russian Archive.

168 "Overwhelming accusations." Spender, 148.

168 "How convinced and happy people are." DD, "Cahier," TS 13.

168 "Breached the trust of a dying friend." Jürgen Born, ed., *Kritik und Rezeption, 1924–1938* (Frankfurt am Main: S. Fischer, 1953), 216.

168 "I explained to Mr. Welk." DD to VZ, November 14, 1929, in Born, 219–220.

169 "Heavy conflicts arise." MB to VZ, October 24, 1929, in Born, 218.

169 "A personal hostility." DD to VZ, November 14, 1929, in Born, 221–223.

169 "All the others who made a mistake here." Ibid.

170 "There is much (unfortunately too much) talking." Ibid.

170 "A vicious circle was in operation." Larsen, 149.

171 "Maria Jelen." DD, Autobiography, Comintern file 495/205/1573/5, Russian Archives.

171 "I know Comrade Maria Jelen (Diamant)." FG, "Auskunft," Comintern file 495/205/1573/7, Russian Archives.

171 "I thank you, but am very sad." DD to MB, May 2, 1930, in Max Brod, *Der Prager Kreis* (Stuttgart: Kohlhammer, 1966), 112.

172 "Franz was actually my teacher." Ibid., 112–113.

172 "I am rather honest on the whole." Ibid.

172 "For even though in great love." Ibid. Translation partially taken from Pawel, 348.

173 "Only in love, and earlier, the belief in God." DD to MB, May 2, 1930; cited in Brod, *Prager Kreis,* 112.

173 "The proletarian struggle with the most revolutionary realism possible." Richard Stourac and Kathleen McCreery, *Theatre as a Weapon* (London: Routledge & Kegan Paul, 1986), 148.

174 "The KPD supports." Ibid., 148–149.

175 "Uniformed officers." Ibid., 148.

175 "After Charlottenburg, I worked for a short time in Zehlendorf." DD, Autobiography, Comintern file, Russian Archives.

175 "She was accused of inactivity in her street cell." DD, Comintern file, Protokoll no. 2245, 495/205/1573/11, Russian Archives.

176 "The comrade Dora Dymant." Ludwig Lask, SED Fragenboden, Bundesarchiv DY30/IV-2/II/V1556.

176 "School for better-class daughters." Berta Lask, Autobiography, DY30/IV-2/II/V1003, Bundesarchiv.

178 "A military dictatorship." Friedrich, 351–352.

178 "Came back to her native Berlin in 1932." Ibid., 372–374.

179 "Less ambitious." Hodin, "Memories," 36.

179 "The economist Ludwig Johann Lask of Berlin-Lichterfelde." Marriage certificate 583, June 30, 1932, stamped by the Preuss. Standesampt, Berlin VIII, PC.

Chapter Fifteen: Exodus from Berlin

180 "Do not let Evil make you believe." FK, *Blue Octavo Notebooks,* 88.

180 "Now we will show them!" Larsen, 178.

180 "Endanger the state." Ibid., 179.

180 "Restore order." Friedrich, 379.

181 "Gentlemen, surely you do not think." Ibid., 381.

181 "Hitler Reichskanzler," Larsen, 171; "We aim to defeat France," Friedrich, 382–383.

181   "The first reaction to his victory." Friedrich, 383.

181   "Wouldn't be seen dead in their company." Larsen, 172.

182   "Bellowing threats." Friedrich, 383.

182   "Suspected in 1933 of distributing documents against the State." Gestapo report no. A092, no 50482, p. 170/38a, October 19, 1937, Landesarchiv-Berlin.

182   "On suspicion of being involved." Ibid., 170/39b.

183   "In protective custody." Ibid., 170/38b.

183   "Confiscated every scrap of paper." Pawel, 438.

183   "Franz's things are gone." Berhard Echte, Brod correspondence list, Mappe 14, 2, AKKA.

183   "Immediately mobilized the Prague poet." Pawel, 438–439.

184   "A portion of the manuscripts remained in Berlin." Max Brod, "Franz Kafkas sämtliche Werke," *Aufbau,* 1937, 23, Adk.

184   "In spite of all attempts no one has succeeded in finding them again." Hodin, "Memories," 43.

184   "Mountainous stacks of paper." Pawel, 439.

184   "Difficulty recalling all of the details." Lutz Lask, Autobiography (1953), DY30/IV-2/II/v1556, 54–57, Bundesarchiv.

184   "You couldn't have it worse." Marianne Steiner, interview, London, 1990.

184   "Germans! Do not buy from the Jews!" Plater Robinson, *Deathly Silence Guide: Everyday People in the Holocaust.* Available at www.tulane.edu.

185   "Cleansing of the German spirit," "Burn Karl Marx!" Friedrich, 385.

185   "Wherever they burn books." Ibid.

185   "Cancelled her registration and travelled to Prague." Landesarchiv, p. 170/38.

186   "In each residence, I was in contact with the Party." DD, "Lebenslauf" autobiography (1937), Comintern file no. 495/205/1573/5–6, Russian archives.

186   "She found his underwear stained with blood." Marianne Steiner, interview, London, October 1990.

186   "Beaten constantly." LL to Central Committee SED, September 15, 1953, CY30/IV-2/11/v1556, Bundesarchiv.

186   "During the first days of the interrogation." LL, Autobiography, 54–57.

187   "Franziska Marianne Lask." Birth certificate no. 142, August 6, 1934, Berlin-Dahlem Standesbeampt, Lask Collection, Berlin.

187   "His brave, upright attitude." BL, letter, April 16, 1950, DY30-IV-2/II/V/1556, 61–62, Bundesarchiv.

187   "Due to the life-threatening illness of my wife." LL, Autobiography, 54–57.

188   "Under police protection." Ibid.

188   "Political emigrant." Ibid.

190   "A Jew is a Jew is a Jew." Lucy Dawidowitz, *The War against the Jews* (New York: Holt, Rinehart & Winston, 1975), 59.

191   "At the head of the table, Dora Dymant." Avrom Nokhem Stencl, "A Mendele Ovnt—in Berlin," manuscript, Mappe 27, no. 31, Elisabeth Wohler Archive, Archiv Bibliographica Judaica, Frankfurt am Main.

191   "I brought Dora to the railway station." Ibid.

191   "The noted Jewish professor." A092, no. 50482, p. 170/38, Landesarchiv.

192   "Ludwig Lask and his wife." Ibid., p. 170/39b.

Chapter Sixteen: The Worker's Paradise

193   "The Revolution evaporates." FK, in Janouch, 120.

194   "All of Eastern Europe rolled up their skirts and joined the dance." DD, "Shlomo Mikhoels, The Jew," *Loshn un Lebn* 97 (February 1948), 5–8.

194   "No-man's land toward Niegoreloye." Adolph Carl Noe, *Golden Days of Soviet Russia* (Chicago: Thomas S. Rockwell, 1931), 17.

194   "Close an eye," "A curse on your father's father!" DD, "Solomon Mikhoels."

195   "Despite what it turned into, the Russian Revolution." Susan Weissman, "The Russian Revolution Revisited," www.Igc.org/solidarity/atc/weissman.

195   "Divine rights of capital." Eugene Lyons, *Assignment in Utopia* (New York: Harcourt, Brace, 1937), 606.

195   "The bureaucracy, was able to grow." Weissman, "Russian Revolution."

196   "Under the heel of arbitrary power." Lyons, 605.

195   "Russian debacle." Ibid., 606.

196   "The land from which their best people." DD, "Solomon Mikhoels."

197   "Try to imagine." Ibid.

197   "Not only Jews but descendants of all races." Ibid.

197   "Volumes." Ibid.

197   "The soul of all this awe-inspiring splendor." Ibid.

197   "It is not pleasant to feel your hope changing." Lyons, 603.

198   "Anti-patriotic," "cowardly defeatism." Walter Duranty, *USSR: The Story of Soviet Russia* (Philadelphia: Lippincott, 1944), 162.

198   "All comrades in Germany." DD, "Formular," 495/205/1573, Comintern file, Russian Archive.

198   "I was born in the year 1898 in Poland . . . then in a children's home, as a house seamstress." DD, "Lebenslauf," 495/205/1573/5, Russian Archive.

199   "1923, I married the German-Czech writer." Ibid.

199   "In each residence I was in contact." Ibid.

200   "To buy the elementary drugs." Lyons, 436.

200   "The gaping gulf between abstract research." Ibid., 437.

200   "Except under unusual circumstances." Ibid., 440.

201   "Undulating forests, blue-green water." Ruth Kedzie Wood, *The Tourist's Russia* (New York: Dodd, Mead, 1912), 211.

201 "Comrade Hess, please excuse my delay." DD, letter to Hess, 495/205/1573/6, Russian Archive.

201 "Ula Wimmler was a friend of Anatoli Becker." Ibid.

202 "An exhausted heart after hard illegal party work." Berta Lask to "Dear Comrade," April 16, 1950, DY30/IV/IV–2/11/V1556, 61–62, Bundesarchiv.

202 "I now know, since death has forcefully spirited." Berta Lask, "An meinen sohn Ernst," Berta Lask Nachlass, BL 413/177, AdK.

203 "Schreiber informs us." Chernomordik to Kornilev, August 29, 1936, 495/205/1573/20, Russian Archive.

204 "He took her for a sympathizer." Transfer protocol, no. 2245, Comintern file, 495/205/1573/11, Russian Archive.

205 "Amazed that such anti-fascist books." Mailloux, 565.

205 "Because he seemed very knowledgeable." DD to NKVD, August 13, 1937, Comintern file, 495/205/1573/19, Russian Archive.

206 "Children's tuberculosis." DD, statement [April 1937], Comintern files, 495/205/1573/17, Russian Archive.

207 "To be allowed to travel," "Assuming that we get the permission." Ibid.

207 "Because the activities of Dora Lask could not be confirmed . . . the KpdSU (B) is currently out of the question and her membership in the KPD since 1930 is merely confirmed." Protocol no. 2245, June 9, 1937, 495/205/1573/12, Russian Archive.

208 "The deterioration of the international situation." LL, Autobiography, 54–57.

208 "Kafka's works are forbidden in Germany." DD to NKVO, August 13, 1937, 495/205/1573/19v, Russian Archive.

209 "A 'Special Consultation' of the NKVD, he had been sentenced to five years imprisonment in a work and reform camp on suspicion of spying." LL, SED biography, October 12, 1953, DY30/IV-2/II/V1556, 25–27, Bundesarchiv.

209 "If it took a miracle to cure the child." Pawel, 439.

209 "Unless one had the permission of the NKVD." Bernd-Rainer Barth, interview, September 24, 1998, Berlin.

210 "Polish Jews were chosen." Ibid.

210 "Dora was the right age." Ibid.

210 "Kicked out of the country." Ibid.

CHAPTER SEVENTEEN: THE GREAT ESCAPE

211 "The world is growing smaller every day." FK, "A Little Fable," in Complete Stories, 445.

211 "All local border crossing control points to immediately arrest all such persons should they attempt to cross the border." Gestapo document R58 3565, p. 4, Bundesarchiv.

212 "She decided to go to Switzerland." MS, interview, London, 1990.

213 "Open the doors of the United States."; "If we are going to keep our country the way it is . . . " Peter Jennings and Todd Brewster, *The Century* (New York: Doubleday, 1998), 206.

213 "After Switzerland, England." MS, interview.

213 "Betrayal at Munich." Asimov, 573, 577.

214 "With her German passport and Russian family." MS, interview.

214 "Grudgingly issued 1,000 Certificates." Herman Carmel, *Black Days, White Nights* (New York: Hippocrene, 1984), 1920.

215 "Quite marvelously." Ibid., 208.

215 "The only car to be had for the journey." Ibid., 204.

215 "All his vital energies." Ibid., 208.

215 "Nineteen or twenty." Ibid., 196.

215 "The first and most important Dutch theoretician." Netherlands Film Festival Web site, October 2002, www.filmfestival.nl.

216 "Spent several hours in animated discussion." Letter from ML, cited in M. ter Braak and E. du Perron, *Briefwisseling 1930–1940,* ed. H. van Galen Last (Amsterdam, 1967), 14:473.

216 "The congruence of humor." Niels Bokhove, "Dora Dymant en Menno ter Braak over Franz Kafka," *In de Waageschaal,* June 25, 1983.

216 "After being returned yet again to the Dutch port." MS, interview.

216 "Divorced." Registration card no. 730855, May 30, 1940, Manx National Heritage Museum and National Trust.

218 "Nice warm blue coat." Sara Baumer, interview, London, August 14, 1999.

218 "A potential security risk." Ronald Stent, *A Bespattered Page?* (London: Andre Deutsch, 1980), 35–36.

219 "Exempted until further order from internment." D. Lask, Isle of Man registration.

219 "Because he thought a life under a German occupation." Leon Hansen, *Menno ter Braak, 1902–1940,* vol. 2, *1930–1940* (Amsterdam: Balans, 2001), 570.

219 "A very large round-up of enemy aliens." Stent, 54, 57.

219 "Is the female of any species." Ibid.

219 "Enemy aliens," "rampant anti-refugee paranoia," "All aliens are a potential menace." Ibid., 60–61.

220 "Internment of all 'B' women." Ibid., 62.

220 "Any incriminating material." Ibid.

220 "Here, come sit on my lap." HL, interview, London, October 30, 1990.

CHAPTER EIGHTEEN: THE ISLE OF MAN

222 "Believing in progress." FK, *Blue Octavo Notebooks,* 91.

223   "If they would be prepared." Miriam Kochan, *Britain's Internees in the Second World War* (London: Macmillan, 1983), 46.

223   "Tough old commandant." Ibid., 55.

224   "Tumbled in, and then tumbled out." HL, interview, Isle of Man, October 2000.

224   "Betrothed and dismantled." HL, diary, late June 1940; HL, interview, Isle of Man, October 16, 2000.

224   "Marianne is a born actress." HL, diary, June 16, 1940.

224   "Temptation to share the spoils." Peter and Leni Gillman, *"Collar the Lot": How Britain Interned and Expelled Its Wartime Refugees* (London: Quarter), 145.

225   "THE event here—for me—up till now is Dora Kafka." HL, diary, June 16, 1940.

225   "His love for all that is genuine." HL, diary, June 21, 1940.

225   "Dora exuded warmth." HL, diary, June 16, 1940.

226   "The specially favorable conditions." Kochan, 53.

226   "Dora Lask provides, again, calm." HL, diary, June 17, 1940.

227   "Technically admirable." HL, diary, June 18, 1940.

227   "The death of the bad witch." HL, diary, June 23, 1940.

227   "Delightful and in high spirits." HL, diary, June 19, 1940.

227   "Separation from family." Kochan, 55.

228   "Canada was ready." Ibid., 59.

228   "Eva is quite tearful." HL, diary, June 19, 1940.

228   "This wild, constant, icy storm." HL, diary, June 25, 1940.

228   "My head feels quite empty." HL, diary, June 24, 1940.

228   "Very soon, Rushen camp was buzzing with schemes." Kochan, 52.

229   "Modern lines," "noted educationalist." HO 215/55, PRO.

229   "Very mixed, very funny 'Variety Show.'" HL, diary, June 26, 1940.

229   "Emphasized the importance of consonants." HL, diary, June 21, 1940.

229   "And Dora! What she's made of this." HL, diary, July 3, 1940.

229   "About a little child separated." HL, interview, London, October 30, 1990.

230   "Without stockings." HL, diary, July 1, 1940.

230   "She was excellent, a wonderful Yiddish actress." HL, interview, 1994.

230   "Dora knew the poem by heart." HL, interview, London, October 1994.

230   "Extend to the opponents of force." *Encyclopedia Britannica,* s.v. "WWII." Available at http:search.eb.com/eb/article?eu=118865. Accessed April 23, 2002.

231   "A little half-pint." DD, letter to Hanny, Easter, March 25, 1951, PC.

231   "Dora made me a jarful of *schmaltz*." HL, diary, November 21, 1940. *Schmaltz:* cooked drippings, usually chicken fat, which is rendered into a spread. Often mixed with chopped liver. The word has also come to mean corny and over-emotional. It also means good luck: "He fell into a tub of shmaltz, that's how lucky he is." Rosten, 355–356.

232   "Useful." Francois Lafitte, *The Internment of Aliens* (London: Libris, 1988), 195.

232   "Dear sweet Kolibri." DD to HL, April 15, 1941.

232   *Bechaint:* charming.

232   *Balebosste:* an excellent housewife or homemaker. "To call a woman 'a real balebosteh' is to bestow high praise indeed; it means the honoree is a splendid cook, baker, laundress, and above all, keeps so immaculate a home that 'you can eat off the floor.'" Rosten, 30.

233   "It seemed to me as if a mystic was singing 'Shir Hashirim,' Solomon's Song of Songs." DD, *Loshn un Lebn,* January 1949.

233   "How lovely." DD to HL, April 15, 1941.

233   *Simmis* or *Tsimmes:* a sweet stew of fruits or vegetables; used metaphorically for a prolonged production, with the end result generally not worthy of the labor and time involved.

233   "Will you, at some time, be able to write?" Ibid.

233   "Have become a 'C.' Ibid.

Chapter Nineteen: Friends of Yiddish

234   "The crows maintain that a single crow." FK, *Blue Octavo Notebooks,* 89.

234   "Connected to the real world." Dr. Derek Matravers, in *Celebration of the Life of Professor Dorothy Emmet, 1904–2000, Emeritus Fellow of Lucy Cavendish College,* Cambridge, November 18, 2000.

235   "A motorcade with Hitler." Dorothy Emmet, *Outward Forms and Inner Springs* (Macmillan, 1998), 105.

235   "The nearest thing I ever had to a conversion." Anthony Wilson, letter, November 26, 2002.

235   "Nature is . . . processes." Alfred North Whitehead, *Science and the Modern World* (New York: Free Press, 1967), 72.

235   "Senior and well published philosopher." Baroness Perry of Southwark, "A Tribute from Lucy Cavendish College by the President," November 18, 2000.

236   "Told her that Kafka's Dora." DE, interview, Cambridge, October 21, 1999.

236   "It was the time of the air raids." Ibids.

237   "When Dora and Marianne were with me." DE, letter to author, July 25, 2000.

237   "Dora didn't answer her letters properly." DE, interview, 1999.

237   "Marvelous cook." DE to author, October 1999.

237   "She made very good soups, which were quite welcome in wartime." DE, interview, 1999. "Especially fond of her." DE, letter to author, July 2000.

237   "Here's a girl who will benefit." Anthony Wilson, interview, Hampstead, October 2000.

238   "Spacious, with the lofty ceiling." Elfrida Foulds, unpublished manuscript, 19–20, PC.

238   "A place where as many children as possible." Ibid., 9.

238   "A very wide range of people." Ibid., 12.

239   "The basis of recruitment broadened." Ibid., 10, 12.

239   "She was subject to dramatic outbursts." Ibid., 86.

239   "The more these demonstrations were ignored." Ibid.

239   "Dora was a cook of character." Anthony Wilson, interview, Hampstead, October 2000.

239   "We were told that Mrs. Lask was 'Kafka's Dora.'" Carol Shaw to author, August 8, 1999.

239   "Today is my first father's birthday." DE, letter to author, October 1999.

240   "Became one of the most helpful children." Foulds, 86–87.

240   "Humorous, charismatic, always interesting." Heather Valencia, *Edinburgh Star,* 28.

240   "Only two authors existed for him: Kafka and Flaubert. He didn't read anything else." MS, interview, 1990.

240   "Refusing to move beyond the frontier of the East End." Ibid.

240   "His first permanent home," "campaign to preserve Yiddish as a vibrant language." Valencia, *Edinburgh Star,* 30.

241   "Immediately after her arrival." "Tsu der erster yortzayt fun der shoyshpiler Dora Dimant," *Loshn un Lebn,* 1956.

241   "The star of the show." Majer Bogdanski, interview, London, 1995.

241   "She was quite capable and very tough." MS, interview, 1990.

241   "It flourished so much I had to get rid of it," "It was too much money. I couldn't bear it." Ibid.

242   "Her designs were extraordinary." HL, interview, London, October 23, 1994.

242   "The best Jewish writing." Joseph Leftwich, *Yisroel: The First Jewish Omnibus: A Treasury of the Best Jewish Writing of the Nineteenth and Twentieth Centuries* (New York: Beechhurst, 1952).

242   "When I was busily occupied." DD, "To Mosheh Oved on His Sixtieth Birthday," *Loshn un Lebn* 69 (1945): 20–23.

243   "Playfulness, his childlike holiday-mood." Ibid.

243   "Free the weekdays." Ibid.

245   "Rehearsed in the Yiddish Theatre." Editorial in *Loshn un Lebn,* 1956.

245   "Teyve the Dairyman," "For Hardt, with thanks for your reading." Mappe 26, no. 18, Elisabeth Wöhler archive, Archiv Bibliographia Judaica, Frankfurt am Main.

245   "Impoverished." DD, "On the Performance of Peretz's 'Three Gifts,'" *Loshn un Lebn* 63 (1945): 24–28.

246   "The first signs in the street." Ibid.

246   "Does this first attempt actually deliver." Ibid.

246   "It was therefore a pity." Ibid.

246   "Full-hearted praise." Ibid.

247   "There remains the principle." Ibid.

247   "See real Yiddish dramatic art." DD, "Dina Halpern in London," *Loshn un Lebn,* September 1946, 51–54.

247   "After so many years of being fed." Ibid.

247   "I have seen Shylock." DD, "Shakespeare on the London Jewish Stage," *Loshn un Lebn,* October 1946.

248   "If a work offends in its essence." Ibid.

248   "Our hope is not yet lost!" Ibid.

248   "The most moving, shocking Shylock." Ibid.

248   "The hatred was at the right place." Ibid.

249   "As lovely as gold and full of charm." Ibid.

249   "A strange and very disturbing phenomenon." Ibid.

CHAPTER TWENTY: SOMETHING INDESTRUCTIBLE WITHIN

250   "Man cannot live without a lasting trust." FK, in Brod, *Biography,* 214.

250   "Marianne Lask is doing well." Foulds, *Yealand Manor Newsletter,* 1947.

250   "The Nazis took that away." Zelig Besserglick, interview, New York, 1999.

251   "Often raped the girls." Sara Baumer-Dimant, interview 2, London, 1999.

251   "Those photos made it possible." Sara Baumer-Dimant, speech at Memorial Service and Stone Setting for Devorah-Dora Dymant-Lask, August 15, 1999.

252   "Repatriation of Jews." Displaced Persons Operations, *Report of Central Headquarters for Germany* (Washington, D.C.: United Nations Relief and Rehabilitation Administration [UNRRA], April 1946), 5.

252   "To inquire into the conditions of the Jews." "Zionism and the DPs," Yad Vashem Holocaust Martyrs and Heroes Remembrance Authority, www.yad-vashem.org.il.

252   "As things stand now." Malcolm Jarvis Proudfoot, *European Refugees, 1939–52* (Evanston, Ill.: Northwestern University Press, 1956), 325.

253   "Palestine question." British White Paper of 1939, Avalon Project, Yale University, www.yale.edu/lawweb/avalon/avalon.htm.

253   "The Arabs of Palestine felt that any influx." Asimov, 555.

253   "We shall fight Hitler." Rabbi Benjamin Blech, *The Complete Idiot's Guide to Jewish History and Culture* (New York: Alpha, 1999), 281.

254   "Simple, discreet and modest." Hanns Zischler, "Kafka's Niece," *Frankfurter Allgemeine Zeitung,* November 13, 2000. Marianne Steiner obituary.

254   "Landless Arab population." British White Paper of 1939.

254 "A hearty Mazal Tov to my only sister." DD, *Loshn un Leben,* October 1948.

255 "Dora was very worried about her." Ottilie McCrea, interview, London 1990.

255 "A strange and disconcerting genius." Edwin Muir, quoted in publisher's note to Franz Kafka, *The Castle* (Vintage, 1974), v.

255 "A religious humorist." Thomas Mann, preface to Franz Kafka, *The Castle*, xi.

255 "An existentialist." Ronald Grey, *Kafka: A Collection of Critical Essays* (New Jersey: Prentice-Hall, 1962), 16.

255 "One can hardly survey the gigantic essay literature." Brod, *Biography,* 213–214.

256 "The inevitable distortion of his image." Ibid., 215.

256 "A sexual development that is by no means normal." Hodin, "Memories," 31–35.

256 "The never-ending debate." Heinz Politzer, *Franz Kafka: Parable and Paradox* (New York: Cornell University Press, 1962), viii–x.

257 Author's note: Since I prefer the original German version of Dora's interview in *Der Monat* (June 1949) to the English translation, which was published first, in some cases I have chosen to use my own translation of Dora's interview, not that of J. P. Hodin, which appeared in *Horizon* in January 1948.

257 "From the mantelpiece over the open fireplace" through "one can live for short moments only." Hodin, "Erinnerungen," 90–96.

262 "Ravishing beauty." Hanns Zischler, Marianne Steiner obituary, *Frankfurter Allgemeine Zeitung.*

262 "She shared his honesty, his clarity, his passion." MS obituary, *The Times* (London), November 22, 2000.

262 "Soon realizing." MS, interview, 1990.

262 "Simply vanished." Mailloux, 567.

262 "Demonstrated once again the courage." Ibid.

263 "The strangest thing that ever happened" through "it was not a dream." MS, interview, 1990.

CHAPTER TWENTY-ONE: THE PROMISED LAND

265 "Splendor forever lies in wait." FK, *Diaries,* October 18, 1921, 393.

266 "War of extermination." Benjamin Blech, *Jewish History and Culture* (New York: Alpha, 1999), 285.

267 "Gruesome events." DD, "Shlomo Mikhoels, the Jew," *Loshn un Lebn,* February 1948.

267 "Two sentences from Psalms 1." Ibid.

267   "Blessed be the man." Ibid.

267   "Constant thought." Ibid.

267   "Marianne Lask was still in hospital." Elfrida Fouldes, *Yealand Manor Newsletter,* 1949.

268   "Engaged in a bitter struggle." DD, "On a Concert of PPYL at the People's Palace," *Loshn un Lebn,* January 1949.

268   "Against forgetting." Ibid.

268 "Conferences, meetings, readings." Marthe Robert, "Notes inedites de Dora Dymant sur Kafka," *Evidences* (Paris) 28 (November 1952).

269   "A task which might one day." Ibid.

269   "What can you do?" DD, "On a Concert."

269   "She stood, confined by a dark curtain." Mendel Mann, "Franz Kafka's Wife," reprinted in Joseph Leftwich, comp., *The Way We Think: A Collection of Essays from the Yiddish* (New Brunswick, N.J.: Thomas Yoseloff, 1969), 2:779. Also translated from the original Yiddish by Hanny Lichtenstern.

269   "Wild enthusiasm of the audience." DD, "On a Concert."

270   "She didn't know Yiddish." Ibid.

270   "Paul was jealous of Dora." HL, interview, October 1990.

270   "It was very cold in that poorly furnished room." MS, interview, London, October 1990.

270   "She was very lively." Ibid., 16.

271   The mayor issued an official invitation for Dora to speak as a guest of the city. The invitation included free transportation from London to Tel Aviv. Bracha Plotkin, interview, Mishmar HaSharon, Israel, 2001.

271   "This whole business still appears." Werner Timm, "Müritz, Franz Kafkas Begegnung mit Dora Dymant," *Freibeuter* 38 (1988): 14, 22.

271   "He didn't have on his hat." Bracha Plotkin, interview.

271   "Dora wanted to become an actress." Ibid.

272   "He felt he owed her a debt." Ibid.

272   "Her visit made her feel like a human being again." ML to David Maletz, September 19, 1952, Yad Tabenkin Archives, Tel Aviv.

272   "Reached the sunny country from the bottom of hells." Baudy, 23.

272   "All too brief stay in Israel." Brod, 215.

272   "An Evening with Dora Diamant at the Habima," Bernhard Echte, Brod correspondence list, Mappe 15, 2, AKKA.

272   "She visited me often." Brod, *Biography,* 216.

273   "It affected her as it had me." Ibid.

273   "His wealth—a beautiful collection of Kafka books." Baudy, 23.

273   "Men formerly reduced to compromise." Ibid.

273   "Had disappeared." Ibid.

273   "Connection during Dora's visit was very deep." Sara Baumer-Dimant, interview 2, London, August 14, 1999.

274   "She was *ganz meshugge.*" Sara Baumer-Dimant, interview 1, London, August 12, 1999. *Ganz meshugge:* Very crazy; also, wildly extravagant, absurd. Rosten, 240.

274   "Dora still had a great love." Ibid.

274   "From him, I learned to make business." Zelig Besserglick, interview, New York, 1999.

274   "Like a lawyer. Everyone went to him." Ibid.

275   "God is dead." Plotkin, interview.

275   "When Zvika wanted to go outside." Besserglick, interview.

275   "Suddenly a light emerged." Tova Perlmutter, address to the memorial service and stone setting of Deborah-Dora Dymant-Lask, London, August 15, 1999.

275   "All the names of each of her family." Sara Baumer-Dimant, interview 1, 1.

276   "The door creaked." Mann, 774–780. Translation in part from the original Yiddish by Hanny Lichtenstern, 1999.

276   "I want to see Madam Dora," through "It creates for them the illusion of real people." Ibid., 523–527.

278   "As the stage for humanity's apocalyptic finale." *Fodor's Israel* (New York: Fodor's Travel Publications, 1999), 229.

279   "She was our guest." Noga Maletz, interview, Israel, 2001.

279   "I felt like she was really interested." Ibid.

280   "These subjects were close to pornography then." Ora Fein, interview, En Charod, May 2001.

280   "Dora asked so many questions." Maletz, interview.

280   "Women didn't have cosmetics available." Ibid.

281   "For your quick return." Inscription on title page of Brod's *Galilei in Gefangenschaft,* published by Mondial Verlag, signed and dated January 19, 1950. Collection of Tova Perlmutter.

CHAPTER TWENTY-TWO: A MEMORY COME ALIVE

282   "Anyone who grasps life completely." Janouch, 128.

282   "Imitators rather than genuine disciples." Heinz Politzer, *Franz Kafka: Parable and Paradox* (Ithaca, N.Y.: Cornell University Press, 1962), 334–335.

283   "Last Friday, a hatless woman." Baudy, 21.

283   "Did you bring?" Ibid.

283   "A Kafkaesque situation." Ibid.

284   "I am convinced." Ibid., 22.

284   "Dora does not wait." Ibid.

284   "His kindness and a sort of glow." Ibid., 23.

284   "The word 'saint.'" Ibid., 25.

284   "A man who knows these things." Felix Weltsch, "Entretiens avec Dora Dymant," unpublished manuscript, 1949–1950.

284   "A high-level Kabbalist." Dr. Mitra Makbuleh, interview, Irvine, California, 2001.

284   "He suffered intensely." Baudy, 25.

285   "Dora had nothing final." ME, 39.

285   "Did Kafka have faith?" Ibid., 39–40.

285   "If one would only listen." Ibid., 40.

286   "Award-winning literary critic and translator." MR obituary, *San Diego Union-Tribune,* April 15, 1996.

286   "In translating an author." Ibid.

286   "To prepare for her final departure." Baudy, 21.

286   "Marianne Lask is still in hospital." Elfrida Foulds, *Yealand Manor Newsletter,* 1950, Susan Hartshorne PC, York, U.K.

286   "Very well indeed." MS, interview, 1990, 10.

287   "His great new novel." Ester Hoffe to DD, June 20, 1950, PC.

287   "Your sister hasn't yet picked up the package." Ibid.

288   "It is the Saturday afternoon literary get-together" through "every possible shade of the human voice." Ravitch, iv.

289   "Marianne has come out of hospital." Foulds, *Yealand Manor Newsletter,* 1951.

290   "Above all, that I leave Marianne." DD, "Cahier," TS 11, PC.

291   "Our argument was that Marianne's English was perfect." MS, interview, 1990.

291   "Although it would have helped them." Ibid.

291   "Begun to systematically." B. Echte, Brod correspondence list, Mappe 15, p. 2, AKKA.

291   "The first step: free yourself. . . . He used up all his strength in the preparation." DD, "Cahier," TS 1–2.

291   "I have already recognized." Ibid., TS 3.

292   "Should I reach my fortieth year, I will probably marry an old maid . . . exposes the upper teeth." Ibid., TS 16.

292   "I hate Werfel." FK, *Diaries,* December 18, 1911, 141.

292   "One passage among many that offers the key." DD, "Cahier," TS 14.

292   "Since I will hardly ever say more." Ibid.

292   "Sensuous like an animal." Ibid., TS 12.

292   "Searching psychoanalysts." Ibid., TS 15.

293   "Totally at home, walking on firm ground." Ibid., TS 3.

293   "I want to say something essential." Ibid., TS 1.

293   "Dreamy, blossom seed-tiny precision." Ibid., TS 4.

293   "Have an unpleasant feeling." Ibid., TS 1–2.

293   "With Franz, there is absolutely no imitation." Ibid., TS 1–2.

294   "At this point," "all exaggerations." Ibid., TS 4.

294   "Who is to gain from this writing!" Ibid., TS 13.

294   "With each new attempt I found out." Ibid., TS 7.

294   "Marianne is very ill." Ibid., TS 5.

295   "I spent the whole day, with great sadness." DD, letter to HL, March 25, 1951, PC.

295   "Everyone had to be ready." Ibid.

295   "All the heavy cases." Ibid.

296   "Hannichen." DD to HL, April 9, 1951.

296   "Spiritual leader." Dora Dymant, open letter to the editor, *Loshn un Lebn,* April 1951, 44–45.

297   *Mitzvah:* a good deed, sanctioned by God, a profound obligation, ideally performed not with a sense of duty, but with joy. Israel Zangwill described the practice of mitzvoth (plural of mitzvah) as the Jew's "sacred sociology." From Rosten, 252–253.

297   "Fright," "sweet and touching," "so lovingly." Ester Hoffe, letter to DD, April 10, 1951, PC.

297   "I'm very happy that you're writing." Max Brod note, ibid.

297   "It is much easier in letters." DD, "Cahier," TS 13.

297   "The perfect honesty accompanies you." Ibid., TS 7.

298   "One human being alone." Ibid., TS 12–13.

298   "Taken by the hand by Franz." Ibid., TS 5.

298   "If such a thought." Ibid.

298   "A mandate." Ibid., TS 2.

299   "I am the life." Ibid., TS 4.

299   "Whoever knew Franz, could do nothing else." Ibid.

299   "The writings in this exercise book." Ibid., TS 9.

299   "How sad it is." Ibid., TS 7–8.

299   "Even Franz, whose span stretches." Ibid., TS 8.

300   "In the bed directly opposite me." Ibid., TS 10–11.

300   "What happens now?" Ibid.

300   "It was the first death." Ibid.

301   "What a lovely idea." DD to MR, May 12, 1951, PC.

301   "The bloodless and muscle-less look." Ibid.

CHAPTER TWENTY-THREE: "MACH WAS DU KANNST"

303   "Beyond a certain point." FK, "Reflections on Sin Suffering, Hope and the True Way," in *Blue Octavo Notebooks,* 87.

303   "The complete fiasco." DD to HL, July 2, 1951.

303   "Hannychen, here I present you." Ibid.

304   "Does the heart suspect something?" Ibid.

304   "I suppose as a man of the world" through "born on the last days of February." DD to Davy Lichtenstern, July 1, 1951.

305   "Not least for the reason." DD to Ester Hoffe, letter drafted after April 11, 1951.

306   "Very silly and impractical." DD to MR, undated (summer 1951).

306   "I am now significantly better." DD to MR, August 25, 1951.

306   "This is not a letter, just a key." DD to MR, undated (c. August–September 1951).

308   "If I'm not ashamed." DD to MR, December 4, 1951.

308   "I got so excited, remembering the pleasure." DD to MR, December 29, 1951.

309   "If you haven't yet received it." Ibid.

309   "Urgent recommendation." Ibid.

309   "I am in favor of this." DD to MR, December 29, 1951.

309   "Could not suppress the feeling of joy." DD, "Cahier," TS 18.

309   "It now seems to me." Ibid., TS 15-16.

310   "Bears the same relationship." W.H. Auden quote (cover) for FK, *Complete Stories.*

310   "Embodying the tragedy of the West European Jew." Ibid., TS 17.

310   "He was (still?) at the stage." DD, "Cahier," TS 12.

312   "Be buried beside Kafka in Prague." B. Echte, Brod correspondence list, Mappe 12, p. 2, AKKA.

312   "It's your birthday." DD to MR, March 1951.

312   "The writing, as it is now." DD, "Cahier," TS 13.

313   "There are few opportunities." Martin Walser, *Werke,* vol. 12, *Leseerfahrungen, Liebeserklärungen, Aufsetze zu Literatur* (Frankfurt: Helmut Kierel & Franz Borsch, 1997), 731–737.

313   "Such tender hands and such bloody work." Ibid.

313   "It was the darkest late afternoon." Ibid.

314   "Her notes, which she penned." Ibid.

315   "He knew by heart." DD, "Cahier," TS 15.

316   "Unfortunately, I have to break." ML to David Maletz, August 21, 1952, Maletz Papers, Yad Tabenkin Archives, Israel, 5/1.

316   "Was very dark, almost black." HL, interview by author, 1994.

316   "We never spoke about her imminent death." MS, interview, London, 1990.

316   *"Mach was du kannst."* Ibid.

Chapter Twenty-Four: Kafka's Daughter

317   "Man's embittered features are often only the petrified bewilderment of a child." FK, in Janouch, 179.

317   "Dreadful storms threatened England." MR, 38.

317   "No writers or journalists attended her funeral." Ibid.

318   "Did not really live in London." Ibid., 38–39.

318   "Among 'her people.'" Ibid., 38.

318   "Dora Dymant did not think she had to intervene." Ibid., 39.

318   "She was alone." Ibid.

319   "They offer little of a philosophical or religious nature." Ibid.

319   "I am writing to you." ML to David Maletz, August 21, 1952, David Maletz Papers, Yad Tabenkin Archives, Israel, 5/1.

319   "Marianne stayed with us for a time." MS, interview, London, 1990.

320   "She was intensely private." Ibid.

320   "Dora and Marianne's relationship was too close." Dr. Michel de M'UZAN, interview, Paris, October 2000.

320   "Marianne could have been." MS, interview.

320   "Mr. Stencl translated it for me." ML to David "Malic," September 19, 1952, Maletz Papers, Yad Tabenkin Archives, Israel, 5/5.

321   "Unfortunately, there are only a few." Ibid.

321   "Her journey to Israel." Ibid.

321   "Mother isn't there." Ottilie McCrea, interview, London, October 1990.

321   "This month, the eleventh of Av." "Tsu er ershter yortzayt fun der shoyshpiler Dora Dymant," *Loshn un Lebn*, August 1956.

322   "Rehabilitated." SED file DY30/IV-2/II/V1556, 14, Bundesarchiv.

322   "On the 26th of March I was arrested." Ludwig Lask, Autobiography, SED file DY30/IV-2/II/V1556, 54, Bundesarchiv.

323   "Eternal exile." Nathan Steinberger, interview, 1997, www.wsws.org/public_html/iwb4-7/ns.htm.

323   "I am sixty-seven years old," "Ludwig has now been imprisoned." Berta Lask to Wilhelm Pieck, April 15, 1946, and August 6, 1946, DY30/IV-2/II/V1556, 80, 84, Bundesarchiv.

324   "Often I have written." Berta Lask to Wilhelm Pieck, August 15, 1947, DY30/IV-2/11v.1003, 90, Bundesarchiv.

324   "Without any particular accusation." Berta Lask to Walter Ulbricht, April 16, 1950, DY30/IV-2/11/V1556, 61–62, Bundesarchiv.

325   "For the period of my imprisonment." Lutz Lask, Autobiography, 56–57.

325   "Expressed the desire." SED report on Lutz Lask, October 12, 1953, DY30/IV-2/11/V1556, 25–27, Bundesarchiv.

325   "Comrade Lask will not travel to other countries, and not to West Germany." Note to file, November 16, 1953, DY30/IV–2/11/V1556, 21, Bundesarchiv.

325   "With a request to find his daughter for him." MS, interview, October 1990.

326   "Her wish was to become a librarian." Ibid.

326   "She worked there for a year." Ibid.

326   "We all loved her very much." HL, interview, 1990.

326   "There was nothing Marianne culd not do." HL, diary, October 20, 1982.

326   "Comrade L. approached us." Note to file, DY30/IV-2/11/V1556, 17, Bundesarchiv.

327   "Always morbidly guarding her privacy." MS, interview, October 1990.

328   "Superb." ML to Hanny and Paul Lichtenstern, December 1, 1962.

328   "You poor frozen souls." ML to Hanny and Paul Lichtenstern, January 18, 1963.

328   "It really is an enchanting place." Ibid.

330   "While I would love to be with you." ML, postcard to Family Lichtenstern, March 20, 1963.

330   "Fairly steadily." ML to Hanny and Paul Lichtenstern, April 29, 1963.

330   "If all goes well." Ibid.

330   "From somewhere in Northern California." Ibid.

330   "A whole, wonderful week in Vancouver." Ibid., May 14, 1963.

331   "The scenery is breathtaking." Ibid.

331   "A dismaying collection of souvenirs." Ibid., April 29, 1963.

Chapter Twenty-Five: A Redwood Grows in Hampstead

332   "You do not need to leave your room." FK, *Blue Octavo Notebooks*, 98.

332   "She never earned much money." MS, interview.

332   "We all stayed close." HL, interview, July 8, 1998.

332   "Marianne came for lunch and tea." Ottilie McCrea, interview, London, October 1990.

332   "The theatre was Marianne's great love." MS, interview, October 1990.

334   "A very pleasant, highly intelligent man." HL to author, July 30, 1998.

334   "Lask was a clever man." MS, interview.

335   "To Mrs. Marianne Steiner all correspondence." ML, last will and testament, 1. Official two-page document dated June 6, 1977, PC, Hanny Lichtenstein.

335   "To pay for the erection of a tombstone," "To the nearest teaching hospital, to use in any way that they wish, either for transplantation of organs, or for dissection purposes." ML, last will and testament, 2.

335   "Miss M. Lask wishes." ML, postcard (inside envelope), n.d., PC, Hanny Lichtenstern

336   "Who's there?" Sara Baumer and Tova Perlmutter, interview 1, August 1999.

336   "We talked about books." Ibid., 4.

336   "She was like a frightened mouse." Moti Perlmutter to author, Tel Aviv, May 15, 2001.

337   "She was blooming." Tova Perlmutter, interview, Israel, 2001.

337   "When Marianne was in her mid-forties." MS, interview.

337   "'Can't you hear them?'" McCrea, interview, 1999.

337   "Kept there for several months." MS, interview.

337   "Diagnosed as schizophrenic." McCrea, interview, 1990.

337   "I have no family!" HL to author, Isle of Man, October 2000.

337   "Dear Sir and Madam." ML, undated postcards (probably 1981) to HL; PC, Hanny Lichtenstern.

337   "I called on her flat." HL to author, November 21, 2002.

338   "Liebe Mariannchen." HL to ML, July 30, 1981, PC. ML reply written on envelope.

338   "3–4 pm. In bath. [ML, diary, December 13, 1982], "alien thoughts," "Gremlins getting through again . . . A kind of subliminal promotional effort" [January 19, 1982], "suddenly felt the old nausea and cold grip me . . . Hardly any 'buzzing,' just a prickling, bubbling sensation." ML, diary, February 10, 1982, PC, Hanny Lichtenstern.

339   "Mr. & Mrs. Lichtenstern." ML to HL, July 18, 1982.

339   "Feared that her sad life." HL, diary, September 1982.

339   "Obviously we do not intend to allow." Brustmix Investments Ltd. to Miss Lask, July 17, 1982.

339   "I owe you £232.00 for same." ML to Brustmix Investments, July 18, 1982.

339   "Again she refused to open the door." MS, interview.

340   "You may remember that I wrote." Graeme Tweedale to ML, August 23, 1982.

340   "Dead on the floor." HL, interview, October 1990.

340   "Left Ventricular Failure." Death entry no. 209, November 18, 1982, General Register Office, London.

340   "We are heavy with guilt." HL, diary, October 20, 1982.

340   "At 2:45, Marianne was cremated." Ibid.

EPILOGUE

341   "There is always something unaccounted for." FK, in Janouch, 116.

341   "Part of Kafka's legacy." Anthony Rudolf, "The Adventures of Kathi and Dora," *Jewish Chronicle Literary Supplement* (London), February 26, 1999, ii.

341   "The chance is not zero." Prof. John Erpenbeck, interview, Berlin, 1998.

341   "Kafka's last love." Zvi Diamant, speech given at memorial service and stone setting for Dora Diamant, London, August 15, 1999.

342   "A certain Lask," "between 1926 and 1936." Niels Bokhove, Kafka Circle of the Netherlands, "Dora Dymant's Course of Life, 1996.

342   "He told me that many had looked for her grave." Zvi Diamant, memorial speech.

343   "Repair this wrong." Ibid.

343   "I am your cousin." Ibid.

343   "I was speechless." Ibid.

343   "To see her father's grave." Tova Perlmutter to author, June 19, 1999.

344   I was so happy to meet you." Sara Baumer-Dimant, words at the memorial service and stone setting of Deborah-Dora Dymant-Lask, August 15, 1999.

344   "Informal yet dignified." Rudolf, ii.

344   "This kind, intelligent and knowledgeable man." Zvi Diamant, memorial speech, August 15, 1999.

SOURCES

The story of Dora Diamant (Dymant-Lask) incorporates information and documents found in the following archives and libraries in England, Germany, Poland, Russia, Israel and the United States.

Archiv Bibilographia Judaica, Frankfurt am Main. Elisabeth Wohler Papers.
Archiv Kritische Ausgabe Kafka, Wuppertal. Telegrams from Herrmann Kafka to Sanatorium Kierling. Bernhard Echte, list of Max Brod correspondence. Dora/Die Schmiede/Max Brod correspondence.
Archive for the History of the Jewish People, Hebrew University, Jerusalem. Diamant Collection.
Bodleian Library, Department of Special Collections and Western Manuscripts, Oxford University. Kafka collection.
Bundesarchiv Stiftung Archiv der Parteien und Massenorganisationen der DDR, Berlin-Lichterfelde. Dora and Lask family Nazi and SED files. Full listing of all German archives researched in "Record of Examined Files," *Kafka Project Final Report,* Berlin Research, June-September 1998, San Diego State University.
Bundesarchiv-Dahlwitz-Hoppegarten. Lask Gestapo file and arrest records.
Dumont-Lindermann Archiv, Düsseldorf Theatermuseum. Dora's theater school records, correspondence, newspaper reviews. Theater poster from Max Brod's *Opunzie, Deutsches Bühnen Jahrbuch 1929.*
General Register Office, St. Catherine's House, London. Death certificates for Dora and Marianne Lask.
Graal-Müritz Heimatstube Archiv. Photographs and documents on Haus Gluckauf and Haus Huten. Old maps of Müritz.
Jüdische Gemeinde Bibliothek, Berlin. Siegfried Lehman, "Erster Bericht, Jüdisches Volksheim Berlin, May-December 1916."
Klaus Wagenbach Archiv, Berlin. Dora's typeset *cahier* and additional writings on Kafka; notes and letters written between 1951 and 1952. Photographs of Kafka, Brod, and Klopstock.
Landesarchiv-Berlin. Der Oberfinanzpräsident Berlin files. Nazi and Gestapo records on Lask family.
Manx National Heritage, Isle of Man. Dora's internment registration card.
Muzeum Miasta Pabianic. Postcards, old city map, genealogical data for Lodz/Pabianice.

National Archives and Records Administration (NARA), College Park, Maryland. American Historical Association, Committee for the Study of War Documents. Microfilm report on Lask family from German embassy in Moscow.

Public Records Office, Kew. Home Office. Enemy alien and internment records.

Rossiyskiy Gosudarstvennyi Arkhiv Sotsialno-Politicheskoy Istorii (Russian State Archives for Social and Political History, formerly Central Archives of the Communist Party), Moscow. Dora's Comintern file.

SOAS Library, University of London. A. N. Stencl Collection.

Staatsbibliotek, Westhafen-Berlin. Newspaper articles from *Düsseldorfer Nachrichten, Neue Zeitung, Jerusalem Post, Tagesspiegel.*

Stadtarchiv Düsseldorf. Dora's civil and residential records.

Stiftung Archiv der Akademie der Künste, Berlin. Kafka Nachlass. Berta Lask Nachlass.

Stiftung Neue Synagogue Berlin/Centrum Judaicum Archiv, Berlin. Berlin Jewish community records.

Urzad Stanu Cywilnego (Citizens Registration Office), Pabianice. Dora's birth certificate.

Yad Tabenkin Archives, Tel Aviv. David Maletz Papers.

Zehlendorf Heimatstube Archiv, Berlin. Articles on Kafka's life in Zehlendorf.

PRIVATE COLLECTIONS

The following individuals generously shared genealogical and civil records, letters, photographs and/or other items from their personal collections: Sara Baumer-Dimant, Miriam and Zeev Bigon, Zvi Diamant, Ulrike Eisenberg, Niels Bokhove, Ruth Lask Kessentini, Noga Maletz, David Mazover, Ottilie McCrea and Michael Steiner. Hanny Lichtenstern contributed the following: personal diary excerpts 1940–1941, 1982, Dora's letters 1941, 1951–1952, Marianne Lask's collected papers and writings, letters 1963–1982, diary and last will and testament, poster of a January 1941 performance at Port Erin Women's Internment Camp.

Michel M'UZAN shared Dora's *cahier,* a handwritten notebook diary written in 1951, Marianne Lask's typed manuscript of the *cahier,* Dora's letters to Marthe Robert, 1950–1952, and Marianne Steiner and Ester Hoffe correspondence with Dora, 1950–1951, from Marthe Robert's literary estate in Paris.

Carol Shaw shared an unpublished novel, "Education for Adventure," by her mother, Elfrida Foulds. Susan Hartshorne shared her collection of Yealand Manor newsletters from 1945 to 1950. The bulk of records of Yealand Manor School are in the Lancashire Records Office at Preston.

Niels Bokhove contributed "Dora Dymant Course of Life," Dutch registration records for the Friedlaender family from 1933 to 1940, photographs of Dora's residences in Berlin, Müritz, The Hague, copies of Dora's signature in Kafka's books, article on Menno ter Braak.

PUBLISHED SOURCES

Selected Books and Periodicals

Baudy, Nicolas. "Entretiens avec Dora Dymant, compagne de Kafka." *Evidences* (Paris) 8 (February 1950).

Bessel, Richard, and E. J. Feuchtwanger. *Social Change and Political Development in Weimar Germany*. London: Croon Helm, 1981.

Blech, Benjamin. *Jewish History and Culture*. New York: Alpha, 1999.

Bodek, Richard. *Proletarian Performance in Weimar Berlin: Agitprop, Chorus, and Brecht*. Columbia, S.C.: Camden House, 1997.

Born, Jürgen, ed. *Franz Kafka: Kritik und Rezeption, 1924–1938*. Frankfurt: S. Fischer, 1953.

Brod, Max. *Der Prager Kreis*. Stuttgart: Kohlhammer, 1966.

_____. *Franz Kafka: A Biography*. New York: Schocken, 1963.

_____. "Franz Kafkas sämtliche Werke." *Aufbau* (New York), 1937, 23.

_____. *Streitbares Leben*. Munich: Herbig Verlag, 1969.

_____. *Über Franz Kafka*. Frankfurt: Fischer, 1974.

Canetti, Elias. *Kafka's Other Trial: The Letters to Felice*. Translated by Christopher Middleton. London: Calder & Boyers, 1974.

Carmel, Herman. *Black Days, White Nights*. New York: Hippocrene, 1984.

Castello, Elena Romero, and Uriel Macias Kapon. *The Jews and Europe: 2000 Years of History*. New York: Henry Holt, 1994.

Dawidowicz, Lucy S. *The War Against the Jews, 1933–1945*. New York: Holt, Rinehart and Winston, 1975.

De Jonge, Alex. *Stalin and the Shaping of the Soviet Union*. New York: William Morrow, 1986.

_____. *The Weimar Chronicle*. New York: Paddington, 1978.

Duranty, Walter. *I Write as I Please*. New York: Halcyon House, 1935.

_____. *USSR: The Story of Soviet Russia*. New York: Lippincott, 1944.

Dymant, Dora. "On the Actress Dina Halpern's Appearance on the London Yiddish Stage." *Loshn un Lebn*, September 1946.

_____. "On a Concert of the PPYL at the People's Palace." Translated by Hanny Lichtenstern. *Loshn un Lebn*, January 1949.

_____. "On a Production of Peretz's 'Three Gifts.'" *Loshn un Lebn* 63 (1945).

_____. "Shakespeare on the London Yiddish Stage." *Loshn un Lebn* 81 (1946).

_____. "Shlomo Mikhoels, The Jew." *Loshn un Lebn* 97 (1948).

_____. "To Moshe Oved on his Sixtieth Birthday." *Loshn un Lebn* 69 (1945).

Friedrich, Otto. *Before the Deluge*. New York: Harper & Row, 1972.

Frynta, Emanuel, and Jan Lukas. *Kafka and Prague*. Translated by Jean Layton. London: Batchworth, 1960.

Giladi, Ben. *A Tale of One City*. New York: Shengold, 1991.

Gilbert, Martin. *A History of the Twentieth Century*. Vol. 1, *1900–1933*. New York: Avon, 1997.

Gillman, Peter, and Leni Gillman. *"Collar the Lot!"* London: Quartet, 1980.

Glatzer, Nahum N. *The Loves of Franz Kafka*. New York: Schocken, 1986.

Goethe, Johann Wolfgang von. *Hermann and Dorothea*. New York: Frederick Ungar, 1966.

Gottgetreu, Eric. "They knew Kafka," *Jerusalem Post,* June 14, 1974.

Gray, Ronald. *Kafka: A Collection of Critical Essays*. New Jersey: Prentice-Hall, 1962.

Haas, Willy. "Kafkas Tod." *Der Tagesspiegel* (Berlin), November 25, 1953, feuilleton 1.

Hackermüller, Rotraut. *Das Leben, dass mich stört: Eine Dokumentation zu Kafkas letzten Jahren, 1917–1924*. Vienna: Medusa Verlag, 1984.

Hayman, Ronald. *Kafka: A Biography*. New York: Oxford University Press, 1982.

Heine, Heinrich. *Jewish Stories and Hebrew Melodies*. New York: Markus Wiener, 1987.

Hodin, Josef Paul, "Erinnerungen an Franz Kafka." *Der Monat*, June 1949.

_____. "Memories of Franz Kafka." *Horizon*, January 1948.

Hoffman, Eva. *Shtetl*. New York: Houghton Mifflin, 1997.

Hoffmann, E.T.A. *Selected Writings of ETA Hoffmann*. Edited and translated by Leonard J. Kent and Elizabeth C. Knight. Chicago: University of Chicago Press, 1969.

Hofmann, Marthe. "Dinah and the Poet: Franz Kafka's Correspondence with a Sixteen Year Old." *Die Österreichische Furche*, October 1954.

Howe, Irving, and Eliezer Greenberg, eds. *A Treasury of Yiddish Stories*. New York: Penguin, 1989.

Institute for the History of the Worker's Movement. *In den Faengen des NKWD*. Berlin: Dietz Verlag, 1991.

Janouch, Gustav. *Conversations with Kafka*. New York: New Directions, 1971.

Jennings, Peter, and Todd Brewster. *The Century*. New York: Doubleday, 1998.

Kafka, Franz. *Amerika*. Translated by Willa and Edwin Muir. New York: Schocken, 1962.

_____. *The Blue Octavo Notebooks*. Edited by Max Brod. Translated by Ernst Kaiser and Eithne Wilkins. Cambridge, Mass.: Exact Change, 1991.

_____. *Briefe an die Eltern*. Edited by Josef Cermak and Martin Svatos. Frankfurt: Fischer Taschenbuch Verlag, 1993.

_____. *The Castle.* Translated by Mark Harman. New York: Schocken, 1998.

_____. *The Complete Stories.* Edited by Nahum Glatzer. New York: Schocken, 1976.

_____. *Dearest Father.* Translated by Ernst Kaiser and Eithne Wilkins. New York: Schocken, 1954.

_____. *The Diaries, 1910–1923.* Edited by Max Brod. New York: Schocken, 1948–1949.

_____. *I Am a Memory Come Alive.* Edited by Nahum N. Glatzer. New York: Schocken, 1974.

_____. *Letters to Felice.* Edited by Eric Heller and Jürgen Born. Translated by James Stern and Elizabeth Duckworth. New York: Penguin, 1983.

_____. *Letters to Friends, Family, and Editors.* Translated by Richard and Clara Winston. New York: Schocken, 1977.

_____. *Letter to His Father.* Translated by Ernst Kaiser and Eithne Wilkins. New York: Schocken, 1966.

_____. *Letters to Milena.* Edited by Willy Haas. Translated by Tania and James Stern. Great Britain: Vintage, 1999.

_____. *Letters to Ottla and the Family.* Translated by Richard and Clara Winston. New York: Schocken, 1982.

_____. *The Trial.* Translated by Willa and Edwin Muir. New York: Vintage, 1969.

Kleist, Heinrich von. *The Marquise of O— and Other Stories.* Translated by Martin Greenberg. New York: Criterion, 1960.

Koch, Hans-Gerd, ed. *Als Kafka mir entgegenkam . . . Erinnerungen an Franz Kafka.* Berlin: Verlag Klaus Wagenbach, 1996.

Kochnan, Miriam. *Britain's Internees in the Second World War.* London: Macmillan, 1983.

Lafitte, Francois. *The Internment of Aliens.* London: Penguin, 1940.

Larsen, Egon. *Weimar Eyewitness.* London: Bachman & Turner, 1976.

Leftwich, Joseph, ed. *The Way We Think: Jewish Essays at Mid-Century.* New York: Thomas Yoseleff, 1969.

_____. *Yisroel: The First Jewish Omnibus.* New York: Beechhurst, 1952.

Lyons, Eugene. *Assignment in Utopia.* New York: Harcourt, Brace, 1937.

Mahler, Raphael. *Hasidism and the Jewish Enlightenment: Their Confrontation in Galicia and Poland in the First Half of the Nineteenth Century.* New York: Jewish Publication Society of America, 1985.

Mailloux, Peter. *A Hesitation Before Birth.* Newark: University of Delaware Press, 1989.

Matthews, Mervyn. *The Passport Society.* San Francisco: Westview, 1993.

Meltz, Eva Stolar, and Rae Gunter Osgood. *And the Winds Blew Cold.* Blacksburg, Va.: McDonald & Woodward, 2000.

Noe, Adolf Carl. *Golden Days of Soviet Russia.* Chicago: Thomas S. Rockwell, 1931.

Pawel, Ernst. *The Nightmare of Reason: A Life of Franz Kafka.* New York: Farrar Straus Giroux, 1984.

Politzer, Heinz. *Franz Kafka: Parable and Paradox*. New York: Cornell University Press, 1962.

Proudfoot, Malcolm J. *European Refugees: 1939–52*. Evanston, Ill.: Northwestern University Press, 1956.

Ravitch, Melech. "Stories of My Life—I am Franz Kafka's Wife." *Jewish Chronicle Literary Supplement* (London), February 7, 1992.

Robert, Marthe. *As Lonely as Franz Kafka: A Psychological Biography*. Translated by Ralph Manheim. New York: Schocken, 1986.

———. "Notes inedites de Dora Dymant sur Kafka." *Evidences* (Paris) 28 (November 1952).

Rosten, Leo. *The Joys of Yiddish*. New York: Pocket Books, 1970.

Rozenkar, Moshe. "The Hebraica Association: The Blossoming of Hebrew Language Restoration in Bedzin." In *Pinkas Bedzin*. Edited by A. Sh. Stein. Tel Aviv: Assoc. of Former Residents of Bedzin in Israel, 1959.

Rubenstein, Joshua, and Vladimir P. Naumov. *Stalin's Secret Pogrom*. New Haven: Yale University Press, 2001.

Rudolf, Anthony. "Kafka and the Doll." *Jewish Chronicle Literary Supplement* (London), June 15, 1984, vii.

Shirer, William L. *The Nightmare Years*. Boston: Little, Brown, 1984.

Spender, Stephen. *World Within World*. New York: Modern Library, 2001.

Stencl, A. N. "A Mendele Evening in Berlin" *Loshn un Lebn*, June-October 1974.

———. "On the First Anniversary of the Death of the Actress Dora Dimant." *Loshn un Lebn,* 1956.

Stent, Ronald. *A Bespattered Page?* London: Andre Deutsch, 1980.

Stourac, Richard, and Kathleen McCreery. *Theatre as a Weapon: Workers' Theatre in the Soviet Union, Germany and Britain, 1917–1934*. New York: Routledge & Kegan Paul, 1986.

Tarrant, V. E. *The Red Orchestra*. New York: John Wiley, 1995.

Thurston, Robert W. *Life and Terror in Stalin's Russia, 1934–1941*. New Haven: Yale University Press, 1996.

Timm, Werner. *Das Ostseebad Graal-Müritz, 1328–1994*. Bremen: Verlag Atelier im Bauernhaus, 1994.

Urzidil, Johannes. *There Goes Kafka*. Translated by Harold Basilius. Detroit: Wayne State University Press, 1968.

Vaksberg, Arkady. *Stalin Against the Jews*. New York: Alfred A. Knopf, 1994.

Valencia, Heather. "Czeladz, Berlin and Whitechapel: The World of Avrom-Nokhem Stencl." *Edinburgh Star*, May 1993.

———. "Yiddish Writers in Berlin, 1920–1936." In *The German Jewish Dilemma: From the Enlightenment to the Shoah*. Edited by Edward Timms and Andrea Hammel. Lewiston, N.Y.: Edwin Mellen, 1999.

Wagenbach, Klaus. *Franz Kafka: Bilder aus seinem Leben*. Berlin: Verlag Klaus Wagenbach, 1995.

Walser, Martin. *Leseerfahrungen, Liebeserklärungen, Aufsätze zur Litertur.* Vol. 12. Edited by Helmut Kiesel and Frank Borsch. Frankfurt: Suhrkamp, 1997.

Wisse, Ruth R. *I.L. Peretz and the Making of Modern Jewish Culture.* Seattle: University of Washington Press, 1991.

_____. *The I.L. Peretz Reader.* New York: Schocken, 1990.

Wood, Ruth Kedzie. *The Tourist's Russia.* New York: Dodd, Mead, 1912.

INDEX

Academy for Dramatic Art of the
    Düsseldorf Playhouse, 154–156
Academy for Hebrew Studies, 14, 54, 63,
    74, 87
ADAM, 309
Agitprop theater, 173–175, 198, 201
Aleichem, Sholem, 69, 146, 245
Alfred A. Knopf publisher, 205
Altmann, Hans (Hans Schreiber), 203–204,
    208
Amerika (Kafka), 156, 160, 162
    See also "Stoker, The"
Anderson, Sir John, 219
Arabs and Palestine, 253–254, 265–266
Askin, Leon, 155
As Lonely as Franz Kafka (Robert), 286
Atkins, Robert, 248
Auden, W.H., 166, 310
Aufbau, 80, 183–184
Auschwitz, 240, 271–272

Baal Shem Tov, 12, 20
Badt, Hermann, 5, 86
Baeck, Leo, 64
Balabanoff, Angelica, 24, 86
Balfour, Lord Arthur James, 22–23
Balfour Declaration, 22–23, 253
Barrault, Jean-Louie, 282–283
Baudy, Nicolas, 283–285
Bauer, Felice, 10, 29, 45, 53–54
Bauhaus movement, 136
Baum, Oskar, 35, 124, 125, 126
Baumer, Abraham, 251–252, 254–255, 266,
    281
Baumer-Dimant, Sara
    at Dora's memorial service, 343, 344
    in Israel, 266, 273–275, 281
    WW II and, 218, 250–252, 254–255
Beck, Oscar, 1–2, 103, 105–106
Becker, Anatoli, 201, 202, 207
Bedzin, Poland
    as Dora's home, 2, 17, 18, 21, 194
    WW II and, 217–218, 251–252, 271
Beggar's Opera (Gay), 167

Beis Ya'acov school, 5, 23–24
Ben-Gurion, David, 253
Bentovim, Pua, 58, 74
Bergmann, Hugo, 13–14, 126
Bergner, Zachariah. *See* Ravitch, Melech
Berliner Morgenpost, 40
Berlin Jewish People's Home/camp, 2, 3–4,
    7–8, 9–10
Berlin's "Golden Twenties," 34, 136–137,
    165–166
Berlin Stories (Isherwood), 166
Bernd-Rainer, Barth, 209–210
Besserglick, Branka/Zelig, 254, 274, 275
Best, Werner, 211
Bogdanski, Majer, 241, 344
Bokhove, Niels, 216, 342
Book of Life, 33
Braak, Menno ter, 215–216, 217, 219
Brecht, Bertolt, 137, 167, 174
Brian, Brenda, 304–305
Brod, Max
    background/meeting Kafka, 36–39
    Dora and, 143–144, 156, 162, 312
    on Dora/Kafka, 12, 75, 215
    Dora's lost letters to, 341
    Dora's writings on Kafka, 291, 294, 297,
        318–319
    Emmy Salveter affair, 35–36, 45, 60, 79
    Israel/Palestine and, 215, 244, 272, 275
    Kafka's Berlin plan and, 26, 30, 35
    Kafka's correspondence with, 28, 40,
        44–45, 59, 66, 67–68, 74, 79, 93,
        103–104
    Kafka's death/funeral and, 122, 124,
        127, 128
    Kafka's health and, 76–77, 88, 95,
        97–98, 103–104, 109–112, 118
    Kafka's lost writings and, 183–184
    Kafka's return to Prague with, 88, 92
    Kafka's *The Trial* and, 143–144, 287
    Kafka's writings/publications and, 29,
        73, 95, 130–134, 143–144, 151, 160
    in literary spat, 168–170, 171–173
    visits to Dora/Kafka, 60–62, 72–73, 85

Brod, Max *(continued)*
    as writer, 38, 39, 70, 125, 126, 215,
        255–256
    Zionist goals of, 10, 25
Broken Pitcher, The (Kleist), 160–161
Brothers Karamazov, The (Dostoyevsky), 82
Buber, Martin, 10, 172
"Burrow, The" (Kafka), 68, 71–72, 84
Busse, Carl, 80

Cabaret (Isherwood), 166
Canada and enemy aliens, 227–228
Castle, The, (Kafka), 144, 151, 152, 205,
        284
Central German Revolt of 1921, 157–158
Chamberlain, Neville, 213–214, 219
Charles-Ferdinand University, 36
Churchill, Winston, 219, 228
Cohen, Shlomoh, 246, 249
Collective Theater of the Rhine, 163–164
Communist Review, 124
Conversations with Kafka (Janouch), 50–51,
        308–309
"Country Doctor, The" (Kafka), 73, 131–132
Cruikshank, Dame Joanna, 223
Cultural Bolshevism, 167
Czechoslovakia and WW II, 214–215

Daladier, Edouard, 213–214
David, Josef (Pepa), 27, 34, 66–67
David, Ottla Kafka
    background of, 26–27, 28
    death of, 262–263
    Dora and, 67, 74, 75–76, 87, 98,
        106–107
    Dora/Kafka and, 66–67, 74, 76
    Kafka's correspondence with, 39–40,
        43, 61, 64, 66, 75, 78
Dawes Plan of 1924, 136
Dawidowicz, Lucy, 190
Demetz, Hans, 127
Depression, global, 170–171, 189
Der Judenstaat (Herzl), 21
Der Monat, 257
Diamant, David, 17, 23, 250, 254, 271,
        274–275, 342
Diamant, Dora
    acting at internment camp, 229, 230,
        232
    acting interests of, 5, 81–82, 135, 136,
        189
    acting lessons/school, 139, 140, 152,
        154–162

acting professionally by, 163–164, 167
autobiography/forms for Russia,
    198–199, 201–202, 207–208
Berlin Jewish People's Home/camp
    and, 2, 3–4, 7–9, 54
birth/early life of, 4–5, 16–25
Brod and literary spat, 168–170,
    171–173
businesses of, 241, 242
correspondence with Kafka's parents,
    96, 97, 98–99, 103, 104, 106,
    113–114, 117
correspondence with Kafka's sisters,
    102, 104–105, 106–107, 108,
    137–139, 141–142
death of, 315–316
description of, 3
education of, 5, 20, 21–22, 23–24, 63
as English "enemy alien," 218–233
escape from Russia, 206–207, 208,
    209–210, 211
escape to England, 213, 214, 216–217
family background of, 16–17, 23
final wishes of, 312
funeral of, 317–318
in Holland, 213–214, 215–216, 217
illness of 1925, 143, 145, 154
illness of 1946–47, 250, 255
illness of 1951–52, 289–300, 301–302,
    303, 305, 308, 315–316
independence of, 4–6, 10, 12, 16, 159
Israel visit, 272–281
Judaism and, 6, 12, 32–33, 49, 63, 146
Kafka's books lost by, 194, 205, 208
Kafka's death/funeral and, 119–124,
    127, 129–130
Kafka's hairbrush and, 121–122, 124,
    281
Kafka's letters/writings kept by, 90,
    133–134, 172, 183–184, 261,
    341–342
at Kafka's parents, 130, 135
on Kafka's sexuality, 292
on Kafka's spirituality, 285, 313–314
Kafka's works burned by, 84–85, 134
KPD membership/work of, 171, 173,
    174, 175–179, 182, 186
on life with Kafka, 257–261
marriage to Lutz Lask, 175–176, 179,
    182, 184, 186–188, 200, 203
memorial service for, 343–344
move/returns to Berlin, 25, 28,
    135–142, 150–151, 152–154

Paris visit, 282–286
Poland return (1925), 143, 145–149
relationship with father, 4, 5, 19, 22,
    23–24, 108–109, 111, 272
royalty checks for, 135, 139, 143–144,
    154, 156, 171, 306
Russia and, 188–190, 191–210
writings about Kafka, 290, 291–294,
    297–300, 310, 312, 315
WW II after internment, 234–244
WW II internment of, 220–233
Yiddish language preservation and, 240,
    241–243, 245–249, 268–270, 318,
    321
Yiddish theater and, 245–249
See also Kafka, Franz, health; Lask,
    Franziska Marianne
Diamant, Dora, and Kafka
Berlin parting, 88–89
Berlin plans of, 14, 15–16, 25–26, 28,
    30–31, 33–34, 35
first meeting of, 6–9
Hebrew language and, 9, 10, 14, 58
Judaism and, 77–78
kerosene lamp and, 58, 260, 277
marriage and, 108–109, 111, 116
in Müritz, 6–16
Palestine dreams of, 13–14, 49
readings together, 55–57, 87
Steglitz apartment (first), 39–61
Steglitz apartment (second), 59, 63–69,
    70–80
Zehlendorf apartment, 80–88
See also Kafka, Franz
Diamant, Gittel, 23, 250, 252
Diamant, Tuvia, 271–272
Diamant, Zvi, 254, 274, 275, 342–344
Diamant family
history of, 16–17
WW II and, 217–218, 250, 251–252,
    254–255, 271–272
Diament, Frajda Frid, 16–17
Die literarishe Welt, 82, 152
Die neue Rundschau, 82
Die Opunzie, 156
Die Rote Fahne, 182, 184
Die Schmiede publisher, 73, 95, 115, 133,
    135, 143–144
Dietrich, Marlene, 178
Dimant, Bela, 145, 159
Dimant, Sara Baumer. See Baumer-Dimant,
    Sara.
Dostoyevsky's writings, 20, 69, 82

"Dream, A" (Kafka), 129
Dumont, Louise, 155, 160, 162, 167
Düsseldorfer Nachrichten, 156
Düsseldorf News, 164
Dymant, Herschel
    background/life of, 16–18, 19, 32, 217
    relationship with Dora, 4, 5, 22, 23–24,
        108–109, 111, 272

Earthquake in Chile, The (Kleist), 56
Einstein, Albert, 136, 178, 179
Eisner, Pavel, 310
Emmet, Dorothy, 234–237, 239–240
Engels, Friedrich, 173, 236, 325
Engels, Mia, 163
Eretz Yisroel. See Palestine
Evereth, Franz, 162

Farben, I.G., 157
Fein, Ora, 280
Feld, Fela, 246, 249
Ferdinand, Archduke Franz, 20
Final Solution, 240
Fischer, Walter, 202
Flaubert, Gustave, 240, 286
Fleming, Alexander, 200
Fool and Death (Hofmannsthal), 163–164
Fortune magazine, 213
Foulds, Elfrida, 238, 239, 240, 245, 250
Fox, George, 238
Franz Kafka: A Biography (Brod), 215
Freud, Sigmund, 136, 286
Friedlaender, Ernest/Ruth
    in America, 219, 327–331
    in Berlin, 177–178
    family reunion of, 334
    in Holland, 187, 213, 215–216, 217
    Marianne's visit to, 327–331
    visits to Dora/Marianne, 303–304, 305
Frietsche, Eva, 165, 168, 199
Fröbel, Friedrich, 24

Gardening School in Dahlem, 8, 28, 57–58
Gay, John, 167
Georg, Manfred, 24, 79–80
Gerer Rebbe, 5, 18–19, 22
Germany
    Kafka's writings and, 205, 309–310
    WW II and, 211, 214, 217–218, 219,
        224
    WW II and England, 224, 230–231,
        236, 244
    See also Hitler; Nazis

Germany's Great Inflation (1923), 40–41, 46, 58, 64, 65

Gestapo, 180, 181–183, 186–187, 191–192, 211

Gide, André, 282

Goebbels, Joeseph, 167, 212

Goethe's writings, 20, 37, 54, 136, 159, 230, 260

Goldman, Dov, 271

Greenberg, Martin, 56

Greid, Hermann, 162

Grindea, Miron, 309

Gropius, Walter, 136

Grosz, George, 141

Haas, Willy, 82, 119, 154, 260

Habima Theater Company, Tel Aviv, 244, 249, 272

Hagadah, 63

Haganah, 254

Hajek, M., 94, 95, 97, 98, 99, 100

Halacha, 63

Halpern, Dina, 247

Hardt, Ludwig, 81, 82, 245

Harrison, Earl, 252, 254

Haskalah movement, 19

Hayman, Ronald, 84

Hebraica Association, 21–22, 23

Heine, Heinrich, 185

Hermann, Elli Kafka, 27–28, 102, 104–105, 106, 108, 113, 262

Hermann, Karl, 96, 102, 123, 262

Hermann and Dorothea (Goethe), 54, 260

Herzl, Theodore, 4, 21, 23, 253

Hindenberg, President, 178, 181

Hitler, Adolph
  as dictator, 181–182
  as Nazis leader, 62, 167, 178, 179
  nonaggression pact and, 210, 217
  purge by, 189
  See also Nazis

Hodin, Josef Paul, 256, 257–261, 284

Hoffe, Esther, 183, 272, 287, 297, 305–306, 309

Hoffman, Camill, 183, 184

Hoffman, E.T.A., 57, 260

Hoffman, Eva, 19–20

Hoffmann, Dr., 104, 116

Hofmannsthal, Hugo von, 37, 163

Horizon, 257

Hovevei Zion (Lovers of Zion), 21

"Hunger Artist, The" (Kafka), 2, 74, 82, 115–116, 131–132, 133, 135, 292

Ibsen, Henrik, 136, 155, 159

"Imperial Message, An" (Kafka), 129

Isherwood, Christopher, 166

Isle of Man, 222–233

Israel
  new nation of, 265–266
  See also Palestine

Jacobsohn-Lask, Louis, 177, 190, 191–194, 200, 230, 240

Janouch, Gustav, 50–51, 272–273, 297, 308–309

Jenufa (Janacek), 35, 88

Jesenska, Milena, 16, 45, 65, 124–125

Jewish Workers Theater, Moscow, 196–197, 267

Jews in German Literature, 79–80

Jordan/Transjordan, 253, 265

Joseph, Emperor Franz, 30

"Josephine the Singer, or the Mouse-Folk" (Kafka), 91, 95

"Judgment, The" (Kafka), 73, 131–132

Kabale und Liebe (Schiller), 163

Kafka, Elli, 27–28, 102, 104–105, 106, 108, 113, 262

Kafka, Franz
  correspondence with parents, 46, 65–66, 96, 103, 111, 117
  descriptions of, 37, 48–51, 68–69
  desires for marriage/parenthood, 15–16
  early friendship with Brod, 36–39
  education of, 36–38
  effect on others, 12, 125–126, 261
  family background of, 10–11, 26–28
  family in WW II, 262–263
  funeral/days after death, 121–127
  ghosts of, 44, 54–55, 65, 84, 130, 259
  gift to Tile Rössler, 42
  girl/lost doll and, 51–52, 138
  independence and, 35, 47, 84–85, 87, 259, 260
  Judaism and, 12–13, 26, 63–64
  literature's importance to, 38, 55–57, 69
  memorial service for, 128–129
  money worries of, 46, 65–66, 77, 78, 85, 93, 94–95
  nature and, 53, 115
  publishing attitude of, 73–74
  relationship with father, 10–11, 29–30, 34, 38, 88–89, 260
  return to Prague (1924), 88–89, 90–91
  Schelesen retreats, 28–29, 30–31

as vegetarian, 8, 26, 45–46, 64
writing need of, 52–53, 54, 59–60,
  70–72, 151–152
See also Diamant, Dora, and Kafka
Kafka, Franz, health
  Conversation Slips, 110–111, 118, 123
  death of, 118–120
  desire to live, 111–112, 114–115, 116
  Dr. Hoffman's sanatorium, 1–2, 99,
    100–120
  nature-cure, 98, 103
  recuperation for, 13, 26, 28–29
  return to Prague (1924), 88–89, 90–91
  Sanatorium Wienerwald, 93–94
  University Clinic, Vienna, 94–100
  winter (1923–24), 75–77, 79, 81, 83,
    85–89
Kafka, Franz, writings
  Brod/publications of, 29, 73, 95,
    130–134, 143–144, 151, 160
  burning and, 84–85, 131–133, 134
  debates over, 168–170, 255–256
  in Germany, 205, 309–310
  Gestapo taking of, 183–184, 261,
    341–342
  growing fame of, 205
  See also specific works
Kafka, Herrmann
  assimilation of, 30
  criticism of Elli, 27–28
  Dora/Kafka relationship, 75–76, 88–89
  relationship with son, 10–11, 29–30, 34,
    38, 88–89, 260
Kafka, Herrmann/Julie
  death of, 262
  desire to visit son (1924), 114, 117
  Kafka's death/funeral and, 122, 123,
    124, 125, 127
Kafka, Julie, 66, 75–76, 124, 130
Kafka, Ottla. See David, Ottla Kafka
Kafka, Valli, 27, 58, 60, 262, 264
Kafka Project, 341–342, 343–344
Kamenev, Leonid, 203
Kayser, Rudolf, 82–83, 260
Kibbutz at En Charod, 279–281
Kindergarten, 24
King Lear, 196–197, 267
King Nicolo, or Such is Life (Wedekind),
  163
Kirov, Sergey, 190
Kisch, Egon Erwin, 158
Kleist, Heinrich von, 55–57, 160, 260
Klopstock, Robert

correspondence with Kafka's family,
  107–108, 112–113, 114, 123, 145,
  153
Dora and, 143, 145, 152–154, 344
Kafka's care by, 107–108, 111, 112–113,
  114, 116–117, 118–119
Kafka's concern for, 44, 78
Kafka's correspondence with, 31, 34,
  41, 74, 80, 85, 87–88, 152
Kafka's death/funeral and, 122,
  123–124
Kafka's health and, 92, 93, 94, 98,
  99–100, 105, 106
meeting Kafka, 92
visits to Kafka, 88, 91, 92
Koch, Hans Hellmuth, 129
KPD
  Dora and, 171, 173, 174, 175–179, 182,
    186
  Nazis and, 180, 182–192
Kristallnacht, 212

Langhoff, Wolfgang (Walter), 158–159,
  174, 199
Larsen, Egon, 170–171
Lask, Berta
  arrest of, 182–183
  background of, 176–177
  escape from Berlin, 185–186, 188
  politics of, 156–158, 176
  return to East Berlin, 322, 323–325, 327
  Russia and, 188, 190, 195, 200,
    202–203, 208, 209, 240
Lask, Emil, 156–157
Lask, Ernst (Berta's son), 178, 195, 202
Lask, Ernst (Marianne's cousin), 322, 327,
  330, 335
Lask, Franziska Marianne
  birth/early years of, 187, 188, 193–194
  death/memorial of, 340, 344
  Dorothy Emmet and, 236–237
  East Berlin family and, 325, 326–327
  education of, 237–240, 243, 286–287
  English citizenship and, 290–291, 319
  illness in Russia, 199–201, 203, 204,
    206, 207
  illness of, 212, 217, 243, 245, 255, 266,
    267–268, 294–295
  internment of, 220–233
  mental illness of, 336–340
  trip to North America, 327–331
  will/testament of, 335
  at Yealand Manor, 237–240, 243

Lask, Hermann, 178, 195, 209, 212, 322
Lask, Ludwig "Lutz"
    Dora and, 175–176, 179, 182, 184,
        186–188, 200, 203
    Gestapo and, 182, 184, 186–187
    KPD work by, 175–176, 177–179, 182,
        186–187
    in labor camps, 209, 322–323
    return to East Berlin, 322, 323–324
    Russia and, 188, 200, 201, 208, 209,
        290–291
    visit to England, 334
Lask, Mira Lose, 327
Lask, Ruth. *See* Friedlaender
Lasker, Emmanuel, 141
Lask family
    at Dora's memorial service, 343–344
    Russia and, 182, 188–189, 190–209,
        322–325
Law for Preventing Overcrowding in
    German Schools and Colleges
    (1933), 185
Law for the Restoration of the Professional
    Civil Service (1933), 184
Leftwich, Joseph/Sala, 242, 296
Lenari and Kafka's books, 205, 208
Lend-Lease Act (U.S./1940), 230
Lenin, Vladimir, 190, 325
Letter to His Father, A (Kafka), 29
Leuna–21 (Lask), 156–158, 165
Lichtenstern, Hanny Metzger
    after WW II, 244, 269–270, 295–296,
        303–304
    internment of, 220–221, 224–233
    Marianne Lask and, 326, 329–330,
        332–334, 337–338, 339, 340, 344
    memories of Dora, 150, 242
Lichtenstern, Paul, 231–232
Liebknecht, Karl, 34, 158
Life and Opinions of Kater Murr
    (Hoffman), 57, 260
Life with a Goddess (Brod), 36
Lindemann, Gustav, 155
Literarishe Bletter, 147
Literary World, 154
"Little Woman, A" (Kafka), 59–60
Lodz, Poland, 146, 236
Loshn un Lebn, 240, 241, 245, 267, 269,
    296, 321
Lowy, Dr. (lawyer), 64
Lowy, Siegfried, 64, 85–86, 88, 108, 123
Ludendorff, General, 62
Lueders, Madeline, 162

Luxemberg, Rosa, 34, 158
Lyons, Gene, 196–198, 200

McCrea, Ottilie, 244, 268, 296, 337
Maletz, David/family, 279–281, 319,
    320–321
Mann, Mendel, 269, 275–278
Mann, Thomas, 56
Marcus, Elizabeth (Betty), 150
Marquise von O— (Kleist), 55–57, 160, 260
Marx, Karl, 176, 236, 325
Masaryk, Thomas, 125
Meditation (Kafka), 132, 133
Meir, R. Issac (RIM), 18–19
Merchant of Venice, The, 247–249
"Metamorphosis, The" (Kafka), 73,
    131–132, 152
Meyrink, G., 37
Mikhoels, Solomon, 196–197, 266–267
Moore, Henry, 309
Mosse newspaper group, 25, 51
Mueller, Alice, 178, 195, 209, 212
Muir, Edwin/Willa, 205, 262, 263, 285
Mussolini, Benito, 194, 224
M'UZAN, Michel de, 306, 319, 320

Narody Listy, 124–125
Nathan, Eva, 225, 228, 229, 231, 232
National School for Drama (Berlin), 139,
    140
National Socialist Workers Party. *See* Nazis
"Nature Theater of Oklahoma, The"
    (Kafka), 160
Nazis
    anti-Jewish campaign by, 184–185, 190,
        212, 217–218, 234–235, 240, 244
    anti-KPD campaign by, 180, 182–192
    "beer hall putsch," 62
    burning books by, 185
    coming to power of, 34–35, 167, 179,
        180–182
    Mussolini and, 194
    purge of, 189
    See also Hitler
Neher, Carola, 201, 202
Nelken, Ludwig, 24–25, 86–87
Neumann, Dr., 105
New York Times, 181
Nietzsche, F., 36
NKVD, 194–195, 198, 202, 203–204, 208,
    209
NSDAP. *See* Nazis
Nuremberg Laws, 190

Outward Forms and Inner Springs (Emmet), 235

Oved, Mosheh, 241–243

Pabiance, Poland, 16–17, 143
Palestine, 4, 8, 13–14, 22–23, 49, 67, 265–266
"Palestine question," 252–254
Pawel, Ernst, 38–39, 183, 184, 209
Peer Gynt, 161
Penal Colony, The (Kafka), 73, 131–132
Peretz, Isaac Leib, 69, 146, 245, 246, 344
Perlmutter, Tova Baumer/Moti, 336, 343, 344
Petain, Marshal, 225
Pick, Otto, 95
Pieck, Wilhelm, 195, 322, 323, 324
Pilsudski, Jozef, 146
Pines, Midia, 82
Pinkas Bedzin (Rosenkar), 21, 22
Piscator, Erwin, 137, 174
Plotkin, Bracha, 217–218, 271–272
Poland. *See* Bedzin, Poland
Politzer, Heinz, 282
Pollack, Josef, 262
Pollack, Valli Kafka, 27, 58, 60, 262, 264
Prager Presse, 95, 124
Prager Tagblatt, 78
Pravda, 192
Prince of Homberg, The, (Kleist), 160, 161
Purple Death (Meyrink), 37

Quakers (Friends), 235, 237, 238

Rainer, Luise, 161, 164
Ravitch, Melech, 146–149, 288–289
Reflections (Kafka), 73
Reinhardt, Max, 136–137, 167
Reymont, Wladyslaw Stanislaw, 146
RGO (Revolutionary Trade Union Opposition), 174, 198
Rise and Fall of the Third Reich, The (Shirer), 41
Rittenburg, Dasha Wendyger, 218
Robert, Marthe
  on Dora, 268–269, 285–286, 317–318, 319, 320
  Dora's correspondence/friendship with, 301–302, 306–308, 311–312, 314–315
Robotnik, 146
Roosevelt, Franklin D., 189, 230
Rössler, Tile, 3, 8, 11, 41–43, 58, 80, 273

Rossman, Karl, 160
Rozenkar, Moshe, 21
Russia
  Lask family and, 182, 188–189, 190–209, 322–325
  reality of, 195–196, 197–199, 200–204, 205, 206–208, 209–210
  Soviet spies, 209–210
Russian revolution, 189, 195–196

Salveter, Emmy, 35–36, 41, 45, 60, 79
Sarwitz, Ilse, 234, 235, 236
Schildkraut, Rudolf, 247
Schiller, Friedrich von, 136, 159, 163
Schocken Books, 291, 309, 311, 312
Schopenhauer, A., 36
Schrammel, Josef, 97
Schreiber, Hans (Hans Altmann), 203–204, 208
Schubert, Franz, 229, 230, 233
Schweiger (Werfel), 83–84
Secker and Warburg publisher, 205
Selbstwehr (Self-Defense), 43, 80, 124
Sforim, Mendele Mocher, 69, 146, 191, 245
Shakespeare's works, 136, 159, 247–249
Shaw, Carol, 239
Shirer, William, 41
"Show trials" in Moscow, 203
Shtetl: The Life and Death of a Small Town and the World of Polish Jews (Hoffman), 19–20
Shylock, *Merchant of Venice*, 247–248
Slezak, Walter, 137
Social Democratic Party, 158, 165–166, 175
Song of Bernadette (Werfel), 83
Soviet spies, 209–210
Spartacist movement, 34, 158
Spender, Stephen, 166–167, 309
Stalin, Joseph, 189–190, 196, 198, 210, 217, 267, 324–325
Stalin purges, 203, 208, 209
Stein, Erica, 225
Steiner, George, 262, 270
Steiner, Marianne
  description/background of, 261–262
  Marianne Lask and, 286–287, 290, 296, 319, 321, 326, 327, 336–337
  meeting/friendship with Dora, 263–264, 270, 296
  memories of Dora, 184, 212, 213, 216, 241

Stencl, Avrom-Nokhem
    Dora and, 140–141, 190, 191, 233
    Marianne Lask and, 287, 320
    Yiddish language and, 197, 240–241,
        242, 245, 288, 296–297
Steurmann, Salka, 154
Stille und Sturm (Lask), 327
"Stoker, The" (Kafka), 73, 131–132, 160
    See also Amerika

Talmud, 15, 20, 78–79
Tawney, R.H., 235
Theatre Marigny, 282, 283
Three Gifts, The (Peretz), 246
Three Penny Opera, The, 167
Tolstoy's writings, 69
Torcziner, Professor, 64
Trial, The (Kafka)
    plays of, 282–283, 284, 287
    publication of, 132–133, 143–145,
        169–170, 205
    theme of, 258
Trotsky, Leon, 190
Truman, President, 252
Tschiassny, Professor, 111
Tselniker, Meyer, 248

Ulbricht, Walter, 195, 322, 323, 324
Ullstein newspaper group, 25, 51
United States, 213, 230
Urzidil, Johannes, 125–126, 127, 130, 138

Verlag, Kurt Wolff, 73, 87, 144, 151, 152
Viertel, Berthold, 154, 159–160
Volksbühne, the People's Theatre, 137,
    152, 154
Vossische Zeitung, 168–170

Wagenbach, Klaus, 184, 341
Waldstaetten-Zipperer, Baroness Henriette,
    113
Walser, Martin, 313–314
Wedekind, Frank, 163
Weill, Kurt, 167
Welk, Ehm, 168–170, 257
Welsh miners, 235

Weltsch, Felix
    Dora and, 48, 272, 284
    Kafka and, 43, 80, 99, 102, 103, 104,
        105–106, 124
    as writer, 125, 126
Werfel, Franz
    Kafka and, 83–84, 97–98, 99, 104,
        260–261, 292
    as writer, 125, 126
Whitehead, Alfred North, 235
Whitehead's Philosophy of Organism
    (Emmet), 235
Wilson, Anthony, 239
Wilson, Margery, 235, 237, 239
Wimmler, Elizabeth (Ula), 201–202,
    207
Wittekind, Hedwig, 202
Wizard of Oz, The, 227
Wohryzek, Julie, 29–30, 111–112
Workers Accident Insurance Institute, 8,
    46, 66, 70, 147
World War I, 20–21
World War II
    beginnings of, 213–214, 217
    displaced persons/camps and, 214–215,
        250–252, 254
    Dora's internment during, 220–233
    end of, 244
    See also Germany
World Zionist Organization, 21, 25

Yealand Manor/newsletter, 237–240, 243,
    250, 267, 286
Yiddish language
    Dora and, 240, 241–243, 245–249,
        268–270, 318, 321
    Stencl and, 197, 240–241, 242, 245,
        288, 296–297
Yiddish theater, 245–249
Yisroel: The First Jewish Omnibus
    (Leftwich), 242
Young Hearts (Maletz), 280

Zetkin, Clara, 4
Zinoviev, Gregory, 203
Zoegiebel, Karl, 165